'Jacob Johanssen ⟨…⟩ light of the older a ⟨…⟩ concepts and bring ⟨…⟩ greatest thanks for this gigantic work.' ⟨…⟩ murderous actions in the ⟨…⟩ her newer psycho-analytic ⟨…⟩ nature of today's world—

From the preface by **Klaus Theweleit** *author of* Male Fantasies

'Jacob Johanssen's *Fantasy, Online Misogyny and the Manosphere: Male Bodies of Dis/Inhibition* is a timely and welcome addition to the growing body of scholarship on anti-feminist formations online. This vibrant psychosocial study explores the psychodynamics of anti-feminist groups and their members, but always within a broader sociological context. Such an approach is especially important for understanding radicalisation processes, which are shaped by complex experiences, fantasies and expressions, as well as by the socio-political factors that enable and amplify misogyny. Johanssen's study neither defuses nor excuses their misogyny, but rather demonstrates how personal contradictions, incoherencies, and ambivalences become channelled into extreme and hateful forms of political dogma. Always attendant to the contextual complexities of neoliberal capitalism, data-driven politics and the dynamics of the alt-right, *Fantasy, Online Misogyny and the Manosphere* enriches our understanding of white male supremacism by adding new lenses and perspectives through which to view the fantasies that drive this increasingly sinister political reality.'

Debbie Ging, *Associate Professor of Media Studies, Dublin City University*

'In a time of political polarisation and multiplying hatreds in the 'real' and 'virtual' worlds – a division that now holds little value – Jacob Johanssen's book is an important guide to some of the most disturbing elements of the 'manosphere'. Addressing the startling rhetoric of incels, MGTOWs, NoFaps and others, Johanssen offers historical context, social and political insight and, most of all, a thorough psychoanalytic reading of this significant and dangerous contemporary arena for the expression of toxic masculinities.'

Stephen Frosh, *Professor of Psychology, Department of Psychosocial Studies, Birkbeck, University of London*

'Jacob Johanssen's *Fantasy, Online Misogyny and the Manosphere* could hardly be a more timely intervention in debates around contemporary masculinities and misogyny in the digital sphere. In this beautifully written and scrupulously researched book Johannsen draws together the disparate communities that comprise what is now known as the 'manosphere' and its discontents. The author's intention, spectacularly realised, is to construct a psychosocial analysis of online misogyny and its connections to fantasy, affect and desire. Given the growth in spaces where these practices take place, in spite of (or perhaps in reaction to) a cultural context in which sexism is increasingly challenged and under threat, a study such as this makes a very necessary contribution to the growing field of literature tackling online misogyny. This is essential reading for anyone interested in the emergence, mechanics and practices of the 'manosphere' and wider cultures of and practices of pernicious toxic masculinity.'

John Mercer, *Professor of Gender and Sexuality, Birmingham Centre for Media and Cultural Research*

'A painful, yet highly necessary, read for any feminist and antiracist, Johanssen's complex study of the online manosphere illustrates the deeply contradictory relationship of misogynistic men to their own identities, desires, fantasies, and dis/inhibitions. Through his poignant analysis of how misogynistic aggression often hides intense insecurity and fragility, Johanssen demonstrates that the world would be a better place if misogynistic men – along with everyone else – understood what Jacques Lacan emphasised, namely that nobody possesses the phallus, that phallic power is a purely illusory construct with no real-life referent. A recognition of this simple fact would open a way toward less toxic masculinities and a way out of the 'us vs. them' mentality that continues to poison the gendered terrain of contemporary life.'

Mari Ruti, *Distinguished Professor of Critical Theory and of Gender and Sexuality Studies, University of Toronto*

Fantasy, Online Misogyny and the Manosphere

This book presents the first in-depth study of online misogyny and the manosphere from a psychoanalytic perspective.

The author argues that the men of the manosphere present contradictory thoughts, desires and fantasies about women which include but also go beyond misogyny. They are in a state of dis/inhibition: torn between (un)conscious forces and fantasies which erupt and are defended against. Dis/inhibition shows itself in self-victimization and defensive apathy as well as toxic agency and symbolic power and expresses itself in desire for and hatred of other bodies. The text draws on the psychoanalytic thinkers Klaus Theweleit, Elisabeth Young-Bruehl, Jessica Benjamin and Wilhelm Reich to present detailed analyses of the communities within the so-called manosphere, including incels, Men Going Their Own Way (MGTOW), alt-right YouTubers and NoFap users. Drawing on wider discussions about the status of sexuality in contemporary neoliberal technoculture since the sexual revolution of the late 1960s, it illuminates how sexuality, racism and images of the white male body shape the fantasies and affects of many men on the internet and beyond.

Integrating a unique theoretical framework to help understand how today's increase in online misogyny relates to the alt-right and fascism, *Online Misogyny and the Manosphere* is an important resource for academics in a variety of fields including psychoanalysis, media and communication studies, internet studies, masculinity research and more.

Jacob Johanssen is Senior Lecturer in Communications, St. Mary's University (London). His research interests include psychoanalysis and digital media, audience research, sexuality and digital media, affect theories, psychosocial studies and critical theory. He is co-editor of the Counterspace section of the journal *Psychoanalysis, Culture & Society* and a founder scholar of the British Psychoanalytic Council (BPC).

The Psychoanalysis and Popular Culture Series
Series Editors: Caroline Bainbridge and Candida Yates
Consulting Editor: Brett Kahr

This series builds on the work done since 2009 by the Media and the Inner World research network. It aims to consider the relationship between psychoanalysis and popular culture as a lived experience that is ever more emotionalised in the contemporary age. In contrast to many scholarly applications of psychoanalysis, works in this series set out to explore the creative tensions of thinking about cultural experience and its processes whilst also paying attention to observations from both the clinical and scholarly fields. The series provides space for a dialogue between these different groups with a view to evoking new perspectives on the values and pitfalls of a psychoanalytic approach to ideas of selfhood, society, politics and popular culture. In particular, the series strives to develop a psycho-cultural approach by foregrounding the usefulness of a post-Freudian, object relations perspective for examining the importance of emotional relationships and experience. We nevertheless welcome proposals from all fields of psychoanalytic enquiry. The series is edited by Caroline Bainbridge and Candida Yates, with Brett Kahr as the consulting editor.

Other titles in the Psychoanalysis and Popular Culture Series:

The Culture-Breast in Psychoanalysis
Cultural Experiences and the Clinic
Noreen Giffney

Post-traumatic Attachments to the Eerily Moving Image
Something to Watch Over Me
Andrew Asibong

Fantasy, Online Misogyny and the Manosphere
Male Bodies of Dis/Inhibition
Jacob Johanssen

For more information about this series, please visit: https://www.routledge.com/The-Psychoanalysis-and-Popular-Culture-Series/book-series/KARNPSYPOP

Fantasy, Online Misogyny and the Manosphere

Male Bodies of Dis/Inhibition

Jacob Johanssen

LONDON AND NEW YORK

First published 2022
by Routledge
2 Park Square, Milton Park, Abingdon, Oxon OX14 4RN

and by Routledge
605 Third Avenue, New York, NY 10158

Routledge is an imprint of the Taylor & Francis Group, an informa business

© 2022 Jacob Johanssen

The right of Jacob Johanssen to be identified as author of this work has been asserted by him in accordance with sections 77 and 78 of the Copyright, Designs and Patents Act 1988.

All rights reserved. No part of this book may be reprinted or reproduced or utilised in any form or by any electronic, mechanical, or other means, now known or hereafter invented, including photocopying and recording, or in any information storage or retrieval system, without permission in writing from the publishers.

Trademark notice: Product or corporate names may be trademarks or registered trademarks, and are used only for identification and explanation without intent to infringe.

British Library Cataloguing-in-Publication Data
A catalogue record for this book is available from the British Library

Library of Congress Cataloging-in-Publication Data
A catalog record has been requested for this book

ISBN: 978-0-367-46866-8 (hbk)
ISBN: 978-0-367-46865-1 (pbk)
ISBN: 978-1-003-03158-1 (ebk)

DOI: 10.4324/9781003031581

Typeset in Times New Roman
by MPS Limited, Dehradun

Contents

Series preface ix
Preface by Klaus Theweleit xi
Acknowledgements xx
Content warning xxii
Glossary xxiii

Introduction: a psychoanalysis of the manosphere 1

1 Male fascist bodies – then and now 28

2 The sexual revolution, the manosphere and (post) feminism 52

3 The backlash against the sexual revolution on YouTube 76

4 Incels and fantasies of destroying/desiring the other 96

5 Men Going Their Own Way – MGTOW: woman shall (not) exist 122

6 The manifestos of mass shooters and the absent father 144

7 NoFap: masturbation, porn and phallic fragility   166

Conclusion: from dis/inhibition to recognition –
a space for hope?   195

Bibliography   214
Index   242

Series preface

Caroline Bainbridge and Candida Yates

The application of psychoanalytic ideas and theories to culture has a long tradition and this is especially the case with cultural artefacts that might be considered 'classical' in some way. For Sigmund Freud, the works of William Shakespeare and Johann Wolfgang von Goethe were as instrumental as those of culturally renowned poets and philosophers of classical civilisation in helping to formulate the key ideas underpinning psychoanalysis as a psychological method. In the academic fields of the humanities and social sciences, the application of psychoanalysis as a means of illuminating the complexities of identity and subjectivity is now well established. However, despite these developments, there is relatively little work that attempts to grapple with popular culture in its manifold forms, some of which, nevertheless, reveal important insights into the vicissitudes of the human condition.

The *Psychoanalysis and Popular Culture* book series builds on the work done since 2009 by the Media and the Inner World research network, which was generously funded by the UK's Arts and Humanities Research Council. It aims to offer spaces to consider the relationship between psychoanalysis in all its forms and popular culture that is ever more emotionalised in the contemporary age.

In contrast to many scholarly applications of psychoanalysis, which often focus solely on 'textual analysis', this series sets out to explore the creative tension of thinking about cultural experience and its processes often drawing on observations from the clinical and scholarly fields of observation. The series provides space for a dialogue between these different groups with a view to creating fresh perspectives on the values and pitfalls of a psychoanalytic approach to ideas of selfhood, society and popular culture. In particular, the series strives to develop a psycho-cultural approach to such questions by drawing attention to the usefulness of post-Freudian and object relations perspectives for examining the importance of emotional relationships and experience.

In *Fantasy, Online Misogyny and the Manosphere: Male Bodies of Dis/Inhibition* Jacob Johanssen provides a highly original and timely psychosocial analysis of the dynamics of contemporary online misogyny within the websites, blogs and online discussion fora that collectively make up what has come to be known as 'the manosphere'. Focusing on the increasingly violent and disturbed modes of online masculinity that exist within that arena, Johanssen returns to Klaus Theweleit's groundbreaking work on masculinity in *Male Fantasies* (Theweleit, 1987, 1989) to shed light on the authoritarian nature of contemporary online masculinities associated with individual and collective online groups.

The author deepens his analysis of the fascistic dynamics of such masculinities by drawing on Elisabeth Young-Bruehl's (1996) analysis of prejudice and Wilhelm Reich's (1936) theory of sexuality and fascism to explore the interrelation between the unconscious, fantasies of sexuality and the body for the analysis of extremism and authoritarian ideologies. A recurring theme of this book is the male fantasy of the impermeable body and a refusal of vulnerability which is projected onto women and the feminine other, who become positioned as objects of contempt. Drawing on examples taken from destructive misogynist online groups, the author links the desire to dominate the other to the experience of castration anxiety, and a profound fear of weakness and disintegration in the face of change and threats to the old patriarchal order.

The subject matter of this book may at times be challenging for the reader, and such challenges are explored reflexively by the author who writes sensitively about experiences of masculinity and its dilemmas. The book provides an important contribution to our series and, more widely, it constitutes a nuanced and complex intervention within the research field of psychoanalysis, sexuality and digital masculinity and its discontents today.

Caroline Bainbridge and Candida Yates

Preface

Klaus Theweleit

Firstly, I have to thank Jacob Johanssen for the prominent place he has given my work *Male Fantasies* from 1977/1978 in his own study on male violence in our society; his great study branches in many directions.

Not much was going on in the previous decades in the field of analytical 'perpetrator studies'. There were studies in history on the German situation after WWI – my special area of work – in the English-speaking world, for instance Mark Jones's book: *Founding Weimar. Violence and the German Revolution of 1918–19,* Cambridge UP 2017; the highly qualified work of a young historian, which combed 'old sources' once more. But, almost nothing is mentioned in the book on specific psychic-embodied reasons of that 'violence', which is in the book's title. That is the crux with professional historians. They work on an 'object' or a 'field', which exists outside of them, study documents, formulate their 'judgements' in a cold subject-object-relation: the historian judges, history is that which is judged, then he proceeds to the 'next object'. He usually does not see himself as a personal part of that 'history' that he has described.

Jacob Johanssen does it differently. He knows that his work, which has male violence as its topic, cannot be written without reflecting on the own historically grown embodiment. One cannot describe this violence without the existing social structures, that is to say for our ruling system: without thinking with the conditions of 'patriarchy' that has been dominant for thousands of years. And part of that structure is every man himself, even if he criticises it: *At the same time, I reproduce patriarchy at least to some degree simply by being a male who is living in neoliberal capitalism.*

Thus, J.J. names the danger, which threatens all work that deals with forms of male violence in the world from 'intellectually and emotionally-superior' standpoints: the danger of unwittingly repeating their central structural features, when they are simply described as 'stupid', 'mad', 'absurd', so being 'of course inferior' to one's own forms of thinking and acting. J.J. notes: When we simply reject the forms of thinking and acting of incels, MGTOWs, NoFap and other groups of the 'manosphere', we reproduce their specific structures, which can be labelled using psychiatric terminology as 'binary and paranoid-schizoid'; but such 'diagnoses' do not liberate us from our own possible entanglement. Particularly the thinking and judging in 'binaries' is disastrous.

Who breathes and lives in our – roughly said – Western-democratic culture and its provided institutional conditions, is not exempt from such conditions through the expression: 'I am different', am no 'perpetrator', do *not* oppress women; am therefore no object of my study, am above my object. This attitude is very common among people, who have not learned to think (psycho)analytically. They tend to situate everything in the outer world that somewhat 'disturbs' or 'hinders' them. 'Evil', 'bad', that which is 'hard to digest', is always in 'the other'. That makes life more bearable (seemingly) but is not a good starting point for obtaining *applicable* insights.

A highly qualified German historian has recently produced a study of 19/20th-century Germany history; a good book with lots of data and names, from which I learn a lot; everything well verified and thought through; for example how the ruling groups and classes of the German empire were already at the end of the 19th century verifiably and with *verve* heading for the war 'in the long distance', which would go down in history as the First World War; he shows how they economically-military downright long for this future war (and world domination); he also does not avoid the presentation of the abominations of the annihilations of Europe's Jewish population in the concentration camps.

But a word such as 'Freud' does not occur in the book; let alone the word 'psychoanalysis'. – Is that possible?, I ask. Can one present the German history of violence, the German history of war, the history of the camps, the German *will of extermination* which showed itself in the attempted destruction of Jewish (as well as Russian) people, without moving into the psychological structures of the perpetrators of such murders – mostly men? I do not think one can; and this applies not least to Anglo-American perpetrators.

When I wrote *Male Fantasies* between 1972 and 1977 – parallel to the developing early forms of (West) German feminism – I was the father of a little boy; newly married to a woman who had begun to work in child and adolescent psychiatry at the University Clinic of Freiburg; connected to all ongoing political discussions, ecological, feminist anti-colonialist; captivated by the 'question of violence': where and when is the use of armed force allowed or even required; a question that threatened to tear apart the – in the self-conception pacifist – body.

And: how does my own 'manhood' relate to that of the killing Freikorps men of 1920; how does it relate to my father's manhood; authority-believing Hitler supporter, Nazi follower. How does it appear in the eyes of my wife; how does our child perceive me? How does my being a man appear in the improvisation group in which I make music?

If you ask today's men of the somewhat older generations, who have managed their lives somewhat 'successfully', about their favourite song, they see their lives, pretty much in unison, bundled under the title 'My Way'. Paul Anka's/Frank Sinatra's, 'I did it my way'; Frankieboy with swollen chest. Last heard this way by German ex-chancellor Gerhard Schröder. 'My Way'; the power macho; unchanged; unchangeable?

'My Way?' I couldn't name my life and actions with that. But rather: 'We did it our way', but even that would be too boastful. Without my wife, without helping, without *resonating* groups of friends, without co-workers and supporters in working groups and institutions, without a share in the changing structures of the *public* in the slowly democratizing society after World War II, without *Black Music*, without constant reflection of one's own state within all these connections, one's own 'thinking' would be rather nothing, it would not be developed at all. In the number '1' the (so-called) individual does not exist at all. '2' is the least, from the baby to the joys of love. The so-called 'autonomous subject' is a philosophical construction (more about this in a moment).

So, first of all, it is a great joy to me that in the year 2021 there is a psychoanalytically thinking person who not only reads with approval the soon 50-year-old *Male Fantasies* (I started writing in 1972), but fruitfully thinks them further. Jacob Johanssen examines today's relevant 'fascist' men and their murderous actions in the light of the older as well as the newer research literature; thinks further newer psychoanalytic concepts and brings them in relation to the changed technological nature of today's world – greatest thanks for this gigantic work; which is always carried by the certainty that in the centre of such efforts diverse human bodies have to stand in the respective different expression of their sexualities.

The individual body – insofar as it compulsively seeks to assert itself as an individual – appears in Johanssen's work, as it does in mine, as a 'fragmented body'; as a body that is partially destroyed in its development, that seeks to armour itself against the threats of the outside world and/or seeks powerful formations with the intention of fitting into them. Fearful, 'threatened' bodies almost always help themselves with violence. The 'fascist' body is filled with fears, especially the fear of being 'swallowed up' by external realities. The central fear of everything 'fascist' is the fear of body dissolution. This is true for 1920, for 1960, for 1990 and for 2020 – with the differences of what surrounds each.

'Today's world': the word/term 'queer' did not exist in 1977; LGBTQ? Unknown. Nor the word/fact 'manosphere' (Incel, NoFap, MGTOW, etc.); nor the word/fact 'internet'. Nor the word/fact 'digitality', at least not in today's relevance.

What has remained the same: 'A real woman is absent and replaced with a fantasy that allows for the control of woman', as J.J. writes. But the forms and conditions of this 'fantasy' have shifted.

Also shifted are the forms of psychoanalytic thinking that seeks ways out of the situation of compulsive (self-imposed) isolation of the manospheres. Thus, Jacob Johanssen continues to think the concept of 'fragmented bodies' within the framework of the work of Jessica Benjamin; her shift of focus from the oedipal/phallic construct to a 'psychoanalysis of relationships'; where one human being recognises another as both equal to and different from itself; where ideas and feelings can be shared and a 'third' can emerge from the mutual recognition and intersection of individuals that belongs to both. This third, says Benjamin, cannot arise under the regime of the phallus, cannot grow in the oedipal Freud/Lacan field, where the father appears as a forbidding instance and threatening castrator. Her constructions of early intersubjective gender relations between mother and child go beyond the evocation of the *pre-oedipal* field of a unity of mother and baby, as Mahler or Anzieu devised it.

'Of course' I can only hint at such complexities here; and this brings me to the main problem of my appreciation of Johanssen's work. I have read his book with great approval; but now, when I try to write about it, I notice that precisely this very far-reaching approval and agreement does not make writing easier, but specifically more difficult. I can't keep saying: 'Right, exactly, I think so too'; 'Well expressed, and it's also true. Admirable!' The chain of quoting would be an endless one; and it would only repeat what is all in the book. That would be a little silly.

So it makes sense to work on some differences. The men of the 'manosphere' that Johanssen analyses are in many respects similar to those I described in *Male Fantasies*, but in some respects they are not. A central observation in *Male Fantasies* is that fantasies about women are usually born out of the absence of real women. This is not so true of today's. Jacob Johanssen writes: 'The men are dependent on the fantasy of woman, because it is the woman, who may (eventually) recognise them and validate their existence.' In the men of the 'manosphere', women are also 'absent', but they are at the centre of these men's fantasies. Nothing is thought or felt without reference to femininity. A *recognition* of their own existence by women is secretly longed for. The anger at women results above all from the fact that they do not want to fulfil this expectation.

To be recognised, to be acknowledged on the part of women was a wish hardly to be found in Wilhelmine-mangled men from 1890 to 1920. The fear of the body-dissolving qualities of women was far too great to allow such closeness. Wilhelmine civilian life up to the First World War was organised in such a way that real closeness between men and women could hardly develop (beyond the sphere of siblings), because there were hardly any public spaces in which the different 'sexes' could have met. The grammar schools were separated into female and male; public dance events did not exist.

All these things have changed fundamentally. Women are now everywhere in the public sphere, they are in workplaces, on the streets, in clubs, in factories and offices. They are no longer locked up in homes and are omnipresent in advertising. The men of the 'manosphere', on the other hand, help themselves with a special fantasy. Johanssen writes:

All of the different communities and men instead construct an other that is there to serve them; as an obedient femininity that should prop up the men's fragmented egos. While they may desire nothing more than recognition, they resort to destruction of the other. Such acts seem to close down any possibility for recognition, mutual understanding, or dialogue. It would seem that if the men desire recognition it is a particular form of recognition: submission. The men, fuelled by their fascist body-fantasies, dream up scenarios in which they are the dominant men who are admired and cared for by submissive women.

A woman is constructed who longs for her own submission. An actual perception of 'the other' and 'mutual respect' cannot arise. Another difference remains unresolved: what are the circumstances that lead men of the 'manosphere' to want to kill 'the woman'? Where is the point where the desire to kill arises; the decision to annihilate the female body; a point towards which many of the male fantasies are heading: a world without women. Johanssen also finds this difficult to decide. Where does the incel, where does the MGTOW man become a killer, an assassin. He does not murder at random; he does not run 'amok'; he makes a decision, that much is clear. Only the precise study of each individual case can help here.

The answer to the central question: 'Where do the destroyed, fragmented bodies come from?' has also shifted in the late 20th/early 21st century. Until the end of World War 2, it was primarily family interventions such as beatings, disregard and mockery of infantile needs, ridicule of 'weakness' and other forms of psychological and physical humiliation that prevented infant male bodies from developing a stable libidinous occupation of their own bodily boundaries. One's own outer skin – that wonderful organ for developing friendly contact with other people – the basis of all varieties of relational capacity, generally remained largely inanimate. Thus, the basis for the development of a stable body-ego in Freud's sense was missing.

The military provided a remedy. Those men who survived the physical tortures of the drill and the systematic humiliation by the officer caste very often experienced it as a 'liberation'; as a breakthrough into a new kind of physicality; breakthrough to a strength they had not felt before. The army, the military formation of which they became a part, replaced the psychologically inanimate bodily boundary for them. They formed what Wilhelm Reich called their 'armour'. A muscular outer ego structured by command and obedience that prevented their bodies from fragmenting as long as they moved successfully within this system. The military terror turned in their bodies into a certainty of strength in coping with external problems. The memoirs of the Freikorps men – who then proudly called themselves 'soldierly men' – are full of descriptions of the *excitement* of reaching this physical stage: freedom! A 'liberated' state – but without the possibility of psychologically sustainable relationships with *anyone*. The almost *logical* consequence: everything that *disturbs* this kind of muscular (constantly fear-threatened) balance cannot be countered in any other way than with violence; with the destruction of the disturbing sources, which include in particular the *liveliness* of women; their (body-dissolving) power of the erotic.

This leads to a frequent question in recent years: how does this work today, when corporal punishment no longer occupies the top position among the 'means of education'? And even the military in this body-stabilising function is only decisive for relatively few of today's young men.

At first, I had in mind other places for bodily workout: sports facilities, shooting clubs, the private training centres that many men regularly visit to 'steel' their muscles, or, to put it simply, to 'keep fit'. All the way to gladiatorial fighting techniques as demonstrated in David Fincher's film 'Fight Club' (1999).

Jacob Johanssen says: the former stabilising function of the military is now mainly performed by the internet. I fully agree with this. The first idea in this direction came to me after reading the 1,500-page manifesto of Anders Behring Breivik, posted on the internet shortly before his Oslo attack and the Utøya murders. Breivik's testimony at the trial that he *had* to commit the murders primarily so that one would notice his internet text underlined this. The perception of his internet appearance was supposed to cement his heroic status; to prove his *supremacy*, which could not be reached by earthly worldly jurisdiction; ultimately: the inviolability of his physicality. The internet as body armour.

The use of the internet as body armour for certain individual men and groups of men became more and more conspicuous in the following period. Jacob Johannsen works this out very clearly in the different (and yet so *similar*) groups of men in the manosphere. A very important point in the physical-spiritual formation of the 'fascist type' is touched upon here; a point that is often overlooked or not taken seriously, or is regarded as 'contradictory'. It is the simultaneity of highly developed technological competences – a characteristic of almost all fascist masculinity – with ideologies of the highest 'backwardness' such as 'blood and soil' among the German fascists, or the talk of the 'natural' superiority of the male over the female body, or the 'superiority' of the white 'race' over all people of colour. One comes to the conclusion that the men of the manosphere are somehow highly modern and somehow highly backward at the same time. But they do not see this as 'a contradiction'. For them, these are parts of a very special kind of wholeness, which they absolutely attest to themselves. Glorification of stone-age gender constructions and virtuoso net mastery or the abilities to build high-tech rockets go hand in hand: 'It fits! Doesn't it?'

This is not about something 'metaphorical'; it is about real bodily states. It is important to understand the internet as a bodily reality; not to distinguish in principle the interconnection (*Zusammenschaltung*) with 'the net' from the interconnection of the 'old style' soldierly man with his machine gun, his motorbike, his tank, his plane. The technical devices are not simply 'dead material'; the psychophysical interconnection with them gives many bodies a kind of special 'liveliness'. Above all, it increases to an enormous extent the feelings of power of those so connected.

Until two decades ago, most of the men of the scattered right-wing branches around the world lived mostly in isolation, without much knowledge of each other; often at loggerheads in smaller groupings. Now there is their international presence; a kind of omnipresence that they are tirelessly expanding and extending. What is now called 'manosphere' is a product of the internet (once intended – by some – to promote grassroots democracy around the world). In being connected to the net, the individual body threatened by fragmentation joins a large overarching whole. Each approving like-click enlarges the person into the superdimensional; we witness a technological re-foundation of the master-race principle. This is not to say anything principally 'against the internet'; on the contrary, it can be used in many ways. The technologies are available to all, including murderers and gangsters who experience its use as an increase in their body of power and violence. 'We' use it differently and should/can use it differently.

A decisive difference to the figure I would call today's 'normal type' is touched upon here. In my opinion, many people in Western democratic societies have fundamentally distanced themselves from the status of a somehow in itself 'coherent' uniformity of their own physicality. I have been trying to grasp this for some time with the term 'segment-ego'. 'Segment-ego' is something like the successful 'overcoming' in civilian life of that type of body that lived in fear of so-called 'schizophrenic' division. This body type dominated until the end of WWII; it saw itself as 'good': good citizen, good family man, good obedient subject, good member of a superior race; it saw itself as 'humane' even if it mass-murdered; *obediently* mass-murdered. The authorities would know what they were *ordering*. Anything that deviated from this threatened the bodies with fragmentation, psychological breakdown. The 'deviant' was – where there was no possibility of physical intervention (=killing) – psychologically *split off*. Those who did not succeed and became conspicuous were considered 'sick'. The *clinically* conspicuous form was called 'schizophrenia'; splitting into 'two personalities' was the 'diagnosis'.

Today's citizens of Western democracies no longer allow themselves to be talked into such dichotomies. They have too many connections to different branches of the actual. One can describe it as follows:

Middle-aged man, employee, drops children off at school, kisses his wife goodbye, arranges a date with secret lover on his way to work, stocks business (real estate, arms trade) in the office at 10:20, makes a donation for starving children in India at 10:50, lays into a subordinate at 11:30 because of his lax attitude to work, is nice to all the surrounding employees during the lunch break (for whose dismissal he pleads in the meeting at 14:30; necessary in the sense of the company). He can be in a church or not in a church, he can be religious for one hour in the morning and again in the evening; he can be a pacifist and child helper for one hour, a war supporter for one hour, in between organising the upcoming lawyer appointments to 'mediate' some of these areas among each other; in doing so, his physicality is also frequently connected to the net. He can then stand at the fence as a good neighbour at the end of the day; tomorrow, however, he can be a neighbourly denunciator in questions of parking or dog poo; he can, as David Lynch demonstrates with a college professor, slap his daughter at the breakfast table because of a little dirt under her fingernails, be a clean father, but at night be 'the ghost' who climbs into her bed and sexually abuses her.

This cannot be accommodated under the figure of a somehow 'uniform ego'. How does this 'normal type' deal with it? As far as I can see, when a change of state takes place, the state that has been abandoned is split off, or better: pushed away, when the entry into the new realm takes place. The decisive novelty: this happens without any feeling of 'sickness'. The switching from one state to the other appears as absolutely ego-syntonic, as absolutely non-pathological. The 'ego' consists of a certain number of segments that co-exist without bothering each other much. Those who can cope well with this can cope well with the surrounding social realities. In addition, today's technologically and socially highly differentiated societies offer the segmented psyche of the individual *scope for action or behaviour*, which in principle allow, for example, any *transgression* as long as it does not appear in the focus of the public gaze: a society of enclaves that leave each other alone.

Men of the manosphere, on the other hand, seem to belong to a species that has not learned such a cultural technique of cool segmentation (of the world and their own psyche) or have failed at it. They strive for a more unified worldview – as Jacob Johanssen emphasises several times – but in view of the many confusing realities in which 'man' has to live, this cannot be achieved except by violence and destruction.

We see other forms of resistance to this segmented world in movements like *Fridays for Future*. They organise the rebellion of younger people against the savvy behavioural tricks of 'the old' that seem 'mendacious' to them; namely, telling something different every half hour and not really sticking to any of it.

For contemporary psychoanalysis, this raises a general problem, namely the question: 'what kind of 'ego' or 'I' are we actually dealing with' when we use the formula 'ego' linguistically; for ourselves or for other 'egos' in society. The question is largely unanswered. Most authors help themselves by simply putting the word 'subject' in their texts, but this 'subject' does not exist – except as an abstract philosophical positing. 'Subject' is an idea, incorporeal. But it is about bodies. About their ongoing attempt to control and organise their individual fragmentalities in such a way that with them 'life becomes liveable'.

It becomes liveable in relationships with other people. This insight makes Jessica Benjamin's psychoanalysis the focus of Jacob Johanssen's reflections on how to escape the isolated worlds of the manosphere. The realisation that 'I' basically does not exist without relation to 'the other' is present in theory, but it has not yet entered the forms of our speech and behaviour. We know only very vaguely what we say when we say 'I'.

Jessica Benjamin's remarks on the power of the vaginal – which right-wing men today fear as intensely as soldierly men did 100 years ago as 'devouring' – also sets the necessary accents here for differentiating new psychoanalytical considerations from the complex of the 'Oedipal' with its tendency towards the binary division of (not only) the gender relations of humanity(ies); this work was only partially complete with Deleuze/Guattari's anti-Oedipus. Here, too, it can be seen that those groups of people who have raised their 'queer-ness' into public consciousness in recent decades aim for much more than just the perception and recognition of their 'deviant' sexualities. In the dissolution of the systems of the 'binary gender order', central forms of organisation and thinking of 'our' society are called into question. One of the consequences is the successive dissolution of all forms of thinking of 'two-sidedness', i.e. heteronormative gender duality as well as what is philosophically called 'dialectics'. Things are not 'two-sided', they (almost always) have several sides; the thought-form thesis-antithesis-synthesis can historically go to the rubbish dump. Also the scheme of proof of 'our' use of language, which (almost always) orders things from a certain point – arranges them *hierarchically* – and from this 'height' seeks to start its 'proofs of truth', has become highly dubious at its core. That it is possible to prove just about anything and everything with 'rational' argumentation was proven not least by Anders Breivik in his speech in court. Everything he presented: always nicely backed up with statistics and tables, every nonsense, no matter how big. Everything 'provable'. Our languages, both everyday and highly theoretical, lag behind the reality of bodies and the actual diversity of social conditions. All the more important is Jacob Johanssen's effort to break through the thicket in fields whose clarity is not exactly increasing.

Less than ever before are we 'at the end' of processes of epistemology. Trump's America has shown us that we do not live in secure 'democratic-civilised' relations. (And it's not 'the only one'.)

The fact that there are men who find life unbearable simply because there are women who are allowed to demand 'equality' is the main problem with the foundations of the 'democratic'. Equality is *unnatural*! (Get it already.)

Klaus Theweleit
10 May 2021
Translated by Jacob Johanssen

Acknowledgements

This book has greatly benefitted from conversations with a number of colleagues and friends. First of all, I would like to thank the editors of Routledge's Psychoanalysis and Popular Culture series, Caroline Bainbridge and Candida Yates, for their encouragement and support with the writing of this book. I am grateful for their critique, suggestions and detailed feedback on the manuscript. The book would not be in its present form without them.

My thanks go to Christian Fuchs for his suggestion that I read Klaus Theweleit's 'Male Fantasies'. Anastasia Kavada provided important advice at an early stage of this project. Steffen Krüger has, as always, been invaluable for discussing many ideas of this book with me and offering feedback and suggestions. Thanks also to Steffen for inviting me to present parts of Chapter 3 during his symposium, Irresistible Forms of Media Interaction. in Oslo on 23 November 2018. I also spoke about parts of this book at the Pleasures of Violence conference at Oxford Brookes University on 7 March 2019. Thanks to the conference organisers, Diego Semerene and Lindsay Steenberg. I also presented parts of Chapter 3 at the Psychoanalysis and Social Media: A Healthy Relationship? symposium at London Metropolitan University on 16 October 2019 and am thankful to Martin Murray and Jenny Harding for the invitation. Thanks also to colleagues at the annual APCS conference in October 2019 and again in October 2020 at Rutgers University, New Brunswick, for useful comments. I am grateful that I had the opportunity to present parts of this book at the Masculinity and National Identity conference in Berlin (17 January 2020), organised by Clarissa Smith and John Mercer. I also spoke about Chapter 7 at the Viral Masculinities online event (01 September 2020), organised by João Florêncio. Thanks to all of you.

Olivier Jutel provided very inspiring comments on the main ideas of the book, which I am very grateful for. I would also like to thank the following colleagues for their support, and conversations about the book's themes:

Bonni Rambatan, Sarah Banet-Weiser, Jack Bratich, Diego Semerene, Tanya Horeck, Jamie Steele, Carolyn Pedwell, Karin Wahl-Jorgensen, Alison Horbury, Glenn Muschert and Greg Seigworth.

Finally, my greatest thanks go to Klaus Theweleit for laying the inspirational foundations on which this book partially rests.

Content Warning

This book discusses toxic, disturbing and offensive data. Some readers may find it difficult to engage with such kind of material.

Glossary

4Chan: Anonymous, image-sharing forum that hosts a variety of sub-fora, dedicated to specific topics, some of which are notorious for extreme and offensive content.

Alt-Right: Right-wing extremist, fascist and anti-Semitic community with a presence online and beyond the internet. The alt-right may have declined in its visibility in the past few years, but its mindset and ideas are still influential.

Beta buxx: A beta male, as opposed to an alpha male.

Blue Pill, Red Pill and Black Pill: Terms widely used in the manosphere and beyond. The blue pill represents mainstream feminism, whereas the red pill is supposed to represent the anti-feminist 'truth': that men are the most oppressed in society. Taking the black pill (a term incels have created) means seeing that everything is broken and there is no hope.

Chad: A derogatory name given to attractive men who are in many sexual relationships with women.

Cuck: Originally refers to a man whose wife is sexually unfaithful. It also denotes a specific genre within porn which shows a white male witnessing sexual intercourse between his 'wife' and a black male. This term has been popularised by the alt-right to describe an allegedly weak man (often used as a term for someone with moderate or progressive political views).

Femoid: A combination of 'female' and 'humanoid' or 'android' that describes women as sub-human or non-human; sometimes abbreviated as 'foid'.

Hypergamy: The alleged act by women of marrying men who are of a higher social class.

Incels: Short for *involuntary celibate*, male supremacist community.

LDAR: Short for *lie down and rot*, used by incels to essentially mean to commit suicide.

LOL: Short for *laughing out loud*. Used to denote something funny.

Looksmatch: Incel term for someone who looks similar to an incel.

Manosphere: Loose clustering of social media profiles, fora and websites that consist of diverse male communities, many of which are explicitly anti-feminist and misogynist.

Meme: Images or short videos that are shared online. Often multiple variations of one image or video are created which rapidly spread on social media and other forms of online communication. Often funny and ironic.

MGTOW: *Men Going Their Own Way*, a community that advocates a male separatist lifestyle and male supremacy.

NoFap: Anti-porn and -masturbation community that mostly consists of men but is also frequented by some women.

Normie: Someone who is average-looking and of average intelligence. Used in a mocking way but also often used to connote envy.

PMO: NoFap term for *porn, masturbation, orgasm*.

Reddit: Platform on which users can create their own communities (or fora), so-called 'subreddits'.

Snowflake: Derogatory term used by the alt-right to refer to liberal, left-wing or 'weak' individuals.

Stacy: Used by incels to denote a woman who has sex with a lot of men (usually Chads) and is stereotypically superficial, unintelligent, beautiful and promiscuous.

Introduction: a psychoanalysis of the manosphere

According to Ian Kershaw, 'Hitler was no "catch" for women' (1998, 44). In his two-volume study of the fascist dictator, Kershaw describes him as an 'outrightly misogynist' man (ibid). The moral code of the early 20th century advocated celibacy until an individual had reached the age of 25. As Kershaw notes, abstaining from sex until a certain time was deemed to be 'healthy, advantageous to strength of will, and the basis of physical or mental high achievement' (ibid). When Hitler left Vienna at the age of 24 in 1913, he had had no sexual experiences. Kershaw reminds us that in 'a city in which sexual favours were so widely on offer to young men as the Vienna of that day, who were widely expected to visit prostitutes while publicly upholding a strict moral code, this was in all likelihood unusual' (ibid). He concludes that Hitler was frightened of women and their sexuality. He was sexually repressed – *inhibited*. A failed man, who saw himself in grandiose terms as an artist destined for greatness. On another level, he was an evil demon – a man who would come to embody the worst and most demonic individual of the 20th century, responsible for mass murder and massacres of everyone who was claimed to be 'other', different or inferior. Hitler was notorious for his hubris, blind rage, uncontrollable anger, (performed) outbursts and 'near-hysterical' states of mind (ibid, 513) – a completely *disinhibited* monster.

Writing about Hitler's failed sexuality is not meant as a joke here. In this example, we see the close links between the fascist state of mind, sexuality and embodied experience. Historically, fascism has had a particular relationship to masculinity, femininity, the body and sexuality – a relationship that finds its echoes and updates on today's screens and within the bodies of many men.

***

Online misogyny has been on the rise on social media such as Twitter, Facebook and YouTube in recent years (Banet-Weiser 2018; Ging & Siapera 2019). Forum platforms like 4chan, 8chan and Reddit have also played a considerable part in the mainstreaming of such misogyny. This rise is

DOI: 10.4324/9781003031581-101

intrinsically linked to the spreading of right-wing and fascist politics and ideas, not just through elections, politicians and governments – Johnson, Trump, Modi, Bolsonaro, Salvini, Orbán, Duterte, Erdoğan, Le Pen – but through their organised dissemination on the internet.

More recently, the spreading of right-wing populism across Europe and other parts of the world (for instance as part of the election of Donald Trump in the United States, the Brexit referendum in the United Kingdom, the anti-refugee discourses by far-right parties in Europe) has also been accompanied by particular forms of misogyny (Walton 2012; Keskinen 2013; Wilz 2016; Ouellette & Banet-Weiser 2018) and a backlash against women's as well as LGBTQI+ people's rights.

In this context, a range of online communities (often collectively referred to as the 'manosphere') have emerged in recent years that specifically circulate hateful posts about women (Gotell & Dutton 2016; Ging 2017; Koulouris 2018; Van Valkenburg 2018; Bratich & Banet-Weiser 2019). Members claim that feminist cis women, LGBTQI+s, left-leaning individuals and people of colour have undermined (white) men and that there is a need for a new heterosexual masculinity, which is constructed in various ways in the manosphere.

Such communities are not only harmful to cis women (and those of other genders and sexual orientations), but put them in actual danger in the case of death or rape threats which have originated from the online communities. They have led to women being killed. Beyond the internet, there have been numerous mass shootings in recent years. White male shooters are often misogynists and racists (Myketiak 2016; Murray 2017a, 2017b; Wilson 2017; Vito, Admire & Hughes 2018) and their views have been amplified by the manosphere and social media. Online misogyny is never just harmless 'virtual' or internet violence; it is and also leads to 'real' violence against women.

We live in a time where certain men seem to desire to hate women. How are such forms of hatred articulated online? Why have they emerged now? How do they relate to wider histories of fascism, the sexual revolution and feminism? Why are they so intrinsically connected to bodies and sexuality? How is misogyny amplified by online communities? What is the role of fantasy in relation to online misogyny? Those questions led me to the writing of this book.

The underlying research question of this book is how misogyny is articulated in different communities of the manosphere. I am specifically interested in making inferences about the men's fantasies, desires and bodily affective states from the data that I discuss. I analyse online misogyny on Reddit,[1] YouTube and online fora as well as in manifestos of two mass shooters.

This book presents essentially a *psychosocial* analysis of misogyny which pays attention to the socio-historical factors that enable or amplify misogyny as a particular socio-political force as well as the subjective-psychological dimensions that are inextricably linked with the former. In her book on misogyny, Kate Manne (2018) has argued against treating misogyny as something purely psychological or subjective-irrational. Misogyny is a practice, rooted in patriarchy with the aim to uphold it, rather than primarily an individual state of mind. What lies behind misogyny for an individual is, for Manne, impossible to scrutinise. However, I think that such an 'either – or' perspective is unhelpful and we need to regard misogyny as a dialectical and psychosocial phenomenon that is situated within the individual and the social. Both are intertwined and embody misogyny in particular ways. It is by trying to understand the subjective dimensions behind misogyny as a social force that allows us to see why misogyny is taken up by particular men who are situated in patriarchy and specific socio-historical contexts.

In my theoretical framework, I draw on psychoanalysis and in particular on Klaus Theweleit's two volumes *Male Fantasies* (Theweleit 1987, 1989). My analyses are also based on Wilhelm Reich's theory of sexuality and fascism (Reich 1997) and Elisabeth Young-Bruehl's work on prejudice (Young-Bruehl 1996). All three thinkers stress the importance of the role of sexuality, the body and the unconscious for analysing extremism such as misogyny and its relationship to forms of authoritarian ideology. If we want to understand the fascination with and the allure of right-wing extremism and fascism today, we must take sexuality into account. Fascism not only promises collective identity, belonging and bodily strength, it also promises a sense of entitlement and freedom from responsibility and a total domination over the other. Such themes are particularly attractive to those who feel castrated, weakened and at the edge of disintegration, as certain men do today specifically in relation to sexuality and women.

The book places a strong emphasis on embodiment, bodies and affect as well as on the social realm through my discussion and development of Theweleit, Reich and Young-Bruehl. Such a psychosocial perspective is useful because the particular fantasies and narratives that I analyse go beyond the discursive or textual: they are shaped by the body, sexuality and affect. While those narratives may constitute written texts that are posted online, they need to be seen as embodied expressions of un/conscious dynamics which relate to the men's psyches as well as to wider socio-cultural dimensions.

Based on Theweleit, Reich and Young-Bruehl, I develop the concept of *dis/inhibition* (that draws from Freud's understanding of inhibition) which I return to at numerous times in the book in my analysis of certain male fantasies. In times of hook-up apps like Tinder, self-produced amateur pornography, and open discussions of sexual practices on social media, sexuality is more liberated and disinhibited than it has ever been. At the same time, such forms of unbounded and visible passion lead to feelings of inhibition and conflict for many individuals. Dis/inhibition serves as a general symptom of contemporary technocultures and how sexualities are experienced, negotiated and thought about within them. The concept is particularly applicable to the cis men discussed in this book. Their bodies are structured by states of dis/inhibition: apathy and toxic symbolic power, contradictions of desire, affective forces and the push and pull of the unconscious. Their egos are fragile, and they feel threatened by women, female sexuality and the (alleged) power women hold today. At the same time, the men feel undesired and inadequate. They respond to such existential feelings of failure by restraining and excluding themselves, feeling alienated as part of particular online collectives and *at the same time* erupting with omnipotent fantasies that put them in control and construct a generic cis woman as Other.[2] This Other bears similarities to how Jews are constructed by anti-Semites and how subjects who are not white are constructed by racists: sexually promiscuous, plotting, deceiving, seductive, contagious.

While there is much literature on the topic of misogyny and social media (Filipovic 2007; Jane 2014, 2016; Rentschler 2014; Massanari 2017; Banet-Weiser 2018; Zuckerberg 2018), the toxic practices of misogynistic male users in relation to online fan and gaming cultures (Mantilla 2015; Salter & Blodgett 2017; Proctor & Kies 2018), and work on right-wing populism and misogyny (Wodak 2015; Lyons 2017; Ott 2017), there is scope to further research the relationship between right-wing ideas, misogyny and social media by paying attention to what kind of content is created online and how such content relates to the (male) body.

This book discusses four types of cis men, male identities and online communities:

- **Reactionary and alt-right YouTubers** who rage against the apparent current moral decline due to the sexual revolution and feminism (Chapter 3)
- **Incels** who dehumanise, yet desire, women (Chapters 4 and 5)
- **MGTOWs** (Men Going Their Own Way) who advocate a male lifestyle without women (Chapter 5)
- **Mass shooters** such as Anders Behring Breivik and Elliot Rodger who killed women because of their own sexual failures (Chapter 6)
- **NoFap** members who abstain from pornography and masturbation but hold equally problematic views of women and feminism (Chapter 7)

In this Introduction, I outline the wider themes and key arguments of this book.

Fascism, the Alt-Right, the manosphere and social media

Right-wing and fascist forces are on the rise on a global scale. That much is certain. In times of complex geopolitical, environmental and economic challenges, renewed forms of nationalism and populist authoritarianism seem to provide easy answers for many. Old ideologies are communicated through new technologies, such as social media (Fuchs 2018). The particular ideologies of nationalism that have gripped many parts of the world today carry inherent racisms, misogyny, sexisms and general xenophobia, as Christian Fuchs writes. This book is about misogyny in times of authoritarian capitalism and the imminent dangers of fascism and right-wing extremism. Many countries have turned to an authoritarian form of capitalism which comes dangerously close to fascism (for example Hungary, Brazil, the USA, or even the UK). Fuchs notes that the differences between right-wing extremism and fascism are that the former tends to accept and use symbolic and real violence against political opponents, whereas the latter tends to accept and use violence against all opponents and scapegoats (ibid, 56). Fascism is a particular ideology and state system. While there were historically very different forms of fascism (for example Nazism under Hitler in Germany and fascism under Mussolini in Italy), there are nonetheless common denominators that help us to understand particular dimensions of fascism as an oppressive, violent, authoritarian form of totalitarianism. Jason Stanley (2018) names the following characteristics of fascism: A referral to a mythic past, anti-intellectualism, a strong emphasis on hierarchy and law and order, a distortion of reality, a feeling of and claiming of victimhood and sexual anxiety.

Right-wing authoritarianism, as Christian Fuchs argues, has the following characteristics:

1. Authoritarianism and leadership: A belief in an authoritarian leader and a strong state
2. Nationalism, ethnocentrism: A belief in the superiority of a particular community or nation
3. Friend enemy scheme: A belief that there are dangerous enemies (Others) that need to be eliminated
4. Patriarchy and militarism: Conservative values, such as sexism, patriarchy, militarism, are spread (Adapted from Fuchs 2018, 53)

Key aspects of forms of fascism and right-wing populism more generally are its conservative gender hierarchy, sexism and often also misogyny. Fascism idealises the body, hard work, male supremacy, and bodily fitness and health. Right-wing and fascist ideologies are dualist and separate genders to the realm of production (men) and to the realm of reproduction (women). The body of the male soldier becomes the ideal body that all men should emulate through physical exercise for example (Fuchs 2018, 68). Fuchs argues that such a dualism (which is also evident in the friend enemy scheme) is ideologically rationalised through patriarchy. Patriarchy is perceived as correct and adequate behaviour, looks and characteristics of what it means to be male and female. 'Women are thereby often reduced to sexuality, biology and housework' (ibid, 240).

Like fascism, right-wing extremist populism is structured by racism, nationalism, misogyny and ableism. It is driven by exclusionary discourses and actions through which a particular group, or a charismatic leader, are presented as embodying the will of the people that seeks to overthrow existing elites and norms. It is characterised by a logic of 'us' and 'them' whereby specific groups (refugees, women, LGBTQI+, disabled or somehow 'different') are seen as the source of a population's problems.

The so-called 'alt-right' has been particularly visible as an amorphous clustering of individuals and groups online as well as offline (Hawley 2017; Wendling 2018). Members of this cluster have moved from a niche position to the mainstream in U.S. and by extension wider Western politics (Wendling 2018). 'The Alt Right helped Donald Trump get elected president, and Trump's campaign put the Alt Right in the news' (Lyons 2017, 2). It is anti-Semitic, racist, anti-feminist and against gender equality. As Hawley argues:

> The Alt-Right is fundamentally concerned with race. At its core, the Alt-Right is a white-nationalist movement, even if many (perhaps most) of the people who identify with the Alt-Right do not care for that term. The most energetic and significant figures of the movement want to see the creation of a white ethnostate in North America. …We can say that the Alt-Right is also an antifeminist movement opposed to contemporary notions of gender equality and in favor of a more patriarchal society. But its critique of feminism is not usually based on traditional religious arguments about gender roles. The Alt-Right promotes what it calls 'sex realism'—that men and women have biological differences that make them suited to different social roles. There is some overlap between the Alt-Right and the so-called Men's Rights Movement, which argues that discrimination against men is now a greater problem than discrimination against women. (Hawley 2017, 11, 17)

This overlap between the alt-right and the current Men's Rights movement is key to keep in mind. As I go on to show, the various male communities and individuals discussed in this book share explicit and at times more implicit connections to the alt-right and the Men's Rights Movement. The alt-right has become an umbrella term and signifier under which a variety of far-right movements assemble. It is leaderless and unhierarchical. It also uses 'resources with considerable skill as well as appropriating practices on the ground usually associated with social movements of the radical left' (Salazar 2018, 136). The technological savviness and skill of members of the alt-right is crucial in understanding how young men (and to a lesser degree) women are captivated by its use of technology (Fielitz & Thurston 2019), such as YouTube videos (Lewis 2018), memes and animated gifs (deCook 2018; Lamerichs et al. 2018), social media presence, tropes from gaming culture and popular culture (Blodgett & Salter 2018), to name a few.

Another key aspect that needs mentioning is the relationship between the anonymous forum 4chan and the alt-right. As Wendling argues, 4chan is a key dimension of the alt-right in so far as it became 'a breeding ground and a destination' (ibid, 51) for many alt-righters. 4chan has effectively no, or incredibly lax, content moderation policies. 'To wade into 4chan as a "normie"—someone who's "mainstream," the least bit conventional, or unfamiliar with the internet's dark underbelly—takes a strong stomach' (ibid, 52). 4chan, like Reddit, can be seen as a nostalgic and regressive attempt to return to an internet that once existed (or possibly never) before the internet became (a) more mainstream and (b) commodified and dominated by big corporations. It has been argued that the 4chan politics board/pol/ (short for Politically Incorrect) was used as a base for launching recruitment efforts for the alt-right and to turn young men into right-wing radicals. The particular ironic and humorous tone of communities like 4chan is a distinctive feature of the new right-wing extremism and how it has shaped other communities such as incels or MGTOW, or the manosphere (Greene 2019; Udupa 2019; Krüger 2021). While the alt-right has been declining in recent years (ca. since 2017) as many prominent members have been banned from mainstream social media platforms, it has not entirely disappeared. One can speak of a prevailing 'alt-right mindset' which articulates itself in various offshoots and attempts by fascists and members of the alt-right movement to regain a stronger online presence (Hermansson et al. 2020).

Adrienne Massanari (2017) and Michael Salter (2018) have both argued that Reddit in particular has amplified the bringing together and spreading of misogynistic communities. It is not a coincidence, then, that all of the communities examined in this book in more detail (incels, MGTOW, NoFap) had and have various subreddits. Massanari (2017) notes that it is Reddit's design, algorithms, and platform politics that support, if not partially enable, the emergence of a hub for toxic masculinity and misogyny. This is also true in relation to other niche communities (such as ones that focus on extreme pornography, or share pictures of corpses for example) that assembled on Reddit and were allowed to exist largely unmoderated for many years until the platform tightened its moderation policies in 2017 and again in 2019 after mounting public pressure. This led to the ban of some of the subreddits. At the same time, as Massanari shows, Reddit as such is not an inherently toxic platform, because there are many feminist, anti-racist communities or simply spaces where individuals form around a particular identity or a hobby.

The Men's Rights Movement is not only significant because of its relationship to the alt-right, MRAs (men's rights activists) are important predecessors and influencers of the contemporary manosphere. MRAs go back to at least the early 1970s in the United States and can be seen as a response to feminism(s). They focus on areas of modern society and developments that, as they argue, negatively impact men, such as family law, parenting, male suicide, violence against men, stereotypical male identities that they need to conform to (Messner 1998). The internet provides new opportunities for MRAs and the manosphere has emerged in the past years on platforms such as Reddit, YouTube as well as singular websites. Hawley defines the manosphere as:

> a loose collection of blogs, Reddit topics, traditional web boards and social media accounts. Some are more or less self-help groups or concentrate on individual campaigns such as combating sexual abuse against boys or agitating for rights of fathers post-divorce. Some communities completely swear off sex and masturbation—while some (like the PUAs) are fixated on sleeping with as many women as possible. Some are obsessed with rape statistics and false rape claims. Some are simply devoted to cataloguing what they see as the evils of modern feminism. (Hawley 2017, 62)

The manosphere, as I go on to show in this book, explicitly borrows from or makes use of alt-right discourses, ideas, images, and terminology.

In addition to the factors, groups and terms I have just outlined, there are four cultural developments and moments of the past years that are particularly important when it comes to understanding current online misogyny. They functioned as scene-setters and originators. They are: *Fight Club* (1999, Fincher) and *The Matrix* (1999, Wachowski & Wachowski), Pick Up Artists and Gamergate.

Blue pills, red pills and snowflakes

Two films which were released in 1999 have taken on a renewed currency in recent years as they have been taken up and references circulate in the communities of the manosphere and the alt-right, respectively. In *The Matrix*, Morpheus famously asks Neo to choose the blue pill or the red pill. The blue pill meaning ignorance and avoidance of reality, whereas the red pill refers to the truth. The notion of the red pill (and its offspring the black pill) has been picked up by the manosphere in particular to denote a truth about a kind of gender order. *Fight Club* is also about questions of facing or rejecting the real world. Men form a proto-fascist group which is inward focused on male brotherhood. *Fight Club* could be read as an articulation and staging of fascist masculinity, because it practices gender segregation and violence. *Fight Club* is significant in another sense, because the term 'snowflake' is used in the story. Tyler Durden uses a megaphone to tell his men: 'You are not a beautiful or unique snowflake'. Snowflake has come to be used by the alt-right to refer to people who are easily offended, weak, or fragile. It closely resembles the terms 'cuck' and 'SJW' (social justice warrior) and is often aimed at individuals on the left.

Commentators have pointed out that the alt-right misreads, or wrongly decodes, those films. However, this argument is problematic, because audiences read media texts in different ways as decades of audience studies have shown (ever since cultural studies emerged). Nonetheless, I would argue that both *The Matrix* and *Fight Club* are neither inherently fascist nor in any way to blame for the culture wars that have emerged in recent years. Both films feature important female characters for example; a fact that is conveniently ignored by the alt-right. We could also read *The Matrix* as a critique of consumer capitalism and the status of digital technologies in shaping our perceptions of and experiences of reality itself. It also offers an implicit critique of fascism where the Agents and the machines are shown as annihilating everything that is different and threatens the system.

Tyler Durden's utopia as it becomes increasingly clear in *Fight Club* is 'an agrarian-oriented hunter-gatherer society where people were attired in all-leather clothes and grew food amidst abandoned skyscrapers and superhighways' (Vacker 2019, online). Vacker notes that Durden's vision of the future reflected those of the eco-terrorist known as the Unabomber in the United States of the 1980s and 1990s. He sent mail bombs to universities and corporations with the ultimate aim to destroy all technology. The final scenes of *Fight Club* come close to such a 'ground zero', a term famously uttered in the first scene of the film by Durden. The greatest fear as shown in *Fight Club* is 'that our mass-produced consumer society is concealing meaninglessness in a universe of expanding nothingness'. The young cis men, and they are often but not exclusively young men, discussed in this book grew up with *Fight Club* and *The Matrix*, as did I. *The Matrix* in particular was a defining film for me and my generation and the ones who would follow. A global pop cultural icon with a lasting legacy. *The Matrix* foreshadowed the deep interconnection and blurring of 'reality' and 'virtuality'. Today's world has moved ever closer to the hyperreal. The notion of self-improvement that is a key part of *Fight Club* is also an implicit thread of this book. The men who I discuss define and debate different ideas of self-improvement and what it might mean in relation to masculinity. 'Self-improvement is masturbation; now self-destruction, that's improvement,' says Tyler to Jack in the film. *Fight Club*'s nihilism is picked up by the alt-right and by the incel community in particular where images, quotes and memes of the film are shared. Incels recognise themselves in the film.

Vacker argues that the men of *Fight Club* are the 'spiritual twin[s] of fundamentalists, religious terrorists, racial supremacists, internet tough guys, and anti-science zealots, those anti-enlightenment tribes who champion premodern superstitions as a guide for hypermodern societies' (Vacker 2019, online). He writes that *The Matrix* shows a similar vision of a life outside of technology. Both films also begin with alienated men (Neo and Jack) who fundamentally transform, revolutionise their own existences. Tyler Durden, a proto-fascist ideologue, is shown as a form of ideal masculinity for the other, weaker men of the film. This is a *key* aspect for understanding the film's appeal and those men discussed in this book who relate to the film. They latch on to those fantasies of transformation. Another key aspect of *Fight Club* is that Jack and Tyler are the same person, thus symbolising the inherent contradictions and struggles of cisheterosexual men today. This contradiction is one of desires and fantasies where men are faced with conflicting ideas and affects. This is a theme I develop at length in the coming chapters.

Either way, both terms of the red pill and the snowflake may have been picked up as mere pop cultural references by geeky, male internet cultures that effortlessly remix and use a multitude of citational practices to fit a particular agenda or argument to their worldview. Many of the communities and men that I discuss in this book are convinced by the notion of the red pill and enthusiastically pronounce their allegiance to, for example, being a MGTOW because they have been 'red pilled' and realised the true nature of this world. For those men, the red pill essentially means knowing (or believing in) a sexual marketplace where women are only interested in high-status men. Status can be obtained by career progression, or other steps to create the appearance of a confident, successful male. The incels' *black pill* takes this further and argues that sexuality is determined upon biological characteristics and looks, such as the jawline of a man. Incels claim that they are oppressed by such a system, because they lack the biological characteristics to take part in it. Another key moment of recent history is imperative in understanding contemporary online cultures and how they are related to the alt-right.

Gamergate

Gamergate is of crucial significance to understand the current communities, some of which were initiated on 4chan, that spread misogyny, sexism and racism. Gamergate was the blueprint for the symbolic and physical *terrorism* of (mostly white) men that women often have to endure today on the internet. It does not matter if they have to endure it directly or indirectly. In 2014, when Facebook and Twitter and other social media platforms started to become fully mainstream, the ex-boyfriend of video game designer, Zoë Quinn, published a lengthy document online. This document detailed the last few weeks of the relationship and included intimate details that should have never been made public. Users of the platforms 4chan and Reddit, homes of online communities and subcultures some of which were frequented by gamers, began a campaign of abuse aimed at Quinn. In a world of male fragility and misogyny, a woman should not be a game designer. Users conjured up conspiracy theories that Quinn was sleeping with male gaming journalists in exchange for positive coverage. Soon other female game journalists, critics and designers were also targeted in a terrorist campaign that lasted months. They were 'doxxed' (where personal details of an individual are posted online) and they received thousands of rape and death threats. Gamergate was the first culture war of the internet. A large group of men set up fake Twitter accounts and pretended to be feminists in order to get ridiculous hashtags, such as #EndFathersDay, trending on Twitter. Male subcultures that had been considered apolitical and harmless up until then exposed their infantile and reactionary face (Massanari 2017; Wendling 2018). Women, ethnic minorities and liberal individuals (often labelled 'social justice warriors' by reactionaries and the far right) were seeking to change gaming culture, to undermine a male domain, and to end such men's virtual existences. 'Political correctness', 'cultural Marxism' and feminism were about to enter gaming cultures. Those were the paranoid and threatening fantasies of the male gamers. They had to fight back (Proctor & Kies 2018). Gamergate brought nerds together with MRAs and catapulted them into the mainstream.

Adrienne Massanari (2017) argues that it was Reddit in particular that helped to not only provide a platform for the aftermath of Gamergate, but also to bring the reactionary and violent aspects of male online communities fully into existence. Reddit was a perfect, less hidden, platform for Gamergaters, MRAs and others, because of its quasi inexistent content and moderation policies.

George Hawley (2017) names Gamergate as belonging to the predecessors of the alt-right. Its persistent, mass trolling and flooding has significantly shaped alt-right tactics. *The New York Times* argued that Gamergate has decisively influenced the mainstream political culture across the West. It is in Trump's tweets, the bot armies on Twitter, fake news and fake hashtags, criticism of the mainstream media, mass death and rape threats against women, LGBTQI+ and BIPOC individuals and above all: the army of anti-feminist YouTubers, social media influencers and politicians (Warzel 2019). Gamergate was the prototype of male online harassment and radicalised some young men into violent misogynists.

Pick Up Artists

Another cultural phenomenon is important for understanding some of the male communities that are active on the internet today: Pick Up Artists (PUAs). PUA goes back to at least the early 1990s and by the 2000s, it had become mainstream in U.S. culture through TV dating shows for example. Pick Up Artistry is essentially a strategy of how to manipulate women in order to have sex with them. PUAs see their efforts as a 'game' where particular rules can be followed that are applicable to all women. PUA is an ideology that sells some straight men the illusion that they can 'crack' any woman. PUAs are an essential part of the neoliberal sexual culture which is structured, at least partly, along the lines of competition and consumption of partners and sexuality (Banet-Weiser & Miltner 2016; Kray 2018; O'Neill 2018; Bratich & Banet-Weiser 2019). The aforementioned notion of the red pill is often referenced in today's pick up communities, for example the popular subreddit *The Red Pill*. PUA designates a strategy that essentially thinks of women and female subjectivity as *machinic and biologistic*. Women are like machines and all it takes is the right male 'algorithm' to get access to them. This form of instrumental thinking is crucial to other male communities, such as incels, MGTOW and NoFap today, and I return to it in the chapters to come. PUA promises traditional male entitlement to heterosexuality and a phallic potency that is amplified through how masculinity is often portrayed in the mainstream media – a masculinity that (cis) men can never obtain in reality because it is constructed as a fantasy. Rachel O'Neill (2018) has demonstrated the way PUA 'trainers' work with some heterosexual men as part of a flourishing seduction industry. She shows that the men she interviewed feel confused and find it difficult to navigate a so-called 'postfeminist' world of dating where women may present themselves as phallic and empowered (see also McRobbie 2009). Having discussed sociocultural developments that form an important backdrop to this book, I outline central concepts in the next section.

Psychoanalysis: fantasy, desire, castration and affect

This book makes a contribution to a psycho-cultural approach to digital media, as developed by the editors of the book series of which it is a part (Bainbridge 2012, 2013, 2019, 2020; Bainbridge & Yates 2011, 2012, 2014; Yates 2007, 2015, 2019). Such an approach draws on psychosocial studies, psychoanalytic theory and methodology as well as work from media and cultural studies. The book is also situated within studies of (social) media that have drawn on psychoanalysis, an area which is growing within media studies (Dean 2010; Turkle 2011; Balick 2014; Horbury 2015; Johanssen & Krüger 2016; Clough 2018a; Eichhorn 2019; Johanssen 2019; Pinchevski 2019; Singh 2019). It is particularly useful because it places an emphasis on messy and contradictory modes of how individuals are implicated by and respond to social forces. It shifts the attention from rationality to contradictions, incoherencies, ambivalent and seemingly nonsensical experiences, thoughts, fantasies and expressions. It also consists of a unique theory about the relationship between fantasy and reality that pays attention to emotional and affective investments in discourses, images and ideas (Johanssen 2019).

A psychoanalytic and psychosocial approach may specifically help us to better understand the psychodynamics of individuals embedded in cultural and social processes resulting from and responding to online misogyny.

From the very beginning, psychoanalysis was concerned with questions of masculinity, femininity and how gender related to sexuality. Sigmund Freud stressed that there is no 'normal' sexuality and heterosexuality is a myth. He also noted that the feminine was a dark continent, or a mysterious riddle without an answer. While his particular theories of female sexuality were critiqued by feminist thinkers (for example, Mitchell 1974), his work proved to be influential for thinking about gender and sexuality for many disciplines and post-Freudian psychoanalysts. Sexuality and related themes have primarily been discussed in clinical terms by psychoanalysts and some have also related them to cultural aspects – an area that has been growing in recent years (Lemma & Lynch 2015; Giffney & Watson 2017; Knafo & Lo Bosco 2017; Lemma 2017; Kanwal & Akhtar 2018).

Psychoanalytic understandings of gender and sexuality have been discussed by a wide range of thinkers (Rose 1986; Pollock 1988; Butler 1990; Sedgwick 1993; Copjec 1994; de Lauretis 1994; Grosz 1995; Dean 2000; Yates 2007; Bainbridge 2008 and many others). There are some authors who specifically discuss masculinity and psychoanalysis (Frosh 1994) and some have also written about misogyny (Moss 2003) as well as more generally discrimination, such as sexism, racism and homophobia (Young-Bruehl 1996; Auestad 2012, 2014; Krüger, Figlio & Richards 2018) and violence (Sinclair & Steinkoler 2019). Prejudice occurs because of a fundamental threat that is individually felt (which is of course not objectively real), consciously or unconsciously, and turned into a specific prejudice (racism, sexism, homophobia, Islamophobia). Elisabeth Young-Bruehl defines prejudices as 'social mechanisms of defence' (1996, 209).

The psychoanalytic notion of fantasy in its Freudian definition is particularly useful and I use it frequently in the book (Freud 1981d). All different platforms and communities can be seen as spaces where fantasies are expressed and commented on by other users, who often affirm someone else's fantasy. Fantasy, which Freud defined in a non-judgemental way, refers to imaginary scenes created by the individual in which they are the protagonist. Freud made an analogy between fantasy and nationalism when he writes that fantasies are similar 'to the legends by means of which a nation that has become great and proud tries to conceal the insignificance and failure of its beginnings' (Freud 1981d, 20). Fantasising often represents a desire for wish fulfilment, the creation of a particular reality (Freud 1981d, e).

For example, the various online communities discussed in this book construct different, misogynistic fantasies of what masculine identity means in relation to a feminine Other.[3] The users construct women in certain ways (for example as having too much power over men, or as being superficial). In response to this, fantasies of masculine identity are created and social-political ideas that echo right-wing populism are evoked (for example that women need to stay at home, or that white women should only be in relationships with white men). From a psychoanalytic perspective, such fantasies and how they are manifested in content online are marked by a (potential) identification of men with highly attractive discourses that characterise them as being powerless victims and as being wronged by particular groups or individuals (feminists, women). Right-wing populism and fascism tap into individuals' existing (un)conscious fears and anxieties which are then exploited and distorted: fears of difference, loss and social change (Auestad 2014). The manosphere operates in a similar way. It makes use of a populist logic of 'us vs. them' (men vs. women) which characterises feminism and women as the problem and promises new forms of masculine identity. At the same time, fantasy also implies an active component where new realities, actions or relations are constructed in the mind. This is a process I detail throughout the chapters of this book as fantasies shift between defense mechanisms and self-victimisation and toxic symbolic power.

Related to fantasy, there are a number of other key terms and concepts that I use throughout this book and it is helpful to briefly define them at this point. They are 'desire', 'phallus', 'symbolic castration' and 'affect'. Desire is closely connected to fantasy and the drive. While this book is not primarily Lacanian (but more Freudian) in its orientation, I nonetheless find Lacan useful in how he developed some of Freud's concepts in relation to questions of desire, sexuality and fantasy. For Lacan (1977), the drive can be imagined as a motion that endlessly circles around its (part)-object, going back and forth in an endless loop, never fully obtaining it. Desire on the other hand is a forward-facing motion, perpetuating onwards with productive force. Lacan (1977) regards desire as first and foremost unconscious and sexual. The aim of psychoanalytic treatment is to render desire conscious through free association. However, there is always an element to desire which cannot be fully known, or which cannot be turned into language.

I use desire in a way to refer to conscious desire in most instances. The online men are (to a degree) *conscious* of their different desires in most cases and they either name their desires explicitly or implicitly. We are able to interpret their narratives to mean or refer to a particular desire even if such desire is not explicitly named. It is the productive force of desire, which Lacan (1977) as well as Deleuze and Guattari have also emphasised in their reworking of Freud (Deleuze & Guattari 1983a, b), that is absolutely essential for incels, MGTOWs, NoFappers and the other men.[4] This desire has unconscious components that frighten those men and which they are torn between. For Lacan, desire can never be satisfied or fulfilled. It is always deferred. It knows no end. It has no final object or is not oriented towards a particular object, even though it momentarily seeks particular objects. In a sense, desire is dependent on 'the unavailability of its object' (Ruti 2018,

141) and leaves us wanting 'to keep wanting' (ibid). Desire is particularly related to other human beings, where individuals seek to be desired by others and recognised by them as subjects. Incels, for example, wish nothing more than to be desired by women, to be seen and valued. Linked to desire is the notion of *the desire to desire* (Deleuze & Guattari 1983a, b) which I develop more in Chapter 7.

With the Lacanian theorist Mari Ruti, we could read the manosphere as a collective embodiment of penis envy (Ruti 2018). Penis envy, for psychoanalysis and for Lacan in particular, constitutes an act of envy of the symbolic (and very real) power and prestige that the phallus brings. The 'penis as a signifier of phallic power is a collective fetish' (Ruti 2018, xi). Yet, the two are not synonymous (see Chapter 1). Those who consider themselves as lacking the phallus, or as having been castrated, envy those who have it. As the many narratives of the men discussed in this book attest, they feel that it is now women who have the phallus and undermine men. The phallus is a key psychoanalytic concept which I return to numerous times in this book. However, it is not sufficient to explain the dynamics and contradictions of those men alone. Related to the phallus is the idea of castration for psychoanalysis. Penis envy goes back to Freud and he argued that initially the girl thought she had been castrated as she spots her brother's or father's penis and realises she has none. The boy thinks the same and fears that he will be castrated next (by the father). This idea has been critiqued and developed to wide-ranging extents. I return to it in more detail in Chapter 1. My discussion of symbolic castration in this book relates to a fantasy of loss of phallic power. For Lacan, castration means 'a symbolic lack of an imaginary object' (Evans 1996, 23) that is universal for all subjects. All must accept castration in order to reach a degree of healthy psychic functioning. However, this does not mean that fantasies of castration (or penis envy) do not present themselves throughout an individual's life. In fact, I argue that the conscious fantasy of symbolic castration – i.e. the taking away of phallic power – is a key component of the psyches of the men that I discuss in this book. As I outline in Chapter 1, there have been many critiques of the phallus as a concept and of (specifically Freudian-Lacanian) psychoanalysis as phallocentric. Such critiques come from both inside psychoanalysis (Benjamin 1988) as well as from other disciplines such as media and cultural studies (for example Renold & Ringrose 2012, 2017). I feel it is useful to deploy the phallus as an analytical category because the narratives I analyse are phallic in themselves (Allan 2016). This does not mean, however, that my analysis is phallic or meant to reproduce phallocentricity. I return to this point in the book's Conclusion.

Finally, affect in its Freudian orientation is an important concept for me as it allows a conceptualisation of the un/conscious entanglements of language and embodied experience (Johanssen 2019). Theweleit also uses it in his work in more implicit terms. Related to dis/inhibition, we can understand affect as the body's attempts to uphold a homeostasis or bodily equilibrium. For Freud, affect in his early discharge model refers to subjective bodily experiences that are felt and subsequently 'discharged', as he called it. They leave the body and fade away. An affective experience, while partially consciously felt, designates a state of momentary bodily dispossession and loss of agency (Freud 1981a), for instance, when my body involuntarily jerks while watching a horror film sequence. We can also think of bodily states of feeling agitated or under pressure as essentially affective states which we cannot fully name, explain or describe. Affect refers to a state of bodily tension. In the context of this book, this refers to a state that can become so severe for some men that they seek to annihilate the other who they think is responsible for it.

Chapter summaries and theoretical positions of this book

Broadly speaking, Chapters 1, 2, 3 and 4 of this book are more sociostructural and Chapters 5, 6 and 7 are more psychological-subjective in terms of their analytical *foci*. The first three chapters of this book set the wider scene and critically introduce important terms and contexts. Chapter 1 introduces my theoretical framework and specifically the notion of dis/inhibition. Chapter 2 provides a review of important literature from feminist media studies and other fields. Chapter 3 discusses the wider sexual politics of alt-right, and reactionary YouTubers which inform the subsequent case studies of this book: incels (Chapters 4 and 5), MGTOW (Chapter 5), NoFap (Chapter 7), as well as the two mass shooters (Chapter 6). It is in those chapters that my theoretical framework comes into full use. Dis/Inhibition is a general conceptual thread that runs through the various chapters as I show how the male fantasies at work in the manosphere are inherently structured by contradictions, defense mechanisms and the creation of agentic symbolic power, passivity and activity and changing forms of desire.

Wilhelm Reich is an important thinker for understanding the relationship between sexuality and fascism. I discuss his *Mass Psychology of Fascism* (1997) in Chapter 1. Reich argued that fascism came about to a strong degree because of sexual repression and sexual inhibition and that the primary roots of fascism were laid down in the nuclear family. The authoritarian father is a representative of the authoritarian state. For Reich, the average human being has inherently fascistic dynamics within them rather than them being caused or inserted into them by fascism. This is an important insight. Chapter 1 highlights four main themes of Theweleit's, Reich's and Young-Bruehl's works which I take up in the book. Those themes are: The fascist character type; questions around sexuality and upbringing; the absent presence of woman; the body armour and the fragmented ego. Those themes are informative for my wider analyses in the coming chapters and I return to them throughout.

The German philosopher and theorist Klaus Theweleit is essential for my wider arguments. This book is in part an *homage* to Theweleit's groundbreaking two-volume work, *Männerphantasien* (1977, 1978) – *Male Fantasies* (1987, 1989) – and its illuminating and highly original analysis of the men of the Weimar Republic. Theweleit shows that a particular bodily and fantasmatic predisposition enabled and eagerly responded to Nazism and the Third Reich. His psychoanalysis of male bodies is, in my view, the best work when it comes to understanding affirmations of fascism and how they are inherently tied to misogyny. Its punchy, witty and wild style whisks the reader away into a jungle of penetrating arguments that go beyond 1920s Germany. Theweleit asks:

> Can we not then trace a straight line from the witch to the seductive Jewish woman? Is the persecution of the sensuous woman not a permanent reality, one which is not primarily economic in origin, but which derives from the specific social organization of gender relations in patriarchal Europe? (Theweleit 1987, 79)

As I go on to show, Theweleit's arguments are not only historical in nature, but can be read as an analysis of patriarchy as a psychosocial ontology that goes back hundreds of years. In that sense, his analysis is ahistorical even though he pays specific attention to historical contexts. His ideas are particularly applicable and can be developed in relation to today's manosphere. Chapter 1 introduces and discusses Theweleit's two volumes. Based on hundreds of novels, diaries, images and other data that Theweleit analysed, he produced a psychoanalytic study of German men, many of whom members of the Freikorps militias, and their bodies, fantasies and unconscious. He argued that those men defended against everything pleasurable and sensual in women and in themselves. Women were either purified as asexual beings or killed as a 'dirty', threatening, phallic, sexualised Other. Killing the other served as a defense against a conscious fear of being castrated. In killing the woman, she is symbolically castrated, and this act brought pleasure to the soldier male. Such acts, along with the feeling of being part of a collective (like fascism), strengthened the soldier's body armour – a term Theweleit develops from Reich. This is also achieved through writing and speaking about women, enemies and the massacres those men engaged in. They are *consciously* constructing barriers and dams against feelings of bodily ego disintegration. This is an absolutely key insight for analysing the men I discuss in this book, for I argue that they are similarly conscious of their own feelings of impotence and disintegration. However, such feelings nonetheless have unconscious dimensions, which I unpack in the coming chapters. Chapter 1 also develops my concept of dis/inhibition mentioned earlier.

Chapter 2 presents a review of literature from feminist media studies, sociology, feminist theory and other fields that discusses the wider themes of this book: the changing nature of sexuality due to the sexual revolution of 1968; evolving feminist movements and the Men's Rights Movement from the late 1960s onwards; masculinity in crisis debates; the alt-right and white supremacy; geek and non-hegemonic masculinity; as well as debates on postfeminism and porn culture. I show how this book relates to such scholarship and what interventions it makes. The themes outlined in Chapter 2 are also regularly mobilised by the manosphere in a very different way to how academics discuss them.

Chapter 3 picks up on the consequences of the sexual revolution of the late 1960s, which has become a key signifier for contemporary conservative, reactionary, and alt-right commentators online. I discuss selected YouTubers in detail and how they construct the sexual revolution as a powerful event that led to moral decline, sexual disinhibition and many other alleged ills of the present. While the sexual revolution was by no means uncomplicated (as I discuss in Chapter 2), the backlash against it from the alt-right and other circles today is unjustified. The consequences of the sexual revolution show themselves in particular in how sexuality has become a commodity that we are surrounded by through advertising and other media images. Sexuality is shown as agentic, lustful and liberated, and particularly in a hypersexualised femininity where women are objectified. This also shows itself in the widespread use of pornography. Such portrayals of sexuality are taken up by some men today and distorted. They blame women and feminism for feeling (sexually) undermined and powerless. They feel inhibited by the images of and fantasies of disinhibition around them. Such narratives also need to be seen in relation to narratives about neoliberalism, evolutionary psychology and how sexuality is embedded in a logic of the market, which I discuss in the chapter.

Chapter 4 focuses on incels and analyses data from Reddit. Incels, who have often never been in a relationship with a woman, demonstrate the fundamental contradiction of many men of the manosphere: a simultaneous desire for and destruction of cis women. I show how incels appear to be exercising defensive, self-destructive and nihilistic dynamics when they endlessly pity themselves and speak of a general hatred of the world and of women in particular. However, at the same time incels are in a state of constant affective tension where they just want to be with a woman. I also show how incels appropriate the discourses and images handed to them by the alt-right and how they discuss questions of race and ethnicity. Incels desire fascist male bodies and many are obsessed about genetics, for example, and the shape of their head or jawline. They move beyond defense mechanisms and construct fantasies of active transformation. Their fora are also overflowing with narratives of symbolic destruction of women, they talk about enacting revenge on women for having been ignored or rejected. Drawing on Jack Bratich and Sarah Banet-Weiser's (2019) recent discussion of incels and neoliberalism and their argument that incels emerge as a particular response to the 2008 financial crisis which resulted in many men losing confidence in neoliberalism and in themselves, I argue that the fantasy of the fascist body provides the men with a toxic form of symbolic power through which they wish to move beyond apathy.

Elisabeth Young-Bruehl and her book *The Anatomy of Prejudices* (1996) provides a sophisticated theorisation of sexism (as well as racism and homophobia) by drawing on psychoanalysis. Her work is introduced in Chapter 5, which discusses another Reddit community: Men Going Their Own Way (MGTOW), a community that finds itself in a similar contradiction as incels. We could say that it is structured in its ontology around the negativity of woman. Woman is constantly present in her absence for MGTOWs as they discuss their male lifestyles of solitude, adventures and happiness. MGTOW ideology is less destructive, but it is just as misogynist as incels are, but the woman is ultimately desired in the same way. The figure of the woman is a necessary fantasy for MGTOWs in order for them to be able to discuss the kind of male camaraderie they advocate. Ultimately, they desire women, even though they would never admit it. I spend the second half of the chapter to argue how both incels and MGTOWs are obsessional characters in the sense of Young-Bruehl's definition (with some hysterical character elements as well). Drawing on the basic character types as developed by Freud (1932), Young-Bruehl discusses in detail how they differ in their embodiment of prejudice. I note that many men of the manosphere, incels and MGTOWs in particular, can be seen as obsessional characters with harsh, controlling super-egos who at the same time blame the other for their misfortune. Such characters are both readily available and formed in those communities, where individuals adapt particular character traits which already map onto their individual obsessional characters. Such character types are consciously modelled and cultivated within those communities as members define and discuss for instance what it means to be an incel or a MGTOW.

I also return to the question of the unconscious and argue that incels and MGTOWs unconsciously wish to supersede and kill their parental *imagos*, their fathers in particular, because they failed to hand down the phallus in an act of intergenerational betrayal. I return to the father in Chapter 6.

In her impressive study of Islamist terrorism, the psychoanalyst Ruth Stein discusses the role of the father in psychoanalytic theory and for men who become Islamist terrorists. I relate Stein's work in more detail to male mass shooters in Chapter 6 where I analyse the so-called 'manifestos' of the mass shooters Anders Behring Breivik and the self-identified incel Elliot Rodger, both of which are littered with misogyny and a hatred of women and feminism, as well as an advocacy of fascist ideas. Rodger in particular is often discussed in the manosphere and regarded as a hero by some. For the terrorists Stein writes about, as for many other deeply religious individuals, God is a father. They worship him and are convinced that it is him who gives them strength, in fact commands of them, to carry out their violent acts. While incels and other men of the manosphere may not believe in God or in a father-like leader, there are nonetheless some similarities in the role of the father for them and the terrorists Stein discusses. The father is constructed as an idealised figure who is desired and yet this desire is disrupted by the real (or fantasmatically 'real') father who has betrayed incels, or failed the men. They desire a phallic father, who guides them and who they ultimately wish to become. Many of the male terrorists, like Anders Breivik and Elliot Rodger, had a fragile or disintegrated sense of masculinity. One that was, on the one hand, threatened by women, and, on the other hand, not nurtured through their fathers. As I discuss in Chapter 6, both had had problems with their fathers and the question poses itself if their actions were final, dramatic attempts at being seen by and castrating/killing/surpassing their fathers.

Chapter 7 focuses on the anti-pornography and anti-masturbation community NoFap and its official forum NoFap.com. NoFap is a self-help forum where men (and some women) who describe themselves as being addicted to porn discuss strategies and document their journey of kicking their addiction. NoFap is less explicitly shaped by alt-right ideas than the YouTubers, incels or MGTOWs, but many men nonetheless portray a problematic understanding of women and unwittingly demonstrate how their desires and images of femininity and masculinity have been shaped by porn. The chapter returns to the notions of desire and fantasy in more detail and spells out further how they look like for the men of the manosphere. I focus on two particular porn genres, which are discussed in many threads on NoFap.com, 'sissy hypno porn' (videos that aim to emasculate men and 'hypnotise' them into being women) and 'cuckold porn' (videos which feature a 'husband' being 'forced' to watch his unfaithful 'wife' have sex with a black man). I relate such discussions to other data from NoFap about racist anxieties, defenses against the consumption of gay porn and the male porn actor in general.

Drawing on Elizabeth Cowie's (1997) theory of fantasy and spectatorship, I argue that the men of NoFap reveal shifting desires and fantasies from identification and a kind of queer desire (for hetero, gay and other porn) to a disidentification and a turning away from such content in order to embrace a traditional heterosexual, hegemonic masculinity. NoFappers also see a feminist conspiracy at work behind sissy hypno and cuckold porn and speculate who may be behind it. I argue that such speculations demonstrate a fear of their own unconscious and its productive force. I draw on Patricia Ticineto Clough's notion of the user unconscious (Clough 2018a) in this context to argue that the very unconscious of those men is born out of their own subjectivities coupled with digital technology (porn-streaming websites, algorithms, big data).

The Conclusion provides a summary of the book's key arguments. I also relate the wider dynamics of the manosphere to contemporary politics and technology. I argue via the Lacanian theorist Olivier Jutel (2019, 2020) that there is a striking similarity between, what he calls, 'techno-liberalism' and the logic of the manosphere. Both operate with a view that postulates that social life can be subsumed under a computational logic of big data analytics and artificial intelligence. At a time when political campaigns and policies are driven by sophisticated computational technology that seeks to automate politics via means of data accumulation and surveillance, the manosphere reflects such a logic in its incessant accumulation of data (articles, posts, videos, etc.) about its 'enemies'. Both politics and the manosphere further a fantasy in which the Other has been excluded and neat virtual worlds are created. However, this desire for phallic mastery, as I show in this book, always fails.

The Conclusion then moves to a new theoretical perspective. I turn to the work of Jessica Benjamin (1988, 2018) and her theory of intersubjective recognition. For Benjamin, recognition is a kind of foundational moment between mother and baby which comes to be a key dimension in the individual's whole life. Recognition means to be able to see the other as similar and different and that the other does the same. If there is one other underlying theme of this book it is a desire for recognition that those men have but cannot bring themselves to fully articulate. Such a desire perhaps presents us with a more hopeful perspective. It can be better analysed through Benjamin and her relational account of subjectivity rather than Freud/Lacan as she foregrounds the pre-Oedipal moment of recognition between infant and mother.

***

Why this book? Some self-reflections

Why write this book? In this final section of this chapter, I wish to provide reflections on my own (unconscious) investments in this project and also address some critical points that readers may articulate.

Research that is influenced by psychoanalysis always takes the researcher and their un/conscious and affective relationship to the topic and data into account. Like many men, I am unsure how I would define myself as a male, or how I would describe a particular sense of masculine identity that I embody. One perhaps cannot help but mobilise particular signifiers that anchor one's identity: White, cis-heterosexual, middle-class, left-wing, feminist. At the same time, I don't feel like those attributes would communicate much about who I am. I am an academic, born in Germany and living in the UK. I would also feel that there is a distinct confusion over my own masculine identity, or rather how I would describe it to others. Maybe I would also describe myself as empathic, thoughtful, reflexive, funny, contradictory, vulnerable, doubtful and self-critical. I am just a man – and such a statement already carries inherent privilege. The writing of this book, then, perhaps was also unconsciously motivated by my own desire to arrive at a clearer understanding or self-description of who I am, or who I am *not*, as a 35-year-old male.

In this book, I try to understand the men I analyse, at least to some degree. While I remain deeply critical of them, I also engage in what the psychoanalyst Ruth Stein called 'identificatory knowledge' (Stein 2010, 3). This designates an essentially impossible act, but one we should nonetheless dare to follow. Trying to understand the minds of those men 'may be terrifying, foreign, and hateful' (ibid, 4) but it produces more complex forms of knowledge rather than one-sided critiques. As a male, I possibly represent precisely the kind of masculinity that the men discuss in this book rebel against (left, feminist, contradictory, etc.), nonetheless I have tried to understand where some of the men I discuss in this book come from. Like Stein, I was driven by an 'ambivalent desire' (ibid, 5) to read more about the men that form the basis of this book – an ambivalent desire that was structured by a kind of voyeuristic fascination, repulsion, anger, shock but also attempts at understanding, empathy, sadness and feelings of hopelessness.

I can also say that as a white male, who regards himself as a feminist and anti-fascist, there have been specific issues that motivated me to write this book. They were, first of all, of a political nature: Recent events such as Brexit, the Trump presidency and the rising right-wing populism across many parts of the world are alarming to many of us. When I first started reading about incels and the manosphere online, I began to see their intrinsic and at times more implicit connections to the alt-right and to fascism. It seemed timely and apt to analyse how such ideas of masculinity were propagated and discussed within those communities through the work of Theweleit, Reich and Young-Bruehl. In that sense, this is a political book that seeks to unmask those men and show to what extent they mobilise fascist ideas, images and fantasies. Such justifications are on the surface and I would instantly name them when asked why I wrote this book. They give it an aura of engaged, political writing. Related to those political motivations are also my own emeshments as a German citizen in the legacy of the Nazi dictatorship and the Holocaust. Being surrounded by the imperative to never forget the horrific pasts of Germany and to do everything to never see a return of democratically elected fascism, the current situation across many parts of the world (and in Germany specifically with the new right-wing extremist *Alternative für Deutschland* party) comes as a particular shock. This book, then, is also an expression of my own anti-fascist history that, like those of many Germans, now more than ever grapples with questions of collective guilt, mourning and working through of the past. It is perhaps also for those reasons that my theoretical framework is very German (Theweleit and Reich) and representative of a particular way of thinking in post-war German scholarship of culture. As a white scholar, my own unconscious bias for particular thinkers was perhaps also evident in such choices.

Additionally, the question of race is of enormous significance in our current socio-political moment of the Black Lives Matter movement and global protests against racism, oppression and racial injustice. While writing this book, I was hesitant to discuss questions of race and how black bodies are talked about by the (mostly) white men of the manosphere for instance. Many men of the manosphere not only use anti-Semitic language, but also racist anti-black narratives. Upon working on the revisions of the manuscript and receiving comments from colleagues, I realised that I should discuss race and whiteness in more detail. The fact that I could have afforded to devote little attention to race and ethnicity shows my (male) white privilege and it is something that needs critical acknowledging.

Yet, I still feel uncomfortable and ambivalent as a white scholar when it comes to such questions. The theoretical framework of this book is very white and I initially possibly made an unconscious decision to foreground themes around fascism and anti-Semitism because as a German anti-fascist I felt I had the credibility to do so. While, as I show throughout, such themes are crucial, they are intertwined with racism and how black bodies are discussed by the incel and NoFap communities for instance. Consequently, I attempt to show how misogyny is often intertwined with fascist and racist narratives in the manosphere.

There were also further underlying, personal motives beneath the surface. My parents were both active in the 1968 German student movement and I have been raised in a kind of post-68 spirit. I am also personally and politically influenced by many of the intellectual voices that were active during the sexual revolution and beyond. For example, Günther Amendt, Gunther Schmidt and Volkmar Sigusch (among others) were key founding fathers of a critical, progressive sexology in Germany. I have an equal interest in the critical theory of the Frankfurt School. In that sense, this book is also an *homage* to those thinkers of the late 1960s and this includes Klaus Theweleit in particular. May their spirit live on. Günther Amendt was tragically killed in a car accident in 2011 when a young driver under the influence of THC, crashed into a group of pedestrians. This occurred about 10 minutes away from where I grew up in Hamburg, Germany.

Secondly, I could also relate to some of those men, incels in particular, who I discuss in this book. In my task of 'identificatory knowledge' (Stein 2010, 3), I realised that not only are such feelings of inadequacy and symbolic castration somewhat universal to all men (and women), but that I and probably many other young people had had similar feelings as incels in my teenage years (without the hatred of women!): am I desirable? Am I attractive? Who am I? Who do I want to become? I can relate to those men and their fears. Like incels and other men of the manosphere, many of whom come from gaming cultures, I was a gamer in my youth, playing online games. In that sense, this book is also about acknowledging similar insecurities and anxieties to those of the men that we all have in us.

This book could also have been written, and I come back to this point a few times in the next chapters, from a different, less phallus-focused, theoretical framework. The overarching theoretical framework (via Theweleit, Young-Bruehl and Reich) is very Freudian. The male fantasies could also have been analysed from an object-relations or relational perspective for example. My initial insistence on the phallus as an analytical tool could be seen as phallic in itself, as my own desire for *analytical mastery* over those men and to exercise a kind of power over them that puts them in their place. This desire probably played a role in shaping my own theory. At the same time, as I discuss in Chapter 1, the material of this book is so phallic in itself (Allan 2016) and therefore it made sense to draw on the phallus amongst other concepts. Below I represent two other main points that could be put forward as critiques.

Reproducing toxicity

Some may argue that the level of detail with which I quote from data and provide analyses is not needed. A criticism might be that the close reading of those communities and men that I studied reproduces the toxic material and further cements women as victims of misogyny, sexism or harassment. I would answer the following to such a critique. It is, first of all, important to quote from the data in detail, because not everyone may have been aware that those communities existed in the first place. 'After all, if we want to challenge the wider economies of power in which we all operate, it is necessary to know as much as possible, in as much detail as possible, about the foundations on which they are built' (O'Neill 2018, 218), Rachel O'Neill writes about her research on the PUA community. I have also restricted the amount of direct quotations that are included in this book. Those quotations are much 'milder' than the majority of the material I have engaged with which I have specifically excluded. Secondly, such a critique relates to wider debates on how we should (or should not) engage with right-wing extremism, fascism and also misogyny today. It relates to debates about calling out toxicity and harassment, as well as to debates about de- or no-platforming and cancel culture (Nakamura 2015; O'Keefe 2016; Vemuri 2018). Some argue that under no circumstances should the voices of fascists, racists and I would add misogynists, be amplified. They should not be given a platform in debates, or through research which analyses them in detail. I do not agree with such a position. I feel that it is important to critically engage with the kind of material that I analyse in this book, precisely to unmask and deconstruct it. Simply banning it does not help and only further adds to discourses of self-pity and self-victimisation that are at the heart of fascism and racism (see Chapter 2).

Writing about the renewed visibility of fascism in many parts of the world today, Laura U. Marks notes:

> It is a big relief to see all that hatred finally on display instead of hidden behind liberal appearances. I think repressed misogyny is much more dangerous than expressed misogyny; and the same with homophobia and racism. That is the danger of liberal discourse that tries to repair politics on the level of representation alone, clearly motivated by many fears. (Marks 2020, 115)

In that sense, the kind of misogyny, racism and fascism we see today unmask themselves in their own discourses rather than being hidden behind liberal ideology which can itself be misogynist and/or fascist. This book also serves to explicitly show the expressed misogyny that is on display today rather than merely paraphrasing, describing or critiquing it without actual data. I also do not feel that a critical discussion of the kind of data I share in this book actually reproduces their inherent toxicity and destructiveness. Nonetheless, there is a tension around the writing of such a book. In reflections on her study of the PUA community, an important work that I return to a few times in this book, Rachel O'Neill writes:

> In order to undertake this project at all, I had to learn how to absorb sexism and misogyny, as it was only by exposing myself to these affects and discourses that I would be able to make sense of the seduction industry as a cultural formation. My fieldwork was thus predicated upon a willingness to silence myself. (O'Neill 2018, 208)

Unlike O'Neill, I did not carry out interviews with the men discussed in this book, I remained a silent 'lurker' who observed their (publicly available) online interactions. I nonetheless similarly had to absorb the misogyny, racism, fascism and destructiveness of those men in order to be able to collect data and ultimately to critically analyse them. This may have been easier for me than for others because I am a white male. Similar to O'Neill, I too stayed silent because if I had started to intervene in the online communities as a 'Normie' or 'Beta', I would have been quickly banned. While I do not feel that I was complicit in the manosphere, it nonetheless formed my research object for some time. At times, I felt sucked into those communities and needed to remind myself to maintain distance and question the kind of narratives I was reading. I often felt deeply uncomfortable and yet strangely drawn to the data at the heart of this book. As O'Neill writes about her involvement in the seduction industry: 'At a psychological and emotional level, it seemed impossible to reconcile my own understanding of the world with that promoted within this sphere' (ibid, 211). I too felt a similar disconnect and often fundamental disagreement between myself and those men. I would argue that this is precisely where critique begins and critical scholarship is initiated.

Us vs. them logic, absent women and lack of alternatives

Related to the above discussion is a critique in relation to the absence of women in this book and that my analyses reproduce a kind of 'us. vs. them' logic that those men perpetrate. Women are to a degree absent in this book because they are absent from the male communities I analyse. Lise Gotell and Emily Dutton discuss a similar point in their analyses of the Men's Rights Movement:

> Scholarly attention can thus have the unintended consequence of amplifying their messages. In addition, serious engagement with the men's rights movement (MRM) reinforces a simplistic 'us versus them' framework that leads to a number of strategic problems. This dichotomized framing can have the effect of shoring up feminism against an external enemy. We can certainly understand the seduction of focusing on an external enemy at a time when feminist politics seems disunified and riven by internal conflict (with feminists divided around issues like sex work and prostitution, for example). (Gotell & Dutton 2016, 70–71)

I too would perhaps regard many men discussed in this book as external enemies, yet I am also mindful of my own implications and reproduction of sexism and patriarchy simply by being a white man. I maintain that one has to, firstly, critically analyse discourses of misogyny in order to be, secondly, able to think about alternatives or pluralist perspectives. I return to this point in the book's Conclusion where I discuss alternative masculinities and (although hesitantly) argue that we can also see hope within the destructive material I have analysed. Such a form of hope allows us to move beyond an 'us vs. them' framework. Before being able to do so, a critical analysis of the manosphere is necessary.

Notes

1 Reddit is a bulletin board style website which provides a platform for special interest communities in so-called 'subreddits'. Users can post text, images, videos, and links. They exchange ideas and opinions around a multitude of topics. Each subreddit has its own moderators, rules and often specific codes and terminology. Posts can also be voted up or down by users and this can influence how they are displayed in the subreddit. Reddit, the self-proclaimed 'front page of the internet', is one of the largest community platforms online (Massanari 2017).

2 Inhibition has been identified as a key dynamic of online communication in John Suler's classic work on the online inhibition effect (Suler 2004). However, in this book I argue that inhibition and disinhibition are never neatly separated, as Suler and also psychoanalysts seem to suggest, but more messily intertwined. Where there is inhibition, there is disinhibition and vice versa. One often requires the other.
3 I mostly do not refer to the Lacanian Other here and in most places in this book. It is clear when the Lacanian Other is meant.
4 There are of course considerable differences between Deleuze and Guattari and Lacan, not least in the way desire and pleasure are understood by them. This book is not a detailed theoretical engagement with their lines of thinking. I would argue that there are some minimal common threads in their work, for example in relation to desire as something dynamic and flowing.

Chapter 1

Male fascist bodies – then and now

This chapter presents and discusses the theoretical framework of this book which consists of work on of fascism as well as on prejudice and character types. Klaus Theweleit's *Male Fantasies 1* and *2* were originally published in German in 1977/78 and in English a decade later (Theweleit 1987, 1989). Wilhelm Reich's *The Mass Psychology of Fascism* was originally published in 1933 (Reich 1997). Both authors provide key insights into a critical, psychoanalytic analysis of fascism and the periods before Hitler came to power in Germany (Theweleit) and the time of Nazi Germany (Reich). Elisabeth Young-Bruehl (1996) makes up the third key theoretical element of this book. Her work is more fully introduced and applied in Chapter 5. Her landmark book on psychoanalytic conceptualisations of prejudice as something that latches on to and articulates itself in specific character types is significant for analysing the typical psyches of the men discussed in this book. I have argued in the Introduction that we are in the midst of an emergence of a particular masculinity which embodies a fascist state of mind. Such a state of mind has overlaps with historically earlier states of mind, which Theweleit and Reich present in their works. It is also intrinsically connected to sexuality, as Theweleit, Reich and Young-Bruehl show. While there are of course differences between the men of those historical studies (Young-Bruehl's character types are more but not entirely ahistorical) and the men of the manosphere, there are also striking similarities. We could say that Theweleit's work in particular anticipated the current authoritarian turn which has fuelled the manosphere. The three authors are crucial for understanding the mechanics of certain contemporary male fantasies, because they place an emphasis on questions of the body, the ego, sexuality, defense mechanisms and agency. Theweleit has provided an especially wide-ranging analysis of male fantasies that are embodied, defended against, and acted upon by proto-fascist men.

The chapter ends with a brief critical discussion of both Reich's and Theweleit's works. Theweleit's book was written in the late 1960s, at the time of student protests and the so-called sexual revolution. I focus on a deeper discussion of the sexual revolution and its consequences for today's

DOI: 10.4324/9781003031581-1

culture of digitally mediated and facilitated sexuality in the next chapter. The sexual revolution at least partly affected and perhaps triggered the contemporary misogynistic discourses that are at the heart of this book. The transformations of sexuality that occurred in and around the *chiffre* '1968' (the sexual revolution)[1] seem like uninhibited forms of being and embodiment, something Wilhelm Reich had strongly advocated in his 1933 *Mass Psychology of Fascism*. For Reich, a key enabler of German fascism was the, in his view, suppressed sexuality and sexual morality at the time. Different sexual cultures and sexualities like the ones of 1968 were needed to liberate the people. At the same time, the sexual revolution of the late 1960s was far from unproblematic or truly liberating, as I discuss in Chapter 2. Today's sexual culture may seem even more liberated than that of 1968. However, this is not the case for everyone and we are, for example, today confronted with authoritarian-fascist developments in many countries which are specifically connected to a backlash against 1968 and the alleged contemporary disinhibited sexuality. It is essential to critically examine the sexual revolution of the late 1960s in order to analyse a different kind of sexual-authoritarian movement that articulates itself in diverse and disparate online communities as well as everywhere else today, as I do in this book. It is equally essential to analyse the wider historical precedents that help us understand such a movement today. We can do so through Theweleit by looking at the male fantasies of the last years of the German Empire leading to Weimar Germany and how they related to fascism. Given the current authoritarian turn in the legal, political and popular discourses of sexual freedom and the world in general, it seems pertinent to re-visit the work of Theweleit to explore how his insights into the growth of fascism might inform an understanding of the contemporary moment.

This chapter, then, presents some key ideas from Theweleit, Reich and Young-Bruehl which I take up in later chapters. They are organised here as four key themes that also run through this book as I return to them in my analyses in the next chapters. They are:

1. The fascist character type
2. Questions around sexuality and upbringing
3. The absent presence of woman
4. The body armour and the fragmented ego

My discussion of those themes culminates in my own theoretical development of the notion of *dis/inhibition* which is a key thread that also runs through the coming chapters as I analyse the fantasies and desires of the different men. Their bodies and fantasies are structured by states of dis/inhibition: contradictions of desire, affective forces and the push and pull of the unconscious. As I show in the coming chapters, the men are defensive-apathic and (symbolically) destructive-powerful at the same time. The notion of dis/inhibition thus enables me to conceptualise those men as contradictory and not just as those who claim to be victims and inhibited by others. They use their victim status to unleash new fantasies in which they are in control.

Following a brief, and by no means exhaustive, discussion of psychoanalytic literature on gender and sexuality as well as a section on racism and psychoanalysis, I devote the majority of this chapter to Reich, Young-Bruehl and to Theweleit in particular.

Sexuality, gender and psychoanalysis

Before presenting and outlining the wider theoretical framework, a general discussion on psychoanalytic conceptualisations of femininity and masculinity as well as sexuality are needed. Questions of sexuality, masculinity and femininity are at the heart of this book and of psychoanalysis as an epistemological paradigm in general. For Freud and the psychoanalysts who went on to develop, challenge or alter his ideas, sexuality is central to subjectivity and all aspects of human life. Like the unconscious, sexuality has a bearing on aspects of life where it would not seem apparent or visible at first glance (Giffney & Watson 2017). 'It was Freud who first bravely placed sex at the heart of psychic development and highlighted its destabilizing power in our psyche and hence the defenses brought into play to manage this' (Lemma & Lynch 2015, 3). As the next chapters show, I make a particular intervention in showing how sexuality is not only at the heart of right-wing populist tendencies today but specifically results in particular defenses as well as the creation of particular fantasies that seek to counter those defenses by some men.

On a more general level, Freud argued that there was no 'normal' or 'natural' sexuality (such as biologically determined heterosexuality for example). At the same time he put forward theories of sexuality that were subsequently critiqued as sexist. There is one strand within Freud that operated on a 'more normative, developmentally oriented path towards reproductive heterosexuality' (Giffney & Watson 2017, 26). This has been echoed by some psychoanalysts who thought (and sometimes still think) that queer, bi- or homosexuality is a pathology (ibid). Psychoanalytic views on sex and gender have been debated within and outside of the profession, particularly regarding transgender and transsexual issues in recent years (Frosh 2006; Elliot 2014; Gherovici 2017) and clinicians have sometimes held outdated and hostile views towards trans people for example. Indeed, Lemma and Lynch observe a 'displacement or marginalisation of sex in some clinical practice where a focus on individual sexuality and conflict is replaced in favour of a focus on attachment, relationships and questions of mutual recognition' (Lemma & Lynch 2015, 4). At the same time, there is a long tradition beyond the clinic which has seen innovative works in feminist theory, queer theory and sexuality studies that have drawn on psychoanalysis to discuss trans and queer issues as well as wider questions on sexuality and psychoanalysis more generally (Rose 1986; Pollock 1988; Butler 1990; Sedgwick 1993; Copjec 1994; de Lauretis 1994; Grosz 1995; Dean 2000; Yates 2007; Bainbridge 2008).

As indicated in the Introduction, this book pays particular attention to the psychoanalytic idea of the phallus and also to castration (as well as to affect, fantasy and desire). In psychoanalysis, there are two thinkers in particular who are associated with both ideas: Sigmund Freud and Jacques Lacan. The phallus (a term that Lacan in particular popularised) has some relationship to the penis, but it is not meant as a synonym (Lacan 2020).[2] As mentioned in the Introduction, it comes to represent (as a signifier) male power, privilege and often dominance (Frosh 1995). It is also strongly connected to the Oedipus complex and the idea that the young girl realises she has no, or lacks, the phallus and turns to her father as an (unconscious) object of desire while competing with the mother for her father's desire and possession. In turn, the young boy competes with his father for his mother's desire and possession. For Freud (and Lacan), then, the phallus is 'the very emblem and embodiment of desire' (Benjamin 1988, 85). In this sense, we could say that the men discussed in this book are very phallic; they desire a heteronormative and sexist logic of sexual difference. Unsurprisingly, Freud and Lacan have been critiqued by feminist and queer thinkers from the 1960s onwards as sexist and phallocentric (see Campbell 2000; Dean 2000; Luepnitz 2003; Huffer 2013; Preciado 2018; McKey Carusi 2020 for overviews and reflections). While criticising Freud, Juliet Mitchell (1974) has argued that we should nonetheless accept (but not affirm or reproduce) the centrality of the phallus as a symbol for desire and power (see also Butler 1990; Frosh 1995; Hsieh 2012). This allows us then to question the phallus, as many theorists have done (Irigaray 1985, 1993; Butler 1990, 1993; Kristeva 1982, 1998).

In acknowledging the real existing power of the phallus, we could nonetheless understand female submission as 'the deep psychic root of patriarchy' (Benjamin 1988, 88). This would also mean that there is no symbol or organ 'to counterbalance the monopoly of the phallus' (ibid, 88). This points to the ideological status of the phallus, *not* any justification of it as such. Isolating the phallus as a symbol of power does not mean that one reproduces it as such; it is merely used for analytical purposes to inquire into its real existing status. Benjamin notes that common images, that go beyond the phallus, of the female only associate her with asexual motherhood or with the 'sexy' (ibid, 78) woman who is an object of the male gaze and male desire. In more recent years, postfeminism has also seen the emergence of the figure of the 'phallic girl', who temporarily takes on male characteristics, in popular culture (McRobbie 2007; Saitō 2011; Renold & Ringrose 2012, 2017). I return to this point in the next chapter. In this book, I follow Jessica

Benjamin's critical arguments regarding the centrality of the phallus. The men of the manosphere precisely seek to reproduce or affirm a logic that grounds the phallus as the anchor of heterosexual power and desire for both men and women.

Benjamin (1988) has further developed the meaning of the phallus in a particularly useful direction. She notes that rather than only regarding the phallus as a symbol of male dominance and female submission, it can be seen as a secondary symbol of the father's power because the child initially wishes to escape the powerful mother. It is first the mother, and fantasies of her vagina threatening to engulf the child for instance, and her power that the child experiences. The child subsequently turns to the phallus, as the psychoanalyst Janine Chasseguet-Smirgel (1986) also argued. The phallus is thus a response to maternal *power*, not lack.

However, Benjamin argues that such an account only serves to replace one type of dominance with another and is therefore unsatisfactory. Instead, she develops a theory of intersubjective recognition to move beyond the binaries of phallus – not-phallus, passivity – activity, subject – object, dominance – submission. I return to Benjamin in the Conclusion of this book. Her work is useful for introducing a further dimension to my analyses and for thinking about what she calls 'the Third' within the narratives that I analyse (Benjamin 2018). However, before doing so, I wish to hold onto the centrality of the phallus for the same arguments that both Mitchell (1974) and Benjamin provide: the phallus, both in reality and fantasy, serves as an instrument of dominance, both sexually and via other means, that mobilises vivid fantasies within the men discussed in this book. It is for those reasons that my theoretical framework places some importance on the phallus, not least because the narratives of the men are so phallic in themselves. I do not mean to be phallocentric or to elevate the phallus to a kind of symbol of sublime power. It serves as an analytical prism, amongst other concepts from psychoanalysis and media studies.

This (Oedipal-phallic) Freudian account of psychosexual development as well as the broader categories of femininity, masculinity and sexual difference have been challenged and also developed by post-Freudian psychoanalysts, for instance by Karen Horney, Melanie Klein, Jean Riviere, Helene Deutsch and others (see Grigg, Hecq & Smith 2015; Lemma & Lynch 2015; Giffney & Watson 2017 for overviews). I cannot expand on those works further here. Due to limited space, I briefly discuss psychoanalytic work on masculinity that specifically focuses on its relationship to sexual difference in the remainder of this section because this book deals with masculinity amongst other aspects.

Candida Yates has argued that '[p]sychoanalysis can help us understand the psychic forces that underpin the binary cultural construction of gender, where femininity becomes the psychic and cultural other of masculinity. Psychoanalytic explanations of sexual difference point to a powerful psychic investment in maintaining this opposition' (Yates 2007, 7). Very similar dynamics are constructed by the men discussed in this book, as I show how their discourses position the female as their Other, who is simultaneously desired and threatening. Yates has argued that many traditionally Freudian psychoanalytic accounts of masculinity are too negative in their portrayal, because they construct it as inherently defensive in relation to Oedipal and parental conflicts. Yates draws on D. W. Winnicott to develop a different model of masculinity which takes account of ambiguities and contradictions today. This kind of masculinity is less idealised and hegemonic, but good enough and also vulnerable. I would similarly situate the kind of masculinities that I write about in this book as defensive *as well as* agentic. The type of men I write about are, however, overall destructive and toxic. It is very hard to see more positive aspects of their discourses. I return to this aspect in the Conclusion. There has also been of course other work on masculinity that draws on psychoanalysis (for example Frosh 1994; Frosh, Phoenix & Pattman 2001; Maguire 2004; Samuels 2018; Quindeau 2018; Neill 2019) which I cannot discuss in more detail in this chapter. Another important aspect to discuss is racism and how it has been analysed from a psychoanalytic perspective.

Racism and psychoanalysis

The topics of psychoanalysis and race, white supremacism and racism have been discussed by clinicians, activists and scholars from across the different psychoanalytic schools as well as other fields. Race is a psychosocial category that is shaped by psychic as well as social factors. It is also inherently intertwined with sexuality, gender, class, religion and bodily ability (Crenshaw 1989; Rustin 1991; Abel, Christian & Moglen 1997; Clarke 2003). As discussed in the Introduction, writing about race as a white scholar already positions me in a privileged (and perhaps somewhat comfortable) position in comparison to writers who have directly suffered from racism and oppression.

Similar to archaic ideas on sexuality as discussed in the previous section, clinical psychoanalysis itself still has questions to answer when it comes to internalised racism, whiteness and ideas of 'neutrality' in light of continued racisms and forms of racial oppression in many parts of the world where psychoanalysts practice. As a profession, psychoanalysis is still not diverse enough and questions of race and racism in the consulting room and in training institutes remain on the agenda (Kovel 1984; Tate 1996; Brickman 2003; Snider 2020). While Freud used problematic metaphors for example in relation to 'primitive' aspects of the psyche or women and 'dark' continents, Daniel José Gaztambide has argued in *A People's History of Psychoanalysis* (2019) that one can nonetheless trace a history of critical and liberatory ideas from Freud's writings to the Frankfurt School and other left-leaning psychoanalysts up to the works and activism of Frantz Fanon, Paulo Freire, and Ignacio Martín-Baró. Cultural studies, postcolonial and critical race theorists have widely drawn on psychoanalysis for example Frantz Fanon (1967), Stuart Hall (1993), Homi K. Bhabha (1994), Edward Said (1978) and other thinkers (see Dalal 2001; Cohen 2002; Khanna 2003; Riggs 2005; Greedharry 2008; Hook 2008 for overviews).

Contemporary psychoanalytic scholarship on race and racism has often been conducted from a Freudian and Lacanian perspective. Scholars, who draw on Freud and/or Lacan, have focussed on theorising race and racism as such, on racism against people of colour and Asian Americans, racism in South-Africa, online forms of racism, or racism and growing nationalism across the world in recent years, to name a few studies (see Lane 1998; Tate 1998; Seshadri-Crooks 2000; Cheng 2001; Hook 2004, 2006, 2018; Bergner 2005; Tuhkanen 2010; Fakhry Davids 2011; Aron & Starr 2013; Auestad 2014, 2017; Krüger 2017, 2018; Sheehi 2020). For reasons of space and as my orientation in this book is broadly Freudian (and to a secondary extent Lacanian), I limit my discussion to a few accounts that draw on Freud and Lacan here.[3] There are also important works that specifically discuss racism and anti-Semitism (Žižek 1994; Ostow 1996; Young-Bruehl 1996; Frosh 2005, 2016) and I return to them in Chapter 5 in more detail.

While racism can be differently theorised depending on a (post-)Freudian or Lacanian perspective, what unites the two and other psychoanalytic approaches as a basic common denominator is that it not only functions through specific actions and discourses but also operates via destructive fantasies which are conscious and unconscious. Race itself, as a psychosocial construct which of course translates into lived experiences for subjects (Lane 1998), gives rise to potent fantasies and actions in relation to the subject who is not white that the white supremacist holds. The racist imagines or re-produces already existing *fantasies* about the other that render them 'dangerous', 'inferior', 'threatening' or any other signifier that is used to discriminate against and oppress the other. Such fantasies are not only held because racists believe in 'pure' nations, want to exploit immigrants as cheap labour power, or are against immigration or freedom of movement of workers for example, as sociological explanations might sometimes argue (Giddens 2009, 639–642). Racism as a psychosocial phenomenon has historical and social dimensions which have shaped particular racist discourses over centuries (for instance racism in the USA in relation to slavery, or racism in Germany in relation to Hitler) and have lasting un/conscious traumatic effects on those who suffer to this day (George 2014, 2016).

The Lacanian scholar Sheldon George has defined race 'as a tool for masking the central lack of subjectivity' (George 2014, 360) of the subject. Or to put it in other words, race itself figures as an un/conscious mechanism through which the subject's existential alienation from their own being is covered over.[4] Race is in itself a fantasy which ideally grounds the subject in containing narratives of who they are in relation to 'their' people and allows them to construct an identity related to other categories such as gender, sexual orientation, etc. Particularly if coupled with fantasies of what constitutes the nation, racial identities are often connected to creating specific in- and out-groups to foster a sense of (nationalistic) belonging by setting implicit and explicit values or rules that stipulate when someone can count as belonging to a nation (Anderson 1991; Billig 1995). George's writing on racism is useful to discuss in a little more detail at this point because he emphasises the sense of excessive enjoyment (*jouissance*) that is inherent to it.

Racism, then, figures as a way to achieve *jouissance*, an affective experience of a surplus of a kind of pleasure-plain (Lacan 1975), for the racist as it seeks to strengthen their Imaginary (fantasmatic) racial identity through the Symbolic (socio-discursive) realm. This (attempt to) strengthen the white racist's identity functions through exclusion of the subject who is not white who is constructed as an Other. 'At the heart of this mode of *jouissance* is the oppression of black others whose supposed inferiority secures for white Americans a notion of superiority and greater being' (ibid, 362), George writes about anti-black racism in the United States. This is an important point to keep in mind and something we can also formulate in more broader psychoanalytic terms without going too deeply into Lacan: racist fantasies and actions in themselves bring a sadistic joy to those who believe in and act upon them (see also Hook 2018). This is a point I will also be making in relation to the racism, fascism, misogyny and sexism that is deployed by the men I discuss in the coming chapters: the very symbolic articulation of such forms of prejudice brings them enjoyment. As Derek Hook writes:

> Cultural otherness is not merely discursively constructed but is experienced, ascertained within the register of the senses and at the level of affect, sensuality, and fantasy. Within this Lacanian account, otherness comes to be marked by disturbing sensualities that not only 'prove' difference but enforce and amplify it at an immediate and visceral level of comprehension. (Hook 2020, 275)

This intertwinement of discourse, fantasy and affect renders racism, and other forms of discrimination, pleasurable as well as destructive and potent for racists.

Related to this question of racist enjoyment is the fantasy the racist holds of having their own enjoyment stolen by the Other or that the Other is able to enjoy better or more fully than they can. The non-white subject's enjoyment is Other in itself: allegedly dangerous, lustful, contagious, excessive. The Other must be annihilated, symbolically or actually. Such fantasies of the threatening Other, which overlap with anti-Semitic fantasies (see Chapter 5), are merged with discourses, often rooted in pseudo-science, about the alleged superiority of the white race, as for example practiced by the alt-right and many other racist groups today (Hawley 2017). Lacanians such as Slavoj Žižek (e.g. 1994), Sheldon George (2016), Derek Hook (2020) and Jason Glynos and his colleagues have argued in their analyses of right-wing populism and racism that it creates such potent fantasies of a theft of enjoyment in individuals: the belief that others (for example refugees) are able to enjoy a far better life than the people 'native' to a country (Chang & Glynos 2011; Glynos & Mondon 2016).[5] This may lead to feelings of outrage, resentment or anxiety. Right-wing populism, racism and fascism tap into individuals' existing (un)conscious fears and anxieties which are then exploited and distorted: fears of difference, loss and social change (Auestad 2014, 2017). The manosphere operates in a similar way. It primarily makes use of a populist logic of 'us vs. them' (cis men vs. cis women and white men vs. BIPOC others) which specifically characterises feminism and women as the problem but often includes racist narratives (see Chapters 3, 4, 5 and 7 in particular). Specific identities (for example incel, MGTOW, NoFap) are constructed and assumed in response to such anxieties. Of course, the anxieties of racists or misogynysts have no grounding in reality or facts whatsoever. While such subjects may have real anxieties about the world or social change, the causes they identify are fantasmatic and illusionary.

The users of the manosphere primarily create particular fantasies about white women (for example how women allegedly are or behave, as allegedly having too much power over men, or as allegedly being superficial). In response to this, fantasies of white masculine identity are created and social-political ideas that reproduce right-wing populism, racism and misogyny are evoked (for example that women need to stay at home to care for the children, or that white women should only be in relationships with white men). From a psychoanalytic perspective, such fantasies and how they are manifested in content online are marked by a (potential) identification of men with discourses that characterise them as being powerless victims and as being wronged by particular groups or individuals (feminists, women, immigrants). I return to this question of self-victimisation in the next chapter.

Fascism presents a form of racism that specifically includes anti-Semitism as a particular understanding of how the state should be organised (see Introduction). It operates through an authoritarian and often dictatorial form of oppressive nationalism, for example in the case of National Socialism in Germany under Hitler (Fuchs 2018).

Members of the Frankfurt School, most notably the works of Theodor W. Adorno (1970), Adorno and Max Horkheimer (1947), Erich Fromm (1941) and Herbert Marcuse (1964), who directly suffered from the German fascist regime and were forced to flee Nazi Germany produced some of the most sophisticated analyses of German fascism, and fascism more generally. They wrote about fascist totalitarianism and drew on Marxist and psychoanalytic thought. *The Authoritarian Personality* study (Adorno et al. 1950) is perhaps as significant as Theweleit's *Male Fantasies*. *The Authoritarian Personality* is also similar to Young-Bruehl's work on character types and prejudice (1996). However, Theweleit makes an important argument, *contra* to Adorno et al., when he notes that fascism is not *per se* rooted in a repression of homosexuality. I further discuss the relationship between fascism, the manosphere and homosexuality in Chapter 5. I have also opted to draw on Theweleit, rather than Adorno or other Frankfurt School thinkers, in this book because he makes a specific link between militarism, the fascist character, embodiment, sexuality and fantasies. This allows for a level of complexity that similar studies have not achieved. Theweleit's work on the proto-fascism of the Freikorps soldiers leading up to the 1930s in Germany is of particular significance in my opinion. He was the first thinker to make an essential link between forms of masculinity, sexuality, misogyny, the body and militarism by drawing on psychoanalysis. He showed how the fascist state of mind is embodied by certain men and articulates itself in fantasies and actions. The next sections introduce him and the other authors who I draw on in this book in more detail.

The Mass Psychology of Fascism and Male Fantasies

A key psychoanalytic thinker of fascism, alongside Klaus Theweleit, is Wilhelm Reich.[6] Reich situated his analysis more directly within Nazi Germany and the fascism of the Nazi party NSDAP. His book *The Mass Psychology of Fascism* was first published in German in 1933, the year Hitler came to power. It is a landmark psychoanalytic study of the origins and characteristics of fascism as such and Nazism in particular. Reich's works were very influential for thinkers like Gilles Deleuze and Felix Guattari, Michel Foucault and others. He was initially largely forgotten after he died in the United States in 1957; it was the 1968 student movement in Germany that contributed to his re-discovery and lasting popularity. Reich, who coined the term 'sexual revolution' in the sense as it is understood today, was enthusiastically read by revolutionary students. In the book, Reich focussed on the authoritarian family as the core unit within fascism, but also as a form of organisation which was readily open towards embracing fascism and Hitler. This is because of repression of sexuality on the part of all family members, something which then articulates itself in authoritarian loyalty and longing for a leader. Fascism, as he argued, also promises a sense of stability and conservatism that is appealing to some. I introduce some of Reich's arguments in more detail in the next section. While I mainly draw on Theweleit and Young-Bruehl in this book, he is an important thinker who was influential for Theweleit. My concept of dis/inhibition is also influenced by Reich's understandings of sexual inhibition and repression.

Klaus Theweleit's *Male Fantasies* is, in my view, the most important psychoanalytic study of fascism (or rather of the fantasmatic development that gave rise to fascism). Theweleit's two books, published in English in

1987 and 1989, which amount to more than 1,000 pages (including notes and bibliographies) consist of long chapters which do not necessarily have to be read in chronological order. Throughout the two books, Theweleit draws on Sigmund Freud, Gilles Deleuze/Felix Guattari, Wilhelm Reich and also Margaret Mahler. His working with psychoanalytic Freudian and post-Freudian theory is loose and at times elusive, and the strength and explosive force of his arguments is first and foremost due to his *own* thinking and analysis rather than an elaborate theoretical framework that he would draw on or specifically develop.

The key underlying aim of *Male Fantasies* is to do as the title suggests: to inquire into the articulation of male fantasies as they were circulated in the forms of journal entries, novels, postcards, artworks, illustrations and plays. In the best Freudian tradition, Theweleit traces the subject constitutions of the Freikorps soldiers[7] and other (young) men through examining their written and artistic outputs. He read through more than 250 novels and memoirs alone. He pays specific attention to the narration of male fantasies about women, violence, the soldier's body, and reports on battles. Those are often, but not exclusively, based on seven men with different biographies, and not all of them would be 'transformed' into national socialists (Niethammer 1979). In the next sections, I present key themes from Reich's *The Mass Psychology of Fascism* and Theweleit's *Male Fantasies*.

The fascist character

Reich, Theweleit and Young-Bruehl are all interested in examining the specific character of prejudiced subjects. They do so in different ways. Young-Bruehl's *The Anatomy of Prejudices* (1996) deals with prejudice in general and specifically analyses racism, anti-Semitism, sexism and homophobia. I discuss her work in detail in Chapter 5 when applying some of her insights to the incel and MGTOW communities. She, drawing on Freud, presents particular character types which are receptive to forms of misogyny, sexism, racism, anti-Semitism or homophobia. She outlines in detail what the psyches of such characters (for example obsessional or hysterical characters) look like, what those characters specifically defend against, what fantasies they have and how they typically act. Young-Bruehl's chapters on sexism are very useful as an addition to my theoretical framework, because she shows how sexism is a socio-collective defense mechanism which corresponds to specific character structures of individuals, who are most often male. I argue in Chapter 5 that incels and MGTOWs in particular are obsessional characters who desire and defend against cis women at the same time.

Wilhelm Reich (1997) was specifically interested in analysing the character of those who actively voted for Hitler in Germany and embraced the Nazi dictatorship. For him, in capitalism, and in forms of authoritarian capitalism such as fascism in particular, there is a fundamental contradiction at the character level of the individual subject.

> The basic traits of the character structures corresponding to a definite historical situation are formed in early childhood, and are far more conservative than the forces of technical production. It results from this that, as time goes on, the psychic structures lag behind the rapid changes of the social conditions from which they derived, and later come into conflict with new forms of life. (Reich 1997, 18)

This is an important insight which I take from Reich: individuals cannot always adapt and lag behind and thus seek to defend against social change which they see as threatening. In the case of the men discussed in this book, this means that they cannot adapt to changing social and sexual relations (see Chapter 2 for a detailed discussion of the socio-historical changes in relation to sexuality, feminisms, and the men's rights movement). I discuss this in Chapter 4 when I outline why incels take up a desire for a fascist identity in relation to precarious neoliberalism. One way of defending is the embracing of fascism, because fascist ideology promises the subject a return to a mythical past in which everything was in order and social change or destabilising forces do not exist (see Introduction). Fascism thus responds to already existing character types that are open to such a worldview.

Klaus Theweleit similarly argues that it was not economic factors, specific events and developments – recession, economic crisis, eroding parliamentary democracy or the First World War – that led to the particular male soldier or a specific type of male. It was rather that this specific type of male *already* existed, playing a part in actively producing what would become fascism and Nazi Germany. A central argument of Theweleit's is that this type of man was already there in 1914, therefore predating fascism.[8] Fascism did not (only) create a specific type of male and specific fantasies of what it meant to be a male, it was rather proactively taken up by already proto-fascistic males. Such male types were created during the 'Wilhelminian peace' – from ca. 1890 up until World War I – a period of peace within a state of implicit war and crises. The peace was always ready to be transformed into actual war. This 'war as peace' (Theweleit 1989, 351) left young men in limbo, longing for *something*. Such types of men were also created in the men's minds following the 'loss' experienced in and through World War I and a shattering of the fantasy that they were born to be victorious warriors. Theweleit strongly rejects the commonly held argument that it was specific economic conditions that led to the establishment of the Nazi dictatorship. Yet, a psychosocial perspective suggests that both socio-economic and wider historical aspects are important to consider when analysing the rise of fascism in Germany. I deploy such a psychosocial perspective in this book which takes account of the social and subjective dimensions within the narratives I analyse.

Theweleit's impressive and meticulous development of a psychosocial predisposition of fascism through (fascist) bodies (and fantasies) is worth unfolding and discussing in more detail. A key dimension to the character types of those men is sexuality, and how they were raised.

Sexuality and upbringing

For Reich, the patriarchal family is the 'central reactionary germ cell' (1997, 89) of fascism. It is particularly, the proletarian family that forces children (and adults alike) to repress sexual desires which are discharged to and expressed as authoritarian loyalty in later life. The child is shaped through the inhibition and repression of sexuality, and other power relations within the family, and becomes 'afraid, shy, fearful of authority, obedient, "good," and "docile"' (ibid, 30). The family often serves as a basic unit for society and mirrors mainstream social norms and structures, power relations between parents and children in particular. '[N]ationalistic sentiments are the direct continuation of the family tie' (ibid, 57). Reich maintained from the outset that fascism 'is only the organized political expression of the structure of the average man's character' (ibid, xiii). This is a key argument concerning a kind of fascist state of mind and body which I draw on in this book while not necessarily placing the emphasis on a specific class, as Reich did.

Theweleit also discusses the relationship between fascism and the authoritarian upbringing of children. In the soldier narratives that he analysed, mothers are described in the grandest of words. They are 'angels', 'above all else' or 'the best of all women' (Theweleit 1987, 104). At the same time, there is an aggression directed at the mothers, Theweleit claims. A motherly warmth, the caring nature of being a mother is split off in the narratives. The soldiers had failed relationships with their mothers from early childhood onwards. They were raised with cold care and a lack of real love. Nonetheless, the mother is 'good' in so far as she can be manipulated/constructed by the soldiers. The desire to kill and be part of the Freikorps militia is in part rooted in the desire to kill the mother and the father as parental *imagos*. 'Thus, according to his analysis, the Freikorps' preoccupation with war served their wish to escape (to individuate themselves) from the hated image of woman and the body that enfolds her sexuality' (Vadolas 2009, 70), as Antonios Vadolas writes. For Theweleit, fascism is thus not about a revolt against an Oedipal father, or about an identification with him. Fathers do not exist; they are 'categorically denied a voice in these books' (ibid, 108). I return to how some of the men discuss their upbringing and parents and argue in the next chapters of this book (particularly Chapters 5 and 6) that similar dynamics to the ones mentioned above are in place. The men of the manosphere also wish to (unconsciously) kill their parents, in order to become full subjects who have cut all ties to their previous lives. I argue in Chapter 6 that the father may play a specific role in the lives of those men. Taking the mass shooters Anders Breivik and Elliot Rodger as case studies, I show how they had difficult relationships with their fathers and sought to (unconsciously) annihilate the father in order to surpass him and be reborn as a new man.

As I show in the coming chapters, many men of the manosphere are only secondarily racist, fascist and anti-Semitic (some not at all) in their discourses. They primarily (desire to) embody a fascist form of masculinity that is both about the desire for and dominance over women. The way their particular fantasies are constructed is also akin to fascism, because they seek to create a specific reality that is both about portraying them as victims of women as well as using destructive symbolic power to negate any self-reflection, as well as any agency of women and others who are not like them. In general, fascism won't have any counter arguments, vulnerability or forms of weakness. The same is the case for the men discussed in this book. As I show in the next chapters, they are highly defensive and at the same time forward-facing. They already have specific desires for a kind of fascist masculinity that comes to be desired and articulated as such because of the rise of the alt-right and associated fascist politics (see Chapters 4 and 5). In the next section, I provide a fuller discussion of *Male Fantasies*.

The absent presence of woman

Male Fantasies 1 (Theweleit 1987) begins with a detailed discussion of how the male Freikorps soldiers of the 1920s talked about their wives and women in general. In a sense, the complete first book deals with how women were perceived and talked about by the male soldiers of the Weimar Republic (and to a wider extent men in general). The men only knew three types of the female subject: mothers, 'white', pure wives, nurses and sisters, and 'red', dangerous, seductive women (prostitutes, female fighters, Jews).

Becoming a soldier, joining the Freikorps, is often narrated as leaving the women behind, as joining in with other men, away from their wives or fiancées. 'Real' men do not miss anything when women are not around. The pure male, who bears no traces of sexuality, is the *real* soldier. Women could not understand them as soldiers. Men could only understand each other. The same dynamics are very much in place in the manosphere today where exclusively male spaces are formed in which particular fantasies are circulated which outline what it means to claim the identity of an incel, a MGTOW or a NoFapper. Both Freikorps soldiers and the men of the manosphere embrace a kind of identity that foregrounds white masculinity and excludes the feminine.

It is not enough to split the woman into a caring, desexualised 'white sister' and a lustful, animal-like 'red sister'. The red sister is destroyed by the soldiers. The act of killing consists of two stages: to castrate the woman in a symbolic intercourse whereby the male phallus (the weapon) destroys the woman's genitalia and thereby castrates her feared phallus. This is a defense mechanism. Secondly, a 'pleasurable perception of women in the condition of "bloody masses"' (ibid, 195) brings the real satisfaction to the soldier. The actions of the soldiers are both defensive and, in a sense, forward-facing. Killing marks the creation of a new reality in which the threatening woman is annihilated.

While the men discussed in this book, for the most part, do not actually kill women, I argue that they wish to symbolically destroy them and at the same time desire them. They are pushing and pulling in two different directions. They defend against and symbolically penetrate the women. In contrast to the soldier males, the men, for the most part, do not split women into good and evil. For them, all women are the same. Theweleit's soldiers also wanted to leave sexuality behind, they defended against everything sexual. The men of the manosphere, however, overflow with a kind of sexual desire which they channel into different outlets, as I discuss in the coming chapters.

The soldier's body: fragmented ego and body armour

A key point which I take up in this book and discuss in relation to the manosphere is that Theweleit argues that the soldier's ego is fragmented and less manifested than in other subjects. Theweleit draws on Mahler and her notion of the 'fragmented ego':[9]

> The fragmented ego cannot cope with changeability and complexities. It cannot integrate and it cannot synthesize. Living objects are much more changeable, vulnerable, and unpredictable than inanimate objects. (Mahler 1979, 176)

Similarly to Reich's argument of the ego that lags behind social change which I discussed earlier, the soldiers must kill everything that is unpredictable and threatening. They desire a trance-like state in which they are themselves dissolved and dissolve other human beings and the planet itself. The fear of being castrated by the *Flintenweiber*, Theweleit notes, goes beyond a mere fear of castration. It is a fear of being disembodied, of being completely destroyed and torn to pieces.

As part of the Freikorps, the soldiers become part of a machine-like totality. The brigade is *one* body. Theweleit argues that the men develop (almost become) a *coat of armour* (see also Reich 1997). This is marked by a process of 'self-distancing, self-control, self-scrutiny' (Theweleit 1987, 302). A 'subduing of affect' (ibid) that opposes the interior and the exterior, the inner and the outer world of a subject. The male soldiers do not have an ego in the Freudian sense, according to Theweleit, that is structured by the Oedipus complex and its eventual dissolution. Their ego has not been formed through identification with external objects (as Freud argued in the Oedipus complex). They are stuck in a pre-Oedipal phase with a fragmented ego. Instead, they are given an ego through external objects. Through military drill, violence and punishments, they have continuously been shown where their limits, boundaries and borders lie. Through their upbringing they are taught to be clean (and all bodily liquids and substances are tabooed) and everything pleasurable is banished. Eventually, they have developed a functioning body armour and they are able to smoothly integrate into wider totalities such as the army. Their body armour is their ego. At the same time, the body armour is never fully complete. The man of steel imagined by the soldiers could never be fully made of steel. The real body armour of those men was fragmented and cracked and so their egos were also fragmented. That is why the army and the leaders were essential. They keep the body armour intact and it is the army's 'totality-ego' (Theweleit 1987, 207) that guarantees the soldier's functioning in tense situations. This was the norm for all men at the time, not just soldiers. In that sense, the subject is *never fully born*. Something bigger has to nurture and birth the subject. Something needs to complete the subject and establish a boundary.

Fascism responds to this and integrates the body into a totality and thereby makes the body feel as a coherent part of that totality. The subject is incapable of binding his libido and is therefore in a constant state of affective tension. I take this to be a key argument that is applicable to the men of the manosphere. They similarly construct a body armour through their fantasies, the collective communities and their posts. They are in constant states of affective tension, or dis/inhibition, and writing serves as a means to discharge such tension and find a momentary relief. Feeling part of those communities strengthens their fragmented egos.

Theweleit emphasises that the men he writes about are not psychotic and that 'their mode of writing is controlled, in a manner which "psychotics" would hardly be capable of, as if a watchful ego were ever occupied in maintaining correct grammar and the proper chronology of events' (Theweleit 1989, 210). For Theweleit, the men instead defend against becoming psychotic by preoccupying themselves with war. They have a fundamental fear of being annihilated, because of the threatening 'red' women and feminine sexuality in general. Feminine sexuality intimidates the fragmented egos of the men and threatens their collapse (which would result in the feared state of psychosis). I would not claim that the men of the manosphere defend against psychosis, but I argue that they do defend against feminine sexuality and also their own unconscious and its uncontrollable forces. This is a point I develop throughout the book.

Being in a state of war results in 'devivification and dedifferentiation' (ibid, 218) for the soldiers. They are unable to form healthy object relations and must kill – devivify and dedifferentiate – everyone else who is living, sexual, different or threatening, women in particular. What is devivified and ultimately killed are the soldier's own female elements within him: softness and passionate, eroticised, female elements.

In addition to the states of dedifferentiation and devivification, Theweleit names a third: 'self-coupling' (ibid, 276) – or 'self-merging', a better translation from the German *Selbstverschmelzung* that he uses. The fragmented ego is being unified through the two actions of dedifferentiating and devivifiying. Those actions lead to the desired state of the soldier: 'he is extinguished and inundated, he transcends boundaries, and reaches his goal' (ibid, 276). This is the ultimate aim, to transcend themselves and leave behind the man they once were. Theweleit thus describes and analyses a transition of the men's bodies from states of feverish disintegration towards massacring and killing othered bodies. All of this is accompanied by complex and contradictory fantasies in the men. I argue that very similar fantasies are present in all the different men I discuss in this book. They all articulate similar fantasies of transcendence and moving beyond their own bodies, of acquiring a new body and becoming a new person. I discuss this in Chapter 4 for example in the fantasy of the Chad that incels wish to become, or in Chapter 6 where I argue that the mass shooters have the unconscious wish to kill their own fathers in order to move beyond their own upbringing and be reborn as new men. Such fantasies are also accompanied by more defensive fantasies of self-victimisation and self-pity.

Theweleit is convinced that the soldier males do not repress anything in that sense, or rather that they seek to repress the unconscious and its unpredictable productivity itself. Pleasure and the pleasure-seeking id must be repressed. I return to this in more detail in the chapters on incels, MGTOW and NoFap as well as in the book's Conclusion. I take those arguments about the fragmented state of the ego to be a key insight of Theweleit's and I make the same point about the men of the manosphere today. They similarly wish to repress their unconscious.

Dis/inhibition

All of the previous discussions, then, culminate in what I call *dis/inhibition*. The men's bodies are dis/inhibited. I unpack this idea in this section and return to it throughout the book.

For Sigmund Freud, inhibition is a central idea. He understood it as a consciously or unconsciously self-selected restriction of a situation by the individual to avert the affective experience of anxiety or unpleasure more generally. In that sense, we may understand inhibition as a barrier between the subject and a particular state or action that stops them from realising or achieving it. While inhibition may be an unconscious or conscious act in itself, the underlying motives for inhibition can remain unconscious. In that sense, inhibition itself can be a symptom (which masks the underlying problem) as well. Freud defined inhibition as 'the expression of a restriction of an ego-function' (Freud 1949, 16). Inhibition thus means that the ego has given up on parts of itself in order not to experience a psychic conflict that would need to be repressed. In this way, inhibition can function to circumvent repression as such. Whatever would elicit the psychic conflict is cathected and maintained in an energised, charged-up state but never released (see also Johanssen 2019, 81). In that way, it works as a mechanism to negate the unconscious itself and its unpredictability (Phillips 2013, 202).

For Freud, inhibition may also serve more banal, commonly understood purposes of averting particular situations that may be considered embarrassing or shameful, such as chatting to an unknown girl for an incel. The super-ego restricts the ego to follow through with a particular desire or activity, because it knows that the outcome would be catastrophic, shameful or embarrassing. The obscene and punishing qualities of the super-ego become apparent in such situations (Johanssen 2019, 80–84).

Inhibition, then, 'distracts a person from the only freedom they have, the freedom to choose an unpredictable future for themselves' (Phillips 2013, 202). Psychoanalysis as such, as Adam Phillips (2013) writes, carefully and steadily works towards easing a patient's inhibitions by enabling them to find the words and ability to realise, think and express particular thoughts, desires, actions that were originally (considered being) prohibited. Working with a patient's inhibitions may ultimately help to ease their pain or suffering. Inhibition always presupposes disinhibition in a kind of sado-masochistic relationship. The inhibited subject has a particular relation to their 'imaginary uninhibited other' (ibid, 201).

There are also natural, or socially agreed upon inhibitions, that are seen as disinhibitions when violated or crossed: respect, public behaviour, common courtesy or the law. In talking about inhibitions, or desires to transgress beyond them, the talking (or writing about them) is significant because it is not the same as actually putting them into action. Inhibitions are tied to the social and something can change from being met with inhibition to being met with utmost affirmation by the subject, as Phillips notes. It then becomes possible to utter that, for example, women are oppressing men, that Jews are conspiring against the ordinary population, that immigrants are taking white men's jobs, etc. because of a changed social environment which encourages a loosening of inhibition. This is echoed in the classic right-wing expression: 'We should be allowed to say this!' Making particular ways of thinking acceptable and mainstream is the first step towards a right-wing and fascist epistemological totality. The unacceptable has been sufficiently re-described, as Phillips puts it (ibid, 202).

Disinhibition, on the other hand, can of course refer to better psychic functioning because one is no longer inhibited. However, I wish to theorise a further escalation of disinhibition as an excessive state of boundaryless modes of being. Essentially, disinhibition may be understood as an opposite state to inhibition. It refers to a state of boundaryless modes of being, acting or relating. It can be understood as a form of excess, challenging set rules and belief systems which may occur outside or inside of regulatory or legal systems. Similarly to its opposite, it is situated within particular social and cultural norms that periodically permit ritualistic (interaction) forms of disinhibition to be lived out in festivals, carnivals or on a 'night out' fuelled by alcohol or drugs. Disinhibition can also be understood as an excessive process, challenging set rules and belief systems which may occur outside or inside of regulatory or legal systems. This is precisely what happened during the 1960s and 1970s in relation to sexuality, embodiment and many other things (see Chapters 2 and 3).[10]

The very practices and narratives I analyse in this book are expressions of inherent dis/inhibitions within those men. This translates to, as I emphasise at various times, particular affective-bodily states of them. This was originally an argument made by Theweleit who argued that the Freikorps men had to act so violently in order to conduct 'self-coupling' and stop feelings of psychosis and disintegration. While I would not go as far as to argue that the online men defend against feelings of psychosis, they *do* defend against feelings of disintegration, castration and a kind of fundamental bodily undoing. This relates to the Freudian model of affect. For Freud, affect functioned along a kind of input-output axis where internal or external stimuli or sensations were discharged and left the body. A key part of his energetic model of the psyche and body, affective discharge serves to re-establish a bodily equilibrium. A bodily equilibrium that is in constant turmoil for those men of the manosphere and the Freikorps soldiers alike. Affects function along an inhibition-disinhibition nexus.

> Affectivity manifests itself essentially in motor (secretory and vasomotor) discharge resulting in an (internal) inhibition of the subject's own body without reference to the external world: motility in actions are designed to effect changes in the external world. (Freud 1915, 178–179, cited in Boag 2012, 124–125)

It is interesting that Freud used the term inhibition above, which is used to denote inhibition in the neurological sense by which a stimuli is inhibited and no longer felt. As I noted previously, the concept of dis/inhibition that I propose is essentially a split or schizoid state of inhibition where an individual's affects but also thoughts, desires and feelings are damned up, clogged up, held onto – and disinhibition where it all breaks free, erupts from the individual, dams break and floods gush. The men try to prevent being flooded and overflowing and at the same time they flood themselves and the internet. The men have consciously and unconsciously dis/inhibited themselves and, so they claim time and time again, are made dis/inhibited by women. The ego has given up on parts of itself while investing highly charged libidinal energy into other parts.

The dis/inhibited men I write about in this book are to an extent id-driven, they act on and act out their drives, while they are also heavily restricted through ego and super-ego dynamics. Be it through the keyboard or an actual weapon. For example, NoFappers seek to restrict their id – at least on some levels – by abstaining from porn and masturbation (see Chapter 7). If anything, the men are consciously prohibiting and inhibiting a particular disinhibition. The YouTubers articulate the need for more inhibition and they lament the disinhibited state of sexuality today (see Chapter 3). A critique which speaks more to their own (unconscious) inhibitions and desires of disinhibition. MGTOWs have inhibited their basic social relating by discussing the need to eliminate women from their lives (see Chapter 5). Incels often lament inhibition (they use the exact word) in social encounters with females and demonstrate a complete disinhibition when it comes to their online lives (see Chapter 4). The mass shooters have struggled with inhibition (Rodger in particular) all their lives and for them the act of killing becomes the final disinhibition (see Chapter 6). Those different bodily states of dis/inhibition all refer to affective processes. They are experienced rather than fully consciously known. Disinhibition may bring the ultimate, while momentary, sense of relief. The men's bodies are locked in an impossible loop of contradictions. To take an example, this is the case for the NoFappers who speak of their sexual drives for porn which are, however, accompanied by a highly unpleasurable affective tone or 'keynote' (as Freud called it) which renders the whole experience of watching porn ultimately unpleasurable (apart from momentary orgasmic pleasure). It is the case for incels, who so strongly desire the Stacy and yet want nothing more than to enact revenge on her for supposed rejections. It is the case for MGTOWs, who are, like incels, obsessed about freeing themselves of women and yet woman always remains as a constant fantasy. It is the case for the mass shooters. The men's body armour is thus always fragile and porous. I discuss all of this in more detail in the next chapters.

Conclusion

This chapter presented and discussed the theories of Klaus Theweleit and Wilhelm Reich as well as ideas by Elisabeth Young-Bruehl which are important for the wider line of argument that this book unfolds in the following chapters. Theweleit's analysis of the fantasies of the soldier males is particularly essential for understanding certain contemporary men. I do not mean to say that Young-Bruehl's, Theweleit's and Reich's ideas can merely be 'lifted and shifted' to a different historical period and dropped there. I show to what extent their ideas are relevant for today's populist cultures and their understandings of masculinity and sexuality. For Reich and Theweleit, there is an essential connection between fascism and sexuality. Or, to put it differently, fascism cannot be understood without sexuality and the body. They also demonstrate the usefulness of psychoanalysis not only for analysing sexuality, but also for understanding the appeal of fascism on an ideological and bodily level.

For both, sexuality when it is inhibited leads to an affective damning up, storing of affect that needs to find a different outlet. Theweleit documents how the pent up soldier males with their fragmented egos needed to kill in order to maintain a bodily equilibrium and defend against feelings of disintegration. We can also understand such bodies as being affectively supercharged and at the edge of explosion. I have discussed elsewhere (Johanssen 2019) that for Freud affect is seen as a subjective, bodily force and intensity. It needs to be discharged, to leave the body. Freud described affect as spread over the human body 'somewhat as an electric charge is spread over the surface of a body' (Freud 1981g, 60). Those men Theweleit writes of were *unter Strom*, which in German translates literally as being electrically charged, but also as being tense because of psychic pressures. They needed to discharge their affects in order to feel a sense of relief. This *motif* of the affectively charged male body is central for my theorisation of the men who I discuss in the coming chapters. They too are fragmented and must devivify and dedifferentiate the other (women). Yet, they also strongly desire women and want nothing more than to be with them. Related to this is the Reichian and Theweleitian notion of the body armour which is used to defend against and ward off specific elements from entering the soldier's body. This is another key concept which is useful for analysing contemporary far-right, misogynistic and masculinist communities.

This chapter has also introduced the notion of *dis/inhibition*. It is a central thread that runs through this book. In its immanence, sexuality works through dis/inhibition too, through restraint and release that can culminate in bodily pleasure in the form of orgasms and other sensations. On a psychosocial level, dis/inhibition figures as a phenomenon that can be seen as an analytical prism through which to understand certain male fantasy and particularly desire – a kind of desire that is enfolded by dynamics of restraint and release in a kind of Moebius strip. Those men, as discussed by Young-Bruehl, Reich, Theweleit and by myself, can be described as being *dis/inhibited*. They are incapable of normal, social interactions as their bodies are in constant crisis and on the edge.

A critical placement

Before closing this chapter, a brief critical discussion of Reich and Theweleit is helpful to situate their works within wider debates. Reich's life took a tragic turn from a talented protégé of Freud's, to chasing UFOs with a 'cloudbuster' and finally dying in prison in the United States. Reich's (and Freud's) arguments in relation to sexual repression may be regarded as having been challenged (if not debunked) by Michel Foucault (1978) and his discussion of the 'repressive hypothesis' in the *History of Sexuality, Volume 1*. Reich placed too much emphasis on the role of sexual repression. A similar critique was articulated by Herbert Marcuse, who noted Reich's sexual reductionism (Marcuse 1955). However, this does not challenge the fact that sexuality is essential to subjectivization and subjectivity. Reich's insistence on sexuality and ideology and how the two shape both material as well as psychological spheres of society is a very important contribution. Some of his discussions of sexuality, childhood sexuality in particular, seem deeply problematic from today's perspective and need to be rejected.

However, Reich's – and Theweleit's – association of fascism with sexuality is an important insight that I want to hold on to for this book. Perhaps we should place an emphasis on the patriarchal, rather than sexually repressive, structure of the authoritarian family that Reich wrote of. It is nonetheless a fact that fascism has a *particular*, and peculiar, relationship to sexuality. Theweleit's, Reich's and Young-Bruehl's works are of immense importance in analysing the contemporary age of authoritarian capitalism and its relationship to sexuality and masculinity, both in ideological and practical terms. Reich's early works on sexuality, fascism and other themes are still important today. We should hold on to his ideas in the light of a dangerous return of fascist populism across the world today. If we want to understand populism and fascism, we cannot ignore sexuality.

The publication of *Male Fantasies* 1 and 2 created a bombshell in the radical left intellectual sphere of 1968 as well as in more mainstream circles and bourgeois media. It became an instant bestseller. This was no coincidence, because Theweleit had hit a nerve in a climate that was marked by working through and revolting against the (proto)-fascist parental generation in Germany that was being shaken up by radical youth. While the two books were mostly unanimously praised by commentators and readers, there was also some critical reception (see Niethammer 1979; Reichardt 2007 for a discussion). Upon re-reading the two books today, the question to what extent the fantasies Theweleit wrote of were generalisable or representative of German men as a whole constitutes itself. Lutz Niethammer noted that 'for instance, a large proportion of fascist sympathisers cannot have gone through what Theweleit regards as the main sites of fascist socialisation (cadet schools, the military drill-ground), because they were simply too young to have experienced these mainly pre-war institutions' (Niethammer 1979, 183). Theweleit slightly dodges this question in the conclusion of MF2 when he writes that those who joined in the fascist mass must have had some sense of (silent or active) affirmation of it. However, Theweleit's analyses are rooted in data which speak for themselves; they demonstrate that fascism was not [exclusively, I should add] about seduction or misconstruing but about 'a specific form of production of reality' (Theweleit 1989, 34). Some have asked how he could draw conclusions from written narratives about the real psychic conditions of the men. Was he perhaps being seduced by their narratives (Niethammer 1979)? It was for example a sign of the times that female names were not mentioned in the literature, not necessarily because the male writers wanted to erase them. Nonetheless, I disagree with the question. Written texts, as Freud showed us, are manifestations of a person's psychic life.

Lutz Niethammer also notes that while women take a central role in the books, they are not examined as individuals with agency, but Theweleit focussed on the male soldiers. Some feminist critiques articulated a similar point (for example Petro 1988; Marks 2020). More specific discussions of the everyday life of the 'ordinary' fascist rather than the Freikorps soldier would have also added more depth to the books. I disagree with such a critique, because, as I read it, it was precisely the soldier males that Theweleit wished to focus on rather than on men as a whole, or the relation between men and women as such. This is a point I return to in the book's Conclusion when I discuss if one can move beyond a focus on the men towards a perspective that focuses on recognition and hope.

The next chapter provides a literature review of scholarship that discusses the history of feminism and men's rights, the sexual revolution and its problems, the alt-right and white supremacy, postfeminism, porn culture and other themes.

Notes

1 I use the terms '1968' and 'sexual revolution' synonymously in the book. My discussion of the sexual revolution, given that I draw heavily on Theweleit's work, also takes (West) Germany as its starting point but also considers other countries and to an extent generalises developments that occurred roughly at the same time in different parts of the Western world (see Chapter 2).
2 Lacan famously differentiates between the Imaginary and the Symbolic phallus and their relationships to different forms of lack, agents (the father), and objects in Seminar IV (see Lacan 2020). This also relates to his discussions of phallic *jouissance* and the '*jouissance* of the other' (feminine *jouissance*). It is beyond the scope of this book to go into more detail (see Lacan 1972–1973, 1974–1975).
3 For non-Freudian or -Lacanian conceptualisations and discussions of race and racism see (Kristeva 1982; Walton 2001; Rasmussen & Salhani 2010; Dalal 2013; Fang 2020). For psychosocial analyses of racism, see especially the work of Simon Clarke (for instance Clarke 2003).
4 This idea relates to the notion of the Lacanian lack and that the subject is constituted as such through a gap in the Symbolic Order. It is attempted to be covered over through Symbolic and Imaginary means throughout one's life (Lacan 1977).
5 Derek Hook (2018) has discussed this 'theft of enjoyment' hypothesis in a critical way and argues that the Lacanian category of enjoyment (*jouissance*) is used too vaguely in such theories. It furthermore depoliticises and dehistoricises racism by

ignoring specific socio-political contexts. It also fails to account for different modes of enjoyment within such racist discourses and practices.
6 Theare are of course many other thinkers within psychoanalysis who have written about fascism and other forms of totalitarianism. It is beyond the scope of this book to engage with them in more detail (see e.g. ffytche & Pick 2016; Krüger, Figlio & Richards 2018 for recent overviews and interventions).
7 The Freikorps were violent militias which formed following the end of the first World War. 'The Freikorps rampaged through Germany in the first few years after World War I. They were halfway between armed bands and mercenary troops. They had partly been formed to fight in the areas of east and central Europe lost to German influence by the treaty of Versailles (for example, the new Baltic states), and they were hired by the central and regional authorities in Germany to suppress workers' uprisings, especially in Bavaria, the Ruhr and Berlin' (Niethammer 1979, 178).
8 The violent oppression of women (and others) has a history that goes back thousands of years and is, we could argue, ahistorical (Theweleit 1987, 1989). One could make the argument that it relates to a fundamental confrontation on the part of the male with the (parts of) the mother who he re-encounters in finding female partners during his life (Benjamin 1988). This book, then, could also have been written from such a perspective and it would have made sense to draw more on thinkers like Melanie Klein (1988a, 1988b,) and her concepts of jealousy and envy and the paranoid-schizoid position for example, or Karen Horney (2015) and her work on womb envy and prejudice against women as a result of Oedipal conflicts and fantasies. However, I specifically wish to link the rise of fascism and wider changes of neoliberalism with the fantasies of the manosphere. I think the theoretical framework that I have opted for in this book opens up the best analytical avenue for doing so.
9 A similar notion of the fragmented ego was of course developed by Melanie Klein. Unlike for Mahler, for Klein the ego is always disintegrated and split, even as it oscillates between the paranoid-schizoid and depressive positions (Klein 1988a, 1988b).
10 Disinhibition is also used in clinical psychology to refer to disinhibited behaviour because of a brain injury for example (No author 2013). I do not use the term in this way in this book.

Chapter 2

The sexual revolution, the manosphere and (post) feminism

This chapter provides a summary and discussion of socio-historical developments in the West since the late 1960s that inform wider questions on the role of male fantasies within the manosphere. I discuss the so-called 'sexual revolution' which was accompanied by the rising second wave feminist movement (from the late 1960s until the 1980s)[1] and (in partial response) the 'men's liberation' (or Men's Rights) movement. A historical perspective on this topic is important because it provides context to the manosphere which often discusses masculine and feminine identities, sexuality, feminism/masculinism and how they have been allegedly shaped by events of and since the late 1960s. While, as mentioned in the previous two chapters, sexism and misogyny have been around for hundreds of years and take on a particular characteristic under forms of fascism, the sexual revolution is significant as a specific anchoring point. It is endlessly mobilised by members of the manosphere as a turning point in history which allegedly led to men being disadvantaged at the expense of women.

In this chapter, I also provide a discussion of the notion that traditional masculinity is in crisis and review wider literature on (post)feminism, the alt-right and white supremacy, geek masculinity and work on non-hegemonic masculinities. I end the chapter by arguing what contributions this book makes to existing debates. I begin with the sexual revolution in the next section.

The sexual revolution of 1968

One key aspect of the developments of the late 1960s was so-called second wave feminism and the demands that were made by feminists in relation to sexual autonomy and to have a right over their own bodies (for example when it came to abortion or divorce). The 1968 student movements in France, (West) Germany, other parts of Europe and also the various movements in the United States which took place roughly around the same time, were all about sexual politics and the politics of sexuality (amongst other things of course such as protests against imperialism, capitalist exploitation,

DOI: 10.4324/9781003031581-2

environmental destruction and racism). Sexuality was one focus, amongst other emphases on politics, civil rights or the environment. Issues were often brought together in order to emphasise the bigger picture and how different modes of exploitation and oppression are intrinsically connected in capitalism. The feminist battle cries 'the personal is political' and 'our bodies, our selves' have been strongly engrained into the collective (un)consciousness of the global North (Schrupp 2017). It is not a coincidence that Wilhelm Reich was taken up by Theweleit, who might have read his books as *Raubdrucke*, pirated copies, perhaps in a Marxist reading group while he was a doctoral student, and many others as part of a general structure of feeling of 1968 which was osmotically open to and devoured Reich's works. If there was ever the time for progressive sexuality, it was then. At least that is what many people thought at the time. It was not only feminist activists and women groups who discovered embodiment and the body, but also men, as Sven Reichardt (2007) notes in his idea-historical discussion of Theweleit's *Male Fantasies* in the context of 1968. The late 1960s were marked by a general opening up towards the body and embodiment:

> One looked for bodily proximity, opened up much space for bodily intimacy, even nudity, in flat-shares, wanted to express oneself through the body – from meditation to sexuality – and placed 'instinctiveness' centre stage of the moral code. (Reichardt 2007, 408, my translation, emphasis in original)

Michel Foucault made a similar observation: what was transformative and different to other revolutionary movements was a focus on the body: 'the importance given to the body is one of the important, if not essential elements' (Foucault 1980, 57) of 1968. In fact, as Foucault argued, it contributed a great deal to the very existence of the sexual revolution.

Such a focus on sexuality and the body also came into being in West Germany (and differently in other countries) as a result of a direct confrontation and debate between university students, young people and the parental generation who had been active (or passive-active) members of the Third Reich. Emancipatory and anti-fascist politics were intrinsically connected to sexuality and embodiment. This included a critical interrogation of ideas of (hegemonic) masculinity. A 'new man' was to be born, one who was to be different than the soldier males Theweleit had analysed. Theweleit also discusses his relationship with his father at the beginning of the first book of *Male Fantasies* and how strict and violent his upbringing under such a father was. Such archetypes of the male were still very much alive in the 1960s and have made an uncanny comeback today. Perhaps they never left (Herzog 2005). They were not restricted to Nazi Germany and the Weimar Republic. As Theweleit writes:

> I don't want to make any categorical distinction between the types of men who are the subjects of this book and all other men. Our subjects are equivalent to the tip of the patriarchal iceberg, but it's what lies beneath the surface that really makes the water cold. (Theweleit 1987, 171)

While the student movement was on the one hand characterised by a revolt against the 'Nazi-connected parent bodies' (Theweleit 1989, 57, cited in Reichardt 2007, 412, my translation), it was on the other hand (and with Reich we know that the two are intertwined), characterised by a creation of new sexualities. A different culture and politics of sexuality and different forms of relationships, sex and being together emerged. This was not the time for queer theory (yet), so the discursive-biological constructions of sex and gender were perhaps not as fully on the agenda as they would be some decades later. New sexualities were not only brought about through philosophy and practice, but were of course facilitated by the pill, and other forms of contraception that had been in development and ultimately in mass supply in Germany and elsewhere since the late 1950s.

> The general societal liberalisation of sexuality, which took place from the mid-60s onwards with the so-called 'sex wave' [*Sexwelle*] and the rise of the sex industry, did not only show itself in bare chested young women on magazine covers, or in the news coverage of partner swapping at parties, or of infidelity. Real changes in the sexual practices of youth had accompanied this media hype und were supposedly influenced by it. Young people had three or four years earlier sexual intercourse than their older siblings. In 1971, every third teenager between 16 and 17 had had sexual intercourse, at the age of 20 more than two thirds of women and three quarters of men. That was a trend that would continue during the 1970s. (Reichardt 2007, 416, my translation)

Trends which Wilhelm Reich would have undoubtedly welcomed and enthusiastically affirmed. If there is one term with which to, at least partly, characterise this historical period, it is transformative *disinhibition* – at least to a strong degree. Disinhibition that took place on sexual and social levels. Given Reich's numerous discussions of sexual inhibition, it appears like his wildest dreams had become reality. Today's culture is more about disinhibition without any transformative effects. Christine Weder (2016) argues in her cultural historical study of 1968 and the role of sexuality and aesthetics, that 1968 was marked by an 'intense thematisation of sexuality' (2016, 12, my translation). This not only happened in academic discourse through the growing discipline of sexology for example, but also in popular culture, and within the 1968 movement itself. But it is more than that. Revolution meant sexual revolution. The Freudo-Marxism of the Frankfurt

School and of Wilhelm Reich in particular situated revolution at the individual body that needed to be liberated and this specifically included genitalia. With such a programme of liberation came a necessary, so it was hoped, change in law and ethics, which at the time of the late 1960s in many Western countries could at best be considered archaic, at worst discriminatory from today's standpoint. Draconic laws on abortion, homosexuality or infidelity were in place – and they were liberalised because of the 1968 movements (Herzog 2005). The year 1968 had long-lasting and undisputed effects which resulted in progressive social change.

Whether sexuality had been repressed or not, and this was and is subject to debate as already noted, it marked *the central* reference point of and for 1968, as Weder argues. In her study, she shows how sexuality was particularly shown and debated in the representational realm: through art, media, literature. This was the case for theoretical works on sexuality that drew on popular culture and the arts, but also academic works specifically from literature and the arts were heavily 'sexualised' (ibid, 18) at the time. There was thus a deep entanglement of aesthetics and theories of sexuality around 1968 – not only in Germany but also in the United States, France and other countries. More importantly, forms of sexuality, as the earlier quote from Reichardt shows, were being transformed as well. Up until the 1970s, there was no sex education in (West) German schools for example. It was a topic that was not discussed by the parents and children of the 1950s and 1960s (or by previous generations). The year 1968 was, at least for some and on some levels, characterised by a different form and embodiment of sexuality.

> The student movement was without question strongly motivated by sexual rebellion against the conformist culture of postwar West Germany. As New Left cultural critic Klaus Theweleit observed in retrospect, a 'special sort of sexual tension was the "driving force" of 1968' [Theweleit 1990, 49] in West Germany. (Herzog 2005, 154)

Young people wanted to talk about and experience sex differently than previous generations and they demanded it. Writing on the sexual revolution in the United States, Eric Schaefer notes that it saw a rise of 'public' sex (2014, 1) – a display and discussion of sex in the media in particular. For second wave feminists and other groups, the sexual revolution meant a revolt against sex as a 'regulatory mechanism designed and constructed to enforce male dominance and female submission' (Jeffreys 1990, 7) – not just in the cinema (see Mulvey 1975 and the many psychoanalytic-feminist film scholars who followed) but in the bedroom and in public. Debates around the female orgasm and sexual agency of women became important for the feminist movement in the United States and elsewhere (Gerhard 2001).

Problems of the sexual revolution

It was the (sexual) body that became the symbol of the revolution. The 1960s also saw the so-called 'sex wave' in West Germany and elsewhere with pornography becoming widely available, in the form of films, magazines and books. Sex became commodified and mediated. This was also, perhaps ironically, a key legacy of 1968: sexuality became part of constructed lifestyles and commodities. Media, sex shops and other commodified forms spread sexuality and forms of pornography to masses of hungry consumers. Sex became omnipresent both through discourses and representations. The linking and lumping together of any imaginable product and sexuality also begun in the late 1960s. Advertising jumped on the new hunger for scantily clad or naked bodies which were used to advertise everything. This, often sexist, legacy continues to this day. The 1960s were responsible for leading to a *public* fascination with everything around sexuality. This can have problematic outcomes, as I discuss in Chapter 7 in relation to porn addiction.

I do not wish to discuss the truth of the idea that the apparent disinhibition of 1968 resulted in inhibition and dis/inhibition of future generations. I think it is interesting how Reich writes of disinhibition and that to him it would result in a more progressive and better society if sexuality was more conscious and disinhibited. 1968 undoubtedly contributed to social change and a more empowered female sexuality in particular. However, I would suggest that there is a fantasy of free love and harmonious hippie culture that we tend to associate retrospectively with 1968. It has become a signifier that is made to signify certain things, while ignoring others. This is particularly true in the popular imagination (see also Herzog 2005).

As Sven Reichardt and many others (Grant 1993; Heidenry 1997; Allyn 2001; Bennett 2016) have pointed out, 1968 was more diverse and fragmented than we might like to admit. There was a backlash against disinhibition and proclaimed new masculinities and femininities within the movement itself at the time and afterwards (see also Yates, Richards & Sergeant 2020). When it comes to sexuality, there is no inhibition without it. 'There is no such thing as a free transgression' (Phillips 2013, 189). The constant demand for embodiment and a questioning of one's own internalised masculinity was criticised by some men and women. The writer Peter Schneider said in 1974 that 'all those mechanistic and cold attempts at sexual disinhibition, which were paraded in front of us on a daily basis, were boring at the end of the day and led to new, namely emotional inhibition' (Schneider 1974, 126, cited in Reichardt 2007, 416, my translation). 'Even during the sexual revolution itself, an uninhibited life of sensuality was less a reality than a product of fantasy' (Sigusch 1998, 356). While the so-called 'male groups' (*Männergruppen* in West Germany) actively debated and critiqued their own masculinities and how they could become 'softer', many also criticised such efforts as being imposed by feminism. A counter-movement emerged that only resulted in strengthened chauvinism and sexism in response to feminism (Messner 2016). This ties in with general critiques of (West German) 1968 as being largely male-dominated and sexist. Many of the heroes of 1968 were men, it was alleged. Sheila Jeffreys (1990) has argued that the so-called sexual liberation was anything but. Instead it served as an ideological mask to hide the continued (sexual) oppression of women. Writing about the Austrian Friedrichshof Commune, David Bennett notes how it was meant to encourage free and disinhibited sexuality. In reality, its leader Otto Muehl was an authoritarian who produced 'fuck lists' on a computer so that each of the 600 communards could have sexual intercourse with as many as possible without repetition (Bennett 2016, 218). Sex had become compulsory. Another, albeit small, dark chapter of 1968 was a harmful and simply wrong advocacy of child sexuality (Baader et al. 2017). By way of conclusion, the sexual revolution was more problematic than it would appear at first.

Feminisms and the birth of the Men's Rights Movement: changing masculinities

A key aspect of the sexual revolution was feminism. The sexual revolution was partly initiated because of a critical disagreement with and reworking of archaic (Freudian) notions of pleasure and female sexuality towards a more agentic and less sexist conceptualisation of female desire and sexuality. Betty Friedan, Shulamith Firestone and Kate Millett were particularly iconic for feminists in this respect. But second wave feminism of the late 1960s and 70s was concerned with radical social change on a broader scale. Feminists protested in order to achieve social, economic, and sexual equality (Schrupp 2017). A criticism of second wave feminism has been that it was largely white and middle class. Working class and women of colour for example felt excluded from it (LeGates 2001).

The second wave feminist movement of the 1960s was more, but not entirely, unified than its subsequent instantiations and from the 1980s onwards different *feminisms* started to emerge and one should write of feminism in the plural from that point onwards. Feminists became (and remain) divided around questions of race and class, sex work and pornography in particular (Scott 1988; Overall 1992; Liff & Wajcman 1996; Bhavnani 2001; Scoular 2004; Snyder-Hall 2010). Second-wave feminism began to decline as a mass movement in the 1980s and third-wave feminism saw a less visible but professionalised and institutionalised form of feminism take hold. This meant a feminist politics that articulated itself through policy and law (in relation to domestic violence or rape laws for example). This form of feminism perhaps became more pragmatic and issue-focused rather than being concerned with the radical social change of second-wave feminism (Evans 2016). Fourth-wave feminism, from the 2010s onwards, has been characterised as more intersectional than previous waves and as specifically using social media and the internet for activism (Chamberlain 2017; Blevins 2018).

Related to critical engagements with sexuality, femininity and masculinity within 1968 is the rise of the men's liberation movement or as it would subsequently be known the Men's Rights Movement. Initially born out of an affirmative response to feminism and the idea that men should be allies to feminist goals, many men soon turned deeply critical of feminism and contemporary Men's Rights Activists (MRAs) are by and large anti-feminist (Messner 2016). As feminism, and different feminisms, moved into third-wave feminism (from the 1990s–2010s) and most recently into fourth-wave feminism (from the 2010s–present), male activists also went along. In his historical overview of the Men's Rights Movement, Michael Messner (2016) has shown that second-wave feminism in the United States (and elsewhere) was met with different responses by men and by male groups: some enthusiastic supporters, some indifferent, some critical. While pro-feminist men of the 1970s acknowledged patriarchy and the role of men in society, they also wished to achieve male liberation i.e. moving beyond an unhealthy hegemonic masculinity (Connell 1987, 1995)[2] which was also oppressive to men. There was a 'tension in men's liberation's attempt to focus simultaneously on men's institutional power over women and on the "costs of masculinity" to men' (Messner 2016, 8). Men claimed they were privileged and dehumanised by their gender at the same time. Messner argues that by the mid- to late-1970s, the movement began to split across different understandings and positions. Some men argued that men and women were equally oppressed by hegemonic notions of gender. This resulted in justified critique from women, because they argued that women suffered under patriarchy more than men. The Men's Rights Movement (from the mid-1970s onwards) began to use openly misogynistic and sexist discourses while sticking to a reactionary understanding of gender and sex. 'The men's rights movement was not simply a kneejerk backlash against feminism; it was a movement that co-opted the liberal feminist language of symmetrical sex roles and then turned this language back on itself' (ibid, 9) by borrowing feminist concepts and idioms and simply applying them to men. Something which has continued to this day and also finds its expression within the manosphere. MRAs claimed that men actually have it worse than women, that they cannot break free from traditional gender expectations as liberated women can, and are often victims of false rape accusations, of child custody cases decided in favour of women, or of alcoholism and other forms of addiction.

Neoliberalism, taking hold under Reagan and Thatcher in the United States and United Kingdom in the late 1970s and quickly becoming the hegemonic economic order across the world, saw radical economic changes that affected men and women alike. Many Western labour markets became deindustrialised, resulting in a decline of traditional 'male' work which was moved to countries like China or India or ceased to exist altogether. Particularly white working class men and men of colour in the global North were affected by this. Service and information work started to become a booming sector from the 1980s onwards which was mostly filled with female workers. Men have referred to this as a 'feminization' of society (Mayer 2013). By the 2000s, the Men's Rights Movement gained in strength because it was pointing to the (allegedly) disadvantaged boys and men who were being left behind in schools and in the workplace as a result of neoliberalism. In addition, MRM activism has often focused on father's rights and paternity laws which, so it is claimed, are often in favour of mothers and have resulted in fathers losing access to their children following divorce and custody legal cases (Hodapp 2017). Online MRM activism has also focused on perpetuating myths about sexual violence: that it is gender-neutral, that rape culture is a moral panic and that sexualised violence against men is rendered invisible by feminists (Gotell & Dutton 2016; Hodapp 2017). Needless to say, none of this is true.

All of the above factors (and others) are often summarised as being exemplary of a *crisis of masculinity* (Horrocks 1994; MacInnes 1998; Segal 1999; Robinson 2000; Kimmel 2013; Roberts 2014; Starck & Luyt 2019). This apparent crisis is often associated with a loss of male authority and a feminisation and emotionalisation of society, whether real or imagined, that men feel (Neill 2019; Crociani-Windland & Yates 2020). Traditional forms of masculinity – the tough male who is the breadwinner – were declining yet also remained hegemonic ideals in Western societies (Gilmore 1990: Kimmel 2008, 2013).

However, there have also been positive developments in relation to changing masculinity. For example, Yates (2007) argues that there has been a greater emphasis on emotion and emotional disclosure both privately and publicly due to the influence of second wave feminism. Traditional traits of the masculine and the feminine were challenged and men encouraged to express a more reflexive and vulnerable sense of self (Yates 2007, 9–10). Different forms of masculinity have existed alongside each other and it is today far more common to embody an emotional, vulnerable and reflexive masculinity (often derogatory referred to as 'beta' or 'cuck' by some men) rather than a machismo kind of chauvinism of the past. Two masculinities, then, emerged in the 1990s in relation to the alleged crisis of traditional masculinity: the reflexive male, a type of masculinity rooted in discourses of therapy culture and the need to be in touch with one's emotions (Yates 2007, 2015; Bainbridge & Yates 2005). Secondly, a consumerist, metrosexual kind of masculinity exists which places an emphasis on fitness, makeup and clothes (Clarkson 2005; Hakim 2019). A third type of masculinity that has emerged in the last two decades is geek masculinity which I discuss in a moment as it is particularly relevant for the manosphere.

The apparent decline of a traditional sense of masculinity is also responded to by the Pick Up Artist movement from the early 2000s onwards, which caters for some insecure men who feel they are unable to date women. PUA suggests that heterosexual men can learn the skills to appear or perform hegemonic masculinity (above all, assertiveness, dominance and self-confidence) and simply need to follow steps in order to convince women to sleep with them (Kimmel 2008; Almog & Kaplan 2017; O'Neill 2018).

The term 'toxic masculinity' is also often used in relation to MRAs and other male behaviour that is considered dangerous, harmful or abusive to others and often to the men themselves. It was initially conceived as a notion in relation to men and their fathers (Haider 2016). 'Some of these analyses focused on the social scripts that surrounded war, presenting an idealised masculinity as a model for heroism and representing war as a ritual transition from boyhood to manhood' (Jones, Trott & Wright 2019, 3). It bears some connection to Connell's (1987) concept of 'hegemonic masculinity'. Toxic masculinity can be seen as a subset of hegemonic masculinity (Kupers 2005; Veissière 2018; Pearson 2019). Toxic masculinity, while being destructive, may at the same time be desired and demanded of men in society. Examples of toxic masculinity include the subordination of women, sexism, misogyny, homophobia and violence. Forms of toxic masculinity function structurally to uphold patriarchy and male power (Manne 2018). In short, toxic masculinity refers to acts of male domination and oppression. Ashley Morgan (2019) notes that toxic masculinity has gained more currency recently in the wake of the #MeToo movement and discussions of masculinity in popular culture. James W. Messerschmidt, a key voice in the development of the notion of hegemonic masculinity has recently argued that it has lost nothing of its salience (Messerschmidt 2018) and that one arena where it is amplified, but also challenged, is the internet. Jones, Trott and Wright argue that the manosphere has provided a renewed platform for idealising and desiring particular forms of toxic masculinity:

> In fact, it is the failure to achieve and fulfil the expectations of what it means to be a man in relation to the narrow definition upheld by hegemonic masculinity that propels these 'beta' men to idealise an identity constructed from the principles of toxic masculinity. (Jones, Trott & Wright 2019, 4)

One such avenue of toxic masculinity is the alt-right and the manosphere can be seen as a gateway drug to it. As I argue in this book, the rise of the alt-right online means that a different, new kind of masculinity is now being presented as hegemonic by that community and taken up by many men (in the manosphere and beyond): a fascist masculinity which is about traditional masculine attributes (toughness, dominance over women, physical strength) coupled with misogyny, anti-feminism, homophobia and racism/fascism. Psychoanalysis can help to analyse this type of new masculinity which is strongly connected to digital culture and the internet.

Whiteness and the alt-right

Writing in 2016, Messner concludes that '[r]ather than overt anti-feminist backlash, I argue that what is more likely to gain traction today in the US is a "kinder, gentler" form of men's rights discourse and organizing' (ibid, 13). Unfortunately, since the election of Donald Trump as U.S. President in 2016, the exact opposite has become the case. It has seen a strengthening of the manosphere and the infusion of MRAs and the alt-right (Nagle 2017). At the time of writing in 2020, no studies had (yet) examined in detail the strengthening of the Men's Rights activism since the popularisation of the alt-right from 2016 onwards. It also needs to be stressed that far right and reactionary men and organisations have *always* been anti-feminist and misogynistic as well as racist (Kimmel 2013).

The so-called 'crisis of masculinity' that this book touches on in relation to its online articulations is predominantly related to white cis men (although there are also many males who are not white who frequent the communities discussed in this book).[3] It thus relates to *race*, as will be made clear throughout this book when I discuss the racist and anti-Semitic language that is often used by such men, as well as to *class*. Messner writes that

> men's rights rhetoric that contains an implicit anti-feminism is likely to resonate with men who feel insecure or embattled. And I would speculate that moderate men's rights leaders' focus on individual choice and their implicit antifeminism resonates best with educated middle class white men who do not want to appear to be backwards misogynists. (Messner 2016, 13)

Messner notes that the aggressive anti-feminism of MRAs, which is amplified by other groups such as incels or MGTOW, appeals to working class men more than it does to middle- or upper-class men. While I cannot provide any meaningful data on the class backgrounds of the manosphere, or supporters of the alt-right, the kind of authoritarian populism of Trump has particularly appealed to working class voters, who had suffered because of a decline in traditional manufacturing in parts of the United States (McQuarrie 2016; Morgan 2018). Additionally, Trump and his sexism, conservatism, racism and above all economic-protectionist nationalism as it articulated itself in the slogan 'Make America Great Again', were particularly attractive to white, working-class male voters (Mutz 2018). Those white male voters not only felt left behind economically (Morgan 2018), but they felt that their very status as men had been weakened by a 'declining white share of the national population' (Mutz 2018, 19) and by the decline of geopolitical hegemony of the United States on the world stage, as Diana C. Mutz argues (see also Reny, Collingwood & Valenzuela 2019).

Nonetheless, Trump was overall voted for by individuals from across the class spectrum (Fraser 2017) and even to a lesser extent by individuals from different ethnic backgrounds. Likewise, the men of the manosphere may come from a range of class and ethnic backgrounds, but I could not tell definitively what their backgrounds are.

Such forms of wrongly perceived male powerlessness not only relate to changes in neoliberalism which I discussed, they also relate to racist fantasies of white supremacism which are implicit and often highly explicit within the manosphere. The manosphere's active mobilisation of alt-right terminology and images perhaps speaks not only to individual crises of the men and a general crisis of masculinity because of neoliberal precarity or wider social change but also specifically to a crisis of whiteness and white masculinity. 'The question regarding the current rise of the new right is whether and in how far western cultures are witnessing a strengthening of whiteness as a hegemonic social and racial formation' (Schmitt 2018, 49). While no definitive data on the demographics of incels and other men of the manosphere exists, it seems that the majority of the men are white. Within the incel community there are also self-described 'currycels' (South Asian and Indian incels), 'blackcels' and many other names to denote specific regional or ethnic backgrounds. It is perhaps not surprising, given the discourses of self-hatred (see Chapter 4), that some but not all of the men who are not white take up racist self-definitions.

Overall, many (possibly the majority) in the incel community and the wider manosphere are white. It is therefore useful to come back to questions of whiteness at this point. While forms of racism and white supremacism are not new on the internet (Daniels 2009), they are specific in how they currently appear in the manosphere. As noted in the Introduction, there are strong overlaps between the manosphere and the ideology of the alt-right. Not everyone in the manosphere is a white supremacist and fascist, and not everyone of the alt-right is necessarily a misogynist, but the two spheres strongly overlap and are also influenced by phenomena that are situated on the fringes or came distinctly before the term 'alt-right' was used (for example the mass shooters Breivik and Rodger who were both racist and misogynists but not part of the alt-right, which did not exist at the time of their crimes). The alt-right is a recent white nationalist-supremacist movement that calls for the creation of a white ethnostate in North America (Hawley 2017). Members of the alt-right play down their white supremacy by focussing on 'protecting' and 'preserving' the white race (Hartzell 2018, 10). Specifically, notions of diversity, difference and identity politics are appropriated by the alt-right and turned upside down when they argue that it is separation between races and ethnicities that acts as the guarantor of diversity.

> Constructing rhetorical distance between white nationalism and white supremacy further enables white nationalist rhetoric to deflect

accusations of hatred and racism by (re)positioning pro-white arguments within a larger discourse of identity politics and arguing that if other groups are able to make identity-based claims to particular rights and protections, white people should be able to make similar claims.
(Hartzell 2018, 10)

Such a strategy makes the alt-right so dangerous, because more traditional forms of racist/fascist ideology and white supremacism are masked through a focus on identity for example. For Hartzell, this strategy is able to achieve a distance from white nationalism and supremacism while simultaneously making claims that are deeply rooted in white nationalism; for example, by emphasising alternatives to so-called 'mainstream politics' and 'political correctness'. As a movement, the alt-right is deeply sexist and often misogynist (Forscher & Kteily 2020). Additionally, the alt-right has also appropriated tactics and visuals from internet subcultures (such as those of gamers), like memes, ironic and funny videos or the remixing of content. As noted in the Introduction, the alt-right has been declining as a coherent movement with a wider presence on social media. However, it has also led to various offshoots as well as attempts to regain in strength by prominent figures.

While this book is not about the alt-right as such, but about the manosphere, it is interesting to note that the narratives of the manosphere are far less strategic and layered than those of the alt-right. Incels, MGTOWs and other men use no symbolism or coded words to lure men in who would perhaps be reluctant to subscribe to more 'traditional' fascist and white supremacist rhetoric. While the manosphere makes use of alt-right language and images, they do so to directly express hatred and toxicity. They are also not actively recruiting new followers, unlike the alt-right does.

The contemporary moment, then, can be seen as a particular response to a (real or imagined) crisis of white-cis (and to some extent any) masculinity. This crisis is also connected to wider geopolitical crises, as Annie Kelly (2017) argues, where national masculinity is in alleged crisis because of an erosion of, or attack on borders, by terrorists for example in the 9/11 attacks in the USA. As the two phallus-like Twin Towers collapsed, right-wing commentators called for the need of America to re-masculinise itself. Such discourse has been widely mirrored in more recent propaganda against refugees in Europe who are described as male invaders with the goal to rape white women. Left or liberal men who support the admission of refugees or feminist politics, are perceived as a threat by the alt-right and reactionary forces and subsequently labelled as 'snowflakes' or 'cucks'. Nations themselves have been portrayed as weak, feminised and passive in that context. Such narratives also relate to anti-Semitism, a key aspect of any fascist ideology, which is also mobilised by the alt-right (Hawley 2017; Kelly 2017) and incels for example (see Chapter 4). Together with left and liberal men, feminist women, Jews and other subjects who are not white are othered by the alt-right and the manosphere. They are blamed for deliberately weakening and subverting nation states and men alike. Such narratives are fantasies. They are fantasies that create a particular reality for the alt-right and the manosphere in which white, heterosexual men are alleged 'victims' of various forces (deindustrialisation, changing job markets, feminism, women *per se*, refugees). In reality, many men today cannot cope with change or adapt to changing socio-economic relations (see Chapter 4). Their 'fear of change, competition, and failure fuel a sense of loss and victimhood' (Boehme & Scott 2020, 178). I return to the explicit anti-Semitism and racism of some of the manosphere communities in Chapters 4 and 5.

Race thus figures in a complex manner for members of the manosphere. It is used as a form of self-hatred by many non-white incels for example who internalise racist descriptors and ideologies. It is also used as an ideological category by white men who advance a particular narrative of white, male supremacism that consists of fascism, racism, anti-feminism and misogyny. The deployment of race is consistent with historical narratives of racism and fascism where the figure of the male Jew or the black male for example are constructed as oversexualised and a danger to 'pure' white women (Theweleit 1989; Crenshaw 1992, 1993; Guillaumin 2002; Collins 2004). White supremacism and how it is drawn on in the manosphere also privileges the fit, white male body over anyone else's (Fuchs 2018). It is in itself also highly sexist and often misogynistic. The racism, anti-Semitism and the kind of misogyny of the manosphere also fundamentally revolve around notions of male entitlement. Incels in particular are of the opinion that they are owed to be in a romantic relationship with a white woman, just like racists believe that they are owed jobs or status because they are white (Kimmel 2013; Jardina 2019).

Compared to the overt racism and anti-Semitism of the alt-right, this version of prejudice is primarily against women and race figures secondarily in the narratives. I show this in Chapter 4 when I discuss the incel community. Incels primarily focus on the white Stacy and the Chad takes a second, but nonetheless important, place in their worldview. Yet, misogyny and specifically fascism are intertwined as they articulate themselves in anti-Semitic narratives in which women and Jews are linked as allegedly having all the fun while incels miss out for example. Racist narratives are also very present within the incel community and the manosphere more widely, for example when it comes to how black male bodies are discussed (see Chapters 4 and 7).

The mass shooters who I discuss in Chapter 6 were similarly misogynists and racists but their hatred was primarily aimed at women and secondarily centred on race.

Another type of masculinity that has strongly informed the manosphere is discussed below.

Geek masculinity

Geek masculinity has also been linked to the emergence, or popularity of, the manosphere and to a lesser degree of the alt-right. Geek men embrace a status of an underdog and outsider, specifically in relation to hegemonic masculinity (Almog & Kaplan 2017). As I discussed in the Introduction, it was the Gamergate harassment campaign which laid the blueprint for some of the current tactics of the alt-right and the manosphere. Gamergate radicalised some 'geeky' and 'nerdy' men into violent misogynists. Geek masculinity signifies a non-hegemonic sense of masculinity in which the geek or nerd is socially awkward, shy, does not conform to standards of a hegemonic male body (muscular, tall, slim), is obsessed with subcultures, fandoms and 'childish' hobbies such as playing video games, or reading comic books. Claiming geek as an identity has become somewhat of a mainstream cultural script – for both men and women (Salter & Blodgett 2017). Representations of geeks in popular culture as well as real geek success stories (for instance Steve Jobs, Mark Zuckerberg and Bill Gates) have led to the figure of the male geek become a desirable archetype for some men, as Solter and Blodgett argue. 'The narrative of the undesirable, marginalized outsider was becoming the story of tomorrow's tech titans' (ibid, 6). Geek masculinity in itself is not problematic or toxic, but can actually figure as a different kind of masculinity that can potentially allow for male vulnerability and reflexivity to be embodied as part of such an identity (De Visser 2017). It was the internet that was not only shaped by geeks in its early days but significantly contributed to feelings of shared Geek communities to emerge around specific games or fandoms (Salter & Blodgett 2017; Salter 2018). This enabled feelings of belonging and community to emerge around a shared object (Hills 2002).

It is perhaps ironic that the representations of masculinity and femininity in computer/console games and many (not all) of the fandoms (for example comics) that geeks engage in are still often deeply sexist and show stereotypical: muscular heroes and passive, objectified female characters (Jenson & De Castell 2013; Hanna 2018). It was precisely this sexism within video games (and the wider industry itself) which was challenged by female game developers and critics which prompted the violent backlash of Gamergate. 'Geek identity is a battleground, its territories demarcated by borders both real and rhetorical' (Salter & Blodgett 2017, 11). Gamergate was a case where geeky men felt that their territories were being invaded by women. Those men circulated the same message over and over again: 'women—and feminists in particular, an easily defined other to identify as representing the supposed influence of the mainstream—are out to destroy geek culture, and these groups of "true" geeks are ready to defend it' (ibid, 12). In reality, geeky men could not come to terms with the fact that their male spaces were being challenged and diversified. Perhaps those men had also been confronted with their own desires of actually *wanting* to surpass their geek masculinity and (unconsciously) defended against those. While geeks are not fascist or racist by default, many geeks perceive themselves as, and embrace the status of being, victims, marginalised and outsiders (Ging 2017), just like the alt-right and the men of the manosphere do. Sarah Banet-Weiser has argued that geek masculinity in general is 'characterized by a kind of overt fragility—and in particular, white fragility. The privilege of whiteness is rarely acknowledged by geeks' (Banet-Weiser 2018, 156). The same is true for the alt-right, although alt-right men seek to compensate their fragility by assuming (or desiring) a kind of fascist, hypermasculinity (see Chapter 4).

The rise of the manosphere and of MRAs on the internet in particular can further be elaborated in relation to postfeminism and changing sexualities as it partly emerged as a response.

Postfeminism, porn culture and irony

In our current era of fourth-wave feminism in the Western world, scholars have put forward that there is an ideological postfeminist sensibility (Gill 2007). Angela McRobbie (2004, 2009) has argued that achievements from second- and third-wave feminism have been actively undermined in the last decades by forces and discourses that acknowledge feminism but argue that we have now moved beyond it. Questions of concern to feminists are apparently no longer relevant or needed, because feminists have apparently achieved so much. Postfeminism suggests that women can achieve everything now, that they are free to choose whoever they wish to marry, they can enjoy their sexuality, earn their own living and live a free life (McRobbie 2004, 2007, 2008). They can be phallic themselves (McRobbie 2007) and exhibit aggression, boldness, confidence and transgression. The phallic girl temporarily mimicks phallic aspects or forms of masculine behaviour. Her phallus is also only possible because any real critique of hegemonic masculinity or patriarchy is suspended by her so that she can join her masculine counterparts (McRobbie 2007; Saitō 2011; Renold & Ringrose 2012, 2017). The men discussed in this book, unlike other men perhaps, seem to precisely rage at the figure of the phallic girl, because to them it is her who has castrated them and should not be like them.

Such forms of femininity were represented in popular culture of the early to mid-2000s such as *Sex and the City* (1998–2004, Star) or *Bridget Jones Diary* (2001, Maguire). They are still very much around today (Banet-Weiser 2018). McRobbie notes that young women would actively disassociate themselves from feminism at a time (during the 1990s–2000s) when popular culture itself became increasingly about representing successful girls and women. Representations which even ironically played with notions of sexism, objectification and feminism, all under the guise of empowerment and irony. Writing about an ad for *Citroen* in the 1990s which showed the model Claudia Schiffer take off her clothes, McRobbie argues:

> Because there is no exploitation here, there is nothing remotely naive about this striptease. She seems to be doing it out of choice, and for her own enjoyment; the advert works on the basis of its audience knowing Claudia to be one of the world's most famous and highly paid supermodels. Once again, the shadow of disapproval is introduced (the striptease as site of female exploitation), only instantly to be dismissed as belonging to the past, to a time when feminists used to object to such imagery. To make such an objection nowadays would run the risk of ridicule. Objection is pre-empted with irony. (McRobbie 2004, 259)

Gill (2007) has also isolated irony as a key dimension of the postfeminist moment where irony allows men (and women) to get away with anti-feminism, sexism, misogyny and homophobia for example, because it was all just a joke or just irony. The so-called 'lads mags' which were very popular in the 1990s and 2000s in Britain and elsewhere mask their heavy misogyny through humour and irony. I would argue that such form of irony and humour contributed to the current usage of irony by the alt-right and by members of the manosphere when they use irony to talk about women (see Chapter 4). Irony has taken on a very different currency in our present moment, where it is similarly used by the alt-right and the manosphere to signify a lighthearted and *nonchalant* form of critique and representation (Greene 2019). The ironic form with which exploitation and sexism were sold as forms of self-empowerment for women has been co-opted by the alt-right to precisely shame and abuse women for empowering themselves sexually and otherwise.

In her influential article *Postfeminist media culture: Elements of a sensibility*, Gill (2007) focussed on postfeminist media culture and regards the media as one particular site where a 'postfeminist sensibility' (2007, 147) is represented. Media texts and specific formats, such as reality and makeover television are often 'beautifying' the female body through 'before-after' shots. While this can also be read as empowering (Thomadaki 2019), it is ultimately often exploitative and reinforces hegemonic ideals of beauty. In general, postfeminist media culture is obsessed with the (female) body and through women's magazines, talkshows and reality/makeover programmes constantly encouraged women to police and survey their own bodies in order to look fit, sexy and desirable (see also McRobbie 2009; Ross 2011). Such practices also occur online on platforms like Instagram for example (Gill 2016; Hakim 2019).

Women are also portrayed as active, sexually desiring subjects rather than passive objectifications of the male gaze (Mulvey 1975) in a culture of postfeminism. The male gaze is internalised and turned into a 'self-policing, narcissistic gaze' (Gill 2007, 151). This also means that pornography has infiltrated popular culture, for example through t-shirts with slogans such as 'porn star' being sold by highstreet chains. Additionally, bodies of mainstream pornography have been exported to wider representations and discourses within the media, for instance when it comes to phenomena like the 'designer vagina' (Jones 2017) or sexual practices. In such a culture, the only woman who is awarded 'sexual subjecthood' (Gill 2007, 152) is cis, young, thin and white. Sexual objectification is thus presented (and perhaps taken up) as something that is freely chosen and embodied by women. This also relates to the wide availability of pornography from the 2000s onwards via the internet (Attwood 2009; Gill 2013). At the same time, women are often shamed as 'sluts' if they have had a range of different sexual partners (Ringrose & Renold 2012). While there are different responses to the idea of postfeminism (Gill 2016, 2017; Rivers 2017) and to pornography in particular (see Ciclitira 2004; Boyle 2014 overviews), the developments that feminist researchers like Gill and McRobbie critically discuss are undisputable. This book is not specifically about contributing to postfeminism or pornography debates within feminism and I do not present particular arguments for or against pornography. Amongst other things, I am interested in thinking about what the ubiquitous availability of pornographic images and fantasies across culture and beyond pornography does to men on fantasmatic and affective levels (see Chapter 7).

Since the notion of postfeminism was first discussed specifically in relation to popular culture by Gill (2007) and McRobbie (2004), feminism has gained new momentum in its fourth wave and acceptance in public, not least because it has been amplified through popular culture and the internet. The #MeToo movement also documented the widespread scale of sexual harassment and sexualised violence against women and queers. Some scholars have introduced ideas around 'post-postfeminism' or the analytic redundancy of postfeminism (Keller & Ryan 2014). In recent work, Gill has argued that postfeminism needs to be interrogated as an ideology more than ever (2016, 2017), because feminism is both present in popular culture and through online activism but at the same time actively undone by antifeminists and reactionary forces. Keller and Ryan (2014) for example have on the contrary argued that it is precisely popular culture, through series such as *Girls* or musicians like Beyoncé, or hashtag campaigns on Twitter or Instagram that has made a form of feminism accessible and of appeal to the masses. Feminism is everywhere and nowhere at the same time. In *Empowered: Popular Feminism and Popular Misogyny*, Sarah Banet-Weiser (2018) has shown how feminism and its misogynistic backlash are more problematically intertwined than one would think at first glance. Such forms of activism and the sheer visibility of feminism have resulted in a reactionary backlash by misogynists, such as Men's Rights groups, who co-opt the popular slogans and identificatory campaigns of feminists in order to weaponise them against them. The logic of the one is appropriated and turned against the other, for example when MRAs claim that men now suffer in confidence and mental health *because* of feminism and the status of women. Popular misogyny is, like popular feminism, networked and makes effortless use of different social media, like YouTube, blogs, Twitter, etc. For every feminist victory or campaign, it is almost certain that there is going to be a backlash from anti-feminists, a backlash that is often co-ordinated via social media.

It is beyond the scope of this book to provide a detailed historical and current review of different forms of feminism and how they may be amplified, co-opted, challenged or undone by digital and social media. Postfeminism, and how it articulated itself, has led to the recent increase in MRAs as there is a greater visibility of female agency and characters in popular culture and wider public discourses (Messner 2016) and has contributed to the growth of the manosphere. The historical developments that I have presented in this chapter are important because, as I show in the next chapters, they have informed and influenced the shaping of the manosphere and to the affective states of those men. Furthermore, developments like the sexual revolution, the different feminist waves, porn culture, or notions such as the crisis of masculinity are actively deployed by men of the manosphere in their narratives.[4]

There is also another legacy of the different forms of feminism, the gay rights movement and queer theory in particular that I think is absolutely crucial for understanding the form that misogyny takes today. It was queer and feminist scholarship that contributed to changing sexualities and gender norms. Gender is now far more fluid than in previous generations and the dramatically increasing number of individuals identifying as transgender and undergoing gender reassignment procedures only attests to this (Bulman 2019). Seen in relation to general shifts of sexuality ever since the sexual revolution in the West of the late 1960s, how sexuality and gender are experienced, portrayed and seen by all of us has changed significantly. This is a change, I argue, that is so *existentially unsettling* to many men today that they resort to defend their masculine identities that are threatened with disintegration. They feel undone by feminism, gender fluidity and the queerness of the world. Needless to say, such responses may seem incomprehensible to us, but we need to hold on to them and see them as instances of impotence and symbolic castration. Forming collective communities functions to create boundaries around the men's bodies and the group acquires an extended body to defend against all the outer threats. Fascism operates with a very similar dynamic.

Beyond hegemonic masculinity?

Is it possible to imagine a different sense of masculinity beyond that of the alt-right, the manosphere or representations in popular culture and Hollywood? I have already mentioned geek masculinity as a form of non-hegemonic masculinity, but it also comes with its own problems and has partially been co-opted by the manosphere.

In *Work that Body* (2019), Jamie Hakim has argued that how male bodies are being displayed through digital media has changed in recent years. The current conjuncture, since the 2008 financial crisis, has seen 'a proliferation of not only sexualised representations of male bodies but also new forms of sexualised modes of male embodiment' (Hakim 2019, xiv). Those include, but are not limited to, the celebrity male nude leak via social media platforms and the rise in (homo)eroticised imagery on platforms such as Instagram by cis-hetero and gay young men. Such representations often embody a sense of stereotypical masculinity: toned, fit, muscular male bodies. Hakim understands them as particular responses to a heightened form of neoliberal capitalism that was brought in with post-2008 austerity policy in Britain and to some extent other parts of the world through which men sexualise their own bodies in order to create value as well as more communal ways of being through for example content shared on social media or the sexual practices of 'chemsex' (where men have sex with other men under the influence of recreational drugs), which Hakim also looks at. This presents a contemporary broader mode of experience where precariousness comes to be lived through and experienced affectively. Other scholars have also written about contemporary masculinities and their (digital and networked) relations to difference, femininity, queerness or trans issues (Semerene 2016, 2021; White 2019). Such works are important because they situate masculinity in relation to aspects that the men discussed in this book violently defend against: soft, feminine, queer elements which are to be found in any male. I return to this point in the book's Conclusion.

The specific, intimate displays of male bodies that Hakim insightfully analyses are an important backdrop to keep in mind when discussing contemporary neoliberal capitalism and its turn to authoritarian capitalism (see Introduction). The 2008 financial crisis not only led to economic recession and austerity, it also contributed in part to the election of right-wing leaders such as Trump, Johnson and others (Cox 2017; Fuchs 2018). There are thus different layers to the current conjuncture, one being the increase in displaying eroticised (and somewhat vulnerable) male bodies on digital media, another layer being the increase in extreme right and alt-right male bodies online. I refer specifically to alt-right male *bodies* here, because I am interested in thinking through the discourses and fantasies that are circulated by those men and how they relate to their bodies and embodiment. While the two kinds of bodies and their usage of digital media are not necessarily connected, we could also read Hakim's case studies of male nude leaks and the male gym photos as representations of what incels call 'Chads': muscular, white, alpha males who are desired by women, according to incels. Those are representations that the men of the manosphere see and engage with. Their desire for a strong and alpha male-like masculinity is thus perhaps not coincidentally intimately connected to the body and to embodiment, given the increase in the circulation of intimate male bodies through digital media. I return to this desire for a particular male body throughout this book. In Chapters 4, I discuss incels and how we can think of them as a particular (embodied) response to the current neoliberal conjuncture. Indeed, Hakim notes that 'the alt-right blames women and feminists and not neoliberalism for the anxious way they feel about their new situations with sometimes murderous consequences' (Hakim 2019, 17). I return to this blame and its connection to neoliberalism in Chapter 3 in more detail. Faludi (1999) argued that the display of male bodies, which began in men's magazines, and has perhaps reached a new stage with the examples Hakim analysed, has created new anxieties and insecurities for men. 'The gaze that hounds men is the very gaze that women have been trying to escape' (1999, 5). This is particularly evident in the incel community and their obsession with the Chad: the muscular, fit male who seems to have jumped straight out of a lads or fitness magazine.

Candida Yates (2007) has argued that there was however a different response to such anxieties and insecurities. A new sense of masculinity emerged in popular culture of the 1990s through films such as *Fight Club* (see Introduction) in which Brad Pitt's body 'conveys a scarred and tortured soul underneath' (Yates 2007, 13). While such an analysis is still valid today, it is complicated by our current cultural moment where there is a renewed backlash against vulnerable, reflexive and emotional kinds of masculinity by forces such as the manosphere. *Fight Club* has acquired a different status today, along with *The Matrix*, than it had in the 1990s and both are used by men to claim that once they have taken the red or black pill, the object of identification becomes Tyler Durden and not the sensitive, vulnerable unnamed narrator/protagonist of the film.

Conclusion

This chapter presented socio-historical developments from the late 1960s up until the present day and introduced debates in relation to the sexual revolution, feminisms, changing masculinities, the alt-right, the manosphere, postfeminism and porn culture. Such debates serve as an important backdrop to this book as the developments I have discussed inform the manosphere in its current form. Members of the different communities of the manosphere (and the male mass shooters who I discuss in Chapter 6) also refer themselves to the sexual revolution, feminism (as a vague and undefined category) or the Men's Rights Movement. The purpose of this chapter was also to introduce and discuss relevant research on those themes. This book, then, makes a number of contributions to the debates and positions discussed in this chapter. There has been no research on the manosphere as a whole which examines some of the communities within it in detail. In general, there is little research that discusses online cultures from a psychoanalytic perspective (Dean 2010; Turkle 2011; Balick 2014; Krüger & Johanssen 2014; Johanssen & Krüger 2016, eds; Clough 2018a; Johanssen 2019; Singh 2019). This monograph provides detailed case studies of particular communities and men by drawing on an innovative theoretical framework which is based on psychoanalysis.

Chapters 1 and 2 have also introduced a wider socio-historical perspective on a contemporary topic. In doing so, I argue that there is a much longer history to the kind of fascist state of mind that I analyse in the coming chapters than some of the current literature suggests. A history that goes back to at least the 1920s and also much farther. Indeed, as Theweleit argued, hundreds of years of patriarchy have created the kind of male bodies and fantasies he analysed. There is thus a connection between the men Theweleit wrote of and the men this book analyses. However, this does not mean that I merely replicate Theweleit's ideas. Additionally, as argued in this chapter, the post-1968 conjuncture and the changes and debates that followed serve as discursive anchoring points for many men of the manosphere. They use them to construct particular ideologies that serve to rationalise sexism, misogyny and also racism (see Chapter 3). Such a socio-historical connection is the starting point for my analyses. I intend to show how misogyny is articulated by particular men via the internet today. Psychoanalysis allows for a complex perspective on this topic, because it pays attention to fantasies, affect, bodies and the unconscious in a way that allows for contradictions to emerge. This notion of contradiction is inherent to the fantasies that I discuss in this book, because they are characterised by defence mechanisms and more active dimensions (such as the dreaming up of a new type of masculinity), as I show. Another example would be the simultaneous desire for and symbolic destruction of women that is present in so many of the data that I discuss. I further develop the notion of a kind of fantasmatic contradiction with my concept of dis/inhibition (see previous chapter) which allows to take the male body into account and how contradiction works on a bodily affective level in a kind of opening and closing, pushing and pulling, restraining and releasing, toing and froing of affects, ideas, fantasies and actions. Such a perspective, then, moves beyond a kind of ethnographic or discursive analysis of text or images alone (as is often done in this kind of research) and allows to make *inferences* from the data about those men's psyches, their bodies, their upbringing, what kind of characters they are and how their unconscious works. This opens up a complex perspective on this topic that goes beyond socio-historical, textual or visual analyses which are common (as discussed in this chapter, see also the first section in Chapter 4). Studies in relation to the wider themes of this book (toxic masculinity, the alt-right, the manosphere) also often aim to maintain a critical distance to their objects. This is very understandable, but I argue that a close reading and specific attention to the kinds of individuals that are part of those communities can help us to analyse them in a more complex manner (see Introduction). At the same time, my psychosocial perspective takes wider socio-historical dimensions into account as well.

Another important contribution this book makes is to move beyond a foregrounding of the notion of victimhood which geeks, the alt-right and the manosphere regularly claim as discussed in this chapter.

Beyond the victim ideology

Such claiming of a victim status, which has been emphasised by many researchers of fascism (Berbrier 2000; Ravetto 2001; Stanley 2018), and of the alt-right as well as the manosphere (Boehme & Scott 2020; Brigley Thompson 2020; Crociani-Windland & Yates 2020) may be correct, but it also risks of cementing this role by reproducing the very term 'victim'. The alt-right is luring in different men (and women) because of a victim narrative (Boehme & Scott 2020) and they respond to such narratives, because they already feel victimised or adopt the status of being victims (they could identify as geeks, MRAs, or just as males). 'Setting up feminism—and feminists—as villains, and men as victims, justifies the networked harassment that often emerges from the manosphere' (Marwick & Caplan 2018, 547). In this book, I argue that men of the manosphere in particular embody fantasies of victimhood (which is of course *false*) but also move beyond it. Victimhood implies apathy and defensiveness. In the context of the manosphere, it is the very epitomy of a defence mechanism *against* those who supposedly make the men victims. This is the case for example with incels or MGTOWs who reproduce endless narratives of how they are the victims of women, feminism, a superficial society, etc. It is the case with the YouTubers I look at in the next chapter and their status as victims of the sexual revolution. It is the case with members of NoFap who are victims of their porn consumption. Victimhood means *inhibition*. Being a victim deprives the subject of agency and symbolic power, at least momentarily, and suggests that the very subjectivity has been undone because of power relations where someone (a perpetrator) or something undermines or subordinates the victim (Dean 2009). The victim is or has been powerless.

None of this is true for the men discussed in this book. They are *already* privileged because they are male and white (Banet-Weiser 2018). The notion of the victim may also reproduce a binary logic of what Jessica Benjamin has called 'doer and done to' (Benjamin 1988, 2018). I return to her in the book's Conclusion. The masculinities and bodily states of those men are more contradictory and complex than mere false victimhood. They affirm and go beyond self-victimisation and assume dangerous symbolic power by creating new realities and desires online. This is a key contribution this book makes to existing debates discussed in this chapter. Their 'aggrieved entitlement' (Kimmel 2013) results in making specific demands what should happen so that they can overcome their alleged victimhood. This means that they create and desire a *new* kind of fascist (alt-right) masculinity. Their absolutely disinhibited forms of communication (and also actions in the case of the mass shooters Breivik and Rodger, see Chapter 6) show how the status of being a victim is used as a springboard in order to formulate and circulate fantasies of power and agency. Such fantasies can be about describing how women are really like or what the ideal male body looks like (see Chapter 4) or in describing their newfound male lifestyles (see Chapter 5), or in discussing kicking their pornography addiction (see Chapter 7). All those examples are instances of assuming symbolic power and having the (privileged) ability to construct fantasies.

My concept of dis/inhibition is particularly useful for further analysing such fantasies, because it takes account of both false victim narratives and other defence mechanisms *as well* as how those are responded to by the alt-right and the manosphere with particular fantasies of strength and agency. Such dynamics also work on a bodily level and I therefore pay particular attention to affect and the body. While I do not disagree with the research that has focussed on victimisation strategies of white supremacists and the manosphere, I contribute to such work by adding another level of complexity that takes account of both victimisation and agency discourses. The real victims of those men are those who they proclaim to be victims of: heterosexual women, LGBTQI+s, refugees, BIPOC – *and, above all, themselves.* The men of the manosphere are victims of their own masculinity and fantasies. This book thus puts forward the argument that the new kind of (fantasmatic) masculinity that the manosphere dreams up is characterised by contradiction, agency, defence mechanisms and other dynamics that are outlined in the coming chapters.

It is for those reasons that I draw on the psychoanalytic concept of fantasy in this book (see Introduction). The creation of fantasies is an (un)conscious process through which the subject becomes their own protagonist in a world of their own. Fantasies can consist of both defensive-reactive as well as agentic elements. For example, when the subject constructs a particular defence against someone or something which is coupled with a scenario in which they assume symbolic power or omnipotence. This also relates to the concept of dis/inhibition which consists of restraining as well as releasing dimensions. Fantasy and dis/inhibition are not meant in a positive or healthy way by me here. Rather, I use both notions to signify and analyse the pathologies through which those men enact particular affective bodily states via fantasies.

How is the alleged disinhibition of the sexual revolution perceived by the alt-right and reactionary men today? I turn to this question in the next chapter.

Notes

1 This chapter cannot provide an extensive overview of the history of feminism and the different forms of feminism, or feminisms, (see for example LeGates 2001 and Schrupp 2017 for overviews and critical discussion).
2 This term 'hegemonic masculinity', coined by Connell (1995), refers to gender as a site of struggle and changing cultural norms and stereotypes that constitute a dominant form of masculinity. There are competing ideas and ideals of masculinity within a given society, but there is one type of masculinity that is able to secure a dominant position which is nonetheless insecure and can be replaced by other types of masculinity. I argue in this book that for some men a kind of fascist masculinity has become hegemonic, or an hegemonic ideal that they aspire to. For a recent overview of masculinity studies see (Gottzén, Mellström & Shefer 2019). Hegemonic masculinity has by some scholars been defined as 'the need to aggressively compete and dominate others and encompasses the most problematic proclivities in men' (Kupers 2005, 713). Connell and Messerschmidt (2005) have however emphasised that hegemonic masculinity should be seen as dynamic, rather than fixed. Hegemonic masculinity is also not the same as 'toxic masculinity', because hegemonic masculinity can take a form that actively distances itself from toxicity (see Yates 2007 for her model of 'good enough' masculinity). However, I argue that for most men discussed in this book hegemonic masculinity is equated with toxicity. Specifically, for some men fascist masculinity has become a hegemonic ideal which is circulated by the alt-right and which those men desire.
3 While the manosphere is predominantly white, many men who are not white also frequent its communities. There is no definitive data on the social and ethnic backgrounds of the men of the manosphere.
4 It is important to point out that feminist research has also examined how women and girls use the internet to fight back and challenge misogyny, trolling and threats (Keller, Mendes & Ringrose 2016; Lawrence & Ringrose 2018; Ringrose & Lawrence 2018; Sundén & Paasonen 2020).

Chapter 3

The backlash against the sexual revolution on YouTube

This chapter outlines how the sexual revolution is discussed by selected YouTubers who range from reactionary to belonging to the alt-right. They isolate the sexual revolution as the key conjuncture in recent history that has brought about alleged moral decline and everything they hate: feminism, so-called 'cultural Marxism', sexual liberation, pornography, homosexuality. Such tirades against the sexual revolution serve as an important backdrop to later chapters of this book. They are part of the manosphere and the wider epistemological universe of the alt-right online and it is safe to assume that such content is viewed by many men today. YouTube in particular is a key platform through which extremist and alt-right influencers (Lewis 2018) disseminate their videos.

The specific psychoanalytic terminology and theoretical application is somewhat limited at this point in the book. This chapter serves as an important epistemological backdrop, along with the previous chapter, to this book's wider aims of analysing the male fantasies of the manosphere. I do so by drawing on my theoretical framework (Chapter 1) and specifically the notion of dis/inhibition. The discussion here then points to exemplary sexual politics of the alt-right, and reactionary YouTubers which inform the subsequent case studies of this book: Incels (Chapters 4 and 5), MGTOW (Chapter 5), NoFap (Chapter 7), as well as the two mass shooters (Chapter 6). It is in those chapters that my theoretical framework comes into full use. The first three chapters of this book set the wider scene and critically introduce important terms and contexts. In the previous chapter, I outlined the history of feminism and the Men's Rights Movement and related it to the sexual revolution, the alt-right and changing masculinity under neoliberalism. I return to neoliberalism in this chapter and specifically in Chapter 4 on incels.

The task of this chapter, then, is to uncover some of the wider sexual politics of the manosphere and the alt-right. They are exemplified by three YouTube videos and their narratives of the sexual revolution and other themes.

DOI: 10.4324/9781003031581-3

The online backlash against 1968

There is a current backlash against 1968 that goes beyond well justified and nuanced criticism. In order to understand some of the narratives from the manosphere and other men that I discuss in this book, it is important to analyse not only the cultural history of sexuality around and post-1968 but also how 1968 has recently been taken up by reactionary, ultra-conservative and alt-right commentators. A search for 'sexual revolution' on YouTube shows many such videos as first results (some of which I discuss in this chapter), perhaps because they are being catapulted to the top by deeply problematic algorithms that push everything that is remotely divisive, extremist or otherwise popular as click-bait (Lewis 2018). On the other hand, it is probably no coincidence that that kind of material has emerged in the last few years. Many videos on YouTube, three of which I discuss in more detail, blame the sexual revolution and its local movements (in West Germany and the United States for example) as responsible for the current 'ills' of Western democracies: feminism, high teenage pregnancy and rising divorce rates, AIDS and other STDs, men being sexually disadvantaged compared to women, drugs, gay and queer culture and other things. The male producers of such videos construct a lasting legacy of a *causal* relationship between the sexual revolution and alleged problems of today. Such videos need to be seen in relation to changing neoliberalism, economic precarity and insecure working conditions that many men (and also women) face today (see Chapters 2 and 4). At the same time, neoliberalism demands that they act as agentic and entrepreneurial subjects (Walkerdine 2020). This form of phallic subjecthood specifically includes sexuality and fantasies around what constitutes 'normal' male sexual subjecthood in times of changing sexuality (O'Neill 2018). The YouTubers whom I discuss on the following pages feel threatened by changing notions of sexuality and masculinity in an age of neoliberal precarity and wider social change. They have lost a sense of white privilege and entitlement and respond with defensive fantasies which seek to re-assert their dominance.

The sexual revolution becomes a powerful signifier that is charged with potency and acquires specific qualities and meanings in those YouTube videos. The commentators are not interested in looking at the sexual revolution itself – they spend hardly any time discussing the events of 1968 in a specific context or in a nuanced way. They are interested in instrumentalising and mischaracterising 1968 in order to advance an agenda for the contemporary age. Given the centrality of the late 1960s to the current moment, which I discussed in the previous chapter, I am interested in analysing how the historical period is discussed by certain cis men on YouTube. Upon entering the search term 'sexual revolution', the videos I discuss in this chapter were among the first results. I have deliberately chosen only to analyse three videos in order to provide in-depth analyses.

Sexuality and post-1968 moral decline

The first video that I analyse is an extensive interview in which an anonymous host, whose YouTube channel goes by the name Vendée Radio, speaks to YouTuber A[1] about 1968 and the sexual revolution. They begin with a focus on West Germany. 1968 is exclusively linked to the terrorist group *Rote Armee Fraktion* (RAF) and leftist terrorism of the 1960s and 1970s.[2] The YouTuber goes on to say that as a response to the terrorist acts committed by the RAF, the German government introduced pornography to pacify the (West) German population:

> 1975, the, first the first response of the German government was to introduce, allow the introduction of pornography into German culture, was very specific, a specific kind of pornography, a very ethnic pornography.... So this is the protest movement, it's focused on Vietnam and it's a worldwide movement, now and in Germany it's a threat to the existence of government, there's no question or the government almost fell because of, the bottom line, okay, because they simply couldn't get it done, so the first response is pornography because that gets you to turn inward. (Vendée Radio 2018, 9.57–12.25)

While the claim that (West) Germany introduced pornography in 1975 to pacify a radical population is arguably a far-fetched hypothesis, the rest of the above quote is embedded in factual discourse. It points to the mixing of facts and fantasies that is so common in alt-right discourses (Hawley 2017). While the late 1960s saw the wider circulation of pornography, as I discussed in the previous chapter, there were no hidden motives behind it on the part of any governments. Pornography is turned into an alleged political means used as a form of state propaganda in the above narrative. Such thoughts reveal a paranoid fantasy of a hidden agenda of the state and are common to many contemporary conspiracy theories which have seen a rapid circulation on the internet and beyond since Donald Trump became president of the USA (Hellinger 2019). Trump and his supporters have been actively promoting conspiracy theories, such as the so-called Pizzagate story or the ideas of the QAnon community (Tuters, Jokubauskaitė & Bach 2018).[3]

What is unique to the kind of fantasies discussed in this chapter is that they specifically link sexuality to forces or events which allegedly seek to undermine heterosexual, white males. Such ideas are shared across the manosphere and wider reactionary and far right communities. It is perhaps no coincidence that sexuality, sexual orientation and specific sexual practices are mobilised in those videos. They instinctively appeal to an existential understanding of subjectivity and identity which is under threat for the producers and viewers of such videos. Sexuality is a key constitutive factor of subjectivity (Zupančič 2017). The alleged decadent and perverted forms of sexuality brought about by the sexual revolution are constructed by alt-right and reactionary YouTubers. Such narratives result in a sense of affective fragility for some male viewers. They feel that their masculinity and heterosexuality are vulnerable. This is all the more revealing when one takes account of the inherent privilege those white individuals have; a privilege that traditionally included phallic sexuality and (a fantasy) of sexual dominance over women. This form of violent male sexual privilege (Sanday 1992) has partly been re-balanced because of achievements by the sexual revolution (see Chapter 2). Sexuality, and how it has changed, is thus used to defend against a (perceived) weakened white hetero masculinity. Such narratives, as the above quotation, are particularly dangerous because they come across as factual and, while conspiratory, are not completely outlandish like the Pizzagate or QAnon stories. They can potentially reach a wider audience of men who believe them. One avenue for distributing such narratives is YouTube and the videos I discuss in this chapter serve as examples.

Another YouTuber whose video I analyse in this chapter is YouTuber B. He makes a similar appeal to facts when he assumes a declining divorce rate resulted from the sexual revolution:

> If you look 1890 through, you know, the, the early part of the 20th century, just a steady divorce rate's still low, steady incline, you get to World War Two and there's a brief sudden spike which coincides with a brief sudden spike in the marriage rate and then it plummets back down again and it starts that gradual incline and then right around the 60s, 70s, 80s that's when it just explodes, there is an explosion of divorce and it stays extremely high for a while now, it has recently been trending back down again, it's still very, very high…. (The Daily Wire 2018, 2.00–3.07)

The video is titled *The Sexual Revolution Ruined Everything It Touched*; it is hosted by The Daily Wire channel (which has 2.4 million subscribers as of November 2020). Other titles include *How Feminism Harms Women*, *What's Wrong With a Straight Pride Parade?*, *Kindergarten Indoctrinating Kids Into Radical Left Wing Gender Theory*, *Inventing Another Fake Environmental Crisis* and many others. While such content may be in line with the wider reactionary and far right material that has flooded YouTube in recent years, the apparent reliance on facts seems at least noteworthy in times of fake news where 'alternative facts' are often made up, misconstrued or when established facts are simply negated, as in the many documented cases of Donald Trump for example. While the mobilisation of some facts may lend authority to figures such as YouTubers A and B in the eyes of some, the causalities they establish seem hard to accept for others.

For both these men and for many other commentators, the sexual revolution caused a general moral decline. In their logic, divorce rates shot up during that time because individuals wanted to live a hedonistic lifestyle of changing partners and sex with as many people as they wanted to. It is more likely that divorce rates went up, because women (and men) felt empowered to annul unsatisfactory relationships. While divorce rates in the United States increased in the 1960s and 1970s, they have in fact been declining ever since the 1980s (Olito 2019). The above quote is exemplary of an ultraconservative belief in traditional families that situates divorce as part of a moral decline brought about, or intensified by, the sexual revolution (Wetzel 2020). Such narratives are particularly attractive to incels, MGTOWs and other men because they appear to be based on facts which are then used by them to stir up hatred. Facts are often heavily distorted, misconstrued or simply invented in such videos. The narratives channel sexism and misogyny into alleged factual discourses which provide those who believe them with a sense of authority and truth. This is reflected in the wider use of scientific studies, crude scientific theories, media texts, YouTube videos and other apparent authoritative resources which are endlessly collected, circulated and discussed by incels, NoFap or MGTOWs in an effort to lend their own ideologies some credibility. While facts and opinions are bent or misconstrued to serve such purposes, they make up a particular worldview for the manosphere and other reactionary men. This worldview is inherently defensive as it seeks to hold onto an authority which is often challenged on social media today by individuals who are not white or male (women, queers, people of colour, and others). As a result of a diversification of social media and online culture, reactionary white men either resort to trolling or abusing others on social media, or they retreat into their own public sphere where they shield themselves from others: the manosphere. Such creation of male spaces in which the sexual revolution and many other specific issues are discussed is underpinned by wider strategies and ideologies.

The above discussions of pornography, sexuality and divorce rates are part of a much wider narrative of the alt-right that specifically connects views against diversity, multiculturalism, equality between men and women, homosexuality and progressive-left views and policies (Hawley 2017).[4] All are made responsible for an apparent decline of Western societies. 'The decline of the West – in its racial configuration, its sexual mores, its consumerism, and the like – is thus not a group of separate causes; rather, it is interconnected' (Gray 2018, 149) for the alt-right and signals a general social decline. For the alt-right, there are specific developments, policies and groups that work against white, heterosexual subjects. Such claims specifically articulate themselves in the form of anti-feminism (Hawley 2017), racism, anti-Semitism (Hartzell 2018), nationalistic statism, economic protectionism and anti-globalism (Mulloy 2020). As discussed in the Introduction, the alt-right, as any fascist movement, constructs specific enemies that are responsible for such a social decline or attack on white heterosexuals: feminists, women, Leftists, black, indigenous and people of colour, specifically Jews, disabled people and LGBTQI+s. The philosopher Jason Stanley (2018) has argued that fascism distorts reality and creates an image of a fantasy of a mythic past in which the current sexual-moral decline did not exist. As this chapter shows, the late 1960s are isolated as a key date for contributing to the apparent current decline and a past is evoked in which a more traditional gender order and hierarchy existed (see also Chapter 6). In this fantasy of the past, masculinity is seen as strong and dominant. Fascism idealises the body, hard work, male supremacy and bodily fitness and health. Right-wing and fascist ideologies, such as those of the alt-right, are dualist and separate genders to the realm of production (men) and to the realm of reproduction (women). All of those characteristics form building blocks of the identity of the alt-right which are presented online through YouTube videos, Twitter and Facebook posts, Reddit discussions, websites and fora. They also reflect wider politics and popular culture such as films and television programmes that are discussed online (see Introduction and my discussion of *The Matrix* and *Fight Club* for example). Those building blocks are taken up by other men of the manosphere and interwoven with their own communities (for example of incels or MGTOW).

'Cultural Marxism'

A key target for the alt-right, far right and reactionary thinkers is what they refer to as 'cultural Marxism'. A term that is meant to signify the alleged dominance of radical leftist (Marxist) thought and practices, brought about by academics, in Western societies post-1968 (Mirrlees 2018). Tanner Mirrlees has written that it is a

> a symbol for every liberal or left-leaning group the right defined itself against, and an epithet for progressive identities, values, ideas, and practices that reactionaries believe have made America worse than before. (Mirrlees 2018, 49)

As in debates about the decline of sexual morality, the 1960s are seen by right-wing and reactionary groups as being responsible for the emergence of a project by so-called 'cultural Marxists' to destroy America and Western societies in general and undermine everything that white, heterosexuals have achieved. The notion of 'cultural Marxism' is a conspiracy theory that is used to spread hatred and abuse against everyone designated an enemy by fascists.

It is a piece in the puzzle of the alt-right identity. '[F]or the alt-right, social unrest connects with civilizational decline connects with multiculturalism connects with "cultural Marxism" connects with disrupted norms, forming a comparatively unified "decline" or "decadence"' (Gray 2018, 144). 'Cultural

Marxism' is specifically used to mainstream and 'advance a white, patriarchal, and Christian conservative vision of America and foment a racist, sexist, classist, xenophobic, and violent backlash against the gains made by the individuals and groups it constructs as cultural Marxist threats' (Mirrlees 2018, 50). Reactionary, fascist and alt-right thinkers alike also refer to specific theorists and academics who are responsible for ushering in 'cultural Marxism' as a form of thinking and practice: The Italian Marxist thinker and activist Antonio Gramsci, Jewish Marxist intellectuals such as members of the Frankfurt School (Adorno, Horkheimer, Marcuse, Fromm), the psychoanalyst and Marxist Wilhelm Reich and other thinkers (Mirrlees 2018).

For example, a hatred of 'cultural Marxists' and its apparent theorists is expressed by YouTuber A – and most famously of all by the Canadian psychology Professor Jordan Peterson in his many YouTube videos (Crociani-Windland & Yates 2020). For YouTuber A, it is Michel Foucault, the 'official philosopher of the United States of America', apparently crowned by 'the oligarchs' who is responsible for institutionalising the moral decay of the spirit of the sexual revolution in American academia and beyond, he thinks. In fact, while in Berkeley in the 1980s, Foucault, it is alleged, had

> this epiphany, he suddenly has this, he calls it his pact with the devil, the devil being the state that he's trying to overthrow and what the, the pact with the devil is basically the pact that he imposed on the left or the left imposed on its dependence on him, he, he imposed on the left or the left imposed on itself and it's basically 'if you give us unlimited sexual liberation we won't criticize your economic system'. (Vendée Radio 2018, 16.38–17.07)

This quote reveals the paranoia and simplistic thinking of the alt-right. Foucault was never in a position to impose anything on the left. In fact, many Marxists were (and are) critical of him for being not critical enough of capitalism and for ignoring/rejecting Marxist categories of class. While Foucault was undoubtedly one of the most important Western intellectuals of his time (and his influence remains extensive), YouTuber A makes it sound like his epiphany resulted in an active stabilisation of the capitalist system by refraining from critique in exchange for unlimited sexual liberation. In this narrative, Foucault becomes a kind of state agent who pacified and dullified the population. Such an ideology is symptomatic of the notion of 'cultural Marxism' as it depicts threats to America and the West. Foucault becomes a powerful figure who allegedly conspired with the state in an effort to be granted sexual liberation in return for ceasing to critique capitalism. None of it is true. Foucault, in fact, can be seen as a representative of a still marginalised group (gay men) because of sexual conservatism. Homosexuality goes against conservative Christian values (that the alt-right is based on). The kind of worldview of the alt-right, then, is specifically and inherently connected to themes and questions of sexuality. It is sexist and misogynist as well as fascist and racist. This kind of triangular ideology (misogynist, racist/fascist, heteronormative) of the alt-right (Gray 2018; Mirrlees 2018) is an important backdrop to keep in mind when reading this book and it is for that reason that I have discussed it here at some length and continue to do so throughout this chapter. It is specifically tied to history and to the sexual revolution in particular.

In the above discussion about Foucault, then, the sexual revolution becomes a form of hedonistic oppression for the alt-right, of repressive tolerance, whereby the state is behind it all in order to control the population. While we may laugh about such ideas and dismiss them, the fact that they are being circulated online shows how history is distorted to fit a particular narrative of critique. In this case, the scapegoat is the sexual revolution. It is mobilised so that others can be convinced of the apparent bad state humans are currently in. Order needs to be restored. The sexual revolution and how it is constructed figures as a defense mechanism for those men to undo and defend themselves against the positive consequences it brought about – above all against feminism and female empowerment. Those are threatening to the men's egos: female sexual empowerment, changing practices and modes of sexuality, the acceptance of non-hetero sexualities and a general popularity and visibility of the liberal left, progressive thinking which became represented in popular culture and the media from the late 1960s onwards. I unpack this idea more in the next sections of this chapter.

Porn addiction, STDs, gay marriage – all caused by the sexual revolution

As we have seen, 1968 has become a signifier that is used to signify all the 'other' and threatening dimensions that the men of the alt-right wish to defend against. YouTuber B says:

> At this point, and we could go down the list of what the sexual revolution brought to us, STD is, that's just one part of the problem.... Well, STDs, when we talk about STDs, let's start with AIDS, okay the AIDS epidemic swept America right on the heels of the sexual revolution and that is not coincidental, you know, you had the hippies with their free love and everything and then boom we have AIDS, okay and then now we have epidemics of gonorrhoea, syphilis, chlamydia across the nation. (The Daily Wire 2018, 0.33–1.45)

Drawing a direct link between hippies, free love and AIDS is too simplistic and factually wrong (Engel 2006). Gonorrhoea, syphilis and chlamydia have no relation to either AIDS or the late 1960s. In the above narrative, AIDS becomes the dark symbol of something ultra-conservative and reactionary commentators want to do away with: sexual disinhibition, polygamous relationships and sex before, or outside of marriage. This form of disinhibited sexuality threatens the very foundations of those male commentators on YouTube. They need to consciously defend themselves against the contagiousness of homosexuality, STDs, becoming gay, watching porn:

> We have the obviously the problem of porn addiction, fatherless homes on and on and on, it even ruined our university system which has turned into this embarrassing orgy of drunkenness and debauchery, which it was never meant to be but that's what it's become now and why.... This is what sexual revolution was all about, taking sex, removing it from marriage and then what happens is number one, you lose the deeper joy that can be found in sex, you've, you've settled for mere pleasure which was already a part of the joy. (The Daily Wire 2018, 6.55–8.13)

The sexual revolution is allegedly responsible for a damaging and unhealthy form of sexuality which leads to divorce, pornography addiction and a kind of unleashed form of sexuality in universities. Such claims are undoubtedly exaggerated and were not (entirely) caused by the sexual revolution. Is there perhaps some truth in the above claims? While I have no interest in defending the institution of marriage, unlike the above YouTuber, many young people who lived through the 1960s have also critically reflected on the incessant need to be sexually liberal and disinhibited (see Chapter 2). This led to problems on multiple fronts. Today it is precisely the promise and fantasy of the sexual revolution that sex has become another good to be endlessly consumed and freely available that may lead to a neurotic sense of sexuality which struggles between infinite, detached but pleasurable sex which is nonetheless situated in a matrix of relationships and desires to belong and be part of lasting relations. Sex becomes a consumer good in the current age, facilitated by digital technology. I think it is important to neither celebrate the sexual revolution as a form of enlightenment, nor to completely dismiss it as alt-right commentators do. The causal link that is drawn between today and the sexual revolution is simplistic and reductionist, but there might be some relationship between the two. The notion of a kind of sexual freedom is problematised in different ways both by media texts and the alt-right YouTubers. While shows like *Sex and the City* (1998–2004, Star), *Girls* (2012–2017, Dunham & Aptow), *Sex Education* (2019, Nunn) or *Casual* (2015–2018, Lehmann) portray it as sexual empowerment which nonetheless has repercussions on people's psyches, the YouTubers portray it as a kind of hell on earth that has destabilised humanity and uncoupled humans from meaningful relationships. For men of the manosphere, such notions are more symptomatic of their *own* defenses and anxieties. They feel threatened. They may be swept away by women or other men into debauchery. They may have certain anxieties about their own sexualities. This is particularly evident in the rages against homosexuality and gay marriage. In the conversation with YouTuber A, the host remarks:

> Vendée Radio: If you look at in this country had, can you believe it, a conservative Prime Minister David Cameron who foisted gay marriage on us and all these so-called conservatives made this argument, that, this kind of dog whistle argument that, look homosexuals they're, they're pretty um, you know, socially disruptive but we can kind of domesticate them by bringing them into this institution of marriage and they end in us, in effect, sort of heterosexualised the homosexuals but in fact the, the reverse has happened, the heterosexuals have become homosexualised....
>
> A: think, I think you're right, I think well this was the intention from the beginning of one of the homosexuals, there was a book that came out in the 80s, something like how the homosexual movement might change the United States of America and it said basically there that everyone will become a homosexual. (Vendée Radio 2018, 38.51–40.09)

In the above, we can see a paranoid fantasy that 'homosexuals' are out there to control the population to convert or turn 'us' (i.e. white, cis men) all into 'homosexuals', or at least make 'us' adopt 'homosexual' characteristics in relationships. While the argument that gay men were being socially disruptive and needed to be pacified by granting them gay marriage was probably never made by any politician, it may be the host's anxiety, of possibly being seduced by a man. It may be that he unconsciously desires to be 'turned' gay and has to defend himself against such fantasies even more, or to defend against the inherent gay elements within him. He does so by first 'domesticating' the alleged wild and contagious affectivity of homosexuality by naming others who have done so. Those who have allegedly done so are the politicians who have allowed men to get married. He then voices his fears of becoming gay as a heterosexual. Such fantasies of becoming gay threaten the very fundamentals of some of today's men's egos.

I argue that there is an uncanny resemblance here to Theweleit's analysis of the soldier males. The solider males constantly felt threatened by living and animated subjects – women in particular – and their egos were fragmented and in danger of shattering as a result. They must act, they must kill, they must do *something* to stop themselves from falling apart. This is achieved through the fascist mass and the killing of others, be it symbolically through words or in reality. The same mechanisms apply to many men today. They must flood the internet, YouTube, Reddit, social media, etc. with endless content against that which threatens them, that which is different and lively: gays and queers, women, feminists, other kinds of men, immigrants, etc. In fact, sex as such needs to be eliminated, it needs to be made sterile and killed off. Sexual intercourse is precisely an affective experience where the body takes over and takes control and acquires its own language, consciousness and rationality are secondary. It is precisely the unpredictability and embodied sexual desire that such narratives seek to massacre through words. It was precisely the sexual revolution of the late 1960s that opened up and gave many a new language to experience such modes of sexual experience (this was not only facilitated by the pill or forms of sex education). A different sexual consciousness emerged. This legacy of the sexual revolution needs to be devivified, deanimated and done away with by those men on YouTube and beyond. Otherwise the sexual revolution, and the things it stands for, get too close to them. This specifically includes gay and queer sexuality, but also a different kind of sexuality, sexuality outside of marriage, as well as within marriage itself. The men defend against their own anxieties and threats.

The sexual revolution is transformed into a fantasy. This fantasy also figures as a way of channelling a particular form of hatred and aggression against Jews and gay men.

Anti-semitism and homophobia

YouTuber A also discusses deeply anti-Semitic narratives, which I have not reproduced here.

Those are also related to expressions of homophobia. The YouTuber mobilises the anti-Semitic suture of 'Jew/money' (Frosh 2011, 97) and associates being Jewish with being dirty, profiteering (Žižek 1994, 48), and sexually perverted. This implicit coupling of Jews and (homo)sexuality is equally rooted in a long tradition of anti-Semitic and fascist discourses (see Chapter 1). It was specifically used in Nazi Germany (Theweleit 1989). Frosh summarises that there is 'the core racist fantasy…of having something stolen. The others enjoy themselves too much; this is envied – there is so much freedom in it – and the question arises, why do they have so much pleasure, and we so little?' (Frosh 2016, 33). This sentiment applies to another group which has been traditionally marginalised and oppressed with specific pertinence today: (feminist) women. Slavoj Žižek has famously made the (very Lacanian) argument that such a theft of enjoyment constitutes an act of stealing something which was never possessed in the first place – a traumatic illusion that is overcome through blaming the other (Žižek 1994, see also Miller 1994). Theweleit makes a slightly different argument in his discussion of the Jew as a bringer of contagious lust which corrupts and infects the 'pure' German population. We can nonetheless summarise those accounts of anti-Semitism (Žižek, Frosh, Theweleit) with the following: 'the anti-Semite lives in terror of the persecutory universe she or he has created, but the benefit is that at least this universe makes sense, and nominates one single, identifiable source of danger – the Jew' (Frosh 2016, 35). The notion of a persecutory universe that needs to be both created and maintained through actions and speech fits well with Theweleit's work (which Frosh refers to) where everything that is 'soft and welcoming' (ibid) needs to be excluded, eliminated or denounced (see my further discussion of this in Chapters 4 and 5). This worldview, as Adorno and his co-authors remarked in the *Authoritarian Personality* (1950), is distinctly structured by paranoia. Fascism is built on paranoia. Such paranoia is also evident within the manosphere. Paranoia is present and escalated in the following exchange between the host and YouTuber A when they discuss the Weimar Republic and its alleged consequences:

> Vendée Radio: And you look at Berlin now just going back to that and, and it's positioning is as this decadent capital, it's just like history repeating itself with Weimar Germany and, and the, the decadence of Berlin then and during the 1930s, in the 20s and 30s you had was it the Human Sex Institute? All these kind of weird, degenerate institutions which were involved with social engineering can you talk a little bit about that?
>
> A: That was Magnus Hirschfeld. He was like the classic Jew of the Weimar period he created this Institut für Sexualwissenschaft, the Institute for Sexual Research, and he attracted homosexuals from all over Europe.... Wait a minute, this is, this isn't science! This is all just, it's, it's a homosexual bordello! (Vendée Radio 2018, 31.00–33.21)

With the above dialogue, we have entered deep, anti-Semitic, fascist territory where Jews are the allegedly lustful, decadent, hedonistic figures of society whose mission it is to destroy the existing social order. The 'decadent' Jews who founded 'degenerate' institutions (another Nazi term) who are out there to manipulate the population – those are fascist narratives.

Terms such as 'degeneracy' and 'decadence' have made a comeback in alt-right circles today. Kelly (2017) writes that degeneracy was originally 'a nineteenth-century eugenicist term to demarcate a lack of supposed white racial purity, degeneracy as a tool of social and cultural critique gained traction under the Nazi regime in Germany to deride art and media perceived as either immoral or unpatriotic' (Kelly 2017, 71–72). In its current usage, the term often refers to a mythic past in which the current allegedly disruptive elements which are responsible for the apparent moral decline did not exist. A myth that in itself never existed. What is noteworthy is the direct and prolonged linkage of Jews and homosexuality in the above narratives. A psychoanalytic perspective suggests that those utterances are defense mechanisms to ward off the unconscious fear of becoming gay, or other 'foreign' elements within the two men that – to them – may be considered 'gay' or 'degenerate'. The inner 'homosexual bordello' needs to be eliminated.

In his writing on fascism in America, Theodor W. Adorno (1970) analysed the speeches of American fascists. He argues that the rhetoric of those 'hate mongers' (Adorno 1970, 119) is so limited that the same tropes and stylistic devices are used over and over again. One speech is enough to know them all. For that reason, I now move on to a different video.

Neoliberalism and the market of sexuality

While I have mainly focussed on two YouTube videos so far, both of which are part of the scene of far-right personalities on the platform, I want to introduce a third video at this point. It is made by the YouTuber The Distributist and named *The Lies of the Sexual Revolution*. It is 52 minutes and 55 seconds long (the video with YouTuber A is 1 hour and 11 minutes, the video with YouTuber B is 24 minutes long). I will be reproducing a number of quotes in detail. The channel is described on the YouTube profile as a 'channel to explore the problems of modernity, the issues of our late political and economic order, and the need for spirituality and truth'. It is rooted in Christianity and ultra-conservatism, but – at least on the surface – is not anti-Semitic or fascist as such and does not belong to the alt-right. The YouTuber has also held debates with left and liberal individuals, most notably the famous YouTuber ContraPoints, and stresses that he is open to debate with others. This makes him a special case as his discussions are certainly far more nuanced than those of the other YouTubers. Nonetheless, he is certainly watched by users who are sympathetic to, or openly members of the alt-right (based on the video comments). He reveals an ultra-conservative and, in my view, deeply problematic understanding of women, feminism and the sexual revolution. Early on in the video, he says that 'we now live in a world where that patriarchal ghost of sexual norms and restraint is totally absent' (2016, 9.21–9.23). His video is a reflection on the sexual revolution and primary its legacy by someone who lives in the supposed age of 'postfeminism' today.

Similarly to the other YouTubers already discussed, the YouTuber laments a hedonistic culture devoid of a moral compass that was brought about by the sexual revolution. We live in a sexual culture of 'almost nothing' which is characterised by gender fluidity and 'fake men' dressing as 'fake women', according to him.

It is particularly noteworthy how he consistently mobilises and evokes the market and neoliberalism in connection to the sexual revolution, femininity and masculinity. In this context, he discusses Dan Savage, a gay rights advocator and commentator, and the kind of sexuality Savage apparently stands for:

In many ways Dan Savage's vision of a purely consent driven, a purely quality driven sexual culture is quite compelling.... It also sells well because this corporate version of sexuality is also a bonanza for people who are trying to sell sex. So we're left asking ourselves, is this it? Have we solved the problem of the sexual revolution? Is there a golden age of coherency once we've accomplished, de-stigmatized in the last few barriers to free consent? Legalized prostitution, legalized polygamy, legalized pretty much anything.... I admit that unlike a lot of elements of feminism there is a hint of truth to this, in fact the free market is a real thing and it applies to value exchanges and sex is a value exchange but that's not really the whole statement of it, the free market is a massively simplistic model. (The Distributist 2016, 18.14–19.36)

This specific thematisation of the market and of sexuality as a commodity is interesting here. There is, to the YouTuber's admission, some common ground between his perspective and feminism's. The 'corporate version of sexuality' that is discussed previously also suits well with how sexuality and dating are portrayed in 'postfeminist' media texts such as *Girls*, *Casual* (and other television series) occurring in an equal(ised) society; where sex, as facilitated through apps and tech, has seemingly become the equaliser for women. It is their sexual agency that marks a pillar of their (alleged) equality in all spheres of life. It is simultaneously enabled and troubled by the sexual revolution.

Such a notion relates to the idea of 'intimate inequality' which is discussed in Rachel O'Neill's (2018) detailed ethnographic study of the Pick Up community (PUA). Many of the men she interviewed were of the opinion that women and feminism had led to 'intimate inequality' (O'Neill 2018, 159) and specific efforts needed to be undertaken for things to become equal again, such as learning the 'craft' of the Pick Up artist. For instance, O'Neill's interviewees complained that women had virtually achieved equality, yet they still expected men to approach them, pay for drinks on a date, and so on (ibid, 160). In the PUA community, getting women to have sex with men, through manipulative moves, is described as patterned, as (so-called) 'tried and tested' procedures that work on women. This ideology 'is a radical emptying out of the intersubjective' (2018, 115) dimensions of meaningful intimacy and sexuality. For the PUA ideologues, sex is seen as (and becomes) a commodity in the free market. It is just about mastering the game of supply and demand in order to manipulate women. Sex is something that is offered and taken, rather than seen as an intersubjective, relational experience, as O'Neill writes. While the previous quote can also be read as being critical of PUA and other sexist ideologies, the YouTuber nonetheless refers to notions of unequal access to the *free market* of sex. In fact, for him, 'sex is a value exchange':

Men and women have different market values which peak and dip at different points in their lives, moreover both genders have very, very destructive instincts. Women have a hypergamous instinct and men have a polygamous instinct, both of which worked at the detriment of developing long-term lasting relationships. When the free market unconstrained is introduced into a system like this, it will only result in disaster. (The Distributist 2016, 21.58–22.14)

Such a statement resonates with those of the men in Rachel O'Neill's study (2018) who lamented that the intimate inequality of dating and sexuality manifested itself in media advice columns aimed solely at women on how to date, or the beauty industry which largely caters for women, and above all, feminism as a practice that was somehow aimed against men. In short, 'women are in a *position* to deny men the freedoms they putatively enjoy' (2018, 168–169, italics in original), as the men think. The Distributist seems keen to criticise the role of sexuality within neoliberal capitalism and positions himself against disinhibited market forces that have devoured sexuality in its pure form and turned into something at the heart of the free market which suggests equality and equal access but in reality masks inequality and different sexual capital.

Yet, the free market is at the heart of gender and sexual relationships for him. Men and women come to the free market of sex with different market values. It is unclear what the YouTuber understands by 'market values', but the expression that they 'peak and dip at different points' in men's and women's life suggests a biological framing of bodies, perhaps in relation to attractiveness, fertility, sexual potency or genetics (Hakim 2010). This relates to another aspect apart from the one of the free market.

Evolutionary psychology and the rationalisation of entitlement

An important discourse that the alt-right and also men of the manosphere employ appropriates theories and ideas from evolutionary psychology. It uses genetic determinism, for example, to explain (and justify) differences in male and female behaviours. One of the most well-known proponents of such theories is the Canadian psychology Professor Jordan Peterson (Crociani-Windland & Yates 2020). Debbie Ging notes that 'the manosphere's engagement with this field is limited to the superficial interpretation and recycling of theories to support a recurring catalogue of claims: that women are irrational, hypergamous, hardwired to pair with alpha males, and need to be dominated' (Ging 2017, 12). This discourse extends to recurring discussions about alpha and beta masculinity (see Chapter 2). It is particularly dangerous because it gives the manosphere a hue of factuality and objectivity. This is amplified by men who recurrently cite from or link to scientific papers and journal articles in efforts to prove or back up their claims. I return to this point in the book's Conclusion.

Such discourses contribute to, what Deborah Cameron (2015) has called the 'meta-narrative of evolutionary psychology', something which extends beyond those who would specifically deal with or research evolutionary psychology (academics). It is taken up in popular culture and popular science discourses, as well as the manosphere (amongst other places). Such a use of evolutionary psychology, Cameron argues, can be used as a weapon against the social changes men see themselves confronted with as a result of feminism (and also the wider economic changes of neoliberalism, I would add). Evolutionary psychology and how it is appropriated 'says that whatever has changed, and however similar men and women might appear, at a deeper level the differences are still there, and always will be there. Whatever inequalities we see now between men are not the result of injustice, but simply the residue of natural difference' (Cameron 2015, 357). To that end, evolutionary psychology is used to undermine feminist theory and scholarship (Cameron 2015; O'Neill 2015; Crociani-Windland & Yates 2020). Gender differences are constructed as biological facts in order to prop up patriarchy as a structural system that is based on misogyny and sexism (Manne 2018).

Given such a meta-narrative of evolutionary psychology, women and men are constructed as essentially incompatible in the above sequence from The Distributist's video, because they are driven by destructive instincts that make them selfish. Men want to be with as many women as possible, at the same time, while women are 'hypergamous' – a key term that is used again and again in the incel and other male communities online. Hypergamy refers to the alleged practice of women of 'marrying up'. Women are genetically hardwired to do so, according to the manosphere (Ging 2017). Women want to marry someone who is of higher social status than themselves and if the opportunity presents itself, they are willing to divorce their current partner if a 'better' spouse is available. It is claimed that such practices are in women's nature, while this position is in reality deterministic, oppressive and positivistic. It is also simply untrue most of the time.

According to The Distributist and men who think alike, such biologically determined instincts of women are only amplified and heightened by the apparently free market of disinhibited sex. As we have seen, he couples biologic determinism with a discussion of neoliberalism in the above quotes. The free market disadvantages everyone because capital is only interested in accumulating more capital rather than facilitating fulfilling or equal relationships. In addition, neoliberal capitalism places an emphasis on the individual, entrepreneurial subject who makes their own luck, including and perhaps *especially* in sexual terms. 'Indeed, evolutionary narratives have much in common with neoliberal rationalities, as both promote a logic of individualism centred on profit maximisation – whether this is defined in terms of finance or progeny' (O'Neill 2018, 148), Rachel O'Neill writes about the PUA community and their use of evolutionary psychology when discussing sexual attraction and sexuality as such. Everything has become self-centred competition in neoliberalism, including sex. Such sentiments were articulated by the men O'Neill interviewed and they are similarly articulated by the men of the manosphere. 'Crucially, then, it is through their convergence with neoliberal rationalities that evolutionary imperatives come to be experienced by heterosexual men as deeply felt and embodied truths' (ibid, 150). The evolutionary aspects of sexuality are intensely coupled with aspects of individual status and economic prosperity for those men in neoliberalism. They feel, as I further discuss in the next chapter, that if they have *failed* in terms of their own looks, career progression, wealth accumulation and overall status, they have *eo ipso* failed sexually and lack a kind of sexual status and confidence.

The phallus is useful as an analytical metaphor here, because it illustrates that, for psychoanalysis, symbolic and actual power can take forms that merge the sexual with the economic. The phallus means male sexual power, but within the ethos of neoliberalism individual power is first and foremost defined in terms of economic success and prosperity. Such embodied truths, as O'Neill calls them, lead to different consequences depending on the communities those men feel part of (for instance incels, MGTOW, NoFap), as I show in the coming chapters. We can see how neoliberalism encourages, in fact *demands*, such fantasies which are inherently phallic, because they are about individual, penetrating, one-sided fantasies of (economic and sexual) power and pleasure for both men and women. As Rosalind Gill argues, the ideology of postfeminism precisely works along similar lines when it is suggested that women can now enjoy their own phallic form of sexuality, economic status and freedom just as men can (Gill 2007). At the same time, women's 'erotic capital' (Hakim 2010) is highly policed and subject to misogynist and heteronormative constraints in relation to what they should and should not do with their bodies. Lacanian theorists have related such fantasies of postfeminism to the general (capitalist) injunction to enjoy. This is amplified in neoliberalism where pleasure, and sexuality in particular, have been turned into the injunction to enjoy (Žižek 1997; McGowan 2004). This demand to enjoy, as I have shown, is a result of the sexual revolution of the late 1960s and today's hook-up and dating apps as well as mediated sexuality are 'the neoliberal offspring of the sexual revolution' (Bandinelli & Bandinelli 2021). Many scholars have argued that dating apps in particular reproduce a neoliberal market logic by which individuals brand themselves and have something to offer. They can expect something in return, after having picked the best match (Heino, Ellison & Gibbs 2010). This also includes cultivating the skills to handle rejections (De Wiele & Campbell 2019).[5]

Neoliberalism thus constructs a particular rational, strategic sexual subject who has been given all the tools to facilitate their own sexual enjoyment and success. Of course, in reality, as I have discussed in the previous chapter, such an ideology works very differently and women and men are far from equal both in terms of economic and sexual power – but not any kind of market value or biological characteristics, as the manosphere would have it – as well as constraints and oppressions. It seems precisely to be men who buy into such a phallic fantasy which is then bitterly disappointed, and they result to blame women for it rather than the ideology of neoliberalism. Such disappointments articulate themselves in toxic fantasies which are shared online and act as a form of affective discharge for those men, as I go on to discuss in the coming chapters.

While men and women may want to express themselves sexually within market-based capitalism, it is the market that serves as a platform for such expressions, according to The Distributist. Such an analysis may have some truth to it. However, the constructions of men and women by The Distributist are very biologistic and essentialising. According to him, the sexual revolution has led to disinhibited sexuality and disinhibited societies that lack forms of control and restraint. The result is apparently terrifying:

> As men became less faithful, women became less trusting of men and openly hostile to men in a lot of very fundamental ways and we started to develop the antagonistic relationship that we see in modern sexual culture where both genders are trying to get the most for themselves at each stage of the process as men let their polygamous natures become more apparent, women let their hypergamous natures become less restricted and as such divorces skyrocketed and trust between all elements of the family disintegrated, this is not something that any one gender did to the other ones, both genders were responding to the incentives that were apparent to them when non-cooperation in marriage became an option to societally acceptable and thus the road to hell was paved by individual rational decisions all the way down. (The Distributist 2016, 44.56–45.45)

Sexuality is described here as a selfish, instinct-driven endeavour which ultimately ruins the relations between individuals. While from the outset, such an analysis might be somewhat in line with psychoanalytic (and particularly Lacanian) understandings of sexuality, the wider discussions of disinhibited men and women, rising divorce rates, eroding trust, and so on, suggest a desire for a kind of White ethnostate type of authoritarian capitalism rooted in Christian values.

In all of the quotes presented in this chapter, a sexual conservatism is laid bare that desires to re-establish a sexual order of the past with clear gender norms, monogamy, lasting marriages, no homosexuality, etc. Such views are not only compatible with fascist views on gender, they show a desire in those individuals for a new authoritarian society, which tightly controlled by a set of principles they have devised. Incels similarly articulate specific fantasies of the future (what they term 'inceldom', see Chapter 4) and MGTOWs dream of a world without women (see Chapter 5). As I go on to show, such fantasies are never as clear cut and coherent as they appear at first glance.

Conclusion

In this chapter, I have continued to discuss the sexual revolution as it occurred in the Western world in the late 1960s and its consequences. Taking the sexual revolution as a starting point is not only important, because of its clear significance for sexualities today, but also because of the 1960s idea-historical relationship to Theweleit's *Male Fantasies* books that I presented in Chapter 1. They were very much a product of the sexual revolution in themselves.

As I read and wrote about the sexual revolution and its consequences in Chapter 2, I coincidentally came across the YouTube videos that I have discussed in this chapter. I was struck by how the sexual revolution figures as an *idée fixe* for those men who vlog about it. They use the term as a floating signifier that they bend and appropriate so that it can signify all sorts of things. The sexual revolution, for those men, becomes the root of all evil. Its feminist dimensions in particular have displaced and undermined men. Sexuality is described as complete disinhibition which occurs at the expense of cis men. It is used to defend against the men's own inhibitions, insecurities and anxieties that may very well have been triggered as a result of female empowerment when it comes to sexuality today. It is also used to defend against their own desires for sexual disinhibition, for example their own feelings of homosexuality, and what we could term the generally *queer* character of desire in its polymorphous perversity. I return to this notion in Chapter 7. With Reich, we can argue that their psychic structures lag behind a world that has evolved. They find themselves unable to adjust to social change and respond with hatred.

The narratives that I have analysed in this chapter are not as heavily misogynistic than others in this book and speak less of women or female sexuality specifically. They can be seen as being about heterosexuality *per se* and how it was apparently shaped by the sexual revolution. There are thus differences between the YouTube videos and the material that I discuss in the coming chapters. The YouTube videos of this chapter are not about male identity, individual male experiences or thoughts, but about an abstract discussion of the sexual revolution and sexuality today that is shaped by neoliberalism, the alt-right and other aspects. A particular worldview is articulated which is nonetheless anti-feminist, misogynist and at times deeply fascist. Such a worldview shapes, is reflected in and shared by the communities and men that I discuss in the next three chapters: Incels, MGTOWs and mass shooters such as Anders Breivik or Elliot Rodger.

In the next chapter, I discuss the incel community and its fantasies.

Notes

1 I have opted to anonymise the two alt-right YouTubers of this chapter in order not to provide a platform for their views. The three YouTube videos I discuss in this chapter were amongst the top search results for 'sexual revolution' and were selected for that reason.
2 The Rote Armee Fraktion (RAF) was a left-wing terror group which was active in West Germany from 1970–1977 (as the so-called 'first generation'). Subsequent further generations followed until the RAF was officially dissolved in 1998. The RAF was responsible for several shootings, bank robberies and bombings (Aust 2008).
3 'Pizzagate' refers to a debunked conspiracy theory which states that politicians of the Democratic Party in the United States are part of a sex trafficking and child sex ring. It was spread during the presidential election campaign in 2016. One of the alleged establishments involved was a pizzeria in Washington, D.C. 'QAnon' refers to a set of false conspiracy theories and a community which actively spreads them online. Its far-right supporters (claim to) believe that a global sex trafficking ring is secretly ruling the world and US president Trump was elected to stop it. An apocalyptic-like event will bring an end to the ring's reign. QAnon originated on 4chan (Tuters, Jokubauskaitė & Bach 2018; Hellinger 2019).
4 The specific misogynist, anti-LGBTQI+, anti-feminist, anti-immigrant and anti-left stance of the alt-right is of course more widely shared by reactionary groups in the US and beyond such as specific groups in the Catholic church, Republican politicians, and other ultra-conservative groups and individuals (Hawley 2017).
5 Coincidentally, incels pick up on precisely this logic and ideology of the dating app and its supposed ability to facilitate matches and dating. There are many posts in which they mock Tinder users, and also often detail experiences of 'catfishing' whereby incels create fake profiles of Chads in order to troll women. We could read such instances as a critical unmasking of neoliberal ideology that is transported through Tinder; Tinder does not always work and this may be one of its most alluring features for all of its users (Bandinelli & Bandinelli 2021). However, we need to be mindful of the hatred and toxicity with which this unmasking is done by incels. They do not make the next step and think about wider relations within capitalism, but blame females who use Tinder, for not going on dates with them.

Chapter 4

Incels and fantasies of destroying/desiring the other

The previous chapter presented analyses of the backlash against the sexual revolution on YouTube. The narratives I analysed were of a general nature and discussed (defences against) socio-historical changes, the relationship between men and women and non-heteronormative sexualities. This chapter presents more particular and specific fantasies in relation to femininity and masculinity. It is based on data analysis from incel[1] communities on Reddit. Many misogynistic online communities have emerged in recent years alongside a palpable rise in un/associated offline misogyny. I focus on the incel community as it constitutes a relatively recent part of the manosphere (Ging 2017). It consists of men who refer to themselves as 'involuntary celibate', (or incel in lowercase), because they have not engaged in romantic or sexual encounters for some time (or never in many cases). Some violent incidents have been linked to incels, such as the Toronto van attack in April 2018 where a man killed 10 and injured 16 people as well as the shooting in a yoga studio in the United States in 2018, where two people were killed. The mass shooting by Elliot Rodger in 2014, who published a lengthy manifesto, is also often referred to in the community and some incels glorify such acts of violence (see Chapter 6).

The term 'incel' was originally coined by a woman in 1993 but it has since been appropriated as a self-descriptor used only by men. In recent years, and partly inspired by media coverage in the wake of shootings by incels, the community has grown and primarily used Reddit to communicate (Bratich & Banet-Weiser 2019). The original r/incels subreddit and many of the communities that followed were shut down in 2017, because of the sheer amount of discussions of rape and violence. When I started researching incel posts in late 2018, a second phase of incel content had come into existence. In that sense, the content that I examined is less toxic than posts which could be found on r/incels, but in no way less problematic or hateful. The majority of posts that I have analysed came from the r/Braincels subreddit which was itself banned in 2019.[2]

Incels believe in a kind of sexual class system or hierarchy. At the top, are the white 'Chads', alpha males who are the most attractive.[3] According to

DOI: 10.4324/9781003031581-4

the community, most women are only interested in Chads. The most attractive women are referred to as 'Stacys'. Stacys, for incels, resemble hegemonic images of beauty that are often portrayed by the media, for example tall, blonde women who look like supermodels. Incels believe that 20% of the population consists of Chads and that 80% of women only have eyes for Chads. The bottom 20% of women are willing to have sex and form relationships with the majority of men, whom incels refer to as 'normies', 'betas' or 'cucks'. At the very bottom of the hierarchy are incels who are destined to be forever alone (Ging 2017). Such a biologistic narrative is similar to some of the reactionary and right-wing YouTube content that I discussed in the previous chapter. Incels in particular make often references to biology and the evolutionary nature of what it means to be male and female. They believe that we live in an age of social Darwinism where women get to pick men based on their looks and income in order to produce the (genetically) fittest children. For incels there are no women left, no 'looksmatch' (in their terminology), who look similar to them. In fact, many are of the opinion that women should somehow be forced by law to be with them if they look similar. Incels rank themselves and others incessantly. A 3/10 woman should be with a 3/10 incel and not with a 10/10 Chad, for example.

In this chapter, I provide extensive quotations from incels in order to analyse what kind of discourses on femininity, their own identity and the male body are presented by them. This helps to further answer the underlying research question of this book on how misogyny is articulated in the selected communities and what fantasies of sexuality, bodies and fascism are associated with it. Incels watch and engage with the sort of alt-right YouTube videos that I discussed in the previous chapter. Their worldview is shaped by 4chan, YouTube, Jordan Peterson, Reddit, alt-right memes, porn, Instagram, Twitter and other social media. They also themselves create memes and other visual material.

The first half of this chapter outlines the defensive actions, and defence mechanisms,[4] that are deployed by incels in order not to engage in any real change and critical introspection. Those defence mechanisms are the use of humour and irony, as well as discourses of self-pity and self-victimisation in relation to mental health and other alleged shortcomings. All are infused with strong misogyny and toxic language. In the second half of the chapter, I detail the symbolic destruction of women by incels when they discuss ways to get 'revenge' for alleged rejections or ignorance. I then specifically focus on a desire for male fascist bodies that they wish to acquire. I relate this desire to how race and ethnicity is discussed by incels. I also look at posts that discuss genetics and male bodies to illustrate this point. The latter half of the chapter's material is less about defence than causing maximum offence and hurt for outsiders. I draw parallels between Theweleit's theorisation of soldier males and the proto-fascist nature of incels when I analyse some data that use anti-Semitic imagery and vocabulary to designate women (and some men) as the ones who have apparently all the fun, while incels get nothing. Incels also articulate distinctly racist fantasies which situate the white body as superior.

In keeping with the notion of *dis/inhibition*, this chapter traces incel discourses from inhibition in the first half (acts of defence, self-pity and a general hopelessness)[5] towards disinhibition and the affirmation of and desire for a kind of hegemonic masculinity (within the alt-right) that is fascist in the second half of the chapter. Incels are thus not only characterised by apathy and the total rejection of change, or even of desire, as recent psychoanalytic work on incels has suggested (Krüger 2021), but by complex and contradictory psychodynamics which will also be further examined in Chapter 5. This movement from inhibition to disinhibition is also marked by a shift for incels from a sense of weakness and powerlessness to a sense of symbolic power, male omnipotence and destructiveness. I do not mean to suggest that this change from inhibition to disinhibition is a linear movement, or on some kind of timeline, but it is more a way for me to organise the various data and their contradictions. As I argued in Chapter 1, dis/inhibition suggests a messy intertwinement and merging of both inhibition and disinhibition. Those fantasies and states that I discuss in this chapter are present all at the same time.

Online misogyny and the manosphere

While many feminist researchers have analysed misogyny online and beyond the internet, there has only been some research on the manosphere, or its specific sub-groups, so far (Gotell & Dutton 2016; Ging 2017; Marwick & Caplan 2018; Banet-Weiser 2018; Hunte 2019; Jane 2018; Van Walkenburgh 2018; Bratich & Banet-Weiser 2019; Farrell et al. 2019; Neumark Hermann 2019). Such scholarship also needs to be seen as being an important aspect of evolving feminist theories and activism (see Chapter 2). There is a long tradition of critically interrogating sexism in societies generally and how different media circulate sexist representations of women in particular (Humphries 2009; Jane 2016; Berns 2017; Banet-Weiser 2018; Manne 2018). Sexism can be defined as naturalising particular ideas about gender differences and inequalities that are often rooted in biologistic discourses. According to Kate Manne, sexism serves to justify the norms of patriarchy (Manne 2018, 88). Misogyny signifies a related but amplified form of sexism which explicitly and specifically features abuse, hatred and often violent threats towards women. In her recent book on misogyny, Manne (2018) defines the term as upholding the social norms of patriarchy. She sees misogyny as a structural phenomenon which upholds male power in society. Manne is critical of a framing or theorisation of misogyny as subjective or with a particular attention to subjectivity. I would disagree with such a position and argue for misogyny as something that is psychosocial; it relates to both structural and subjective-psychological features (Benjamin 1988; Young-Bruehl 1996).

While misogyny and sexism have been around for thousands of years, scholars have emphasised that they have been particularly amplified with the mainstreaming of the internet and the widespread use of social media platforms and websites, such as Facebook, Twitter, Reddit or Instagram, in the last decade. Harassment and online misogyny can be targeted at a specific individual, a group of women or women *per se*. A blueprint for current online misogyny and patterns of harassment was laid, as noted in the Introduction and Chapter 2, with Gamergate which included organised and targeted harassment campaigns against specific individuals and also women overall. Such efforts have been named 'networked misogyny' by Sarah Banet-Weiser and Kate M. Miltner (2016) and present coordinated efforts to humiliate, silence and (symbolically) destroy women (see also Banet-Weiser 2018). Online misogyny often includes abuse, insults, trolling (the deliberate harassing, provoking, upsetting or insulting of someone), death threats, doxxing (where personal information is published online), stalking, rape threats, death threats, revenge porn (where pornographic material that may have been recorded with or without consent of the individual is published against their will) or other threatening or abusive actions (Phillips 2015). Harassment, especially in recent years, has been normalised on social media:

> Regardless of how harassment is defined, women, especially women of color and queer women, are more susceptible to online harassment and more likely to consider negative behavior to be harassment, to the point where young women may see it as a normal part of online experience. (Marwick & Caplan 2018, 545)

While the material that I discuss in this book may not constitute targeted harassment campaigns against specific individuals, it nonetheless forms part of the wider nexus of online hatred that is directed against women (as I show in this and the subsequent chapters). It is thus part of structural sexism and misogyny which affects all areas of society, but especially media and the internet (Mantilla 2013; Banet-Weiser 2018).

The manosphere constitutes a relatively recent (the term was coined in 2009 by a porn marketer) but intensified clustering of male groups online. Debbie Ging (2017) has argued that it is a large network where local, regional and global contexts overlap. The anonymous nature of the internet also further complicates any substantial empirical data on who precisely the men of the manosphere are, because they create avatars, nicknames or fake profiles. It remains thus somewhat speculative to argue, as I would nonetheless do, that most men of the manosphere are young (between their teens to their mid-30s), white, heterosexual and thus *already* privileged (see also

Marwick & Caplan 2018), even though the latter is something they fiercely contest.

Alice E. Marwick and Robyn Caplan (2018) have argued that the recent surge in misogynistic harassment and social media posts has some connection to the Men's Rights Movement (see Chapter 2) and how it has been transformed online. They define the manosphere as a lose collection of groups and communities which revolves around some shared viewpoints:

> While the manosphere includes a variety of groups, including MRAs, pickup artists, MGOW (men going their own way), incels (involuntary celibates), father's rights activists, and so forth, they share a central belief that feminine values dominate society, that this fact is suppressed by feminists and 'political correctness,' and that men must fight back against an overreaching, misandrist culture to protect their very existence. (Marwick & Caplan 2018, 546)

While I already discussed the articulation of such a worldview in the previous chapter with reference to the YouTubers and their propaganda against sexual liberation, queer and homosexuality and female empowerment, there is a specific connection between the alt-right and many members of the manosphere (Nicholas & Agius 2018; Bratich & Banet-Weiser 2019; Lumsden & Harmer 2019, eds). This was shown in the exemplary quotes in the last chapter and I return to it later in this chapter when discussing how incels use anti-Semitic language, alt-right vocabulary and memes to talk about women.

In their research on the manosphere, Marwick and Caplan (2018) focussed on the use of the term 'misandry' by men to continue the myth that men are hated by women and feminists in particular, and need to construct a new masculine identity. They show that MRAs and their use of the term goes back to the early days of the world wide web of the early 1990s. There have been online discussions on this topic ever since and they also feature prominently in current MRA communities on Reddit and YouTube for example. Farrell et al. (2019) have shown in their linguistic analysis of a large data corpus that the 'amount of misogyny, hostility and violence is steadily increasing in the manosphere' (ibid, 87). The manosphere, and men in general beyond the internet, use their tactics to try and silence women and drive them out of online spaces or spaces that were traditionally deemed 'male'. Gamergate serves as a key recent example to illustrate the alleged dominance of women or weakening of male voices in games journalism and online spaces more generally, and the 'need' for men to combat it. In reality, those men could not come to terms with the fact that the once exclusively male site of games journalism was being diversified with women and also men who were not white, or heterosexual.

In her work on different masculinities within the manosphere, Debbie Ging (2017) has argued that it is also inherently Islamophobic and displaces rape culture onto men who are not white (refugees for example) who would be purely responsible. While such acts are political, and as I go on to show, often make use of racist and fascist discourses, Ging has argued that discourse within the manosphere is often cultural, focussing on personal relationships, mental health or personal experiences rather than 'collective political action' (2017, 11). Such discourses are coupled with a heavy reliance on visual material, like mash-ups, emoticons, memes, gifs, clips and are merely symptomatic of wider trends of social media and meme culture in the last few years (Denisova 2019). Yet, as I show in this chapter, discourses within the manosphere remain deeply political *and* personal as they often merge fascist, misogynistic discourses with personal narratives about lived experiences. There is scope to contribute to the studies outlined here, by paying particular analytical attention to the kind of misogyny and other themes that are circulated within the manosphere. Psychoanalysis then allows me to make inferences about the men behind the posts and what their desires, fantasies and unconscious look like. I do so while situating those narratives within sociohistorical contexts (see Chapter 2). This *psychosocial* perspective on the manosphere adds further complexity to existing scholarship.

Jack Bratich and Sarah Banet-Weiser (2018) have emphasised the link between changes in neoliberalism and incels. They argue that there has been a shift in masculinist ideology from Pick Up Artists as well as red pill ideology to incels in recent years. Ever since 2007, which marked a height of the PUA ideology which was widely covered in popular culture at the time, there has been a shift in neoliberalism, particularly triggered by the 2008 financial crisis, which resulted in a decline of neoliberalism's power to subjectivate individuals. This recent version of neoliberalism 'cannot take care of its failures' (Bratich & Banet-Weiser 2019, 5006) anymore and sees the 'subject's inability to restart itself as a subject' (ibid.). As a result, incels form around a rejection of neoliberal values (such as meritocracy) and demand that women provide them with (sexual) confidence and nurturing. As I show later in this chapter, incels partly move beyond such a rejection of neoliberalism when they create and embrace fantasies of fascism.

Following this discussion of literature on the manosphere, I now turn to the analysis of incels. They as well as other men of the manosphere make use of highly misogynistic and toxic language that is difficult to stomach.[6] Women are portrayed as objects or superficial subjects who are only interested in good looking (and rich) men. This is a kind of foundational layer of the misogyny spread by incels.

Misogyny and humour

What is very striking about the type of misogyny in the various incel communities is its immaturity and dependence on the kind of humour that some boys in puberty would share with each other. It is consistent with other communities on 4chan and Reddit that feature 'geeky' or 'nerdy' humour, a heavy reliance on memes, animated gifs, funny videos, mash-ups and remixes. Such 'fast food of the internet' (Denisova 2019) gives a particular tonality to this community. As with other kinds of humour that is at its heart racist, sexist or, otherwise xenophobic, it is never quite clear what is meant to be humorous and what is, in fact, intensely serious (Greene 2019). Such toxic humour is never funny. The humoristic tropes incels deploy are both an illustration of how fatal and doomed their destinies in life are – all that is left is to make jokes about the miserable state they are in – as well as a weapon to be used against others: Stacys, Chads, Normies. A post exemplifies this logic:

> I would use my powers to destroy 90% of the population and recreate the world with enforced monogamy and assigned partners. I would cure depression and rule the world to make it a better place. No more incels, chads, and stacys. (Reddit 2018a, online)

The role of humour should not make us perceive such content too lightly or as being light-hearted, harmless, geeky humour. Humour masks, in fact amplifies, vitriol and a toxic worldview. At the same time, as Krüger (2021) has shown in his discussion of humour in the incel community, it is a central component of the kind of online subcultures that gave rise to incels: 4chan, nerd culture, Gamergate and the hacker collective Anonymous (see also Coleman 2014; Greene 2019). Humour and in particular irony are used by incels to manoeuvre themselves into an impossible position of lethargy and apathy.

Many of the posts shown in this chapter are of an imbecile and destructive-playful nature. There is a sense of bravado and trolling behaviour present and the incel fora are rife with it. Steffen Krüger (2021) argues that incels, and other men's rights groups, take up trolling behaviour and ironically play with it while at the same time identifying with their own (self)-stigmatisation. This identification is auto-aggressive. Incels have identified themselves with their own stigma (that of the ugly, lonely geek). Whereas the earlier subcultures on 4chan and related spaces played with their own difference and alterity in progressive, frivolous, provocative and often funny ways, incels – who have at least partly come through this lineage as a rite of passage – transform such an alterity into a sado-masochistic complex which is loved and hated by them (their own ugliness, the figure of the Stacy, the Chad, etc.). Incels have created an image of a castrated, oppressed and soiled man (Krüger 2021).

Humour, then, functions in complex ways here. Humor, self-victimisation and self-pity are weaponised and become a form of narcissistic power for those men. A weapon which gives them a sense of agency, at least on the internet. At the same time, ironic humour serves as a defence against commitment, or any serious engagement with questions of masculinity, femininity or the individual experiences of incels. Like the alt-right, humour figures as a form of ironic distance: 'a shield to protect against charges of racism and their potential consequences' (May & Feldman 2019, 26), as Rob May and Matthew Feldman write about the alt-right. The same goes for incels. Humour is a shield, or *body armour*, to protect against vulnerability, self-critical engagement with masculinity/femininity and forms of sexuality beyond heterosexuality. May and Feldman argue that irony and humour are specifically used as strategies by the alt-right in order to widen its appeal and to distance itself from previous fascist groups. In the case of incels, such a strategy seems to work as they keenly adopt the tools and ideas that are provided by the alt-right. Humour thus serves as a form of imbecile *nonchalance* (Krüger 2021) which is specifically used to anger, provoke or hurt women and others while rejecting any seriousness. 'It is all a joke, don't you have a sense of humour?', incels might say. Humour is a defence against any engagement with women or other men within the incel communities (and in many other groups of the manosphere) where it is used for maximum effect of offence and outrage. It creates a barrier or border between the community and the outside world. It is also an instance where the irony of postfeminist advertising and popular culture (see Chapter 2) is co-opted by incels in a perverse form not only to be weaponised as irony, but they also often *refer* to the ironic texts (for example, advertisements or media texts that are inherently tongue-in-cheek with their sexism) to highlight the alleged nature of women today: phallic, confident, beautiful, highly sexualised and empowered. Incels fail to see that such images, of what they call Stacys, are of course a cultural construction by the media and *not* the reality.

Above all, such humorous content refers to the notions of the red pill and the black pill (see Introduction). Incels believe in the black pill, that they are essentially doomed and cannot get out of their situation. The ironic and nihilistic humour serves one purpose for them: to defensively shut down any possible form of change, transformation or agency – as well as debate. Irony serves as a form of nihilistic dogmatism and assertiveness. Incels are done with the well-meant advice from others. They think that there is no point. This is further amplified by the responses they receive to their posts where, instead of being cheered up or genuinely helped, they are most often assured by others about how horrible everything is. This kind of self-victimisation is a key characteristic of right-wing groups and the alt-right (Hawley 2017). It is the other who is allegedly responsible for their misery. There is nothing one can do.[7] Such discourses of self-victimisation and self-pity, coupled with humour and irony, are also often related to accounts of the individual lived experiences of incels.

Mental health and responses to neoliberalism's failures

'It's over', writes one user, to which another replies: 'It never began' (see Krüger 2021). Many users write about their mental health and that they are depressed, or feel excluded and ignored by the rest of society. Incels blame others (most often women) for not understanding them. They feel undesired, unwanted and alone. As a result, they allegedly suffer from various mental health conditions. Such states of alleged misery are commonly responded to and debated within the community in two ways: by aggressively *demanding* that (attractive) women see/recognise incels or by concluding that no hope is left and that they are on their own.

While such narratives are deeply problematic because they also articulate a hatred of others, they nonetheless reveal a complex mixture of a sense of entitlement to be with women and to have sex, as well as apparently dealing with suffering and mental health problems. Incels, like the PUA men Rachel O'Neill interviewed in her study (2018), feel that there is a double standard when it comes to women and what is expected of them as men. However, they mistakenly attribute the ideological construction of femininity (and masculinity) to women and feminism today, while in reality it is advanced by capital and consumer capitalism. There are undoubtedly ideological notions of what it means to be beautiful and those who do not conform to those attributes may suffer as a result. Nevertheless, this applies to a multitude of bodies, not just male ones: disabled individuals for example. Such a wider and more nuanced perspective is absent from the manosphere. Incels have made themselves convinced that it is superficial 'lookism' coupled with feminism that has put them in such a miserable place. That is without doubt not the case. At the same time, we live in 'a culture that scorns weakness and punishes vulnerability, especially among men' (O'Neill 2018, 213), as Rachel O'Neill writes. Incels rebel against such a culture but make very wrong conclusions. We can see how particular forms of neoliberal ideology and hegemonic masculinity (and by extension femininity of course) are not only unconsciously internalised by subjects today, but that some fail at doing so. Such failures then result in intense affective and psychological responses which take the form of abuse in the case of incels.

Jack Bratich and Sarah Banet-Weiser's work (2019) on the failure of the current neoliberal conjuncture (which is characterised by economic crises, austerity measures and changing jobmarkets) to ideologically and practically secure and fix subjects is useful to further discuss at this point. They argue that there is a failure within current neoliberalism's practices of subjectivation to govern and transform the subject into a self-sufficient, productive and successful agent. The individual failures of the male subject (whether they are economic, romantic or of a different matter) find expression within online communities such as incels.

Thanks to emerging networked misogyny and its mediated forms of support, the feeling of failure is no longer absorbed as one's own responsibility, but combined and accelerated. The result is a networked masculine subject that feels threatened, and a collective figure is to blame: women. (Bratich & Banet-Weiser 2019, 5007)

Bratich and Banet-Weiser argue that the ideological impetus of neoliberalism (one can make it if one works hard, overcome obstacles, etc.) is laid bare and unmasked particularly since the global financial crisis of 2008 as a result of which individuals lost their jobs, governments introduced austerity measures and spending freezes and general economic insecurity prevailed for some years (Stanley 2014; Bhattacharyya 2015; Walkerdine 2020). The markets had lost confidence and so had many men. We could also put this in psychoanalytic terms and argue that the phallic power of neoliberalism began to fade from 2008 onwards. Loss of confidence means a loss of the phallus, symbolically speaking. Such a loss of confidence is also responded to with a demand, by incels for instance, that it must be compensated by women who should provide for men, build up their confidence and make them feel desired. Bratich and Banet-Weiser focus on confidence as a key aspect of neoliberal ideology whereby the individual must learn to be confident, or at least perform it, as well as needing to *have* confidence in the workings of neoliberal class mobility, entrepreneurialism and success. This promise is at the very core of neoliberalism: if you believe in the system, think positively, act proactively and work hard, you will make it (Gilbert 2013; Walkerdine 2020). Such an ideology is shattered by incels. Whereas confidence figured as a 'confidence game' in the case of the PUA worldview, which suggests in true neoliberal fashion that men only need to *act* in a certain way in order to appear confident, successful and desirable for women, such mechanisms are rejected by incels. For them, confidence is not something to be learned or performed. This is one of neoliberalism's failures; it fails on an affective level to contain subjects who have failed (to believe in) its framework. Incels believe that they can never make it (the black pill worldview), because they are too ugly, too depressed, lack economic status and many other reasons. As a result, women are expected to, what I would call, contain[8] such men, to soothe their egos and anxieties and nurture them. Rather than blaming neoliberalism or the PUA ideology, incels and other men of the manosphere place the blame on women for not giving in to their demands. 'Contemporary incels are thus birthed in an inwardly focused, mutually assured antisocial sociability' (ibid, 5017).

Incels have thus created an identity which consists of feeling undesired, marginalised, geeky, nerdy and mentally unstable (Massanari 2017; Blodgett & Salter 2018; Mountford 2018; Krüger 2021). A profound sense of sexual entitlement is expressed by incels. This sense of entitlement is then coupled with discussions of mental health in a defensive move which, again, places the blame on the outside world and on everyone apart from themselves. Their narratives express an internalised neoliberal logic which the men nonetheless struggle with, because it has failed them. They express that they have fallen into the cracks of the system and are nothing without being desired. For them, being successful in neoliberal terms is strongly associated with sexuality and relationships. While I am not entirely convinced if neoliberalism has ever fully managed to ideologically contain its subjects, as Bratich and Banet-Weiser imply when they argue that it has recently become unable to do so, the changes and economic insecurities they write of are real. We could argue that incels reject, or unmask, the failures of neoliberalism and occupy defensive subject positions as a result. They do not conform to hegemonic masculinity and neoliberal notions of the productive, agentic subject. This and the previous section of this chapter would support such an argument. Incels use humour, irony and discourses of self-victimisation and self-hatred to retreat into apathy and hopelessness which s coupled with toxic and abusive posts about women. This also often goes hand in hand with a specific rejection of all forms of therapy, another one of neoliberalism's promises being that by undergoing therapy the subject can transform themself (particularly in quick, cost-effective, non-psychoanalytic therapies). Bratich and Banet-Weiser argue that a further response is actual violence in the case of incels who have committed mass shootings (see Chapter 6 for more discussion on two mass shooters).

I think there is a further dimension to this argument about neoliberalism's failures which relates to the popularity of the alt-right in spaces such as 4chan and Reddit. It is not a coincidence that rightwing extremism and the alt-right in particular are popular amongst certain men today. Like previous instances of fascism (for example in Germany from the late 1920s onwards), they respond to economic decline and crises by constructing fantasies of who is to blame, what the solutions are, etc. Where current neoliberalism has stalled, the alt-right and a particular form of authoritarian capitalism take over (see Introduction and Chapter 2). Incels embody complex and contradictory psyches which are characterised by dis/inhibition – apathy and symbolic agency. I argue that posts which shame or abuse women need to be regarded as particular forms of (toxic) symbolic power, because they create reality anew rather than only simply critiquing or reaffirming a reality of contemporary neoliberal austerity and crises. This creation of a reality is further amplified, as I show later in this chapter, through the fantasy of becoming a Chad and embodying a particular kind of masculine strength which I define as fascist.

Up until this point then, I have discussed incels as defensive-inhibited and reacting to particular socio-cultural formations in an apathic way. They both affirm/desire neoliberal ideology (having to look good, using ratings based on looks, being a successful male both in sexual and economic terms) as the *sine qua non* and yet also consciously unmask and reject it as superficial and damaging. However, it is women who are blamed for both neoliberal ideology and its failings in providing incels with status and prowess rather than neoliberalism and its ideology as such. We could say that incels as a result respond to a particular version of authoritarian, fascist ideology which they happily affirm: a kind of fascist masculinity which holds promises of agency, fitness, bodily strength and being desirable.

The first two sections in this chapter, then, can be seen as instances where incels construct their body armour through inhibition, defence mechanisms and fantasies, the next two sections show how such body armour is then put to work in a disinhibited imaginary struggle with women and incels' own male bodies. All of such instances are psychosocial, meaning that they are articulations of both subjective-psychological as well as socio-economic-structural phenomena and developments (such as the sexual revolution and its consequences, the changing nature of neoliberalism since the 2008 financial crisis and the rise of the alt-right and white supremacy).

Destroying and desiring women

There are many narratives by incels that use a more active prose and detail violent fantasies of actions, specifically of getting revenge on women for allegedly being ignored, ridiculed or rejected. Yet, as I show in this section, they are also coupled with desire and wanting to be with such women at the same time. Those men desire to be Chads and be with a Stacy. In discussing different fantasies about women, such as those about revenge, what women are really like, how they think and so on, incels assume a form of symbolic power which has no consequences or weight outside of their online communities. It only matters online. Incels, who embody a weakened and failed masculinity which is brought about both by themselves as well as by wider socio-cultural changes, as discussed in the previous section, can circulate and discuss a particular version of reality (which is of course a fantasy) online. Thereby they assume a minimal quantum of agency which only exists on the internet. Such dynamics reveal a disinhibited power that is displayed online. A power that equips them with a sense of grandiosity that they feel is lacking in reality. They can dream up scenarios of enacting revenge and it does not matter if they will ever become reality. They have posted them online and at least through such acts they materialise as *something* that exists and remains stable and fixed for those men, in a world of rapid socio-economic and sexual change.

Such form of perceived powerlessness not only relates to changes in neoliberalism which I discussed, it also relates to racist fantasies of white supremacism which are implicit and often highly explicit within the manosphere (see Introduction and Chapter 2). Incels' active mobilisation of alt-right terminology and images, as I show in the remainder of this chapter, perhaps speaks not only to individual crises of the men and a general crisis of masculinity because of neoliberal precarity and other reasons (see also Chapter 2), but also specifically to a crisis of whiteness and white masculinity. The majority of incels and other men of the manosphere are white and respond to their own feelings of inadequacy by embracing racist, anti-Semitic and misogynist narratives from the alt-right as well as constructing their own.

This crisis of white masculinity is responded to with desires and fantasies that revolve around fascism where an Other is created that is attacked. This Other is, above all, a woman for incels and other men of the manosphere. Nonetheless, incels simultaneously desire and reject women. The following post further illustrates the complexities of desire and revenge:

> There is this girl at work I kinda caught feelings for. I didn't plan on it but I found her very attractive and always made an effort to smile when we walk past each other. Unfortunately the bitch always just blanks me and stares at the floor and passes me in silence. No doubt she is thinking 'oh no, here's that creepy guy again...ugh' everytime we see each other. We have never actually spoken but she seems to have no problem giggling and chatting with everyone else. The other night I looked her up on Facebook and my suspicions were confirmed. Picture after picture of her with her chadlite boyfriend.... I just didn't like her anymore. So today, she was sitting outside for lunch and she left her shoes under her desk. I grabbed the condiment dispenser from the canteen area and pumped her shoe full of tomato ketchup. I wasn't there personally to witness her putting her shoe back on (didn't want to incriminate myself) but apparently she stuck her foot right in and tomato sauce shot right out!!!... (Reddit 2018b, online)

Through posts such as the above incels go beyond self-pity and self-victimisation and enact particular forms of agency which may often remain on the symbolic level by detailing what incels will do, or would like to do, in the future. As far as the post above is concerned, we do not know if the man really did squirt ketchup into the woman's shoe. Either way, it remains an act of violent invasion. If the incel could not get to the desired woman, to get into her sexually, squirting ketchup in her shoe serves as a displaced fantasy of intercourse that is enacted. Semen becomes ketchup. Women are constructed as fantasmatic figures in those narratives and made to embody and do particular characteristics and things (for example being superficial, rejecting incels, being dangerous). Incels themselves feel invaded and castrated, so such feelings are turned into active prose in the above quote. The post is also used in a kind of perverse communal spirit to show to others what the man has (allegedly) done so that he may receive affirmation and encouragement by other incels. Writing about it is significant because it can be commented on and therefore further validated and made even more real by other men. Whether such a post was pure fantasy and never happened, or if the incel really did attack the woman's shoe with ketchup, the act of circulating it on Reddit further validates and verifies it for him, because it has been put into words and thereby an act of affective discharge occurred (Johanssen 2016, 2019). It has become reality for the man, irrespective of whether or not it really happened. By devivifying the woman in the above narrative, the incel has discharged his affective tension and can feel a momentary sense of relief (deCook 2021).

Such posts also show a level of hatred and rage directed against women and female empowerment because the particular user has probably been ignored or rejected by women. The paradox of rejection and desire for women is at the heart of incels and it serves as a kind of mirror for what they may have experienced themselves. They have been rejected, or ignored too many times and this rejection is then turned into a universal rejection of and by women. This serves as an attempt to banish the desire for women that nonetheless persists. The anguish of being rejected (or perhaps rather having *never* really meaningfully interacted with women) and nonetheless desiring women, of hating and wanting them *so* badly at the same time is agonising for incels. Often coupled with a kind of immature, pubertal hormonal body, we get some of the narratives that are shown in this chapter. This means that incels are in bodily states of dis/inhibition, of desire and destruction that struggle between restraint and release. Such contradictory states can be further discussed through the below example:

> I know a guy who's 5'1" with a bad face. He's in undergrad and he just gave up cuz women kept rejecting him.
> Then he basically studeycel'd [studied] himself to death and somehow got a job that's way out of his league. I mean, mid six figures.
> So he's in his senior year of uni and earning six figures. So he decided to play a joke on the foids [women]. He wore a fancy suit under a trashy hoodie and started asking out hot foids who were shorter than him. He would ask if they're free tomorrow night. They would always reject him and say that they're busy. Then he would take off his hoodie and say, 'Well, you're really pretty so take my hoodie as a gift anyway.' And the moment they saw his fancy suit and jewelry they always changed their responses and were suddenly free tomorrow night. And btw none of them were flattered by the trashy thrift store hoodie.
> Cuz they know they'll never find a better betabux [beta male] than this guy. (Reddit 2018c, online)

The above user goes on to write that women would take advantage of the 'guy' and pursue Chad behind his back. Yet, the 'guy' is 'redpilled' (believes in the red pill worldview) and has allegedly only pretended to be a beta male in order to attract women.

Is the person named above as 'a guy', not in reality the user himself who posted the thread? The fantasy of unmasking himself, of shedding his ugly incel side and revealing a handsome, suited male reveals his desire for transformation – a very neoliberal but also human and universal one: to be accepted and (sexually) desired by others. The ending of the fantasy is significant, because it shows how the contradictory feeling of wanting to possess and reject females is managed. Even if women desire the other guy, they would *still* apparently 'fuck Chad' behind his back, because he is a beta male and not an alpha male like Chad. This misogynist fantasy of revenge is thus rooted in the old pattern of incel discourses, because the female is constructed as a someone who cheats on the hard-working, good-natured beta male. The desire for the female that comes too close to them, is thus muted by articulating that all females are sleeping around with men. The incel can stay true to incel ideology and his fellow incels.

However, the last sentence reveals perhaps a way out for the incel. A way out of his own fantasy world where he desires and rejects women at the same time: 'the guy' *knows* all of this – he is redpilled – he is only pretending to be a beta male in order to have sex with women, he is in reality a Chad, as the user writes. According to him, the person named in the above post understands the 'game' and uses it to his own advantage. The above serves as an archetypical narrative of how the complexities of desire and contradictory sexual fantasies are negotiated in incel communities. Incels fantasise about a transformation where they are turned into Chads, desired by Stacys, and yet have been blackpilled and can continue to cultivate their hatred of women. I return to this point in the next chapter. The Chad is cast as the decadent playboy, like the figure of the Jew by the anti-Semite, who was seen as decadent and sexually contagious to all women in the German Nazi propaganda (Theweleit 1989) or the racist figure of the sexually potent black male (see Chapter 7). The above narrative is a fantasy of omnipotent control where the man manipulates everyone around him. It is in fact similar to PUA ideology, which incels nonetheless reject, because the PUA trainers also promise to the men who attend their workshops that they can turn them into masters of manipulation who can follow specific steps to 'crack' any woman, as Rachel O'Neill (2018) has shown in her study. The above post articulates a similar desire for control and mastery of women. It becomes clear that incels, and other men of the manosphere too, go beyond the status of a victim and the defence mechanisms that come with it and actively construct a toxic reality in response, as I have shown in this section. I further examine this below.

Fantasies of masculine strength

While feelings of inadequacy, impotence, self-loathing and self-destruction are frequently voiced by incels, there are also narratives that seek to combat and counter such states, as I have just discussed. Such narratives are further amplified in some posts that specifically allude to masculine strength and discuss male bodies. For example, posts often express the fantasy that women are only attracted to muscular men, criminals and members of gangs. Such narratives also carry explicit racist undertones when it is alleged by incels that Stacys desire black, criminal men for example. This may also be shaped by wider popular culture when criminality for example is depicted or rather *misread* by white men such as incels as racialised, agentic and desirable in films or music videos where black male actors often portray criminals (Balaji 2009; Belle 2014). Incels claim that many white women desire black men who are 'tough guys', just like in popular culture. Such racist narratives stigmatise black individuals as criminals and as dangerous to, yet desired by, white women. They also relate to fantasies which go back to the years of racial segregation in the United States where it was often alleged that white women had to be 'protected' from black men's allegedly lustful desires (Fanon 1967; George 2014). I return to the racist fantasy of the black male as dangerous and hypersexualised in Chapter 7.

Narratives of race figure in a complex manner in incel discourses as many incels who are not white articulate a form of internalised racism when they lament the alleged impossibility of dating (white) women as an Indian or Southeast-Asian male for instance and proclaim a hatred of their ethnic background. Incels allege that white men in particular have a better chance of dating women of any ethnicity compared to men who are not white. This specifically extends to the discussion of alleged shortcomings of the male body that is not white which conform to classic racist narratives such as the ones of the eugenicist Hans F. K. Günther (1933) which I discuss in the below section. Incels, who are not white, lament that their bodies can never match the idealised tall and muscular bodies of the so-called white Chad or black Tyrone. Phallic masculinity is often presented in such accounts through a binary fantasy of the white or black, muscular male. This extends to the racist usage of the term 'cuck' (denoting a white male who is forced to watch a black male have sex with his wife) which I specifically discuss in Chapter 7. Ultimately, the white male is most desired by incels and articulates itself in the construction of the fantasy of the Chad.

The incel community, then, is one in which male supremacism and white supremacism frequently overlap. White masculinity is constructed by incels as a fantasy in which a muscular body figures as the key to a successful (romantic) life. This latent (homo)eroticisation of the white male body is partly brought about by the large increase in the display of eroticised male bodies on platforms like Instagram, as Jamie Hakim has shown (Hakim 2019). Incels and other men engage with such representations (see my discussion in Chapter 2). I return to the question of homosexuality within the manosphere in the next chapter.

This form of hypermasculinity is desired by incels and frequently discussed through the figure of the Chad. This is also often tied to what incels call 'ascending' – a transformation from incel to Chad. The desire to be a strong male, a Chad, an alpha male is very present for incels. In articulating this desire, which is at the same time defended against because the Chad is a figure of hatred, references to the current fascist climate online which is facilitated by the alt-right are frequently made. Cis females and males are equated with Jews and they are accused in classic anti-Semitic fashion of stealing the enjoyment from incels.

> ***I don't think a lot of you guys understand the extent to which Chad and Stacy enjoy life***
> It's not just sex, it's the gluttonous extent of their debauchery which blows my mind. People call us entitled because we desire a basic human act while these absolute degenerate Chads and Stacys engage in the most filthy excesses imaginable. Don't believe me? Just browse instagram lol – they flaunt their excessive lives, revelling in it, calling it 'flexin' etc. Pure genetic chaos has brought them good fortune and they act as if THEY were always entitled to it, as if somehow THEY deserved it.
> We need a new Reign of Terror to thin out these debased genetic aristocrats. (Reddit 2018d, online)
>
> When you post about being shocked by the absolute cucked [weakened] state of the world, remember that our hooked-nose friends are in their mansions JFLing [just fucking loling] at their perfect success and at our misery 24/7. (Reddit 2018e, online)

It is at this point that it becomes clear how deeply intertwined alt-right fascist ideas and those of incels often are. Females and Jews are allegedly enjoying themselves to an excessive degree and have 'cucked' (another alt-right term which signifies emasculated and weakened, often also liberal and left-wing men) everyone else. Incels were not only partially born out a dangerous merger of 4chan, MRAs and other right-wing groups, but they actively make use of tropes and devices handed to them by the alt-right. Such narratives go beyond trolling or a particular understanding of humour which is characteristic of online subcultures, they are actively participating in spreading of fascist ideologies on the internet. The ultimate masculine strength that incels aspire to is that of fascist men. Such fantasies are so deeply irrational. Why do they acquire such an affective force and currency for incels? Stephen Frosh has written about the importance of the Jew for the Anti-Semite (in Nazi Germany) that:

> the Jew is a figure chosen initially for its cultural congruence as a hate object, but is then excessively invested in as a carrier of all this otherness;

conspiracy is to be found everywhere. This produces a spiralling of paranoia and hatred, as the Jew serves both to contain and to exaggerate the projected impulses of the anti-Semite. Psychosis is in the air, kept at bay only by endlessly increasing rigidity and escalating anti-Semitic hate. The Jew is a safety valve for destructive impulses, but this use of the Jew has a profound personal and social cost. (Frosh 2016, 35)

The Jew thus serves as an outlet for projections that never goes away, no matter how ruthlessly annihilated the Jews were in Nazi Germany for example. It is the Jew's fantasmatic dimensions that carry such weight for the anti-Semite. They never fade away, because the Jew has been constructed through fantasy. 'Being unreal, being fantastic, the hated other cannot actually be eradicated; in a sense, the perfect enemy is the one who does not exist' (Frosh 2016, 65). Likewise, the Stacy or Chad do not really exist. They are fantasies. The Jew or Stacy or Chad is seen as responsible for everything that brings misery. For Frosh:

The anti-Semite is attracted to 'irrational' beliefs precisely because they express the turmoil of a mind at war with itself and with the world, yet one that is structurally and socially weak, and needs the prop of its containing madness to keep itself sane. (Frosh 2016, 39)

Many of the narratives I have examined in this chapter detail a similar turmoil of the mind. It needs figure of hatred which is simultaneously desired to maintain some sense of functionality. Such figures are the Stacy and the Chad. Yet, both are also intensely desired. I return to this paradox in the next chapter.

There are also many narratives that frame incels as a 'rebellion' which will lead to 'inceldom' and overthrow all Chads and Stacys, like the Freikorps men who would violently fight to establish the German Reich, incels outline a form of right-wing terrorism. It is rooted in their misogynistic paranoia and a fantasy of omnipotence. This kind of version of masculinity has a strong resemblance with how Theweleit describes the Freikorps soldiers and goes beyond claiming the status of a victim. Consequently (and perhaps not dissimilar from Theweleit's Feikorps men), the users resort to symbolically destroying such women. This may give them a sense of agency over their own (libidinal) frustration and sexual-economic failure. As a result of this symbolic power which articulates itself online, incels frame themselves as stronger than they really are; as 'brave warriors' who will bring about a different kind of sexual revolution. It is not a coincidence that such fantasies and narratives emerge at this point, they are enabled, amplified and encouraged by the wave of right-wing populism and the culture of the alt-right that has flooded the Western world and certain online spaces as well. This not only articulates itself in the language used in posts and in many memes that are shared on the subreddit, many of which feature symbols and imagery popularised by the alt-right, but through an implicit and sometimes also explicit desire and articulation of *becoming* a fascist *body*. Many posts also discuss genetics, family heritage, specific bodily shortcomings and how cosmetic surgery and exercise at the gym can help. I refer to some posts now that exemplify this in order to further analyse how incels make the leap from defensive narratives of self-victimisation towards narratives that emphasise symbolic power.

Fascist bodies

Apart from the Stacy, the Chad figures as a central aspect of the incel worldview. As I have alluded to in this chapter, the Chad is a kind of male equivalent of the Stacy. He is intensely hated and desired by incels. They want to become Chads. The Chad is attributed with certain qualities and imagined to be an archetypical male. Strong, muscled, handsome, outgoing, oozing testosterone. A kind of mixture of a Hollywood actor and a porn star that has been concocted in the incels' minds. He is an alpha male. He is also depicted as white (in illustrations, posts, or images for example).[9] The website IncelWiki describes the Chad as follows:

> A chad is someone who can elicit near universal positive female sexual attention at will. A chad tends to be between an '8' to a '10' on the decile scale [physical attractiveness scale], has an extremely high income and/ or an extreme amount of social power. Even though chad can get almost any woman he wants, he tends to go for Stacy instead of Becky ['average' looking woman]. (IncelWiki 2020, online)

The Chad, then, becomes another object of desire for incels. As well as being shaped by the increased display of (semi-)naked, fit male bodies on social media (Hakim 2019), it is closely influenced by body ideals shared across the far-right which have acquired a wider presence on the internet in recent years. The 'far-right body is averse to pornography, physically fit, and mentally sound. It procreates and spends time in nature' (Strick forthcoming), Simon Strick writes about contemporary constructions of the alt-right male body. Such fantasies of bodies are closely linked to discussions of genetics, race theory and other crude pseudo-scientific ideas by incels.

As a 'science', or rather pseudo-science, physiognomy became more influential across Europe from 1775 onwards when Johann Caspar Lavater published four volumes on the subject. 'Even before 1933, a lot of physiognomic thought got mixed up with 'race science' and anti-Semitic propaganda' (Daub 2018, online). From the beginning, such ideas *'lent themselves* to and *even* invited interpretation along racially discriminatory lines', as the historian Richard T. Gray argues (Gray 2004, 331, italics in original). Nazi race science, eugenics, subsequently took up physiognomy and combined it with crude genetics and biometrics. Aryan bodies had to resemble particular characteristics. So-called 'race hygiene' was 'central to the new order' (Weiss 1990, 41) under Hitler. Racial laws soon stipulated what was deemed Aryan and what was 'unworthy life' and culminated in the Holocaust. One aspect of the Nazi regime policies was the *Ariernachweis*, a document that certified that a citizen as a member of the Aryan race. It marked the exclusion of non-Aryans (Jews for example). The *Kleine Rassenkunde des Deutschen Volkes* (Small Race Study of the German People) was published in 1929 by Hans F. K. Günther. The writer and eugenicist's race theory of the Nordic race and allegedly inferior other races was so influential that Hitler made it one of the basis for the Nazi euthanasia and eugenics policies. Günther wrote for example about the Nordic race:

> The face is narrow with a very narrow forehead, slim, high-rising nose and narrow lower jaw with pronounced chin. The facial features of the Nordic race seem – at least for the man – curiously brave due to a triple emphasis of the line of the facial features. (Günther 1933, 9, my translation)

Similar crude theories still exist today and it is for example a common conception that it looks particularly 'manly' if a man has a pronounced, strong jawline and chin. Such ideals of the male white body are particularly present in fascist ideology (Theweleit 1987, 1989). It is an ideology that has increasingly spread online ever since Trump was elected president in 2016 (Wendling 2018). This idea of the strong male body is fanatically taken up by incels of all ethnicities who discuss human genetics and a focus on the jawline in many posts. There are many discussions of genetics, physiognomy and body types that bear an uncanny resemblance to how the Nazis thought about 'Aryan' bodies. Paradoxically, the white, fascist body comes to stand as a universal object of desire for many incels, no matter what their ethnicity is. Such a fantasy of the white body is not only influenced by the alt-right as well as the increasing display of fit male bodies on Instagram, it is also shaped by wider (Western) popular culture where most men who are shown in adverts, TV shows and films are still white and men of other ethnicities often remain under- or misrepresented. While media content has become more diverse and less stereotypical in the last two decades, questions around misrepresentation still remain (Besana, Katsiaficas & Loyd 2019; Stamps 2020).

For incels, it is their bodies that do not conform to hegemonic beauty standards in combination with superficial Stacys that have allegedly led to their misery. Many incels discuss what they call 'looksmaxxing', 'surgerymaxxing' or 'gymmaxxing' (improving their looks, undergoing surgery or going to the gym) in order to improve their bodies. It is probably no coincidence that there is an explicit reliance on physiognomy by incels. They take up the notion that looks matter in society and the cultural stereotype that once one looks particularly manly, one can 'have' any female. In the subreddit r/incelselfies, incels post pictures of themselves in order to get advice on their looks and if they really are incels. One user writes of his 'misshapen jawline'. Someone responds: 'Above average jaw, I can tell from this pic that you're probably a very good looking person. I wish I had a jaw like yours'. A second user posts: 'naw you're good, what wrong with your eyes? negative canthal tilt? you can probably fix them up w some surgery' (Reddit 2019a, online). Like the Stacys who they so vehemently criticise for it, incels obsess over their looks. They compile endless links to and cite scientific studies that discuss perceived male attractiveness by females, facial symmetry and harmony, universal beauty standards, or what makes men sexually attractive. Many incels also discuss cosmetic surgery in order to alter their appearance and get closer to that of Chad's. A strong body will result in a strong mind and a better life for incels. It will finally allow them to be in a relationship or to have sex. Such fantasies mark the ultimate step in the move from apathic defence towards the creation of a fantasy in which incels have become fascist Chads.

Conclusion

This chapter presented a detailed analysis of various data from incels. I was able to show the complexities of desire and rejection and how they shape particular male fantasies about women. Incels are deeply misogynistic and have buried themselves in self-destruction and self-pity. For incels, woman becomes a universal signifier that is both desired and hated with passion and a fantasy that is destroyed and yet embraced all at once. Such narratives go beyond a mere articulation of misogyny, they present a contemporary form of misogyny that is strongly infused with alt-right rhetoric and a kind of fascist affect. Incels frequently make use of terminology and imagery that has been popularised by the alt-right. This chapter began with a focus on the defensive strategies that incels employ to narrate stories of victimhood. I have discussed the use of humour and irony as well as narratives of mental health issues by them and linked those to Jack Bratich and Sarah Banet-Weiser's argument on the emergence of the incel as a particular identity formation in response to the financial crisis of 2008 which resulted in a loss of confidence in neoliberal capitalism for many men.

> Neoliberalism's social care deficit means there is no social support, only antisocial support. incels are mutated entrepreneurs—men of action, turning others into instruments, but now subtracting the creative from 'creative destruction.' Their techniques of disruption are increasingly techniques of pure negation. (Bratich & Banet-Weiser 2019, 5020)

I focussed on such actions in the subsequent sections of this chapter by showing how the fantasies that incels circulate online create particular forms of toxic realities by being written and posted. Realities in which women embody certain characteristics, incels describe things they have done or would like to do to women, and lastly how incels describe their desires for a fascist Chad body. While Bratich and Banet-Weiser have argued that incels are no longer held or fixed by neoliberalism's promises of confidence and success, I would argue that the fantasy of fascist transformation that I have detailed in this chapter shows perhaps ultimately a deeply held belief in neoliberalism after all (even if it is also coupled with rejecting it via the black pill as I have shown), or perhaps a desire to replace it with a fascist dictatorship which would nonetheless be rooted in neoliberal values of entrepreneurial individualism. The fantasy of individual transformation from a nobody to successful, desired subject is at the heart of neoliberalism. Incels are thus more receptive to neoliberalism than they would like to admit.

Conscious fantasies

The male fantasies of the incel community bear some resemblances to Theweleit's theorisation of the proto-fascist male body. A male body that destroys women, while at the same time appropriating them. A male body that is obsessed about its own embodiment and signs of masculine strength. A male body that has constructed its own version of reality which other men supposedly need to wake up to.

What is very striking about the posts and interactions discussed in this chapter is that those narratives and fantasies are very *consciously* named and discussed. This also relates to Theweleit's description of the Freikorps soldiers. Both kinds of men have a desire to verbalise and articulate their fears of women as well as their hatred of and desire towards them. The fear of castration, as Theweleit argues, is conscious:

> as far as I'm concerned, we really can't talk about an unconscious displacement, or an unconscious fear. On the contrary, it strikes me that concealing the kinds of thoughts we've been discussing, the ones traditional psychoanalysis would call 'unconscious,' is the last thing on earth those men would want to do. They're out to express them at all cost. The 'fear of castration' is a consciously held fear, just as the equation of communism and rifle-woman is consciously made. All of this leads to the conclusion either that the men are repressing precious little, or nothing at all.... (Theweleit 1987, 89)

The narratives on Reddit almost bear no symbolism, no unconscious or hidden meanings. Everything that is written is all out there in the open. Nothing can be deciphered or read as a particular expression of the unconscious. I return to this point of the status of the unconscious in more detail in the coming two chapters. The incel posts are also tied to how the men were raised in neoliberalism where an active sex life is a requirement of full (sexual) subjecthood (Gill 2007). Theweleit writes in a similar context about a much earlier time:

> The young boy is trained in puberty to the point of near madness to live his whole life within the structure of a fictitious before-and-after construct. 'Once I've had a woman—the woman—then...' This 'then' covers everything: guilt, fear, uncertainty, feelings of inferiority will all vanish; life will begin; I will be strong; I will defeat my father; I will leave him; my potential will unfold; SHE will belong to me, and I will protect her. (Theweleit 1987, 376, emphases in original)

The same is true for incels and other men today. This sort of desire also translates into a feeling of entitlement which is disappointed. Incels fundamentally believe that they are *entitled* to women and sex, according to their own rules. They have a burning, hormonal, desire to be with a woman. Finally, to be in a relationship and everything will be fine. This disappointment is met with the articulation of revenge fantasies which find a home in the alt-right discourse.

The incel's psyche and Reddit

Theweleit argued that the soldier males develop a body armour through the totality of fascism and painful bodily drill. The ego is formed in this way. At the same time, the body armour remains fragmented and cracked and with it the men's egos. Everything is held together by the 'totality-ego' (Theweleit 1989, 207) of the army and fascism. Incels of course do not have a leader. They are a leaderless community and in that sense very different to other fascist movements or the Freikorps militias. They are atomised and feel part of a totality through Reddit. Is Reddit then a totality-ego coupled with alt-right discourse? Reddit, and other platforms like 4chan, are not only profoundly anti-mainstream and to a degree anti-establishment and therefore give a platform to fascists and other movements, it started out as a platform that actively enabled and encouraged users to form communities around outlawed, hateful or disgusting topics (amongst many benign communities as well of course). Such controversial content would guarantee engagement and high numbers of users. Reddit's business model is based on advertising. While Reddit has taken more steps towards content moderation in the last couple of years (as noted, the first and biggest incel community was banned in 2017 and other racist or misogynist communities were banned in 2019), its 'geeky' and simple infrastructure encourages users to form communities around a particular topic.

The mass of posts on some subreddits (often between a few and many per hour) works as a similar stream of totality to Theweleit's army. A stream of hatred in order to keep out the female bodies that seek to castrate the incels (in their fantasies). Reddit, like fascism, but to a much lesser extent, manages to integrate the fragmented ego into a feeling of totality, of communion. Reddit acts as a form of body armour. Incels' egos are in a constant state of chaos and are threatened with disintegration. They need to do something, to write against such feelings. Such acts that bring a sense of totality are established through posting and interacting with others in the specific subreddits. What is ultimately killed are the incel's own female elements within him: softness, passionate, eroticised, female elements. The specific narratives of incel revolution and rebellion are also significant because they go beyond individual discussions of incels and appeal to incels as a force, as a mass that will bring about change. For a quasi-fascist movement like that of the incels, like 'ordinary' fascism, the mass and feeling to be part of a mass is foundational.

A 2019 *New York Magazine* feature includes some interview data with an incel who underwent extensive cosmetic (jaw) surgery. He is quoted as saying:

> 'My self-image fluctuates all the time,' he wrote on the forum as he waited. 'I want to live in a plastic surgeon's office. I just want to have a bed in one of his labs. Just a bed, a small kitchen, and an internet connection. I want to feel pure within my body and self-validate by looking in the mirror and seeing the flawless skull. When detecting a tiny deformity, I call the surgeon and he'll be there immediately, along with his assistant and a knife in his hand to cut me open.'... 'The prospect of a better surgery result is keeping me alive,' he tells me. (Hines 2019, online)

Such a state of fluctuation and restlessness serves as a graphic illustration of what I have outlined. The incel's sense of reality and self-worth is entirely dependent on, even generated by, his self-image. He discusses a fantasy of living in the plastic surgeon's office so that he can constantly alter his appearance. But he will never achieve satisfaction. The prospect of the next surgery is literally keeping him alive, serving as a dam to patch up his fragmented and restless ego. The prospect of 'self-coupling' (see Chapter 1), of transcending and becoming a new man serves as a machinic fantasy that generates enough energy for him to live.

I turn to another male community in the next chapter, which is different but to a degree also similar to incels: Men Going Their Own Way (MGTOW). I also return to incels and outline the similarities that exist between the two communities. This chapter has, overall, continued themes from the previous chapter and focused on a structural-conjunctural discussion of wider socio-economic developments (post-2008 neoliberalism in particular) and how they relate to defensiveness and agency. The next chapter specifically advances the psychoanalytic analysis of the manosphere by paying particular attention to the subjective-psychological elements through a focus on what kind of characters those men are. This also allows me to pay more attention to the unconscious and to dis/inhibition.

Notes

1 Incels refer to themselves in lowercase. As the word is a portmanteau term of 'involuntary celibate', I have uncapitalised it in this book except for the beginnings of sentences.
2 Reddit banned the Braincels subreddit in October 2019. This means that much of the data referred to in this book can no longer be accessed. I nonetheless provide the original URLs. In one of the biggest incel communities on Reddit – the original r/incels – there were many explicit discussions of rape and raping women was deemed acceptable. Such content had disappeared from the incel communities that I examined, because it had subsequently been removed or banned by the site. It is for that reason that I do not discuss rape in this chapter; this does not mean that rape would not play a role in the incel worldview. This chapter also cannot adequately reproduce the variety of visual data that can be found within the incel community and the manosphere in general. It plays an important part in the manosphere and how fantasies are circulated through visual representations.
3 Race is an important aspect of the manosphere and how men who are not white articulate their subject positions in relation to whiteness. Specifically, incels who are not white often write that their chances of dating women are further diminished compared to white men because of their ethnicity. This leads to forms of internalised or self-racism in which some incels describe themselves as 'currycels', 'blackcels', 'ricecels', or other terms (see Chapter 2). In that sense, such forms of self-racism are consistent with the general incel worldview which articulates a profound self-hatred. Some men have also formed their own versions of the manosphere for black or Latino men for example in order to discuss the same questions as the manosphere but without the white supremacism (Fountain 2019). Such communities are smaller than the larger fora on Reddit that I examined in this book. Further research is needed to specifically analyse whiteness and race in the incel community and the manosphere more widely. While I discuss race and fantasies of whiteness in this book, I have chosen to specifically focus on the fascist and anti-Semitic dimensions of incels and the manosphere in and how they come to be transferred onto women. Nonetheless, misogyny and racism frequently overlap in the manosphere.
4 Psychoanalysis understands defence mechanisms as un/conscious mechanisms to protect the ego against external threats that may cause anxiety or other states perceived to be as harmful by the ego. They distort or manipulate reality (Laplanche & Pontalis 1973, 103–107).
5 There are many threads in which incels discuss their *inhibition*; they mention the specific terms 'high' or 'low inhib' to denote that they feel too inhibited to interact with females in real life. We could frame such narratives in terms of social anxiety or inhibition, but the absolutely *disinhibited* behaviour that incels display online seems to serve as a way of symbolically countering their real inhibition. In fact, some incels have written that being and feeling part of the community has made them less inhibited in social situations.

6 Throughout the book, thread titles of forum posts are shown in bold and italics. Mistakes and typos in posts have been retained.
7 This retreat into isolation is often discussed as possibly leading to suicide (what incels call 'roping' or 'suifuel' = when they see content that only amplifies their thoughts to commit suicide, or LDAR = 'lie down and rot'). Such posts show the incel as a loner who perhaps finds commiseration in being online with other incels.
8 Containment is a psychoanalytic term by Wilfred Bion (1963) which describes an intersubjective model in which someone (the infant or the patient) who experiences something (pain or dissatisfaction for example) and is in search of and being found by the mother/the analyst. The mother/other can sense the infant's/patients feelings (distress) and reacts to them in a manner that is soothing. In this dynamic model there is simultaneously a 'searching' and a 'being found/responding' (Ogden 2004, 1345).
9 The figure of the black Chad is called 'Tyrone' by incels and featured less in the data that I examined for this book. There is thus an explicit focus on whiteness that is apparent in the incel community.

Chapter 5

Men Going Their Own Way – MGTOW: woman shall (not) exist

This chapter discusses data from another community within the manosphere: Men Going Their Own Way, or MGTOW. The community consists more of a diversity of ages than incels. Members often write about their backgrounds, but there is no accurate data on the class and ethnic backgrounds of MGTOW available. I analyse some material from the r/MGTOW subreddit in order to further inquire into the kind of male fantasies that are produced within the manosphere. I also return to incels, as there are many similarities between the two communities. This chapter engages more fully with the work of Elisabeth Young-Bruehl (1996). Her book on prejudice has lost nothing of its importance. I discuss Young-Bruehl's development of Freud's character types in order to argue, based on data from the last and this chapter, that incels and MGTOWs are obsessional characters whose fantasies revolve around women. As I go on to show, those men also display hysterical character traits which they first introject and then project[1] outwards: a desire for women. This desire for, and love of, women is so intolerable, as it is in tension with the obsessional hatred of women, that it is (attempted to be) suppressed. Such dynamics are further illustrations of the states of dis/inhibition that those men of the manosphere are in. In this chapter, I outline what kind of men those men (typically) are and what their characters are like.

I also discuss the question why the kind of fascist masculinity that those men (desire to) embody is so appealing to them. This points to questions of homosexual erotics within fascism and I consider if the men of the manosphere are also drawn to forming such male spaces because of latent homoerotic feelings. I end the chapter by returning to questions of the unconscious and point to data from incels and MGTOWs that discusses their parents. They wish to unconsciously annihilate their parental *imagos*, because they blame their parents for their miseries. This is a theme I fully develop in the next chapter by focussing on the status of the father for the men of the manosphere and beyond.

Men Going Their Own Way is a community of men who either think of, or have actively, left women behind. They are on their own and claim that they

DOI: 10.4324/9781003031581-5

are finally able to enjoy life. The community is full of posts and also photos where men show their newly found solitary and masculinised lifestyle. The Southern Poverty Law Center argues that MGTOW is situated on the fringes of the incel community (2018, online). While the definitive origins of MGTOW are unclear, the term has been around since the early 2000s. There is some evidence that the community emerged in its current form out of the Red Pill community around 2015 (Zuckerberg 2018). MGTOW is a male supremacist community which advocates male separatism and often strongly overlaps with the alt-right. There are different social media presences and websites of MGTOW, including a strong presence on YouTube. There has been little research specifically on this community (Lin 2017; Jones, Trott & Wright 2019). In her analysis of MGTOW, Jie Liang Lin writes:

> MGTOW believe modern women have been 'brainwashed' by feminism to believe 'they are right no matter what.' She will 'ride the cock carousel' with as many men as possible, most of whom will mistreat her and valorize her feminist claims of victimhood. When women do decide to settle for a man, he will be a passive 'beta-type,' whom she will boss around and target for his 'utility value'—financial assets and stability. (Lin 2017, 89)

Like other communities in the manosphere, MGTOW is made up of individuals with varying viewpoints and degrees of separatism. Some argue that men should avoid all contact with females and 'go monk' and abstain from sex and masturbation. Others oppose such views. As Lin (2017, 93) argues, what unites all MGTOWs is that they 'had alienating experiences, which consequently made them realize double standards exist that do not work in their favor. They realize they have been taught to buy into this unequal system by seeking validation in women'. This of course does not mean that such a worldview is the truth. It is how some men feel.

On the MGTOW subreddit, there are also many photos uploaded by users that seems to document a blissful and *aestheticised* life experience which shows what their male lifestyle looks like, for example by posting photos of travelling alone, or treating themselves to an expensive purchase for example. The MGTOW community is full of narratives that celebrate male solitude and male independence. Men congratulate each other for their achievements. In a sense, MGTOW is the next step from the incel community. While incels are locked in a complex mode of desire that focuses on the destruction and wanting of females, MGTOW men have left such a conflict behind. They are free and can freely articulate their rejection of women – or so it seems. While anti-feminism is a strong theme of MGTOW, the community, compared to many of the incel discussions, also features more banal and communal discussions about life and a male lifestyle in general such as discussions about cooking or other hobbies. The overall tone and atmosphere of MGTOW is more benign and positive than that of incels (many MGTOWs do not follow the idea of the black pill and often have a more positive outlook on life); this does not mean that it is not coupled with deep misogyny and hatred. There are broadly speaking two types of MGTOW posts; one that celebrates male independence and strength (which seems to be in the minority) and the other that discusses the 'evil' nature of women and highlights how men have been oppressed, abused or deluded by women (which seem to make up the majority of posts on r/MGTOW). The below post presents a good summary of the MGTOW worldview.

> *What They're Actually Like*
> One thing I've been thinking about is the colossal disparity between the actual nature of women and what we read in the media. For example, you have all the press about the pay gap, Me Too, rape, 'grab them by the pussy' and on and on and on. And yet, Fifty Shades of Grey sold 125 million copies, and was translated into 52 languages. Obviously, that novel, which is about BDSM, degradation, submission and so on, really appealed to a lot of women. Like, a world record number of women. (Reddit 2019b, online)

Such narratives are very similar to incels and other men of the manosphere. A recurring theme is that there are apparently double standards when it comes to how women behave, and that men need to understand and wake up to them. Themes such as hypergamy and the alleged superficiality of women that I discussed in the previous chapter also appear in the above posts. A nuanced understanding of female empowerment, desire or consent is completely absent from the above narrative. It seems unthinkable for those men that particular forms of sexuality and feminism can go together.

The same move as in the incel community is deployed over and over again in MGTOW as well. A singular experience is abstracted into generic, universal laws that concern all women. One user writes that he was cheated on by his wife and as hurtful as such experiences are, he concludes: 'I will never view anything the same ever again'. Such thinking may perhaps be characterised as immature and as occurring in the moment, a passionate reaction to hurt feelings or particular experiences. Nonetheless, such responses are recorded online and are shared widely in many different forms, thereby contributing to a *cementing* of particular beliefs and ideologies. We may describe such narratives as immature and paranoid-schizoid in the Kleinian sense. MGTOWs and incels are unable to differentiate and see nuances between others. All women are the same and this worldview is hammered into their brains by the men, who remind themselves and affirm those sentiments. As with other communities of the manosphere, MGTOW has grown and been amplified by the surge in anti-feminist and misogynist content online ever since the Trump election campaign of 2015 and the rise of the alt-right (Zuckerberg 2018).

What is the consequence of such a masculinist worldview? GYOW, in MGTOW terms. Go your own way. Such narratives of newly found freedom and independence are often discussed in the community. I explore them in more detail in the next section.

MGTOW and the necessary fantasy of woman

In this section I show how MGTOWs and also incels depend on the fantasy of women which is upheld rather than being rejected or left behind. While the MGTOW lifestyle seems about a life without women, the men depend on a fantasy about the cis woman as an abstract, universal category. I further analyse this fantasy through psychoanalytic theories of anti-Semitism and prejudice, because the same dynamics are in place here. Two users write about their new lifestyles of alleged male solitude:

> *You can do it too!!*
> I work a $16/hr job (full time) and can afford a $1k apartment. Single and happy. Everyone asks me why i dont have a girlfriend and i tell them i simply dont want one. The average response to my rent cost is 'wow thas alot' (its not lol) After bills im left with $1200 per month to spend however i want. I can cook whatever i want anytime of the day. I can try new restaurants and i can pick whatever one i want without a second opinion. I can go fishing whenever. If i want to move to a new neighborhood/state, no problem! I dont have to fight over the tv or when its time to stop playing ps4. I can leave the toilet seat up for a quicker pee. Its not much but i cherish this freedom. They say money cant buy happiness but having this money to my self somehow makes me more happy than sharing it with a gf. That says something about the modern woman. (Reddit 2019c, online)

> *I am honestly three times more happier since i follow MGTOW*
> I look back at all my past relationships and all the wasted time and I feel like a fool, but also I am gratefull because if it wasnt for all that heartache i will have never evolved into what I am today. I was always depressed because my whole existence was based on getting women. Once i removed that completly I lost 100 pounds got jacked got rich started learning 3 more languages graduated college stoped using drugs and now I am never bored. I use all 24 hours of the day to keep evolving I dont use them tryng to get the love of my life (LOOL i know) and now I get 4 times more Women than before they harrass me now but I dont even want them anymore. I jerk off and continue with my life each time I have an urge. Right now I spend my time traveling and working out and I love It. (Reddit 2019d, online)

Another man is 'living on a sailboat', to which another user replies: 'Living the dream. Steady winds and don't get distracted by the sirens'. I would not necessarily want to critique such narratives of male solitude, if they were not coupled with the misogyny and hatred discussed earlier. While the men may genuinely enjoy the kind of MGTOW lifestyle they detail online and it seems that many of them in fact practice it, there are still strong fantasmatic components to it which are worthy of unpacking further. The men detail a kind of solitary enjoyment without women where men can live a type of nomadic life amongst themselves with no females in sight. At the same time, even those who have supposedly succeeded in becoming MGTOW still continuously post *about* MGTOW and women online. Their detailing of their successful transformations is still implicitly (and also often explicitly) referring to those who they have seemingly managed to exclude: women.[2]

One user who Lin (2017) interviewed for her study, wrote: 'It may sound contradictory, but like the Buddhist enlightenment once a person has embraced MGTOW they no longer need MGTOW' (Lin 2017, 87). This is a denial of the role that women play in the fantasmatic construction of MGTOW. They and MGTOW cannot be left behind by the men. The fantasies of complete male solitude can only work *because* they depend on women as a fantasy construction. As we saw in the previous chapter, the more the Jew/woman is annihilated, the more vivid they become for the anti-Semite/incel. For MGTOW alike, woman is the 'perfect enemy…who does not exist' (Frosh 2016, 65) but always persists (see also Frosh 2005). As Slavoj Žižek writes: 'This paradox, which has already emerged apropos the Jews in Nazi Germany…the more they were ruthlessly exterminated, the more horrifying were the dimensions acquired by those who remained' (Žižek 1994, 78, cited in Frosh 2016, 65).

This leaves us with two questions: would MGTOWs who have gone 'full monk' as they call it or live in a kind of male solitude, still post online? Who would they blame for any hang ups, problems, or worries that occur to them as part of the MGTOW lifestyle? The answer, according to Frosh and Žižek, would be: women. MGTOW and the manosphere in general depend on women as the Other. If all women were suddenly gone, their communities and egos would collapse. Woman is thus both symbolically 'written off' in such narratives and at the same time fantasmatically held on to.

Such dynamics can be further analysed through Young-Bruehl and I introduce her theory of prejudice in the next section. It is useful in order to examine the kind of characters that MGTOW and incels are.

A psychoanalysis of MGTOW and incel characters: affirmation and denial of difference

In *The Anatomy of Prejudices*, Elisabeth Young-Bruehl (1996) writes that sexists are 'people who cannot tolerate the idea that there exist people not like them. Their prejudice has a narcissistic foundation' (Young-Bruehl 1996, 35). Male sexists feel challenged by women's gender identity and threatened with castration, for that reason they need to insist on boundaries and 'genital intactness' (ibid, 35). For Young-Bruehl, sexism is a manifestation of men's fears of becoming women. It is for that reason that sexism seeks dominance and control over women, in particular women's sexuality and reproduction. As she argues, sexism is multi-layered and simultaneously insists on gender differences and denies differences at the same time. This dialectical view of prejudice makes Young-Bruehl's position so useful for this book. I argue that the men of the manosphere both desire and deny dependence on and romantic attachment to women. This contradictory desire is characterised by dis/inhibition, and also un/conscious dimensions, as I outline in this and the coming chapters.

Young-Bruehl advances this idea of insistence and denial of (sexual) difference by discussing different prejudices (see Introduction in this book) and argues that underneath them all lies a layer that *denies* difference, a layer that wants to abolish difference and otherness rather than maintain it. This goes against common theories of prejudice that argue that there is an other that needs to be maintained as a scapegoat, space for projections and so on (ibid, 134). She introduces a nuanced differentiation between sexism and racism and anti-Semitism in her book. While I have conflated the two up to this point, and I think there are many similarities, it is useful at this stage to discuss how sexism is different from racism or anti-Semitism. Young-Bruehl would have possibly disagreed with Stephen Frosh's and Slavoj Žižek's conceptualisations of anti-Semitism as needing to *maintain* the Other: 'The antisemite does not want to keep the Other in place; he or she wants to attack the Other...and cleanse the world of him or her' (ibid, 134). I agree with her arguments but would try to integrate the two views on prejudice by her and Frosh/Žižek. For example, one can say that whilst sexism is similar to anti-Semitism, it operates through a double layer of rejection *and* (desire of) affirmation. Integrating the view on prejudice that argues that it is about a fantasmatic maintenance of the Other with the view that racism, fascism, sexism or misogyny are about annihilation of the Other is useful because both dimensions are inherent to the male fantasies that I discuss in this book. In such fantasies, the female Other is both denied and desired.

This double layer of rejection and desire within prejudice is the case for the manosphere where the ultimate layer of an annihilation of the Other and thereby of difference is at its core. To be sure, this layer is only perpetuated through the unconscious (sexist-misogynist) emphasis of and *desire of* sexual difference. This is, as I have outlined, certainly the case for incels, who desire and reject women. It is even more so the case for MGTOW who, at first glance, are all about rejecting women but this rejection is perpetuated through an underlying layer of heterosexual desire for women. In that sense, and this is perhaps not surprising, sexism (and by extension misogyny) is more life-affirming in its destructiveness than anti-Semitism or racism.

Young-Bruehl argues that sexism is multi-layered and structured by two intertwined forms of sexism, which she refers to as 'sameness sexism' and 'difference sexism' (ibid, 419). Sameness sexism is a kind of originary, or earlier, form of sexism that denies difference and narcissistically affirms sameness by postulating that women are inferior or weaker men. Young-Bruehl writes that sameness sexism is found in early biological theories which described women's bodies as being similar but inferior versions of their male counterparts when for example women's genitalia were described as inward-shaped penises. However, as 'women keep stepping out of their definitions and the reality of sexual difference keeps reintruding' (ibid, 420), difference sexism starts to take hold. Women assert themselves and are seen as different beings with their own identities, desires, lives and motivations and this brings about 'the greatest uncertainty' (ibid, 402) in men. Woman is pushed away (into the private realm) and becomes an Other for men. Femaleness is driven 'beyond the realm of the human and into nothingness' (ibid, 422). Nonetheless, as I read Young-Bruehl, one can see that those two forms of sexism are somewhat intertwined. Sameness sexism 'is always underneath' (ibid, 419) difference sexism and the two 'do not appear in completely discrete individual or social forms' (ibid). I would argue that they are messily intertwined, rather than neatly layered on top of each other as Young-Bruehl seems to imply. Such a conceptualisation of sexism allows us to see its inherently affirming and negating qualities. While there are differences between misogyny and sexism, as discussed in Chapter 4 and below (Manne 2018), I would nonetheless argue that Young-Bruehl's theorisation of sexism can also be applied to misogyny. Misogyny can be seen as a particularly violent form of sexism which serves to strengthen male power and harm women.

But are sexism and misogyny sufficient as categories to analyse incels and MGTOW? If misogyny is a crass form of sexism, a particular hateful version of sexism, the MGTOW and incel and other men's communities are deeply fearful of women and of changing gender relations. Sexism and misogyny are about putting women in their place so that male privilege can be sustained. Both operate with a complex dialectic of embracing/constructing and destroying/castrating the figure of the phallic woman. Sexism and misogyny work through a strange non-/relation between women and men (or other gender identifications). Such discourses are dependent on women so that they can be endlessly taken up and discarded discursively, picked up again and thrown away again.[3] Is MGTOW then post-sexist in some sort of way? No. On the one hand, as I have shown, MGTOW and incels are clearly misogynistic and sexist in how women are framed. On the other hand, many MGTOWs wish to leave women behind altogether. They are done with women. They dream up defensive fantasies of male brotherhood and camaraderie, represented as a kind of blissful male solitude. They seemingly do not need women any more in actual terms. While their inner worlds are structured by a dialectic of expulsion of and desire for women, as I have outlined, their actual, day-to-day interactions are – so they say – different. Many men write about how they have moved on and have gone their own way. The following example further illustrates my argument.

In/dependence

The popular MGTOW YouTuber Sandman discusses an experience another user wrote to him about. He reads out a message from the user first:

> I'm an 18-year-old college student who's fed up with the barren wasteland known as dating. Growing up girls always attack me for no apparent reason. I've heard that apparently I look like a paedophile or that I'm not actually that good-looking and other insults from girls all the way back to middle school. After not only these constant put-downs from girls but constant rejections I then decided it wasn't worth my time trying to find a worthwhile female.... Fast forward to now and I actually have no desire to date women at all. I see my male friends and relationships in living with their girlfriends in college, the best four years of your life, and I've completely focused on myself. I play football, wrestle and kickbox as well as an athlete on the rise. (Sandman 2016, 0.18–1.25)

Sandman, who has hundreds of MGTOW videos on YouTube, advises the other user to reject women if they approach him and want to be with him. He goes on to talk about how young athletes should focus on their careers and ignore women until they are ready to settle down. Being in a long-term relationship 'lowers a man's testosterone' and he has to work harder to keep it up. For that reason, women should be rejected. According to Sandman, we live in a society

> where men are being stripped of legal power in marriages, have to beg women to go out on dates with them and are basically lucky enough to find someone at all. The only real power we have is to reject women, women know this and they hate this and that's why they actually hate it when men go their own way. (Sandman 2016, 8.29–8.38)

Such a narrative is consistent with MGTOW and to a degree with a lot of the Men's Rights movements of pre-alt-right Reddit spheres as well as the contemporary MRAs. Leaving the weird and nonsensical 'arguments' aside, what seems striking about those MGTOWs who are allegedly going their own way is that they need to keep returning to the communities and to women. Their fantasy world is structured in a circular motion that revolves around women and *the need to write/post about them online*. Both the college student and Sandman proclaim that they have emancipated themselves from women and yet they still need to talk about women. Women haunt their fantasies, while the men may be able to avoid contact with them in their everyday lives or at least keep it to a minimum.

Sexism and misogyny thus operate here in a slightly different way than Young-Bruehl conceptualised it; for her sexism is about rejecting, then dominating the woman as Other. The kind of MGTOW narratives that I have discussed lay bare the complexities of a misogyny that is about a desire that is in itself split and painfully distorted at the intersections of wanting and hating women but ultimately manages to leave women behind on a practical level, to annihilate them symbolically, by ignoring and rejecting them (as detailed above). This means however that women continue to haunt the men as ghost-like figures, and it shows that for some of the MGTOW men, misogyny is similar to anti-Semitism or racism where the Other needs to be annihilated and left behind – rather than simply put in their place or dominated in the case of sexism, as Young-Bruehl argues. Of course, MGTOWs do not advocate the murder of women but they strive for a male solitude and an intimate life that is devoid of females. Having made the argument that MGTOWs and incels depend on the fantasy of woman so that their own identities can be sustained, I present more analyses of the character types that MGTOWs and incels are in the next section.

Incels and MGTOWs as obsessional characters

I also want to return to incels and the question of their psyches in more detail at this point. I discuss the commonalities between MGTOW and incels as far as their characters are concerned. In her landmark work *The Anatomy of Prejudices* (1996), Young-Bruehl isolates specific character types as being particularly receptive to prejudice.[4] There is one that can be directly related to the manosphere today: Obsessionals. Incels, MGTOWs and other misogynists on the alt-right have *obsessional* characters. While I have spent some time in the previous chapter outlining incels as proto-fascists who share similarities with Theweleit's soldier males, returning to them now and asking again 'What kind of people are incels or become incels?' will help to add further complexity to the wider arguments. Before doing so, I outline Young-Bruehl's discussion of the obsessional character type in general. Drawing on Freud's discussion of three basic character types (Freud 1932, 1981c), erotic, narcissistic and compulsive, she goes on to construct obsessional, narcissistic, hysterical character types in impressive detail. Young-Bruehl's intricate knowledge of psychoanalysis and how she critically synthesises psychoanalytic and more sociological and philosophical texts make her work truly psychosocial and of immense value for this book. She is interested in crafting a developmental theory of character types, with specific attention to prejudice, that is combined with questions of the social character and how societies encourage or shape particular character types. Her characterology presents characters as ideal types and there are of course variances and differences if we were to break down an obsessional character for an individual person for instance.

Obsessional characters, or individuals with obsessional character traits, are rigid, well-organised individuals, neat, 'aversive to dirt' (ibid, 210) but might also live in a chaos that they consider orderly and organised. They are 'mentally lucid' (ibid) and often of high intellectual capacity. They may become fixated on certain (mental) acts that are also tied to organisation, such as creating lists, going through motions mentally, creating scenarios which they endlessly repeat in their minds. This may also relate to actions which one might consider obsessive-compulsive, such as needing to perform certain actions over and over again, like hand washing. 'Obsessionals may rely on an *idée fixe* to organise themselves' (ibid, 211). They often idealistically and nostalgically refer to a mythic past and eclectically refer to ideas that they regard as pure or 'unsullied' (ibid, 211).

Obsessionals devote themselves to projects or tasks with painstaking attention. Only a task that requires great effort is worth doing in their eyes. Such activities can take on self-punishing qualities and obsessionals admonish themselves if they make mistakes or waste time. They 'find it difficult to admit defeat' (ibid, 212). Obsessionals associate themselves with categories and roles and often wear a uniform:

> Along with their tendency to identify with their tasks or projects or causes, obsessionals tend to identify with particular roles or social categories. They designate themselves as an 'X' (whether this is a religious group, a profession, an ethnicity, a gender). When they have assigned themselves a role, they feel secure in carrying out what they take to be its requirements. (Young-Bruehl 1996, 212)

Such pathological emphasis on routines not only stabilises the obsessional's psyche, it gives them a sense of worth and self-love, because they convince themselves that they are better, cleaner, more efficient, superior than others.

Freud drew a lineage between obsessionals and their childhood, specifically in relation to the anal phase. Obsessionals may be collectors or hoarders. Their character is linked with 'childhood anal retention and expulsion – manipulation of anal functions designed to control others, to be in command of situations that are threatening' (ibid, 213). Theweleit (1987) also argues that the male soldiers had a specific relationship to their bodies which is characterised by a negative perception of all bodily liquids, excretions, etc. The same goes for that of other bodies. There is a repulsion and attraction to them. Touching them, engaging with them, is seen as distinctly unmasculine. It is associated with cleaning, cleaning children, or cleaning the house. The soldier is afraid of and yet attracted to them. Theweleit traces this back to the development of the baby. For the baby, liquids and other substances and in particular their expulsion (crying, peeing, defecating, spitting, vomiting, etc.) are a form of release of affective tension. If such acts are then responded to with disgust and negation by the caregiver, the subject will eventually recognise them as bad. The Wilhelminian boy and young man is raised in strict opposition to such phenomena. They are banned unless they occur in their specific, sanitised spaces. With this cleanliness training comes a negation of sexuality and a fear of anything sexual. The body is banned from being used for sexual purposes.

Obsessionals often work in large, bureaucratic organisations where they can both be lost as one of many and figure as a powerful wheel in the grand scheme of things. Organisations where obsessionals have (the illusion of) power attract them: hospitals, psychiatric institutions, care homes, prisons. Places where they can call others 'messy and messed up' (ibid, 214). The obsessional defends in this way against their own dirty and messy desires – 'usually of an anal or sadomasochistic sort' (ibid) and connected to a desire where they want to be the opposite sex. 'The "others" are dirty, nasty, assertive and attacking' (ibid). The obsessional's desire to become the opposite sex is tied to passivity; they want to become a passive male or female. It is the others who are seen as attacking, dirty, filthy. The obsessional's ideal self 'is filtered of all impurities, all temptations, an imperturbable, perhaps even saintly self that cannot be attacked' (ibid). Their lives are rigidly organised so as to 'keep out of bounds all tempting states of relaxation or spontaneity that could allow them to be swept away, overwhelmed, or overstimulated' (ibid). Such processes render obsessionals incapable of introspection; everything is directed outward, purged out towards the other. The other's 'aggressive activities and plots and machinations need constant attention' (ibid, 215). A defence mechanism to deaden the obsessional's tabooed desires and self-questioning. In that way, obsessionals are free from guilt or blame. It is the other that is to blame for their problems and unhappiness.

At the same time, obsessionals have harsh, controlling, punishing superegos. If they are unable to fully offload their feelings onto the other, they resort to criticise themselves. They

> constantly complain of their own inadequacies – they should do this or that, they say; they must get organized, and be more disciplined, less wasteful and more productive, more able in relationships; they should be better more considerate, more self-sacrificing, and so forth. If only they could be good, they lament. Unable to displace blame, in a defeatist mode, they may say that they never will be happy, that they are bad people, whom no one should or could love. (Young-Bruehl 1996, 215)

In order to relieve themselves of their punishing super-egos, obsessionals must discharge such affective bodily states and shift them onto others. The same others who are designated as filthy and dirty are equipped with overwhelming intellectual power. 'They are powerful enough to run the world, to constitute an international conspiracy, to have a monopoly on shrewdness for amassing wealth' (ibid, 215). It is evident how anti-Semites and racists fit into this character category in how they think of the Jews or other groups. The other is thus both hated and envied.

The other is seen as a penetrator by the obsessional that must be gotten rid of symbolically as well as practically if conditions allow it. They are feared to be anally penetrating the obsessional, sneaking up from behind and stabbing them in the back. We can see strong similarities between the symbolic and physical annihilation of the other (woman, Jew, communist) that the Freikorps soldiers engaged in and that has been so vividly documented by Theweleit. Theweleit's soldier males were likewise obsessional characters who hated women in particular. Women were perceived as penetrating, phallic beings who threatened the soldier males with castration. The soldier males did not desire women in the way that obsessional incels and MGTOWs do, but the basic common denominator between the two remains. For both, anxiety 'about being overwhelmed, rendered ineffectual or inactive or passive, is key' (ibid, 219). I argue that both represent a heavily obsessional character with some elements of hysterical character tropes.

Young-Bruehl's study of the obsessional character, to me, reads like a psychoanalysis of incels and MGTOW. As other obsessionals, incels seem similarly aversive to dirt when they describe females as dirty and filthy (as they do in many posts). The same holds true for Theweleit's soldier males who experienced women as filthy floods who threatened to castrate and overwhelm them. As noted, obsessionals rely on an *ideé fixe* that organises their worldview. For incels and MGTOWs, this *ideé fixe* is women (and to a lesser degree Chads in the case of incels). As I have argued in detail in Chapters 3 and 4, the alt-right and its misogynists today refer to a mythic past, which was somewhere before 1968, in which (allegedly) a different gender order existed. This mythic past was orderly, pure and free of dirt. While I cannot say if incels or MGTOWs devote themselves to projects or tasks with painstaking attention, the attention with which they subscribe to their respective misogynistic ideologies is structured by detail, devotion and endless habitual repetition of discourses, ideas, fantasies and images. Incels and MGTOWs certainly have great difficulty in expressing that they might be (partly) in the wrong or admit defeat. By assigning themselves the role and collective identity of 'incel' or 'MGTOW', the men find security and a sense of belonging. This is only strengthened by their implicit and explicit allusions to fascism, as I have previously discussed. Such identifications with, and taking up of roles, can 'go to the point of self-caricature' (ibid, 212), as Young-Bruehl notes. This is certainly the case for the manosphere, at least to outsiders.

Incels and MGTOWs may not share the aspect of classic obsessionals with regards to keeping out everything that is filthy and dirty. In fact, incels, as Krüger notes (2021), demonstrate a kind of defiant self-soiling. At the same time, they, like obsessionals, defend against all spontaneity, passion and chance in order for their fragmented egos not to be overwhelmed. Theweleit discusses this similarly in relation to the Freikorps men.

All three (incels, MGTOW, Freikorps soldier males) show an incapability of introspection and self-criticism. Incels' destructive self-undoing is devoid of any nuanced introspection. All fault lies with the other. Incels – unlike MGTOW who have left that stage behind – also can often be seen complaining about their own inadequacies; while the blame is shifted onto the other.

At the same time, as Young-Bruehl notes, the other is also envied; ascribed with enormous power and capable of running the world, pulling all the strings. This is certainly the case for incels and MGTOW who designate women, quite literally, as the new Jews (see the previous chapter and earlier discussions in this chapter). Additionally, incels and MGTOWs also show hysterical character traits.

Hysterical characters

Young-Bruehl goes on to discuss hysterical characters.[5] Hysterical characters are more explicitly tied to the erotic than obsessionals are. They are attractive and manipulative. They are vain and concerned with appearance. They are seductive and always in relationships – whether in reality or in fantasy. Perhaps we could say that the quintessential image of agentic, male and female sexuality today is that of the hysterical. Hedonistic, appearance-based and selfish. Hysterical characters are the Chads and Stacys of our time, ultra-masculine or ultra-feminine. They regard life as exciting and often take part in risky or even illegal activities. While incels are by no means archetypical hysterical characters, they nonetheless bear some character traits of hysterics that are specifically connected to desire. An obsession with strength, sex and appearance. Young-Bruehl outlines the hysterical character type:

> Both male and female hysterical characters tend to rely heavily on projection for defending themselves against their libidinal and aggressive impulses – they unconsciously make over or transfer to others their impulses. When they are prejudiced, as I have noted, they have projected their desires onto the objects of their prejudice, the others have become an image of their forbidden or frustrated desires. But this means that the others, while classified as forbidden, are also alluring, as the drives they bear are still alluring (which is not the case with the

people who become the vessels for the obsessionals' displacements, who are judged disgusting and repellent). Hysterical types protectively identify with the people who bear their projections, they are bound to them, like doubles, even while they fear that the victims may reveal or expose them. (Young-Bruehl 1996, 229)

The Freikorps soldiers bore no characteristics of hysterical characters, quite the opposite. However, incels bear some hysterical elements. They are obsessional first and hysterical second, but they also project their sexual impulses onto Stacys and Chads. The Stacy and Chad bear the image of the incels' *frustrated* desires of strength, beauty and oozing sexuality and constant sexual availability. Such *imagos* are influenced by the wider diffusion of mainstream pornography, whereby porn actors are essentially presented as hysterical: hypermasculine or -feminine, superficial and obscenely sexualised. The mass circulation and consumption of images of perfect bodies via Instagram and other platforms has also shaped the construction of hysterical characters both in how ordinary users present themselves and how the men of the manosphere perceive others to be (see Chapters 2 and 7).

For hysterics, it is the other who is having too much fun and getting too much erotic satisfaction from life. By rendering the other as uncivilised, raw and sexually restless, they are lowered and denigrated by hysterics, kept in his/her place and deprived of (sexual) agency. The Stacy and Chad are highly alluring, sexually potent and simultaneously constructed as forbidden, as I have shown. At the same time, they are rendered disgusting, dirty, superficial, etc. as an obsessional defence mechanism against such hysterical projections. However, incels are by no means, by their own admission, hysterical characters. They are not seductive, attractive or manipulative.

How then can they bear some character dimensions of hysterics? I argue that there is a temporal stage *before* the projection (that Young-Bruehl details in relation to hysterics) that takes place for incels. As obsessionals, they firstly *introject* the Stacy and the Chad. Such psychic mechanisms are so conflictual and tense for incels that they must project them outwards again onto the Other. They must defend against the very sexual desire and superficiality they have taken in and which is consequently projected onto the Stacy/Chad. The Stacy/Chad is desired and incels want to be Chads and be with a Stacy, and rejected, because incels are *betraying their own obsessional character by allowing themselves to be hysterical*. Those are dis/inhibition dynamics. For that reason, the allegedly dirty, lustful and superficial Chad and Stacy are rejected and need to be destroyed. Incels find themselves in a conflictual and contradictory *double-bind* position which is revealed through the different themes that I have discussed in the previous chapter. Love and hate, powerlessness and agency, self-victimisation and toxic power.

'For obsessionals, women are impure, sullied creatures, oversexed, aggressive, and corrupting. Both the hysterical character, and the obsessional operate narcissistically when they exhibit sexism or misogyny, but the narcissistic character thinks more generally and centrally in sexual terms of us and them' (Young-Bruehl 1996, 239). MGTOW in a sense present a similar psychodynamic to incels, but they appear to grapple with such contradictions differently by stressing their male independence in relation to women, rather than only discussing their frustrated desires (which nonetheless persist).

Incels and MGTOWs bear many traits of the obsessional character in how they present themselves online and they are also *cultivating* such a character at the same time, carving it out of ideological building blocks, handed to them by MRAs and the alt-right. This cultivating of the incel or MGTOW as ideal type is done consciously through creating a group identity that men can identify with and by writing what incels should do, be and feel. How they should act in response to women, as I have shown in the previous chapter. Such a character becomes self-perpetuating and is amplified through the thousands of posts online that lay the foundations of what it means to be, and claim to be, an incel or a MGTOW. My discussion here presents a development of Young-Bruehl's theory of the obsessional character, which she conceptualises as being largely fixed and as being kind of statically deployed by obsessionals towards an other. Such character types, while already in existence before certain men join the manosphere, are (re-) created and appropriated through the creation of symbolic identities within it. The character types have also emerged because of particular sociocultural conditions (see Chapters 2, 3 and 4).

I have argued so far in this book that the men of the manosphere embody a fascist state of mind, but they do not necessarily need to be fascists in order to do so. There are also presently no outright fascist societies in the Western world. It is worth asking, then, why fascism presents such a seductive and appealing worldview for many men today.

The erotics of fascism?

All this being said – there remains an underlying tension between my arguments in relation to the alt-right and the manosphere and their desire for fascism. We do not presently live in a fascist era, although many countries in Europe, but also the USA, or Brazil come dangerously close to such an era, but instead authoritarian capitalism is being attempted to be put into effect through right-wing populists (Fuchs 2018). There are specific economic and cultural conditions which have allowed for fascism to emerge again as a threat in many parts of the world today – for example rising unemployment, precarious and insecure working conditions, a growing number of refugees or global economic disputes (see Introduction and Chapter 2). In contrast to Theweleit's Freikorps soldiers, who were (proto-)fascist and were actively massacring their way towards the establishment of the Third Reich, many men today implicitly or explicitly *desire* fascism. It remains a fantasy that they conjure up or hope to bring about, but no practical reality. On a superficial level, the allure of fascism is evident for those men and this is discussed at length by Theweleit (see Chapter 1). Fascism produces and provides the body armour to patch up the men's fragmented egos. Fascism also consists of an inventory of images and belief systems on how men look like and who should be in control of women. Fascist prejudices against Jews and other groups are appropriated by the alt-right and the manosphere against women, as I have discussed in this book so far.

Are there deeper, underlying factors that speak to the mobilisation of fascist images and discourses by those groups? Many authors, including Young-Bruehl, have specifically discussed the erotic qualities of fascism. Klaus Theweleit has argued that the soldier males of the 1920s wished to do away with sexuality and drives as such. It is by becoming a soldier that women and sexuality can finally be left behind. It is the act of killing that specifically desexualises the men's lives. For Wilhelm Reich, fascism was also characterised by sexual repression. Fascism seeks to extinguish sexuality. Susan Sontag similarly described fascism as a channelling of sexuality into energy: 'The fascist ideal is to transform sexual energy into a "spiritual" force, for the benefit of the community. The erotic (that is, women) is always present as a temptation, with the most admirable response being a heroic repression of the sexual impulse' (Sontag 1981, 93). In her essay *Fascinating Fascism*, Sontag characterises fascism as:

> The fascist dramaturgy centers on the orgiastic transactions between mighty forces and their puppets, uniformly garbed and shown in ever swelling numbers. Its choreography alternates between ceaseless motion and a congealed, static, 'virile' posing. (Sontag 1981, 91)

Inhibition-disinhibition dynamics are at play in fascist movements. A kind of release and restraint representation of bodies and masses where 'movements are confined, held tight, held in' (ibid, 93). For Sontag, it is in particular the visual aspect of fascism (that is German National Socialism in her case) that is alluring and has in fact been taken up by artists who are non-fascist but nonetheless play with fascist symbols and imagery. It is also been taken up in a kind of BDSM (bondage, discipline, dominance and submission, sadism and masochism) style by erotica and pornography. For Sontag, the practice of BDSM is itself fascist. 'Sadomasochism has always been the furthest reach of the sexual experience: when sex becomes most purely sexual, that is, severed from personhood, from relationships, from love' (ibid, 105). Sontag goes on to note that it 'should not be surprising that it has become attached to Nazi symbolism in recent years. Never before was the relation of masters and slaves so consciously aestheticized' (ibid). Fascism in itself not only has an erotic dimension, but it has been taken up and specifically eroticised by cultural practices. This point is critically and nuancedly explored by Laura Frost in *Sex Drives: Fantasies of Fascism in Literary Modernism* (2001). She argues against an inherently erotic or alluring-arousing dimension of fascism. Instead, Western fascism is sexualised in an anti-fascist culture following 1945. Psychoanalytic theory itself has contributed to this eroticisation of fascism. Contra to Sontag, Frost notes that sexually deviant or allegedly abnormal practices (like BDSM) were often named fascistic by commentators in order to outlaw or banish them from what was considered the norm. Fascism is not inherently erotic, but is taken up as a stylistic device and eroticised by writers, filmmakers, artists, etc. Michel Foucault made the same argument when he noted that Eros was completely absent from Nazism (Frost 2001). 'The discharge of sanctioned violence serves to maintain the fascist machinery, whereas orgasmic discharge threatens to dissolve its unity' (Frost 2001, 111). Fascism is thus imagined as a particular sexual dynamic which is exaggerated by those who want to render it particularly sado-masochistic, homosexual, or in any other form sexual.

However, such arguments can, in my view, not completely disempower the argument that fascism, or German Nazism in its specificity, was inherently asexual or desexualised. In its delibidinisation of sexuality and in shifting the emphasis away from sexuality – for example through propaganda, through the killings of gays and lesbians, through the desexualised Freikorps (and later SS) men who Theweleit describes – fascism nonetheless maintained a kind of relational non-relation with sexuality, or a coupling with sexuality in its negativity. Fascism as a propaganda machine and authoritarian system may *promise* to do away with sexuality, but in reality could, of course, not eradicate it or channel it exclusively into a pure, desexualised culture. Fascism as a form of male bonding is, for Theweleit, also not specifically tied to homosexuality or a latent form of (prohibited) homosexual desire. While incels and MGTOW are characterised by their male exclusivity and banishing of female users, their virtual bonding does not seem to be of a gay nature. In fact, references to homosexuality are scarce within the communities. However, I argue that it is the *phallic* nature of fascism that is so attractive to incels and other men today. Such an attractiveness has at least *some* sexual and erotic undercurrents that may remain unconscious to the men. They may be drawn to the fantasy of masculine strength of fascism because it stimulates latent homoerotic feelings and is narcissistically arousing. On the surface, fascism is so alluring to incels because it promises strength and a defence against female sexuality.

> The fascist treatment of woman promotes a female image that extends grandiose imaginary ideals of masculinity (e.g. toughness, bravery, self-discipline, self-determination etc.). This bolsters male domination and

the image of the vigorous superiority of man, which feminism opposes. (Vadolas 2009, 72)

Fascist 'masculinity is formed by the fear and loathing of the feminine as the image that haunts male fantasies and nurtures destructive impulses' (ibid, 71). Fascism is taken up very consciously by incels and other men on the internet and beyond today – but what about the unconscious that pushes them towards fascism in the first place? As I have discussed in Chapter 1, Theweleit argued that the soldier males almost had no unconscious. Their fears were conscious to them and they acted to counter them, but there are some unconscious aspects of the incel and MGTOW discourses.

Where is the unconscious?

It was alluded to in the last chapter that incels thematise their families and ways of upbringing when they evoke genetics and discuss their looks. They blame their parents for their ugliness or deficiencies. There are also threads that specifically discuss the incels' mothers and fathers. Two users write:

> ***My chad brothers***
> I fucking hate myself for being such a loser compared to my brothers. I've accepted that I'll never be as good as them and am haunted by memories of them picking on me and thinking of me as no more that a little annoyance. I'm mentally and physically inferior as my mother chose to have me at the age of 32. She didn't help either as she only serves to lay a good thick layer of wording on me about how disappointed she is, and she is unaware as to how depressed I felt ever since I was 13. (Reddit 2018f, online)

> ***daydreaming about the life i would have wanted***
> just try to imagine.......being born in a nuclear family, having a dad around growing up, to share his life experience with you and help you avoid whatever mistakes he might have made. seeing your parents as people you can trust and work with, not entities you are deathly afraid of and must strive to appease in order to avoid their wrath ... bust no. i got what i got. (Reddit 2018g, online)

Two users reply to another user's question about what their family backgrounds are:

> abusive single mother told me i was an accident and parents got a divorce after i was born. Not a looksmatch [no potential female partner who looks like him] as dad was a betabux [beta male] (Reddit 2018h, online)

> My parents are not bad people but they make a shitty family. My dad had severe depression when he was young and always lived in his own world: he doesn't care about anything or anyone but himself. My mom has anxiety problems since she had and heart attack years ago. This + the emotional baggage she had from her childhood made her unstable emotionally, and she projected this on me. The result? I am an insecure and awakward idiot. Plus they fight continously and this led me to some nervous breakdowns. (Reddit 2018h, online)

In the above, we can see similar dynamics of individuation to Theweleit's discussion of the soldier males who want to overcome and destroy their parental *imagos*. Incel and MGTOW men wish to annihilate their mothers and fathers, because it is *them* who they blame as being responsible for the misery (in how they look, act, are). They have the unconscious wish of killing their parents. Parents, who have castrated them or not provided them with the phallus (as far as incels are concerned) and the men are then castrated a second time by all the women that follow. Only by doing so can they 'ascend', as incels call it, and be reborn as a fascist Chad. Like the soldier males from Theweleit's books, some contemporary men wish to transcend themselves and become a new man. However, most incels do not do so. They do not kill their families (or others) and while they are conscious of their hatred for their families, their wish for destruction of them remains unconscious. Except some men do and commit violent crimes, as I discuss in the next chapter.

Conclusion

This chapter discussed the MGTOW community and how their desires are structured around the contradictions of an *absent presence* of woman. While they may not be as overtly destructive, racist and political as incels, men who post in the community still present strong misogynistic and sexist views. I have underscored this through the discussion of a video of the popular MGTOW YouTuber Sandman. I then proceeded to argue that incels and MGTOW constitute obsessional character types, and in the case of incels with added on hysterical characteristics.

The obsessional character is of course at least in part also formed through childhood and adolescence, before men go on to join an incel or MGTOW forum; there are predispositions for such a character. But such predispositions are taken up and manoeuvred into becoming fully incel/MGTOW by the men online when they endlessly discuss *what* and *how* incels/MGTOWs are and are not. Young–Bruehl also traces the formation of specific character types back to an individual's upbringing and subjectivisation (see Chapter 1). Incels – unlike MGTOW which consists more of a diversity of ages (but this is difficult to say for sure) – seem to largely consist of young (mostly white) men between 15 and 30 years. (incels have conducted some surveys of their own communities which suggest this.) The adolescent male is of course of a specific character. While I do not want to mobilise the immaturity or youthfulness of incels to explain or excuse their misogyny, it is nonetheless a potential factor that needs to be mentioned. Young-Bruehl writes about adolescents:

> Most ominously, an adolescent whose anxiety over object ties is especially strong may escape them by regression in all parts of his or her personality. The boundaries of the ego become permeable, and the objects may be drawn into it (a process of identification), or the ego may become involved in projections that obscure the difference between the internal and the external world. Such efforts, towards delibidinizing the objects, may reduce anxiety, but they also create another anxiety at the possibility of what Anna Freud termed 'emotional surrender, with the accompanying fear of loss of identity'. (Young-Bruehl 1996, 314)

Prejudices provide an identity in such a situation and create boundaries and stability. 'I hate, therefore I am' (ibid, 315). Incels may have a similar anxiety over object ties and respond with a mixture of projection and identification. Like children, incels (no matter their age) and MGTOW divide the world into good and evil – a fundamental manic characteristic of the alt-right in general. The Freikorps soldiers, incels and MGTOW all feel threatened by a phallic woman. For Young-Bruehl, 'the narcissistic fantasy of the phallic woman is at the motivational core of the many layers and forms of sexism' (ibid, 297). Men feel undermined by women and resort to sexism or misogyny. 'Of all the types of prejudices, the obsessional prejudices are the most ambivalent' (ibid, 348), as I have shown. For incels and MGTOW, 'the group that is feared as corrupting and destructive is also the group that is, without acknowledgement, unconsciously, the most alluring' (ibid, 348). Young-Bruehl argues that such ambivalence manifests itself in doubt and indecision, which is curtailed by a leader figure. MGTOW and incels have no leader, they embody a kind of collective function and regularly remind themselves (incels even use the expression 'daily reminder' for this) to 'never waver, never turn back, never reconsider, never be anything less than hard, steely, a beacon in any darkness' (ibid, 348). The latter aspects (be hard, steely and a beacon) are, as I have shown, expressed as desires by incels. They want to become hard, fascistic men with bodies of steel.

Young-Bruehl writes about the leader of obsessionals that: 'People outside of the group may find the leader fanatical, but the followers feel the leader's rigidity as – to use metaphors that are psychoanatomically precise – their backbones, their sphincter control' (ibid, 348). Such dynamics of restraint and release, quite literally of shit (Krüger 2021), are taken care of by incels themselves. They do not need a leader. Incels in particular, as such dynamics are less but still observable for MGTOW – present dynamics of dis/inhibition through which they not only attempt to (unsuccessfully) control their own desire, but also describe the Other as disinhibited and overwhelming.

Such alleged disinhibition is responded to with *dis/inhibition*. Inhibition by restraining themselves from being friendly and loving with a female; disinhibition by pouring out their hatred of females online. Their own contradictions are also inhibited and negated. Their own soft elements, female dimensions and desire to be loved by others are inhibited (but never go away completely). Such problems relate to more general dilemmas of today's neoliberal consumer capitalism as I have shown in Chapter 2. While incels and MGTOW and the progressive, liberal characters of shows like *Girls* or *Casual* could not be further from each other, both struggle with fantasies of sexual desire as they are shaped by ideologies and images circulated through digital media. Both can be seen as symptoms of a wider cultural development in neoliberalism centred on choice and sexual agency, which was partly enabled through the sexual revolution, the ideology of postfeminism and the current mediated form of sexuality through hook-up apps.

Contemporary capitalism suggests that one can have it all when it comes to sex but because humans are to a degree inherently neurotic when it comes to relating to each other, such a fantasy is necessarily disappointed. It is responded to by reactionary and alt-right YouTubers by mobilising a kind of hell on earth scenario where feminism and other developments are the cause. It is responded to by the manosphere, incels and MGTOW in particular, by expressing their own kind of dis/inhibition that turns away from women while inherently being connected to heterosexual desire of them. All such forms of dis/inhibition relate to underlying anxiety. Anxiety about attractiveness, being desired, desiring the other, as well as a perverted notion of sexual market value which both wider mainstream culture and incels evoke in discussions of attractiveness, Tinder and hook-up apps, sex and detached sexuality. They may also relate to the crisis of masculinity that I discussed in Chapter 2 and in the previous chapter with reference to neoliberalism.

Wilhelm Reich was wrong when he hoped that a progressive and educated form of sexuality would serve as a kind of bulwark against fascism (Reich 1997). Sexuality has in part been co-opted by capital. For some men today, it is the very culture of sexuality that leads them to desire fascism both in its bodily and regulatory form where the mythic past of fascism promised a different kind of sexuality. For some men, posting online about such themes is not enough; they kill others. The next chapter discusses two mass shooters and their misogynistic fantasies.

Notes

1 The psychoanalytic notion of 'projection' may be defined as a process where an individual unconsciously makes an external object embody certain attributes. It is a subjective process but the individual believes it to be an objective one. They may place thoughts, actions, narratives or interpretations in another subject and attribute them to the other. The individual has essentially displaced something but believes this is an objective, external phenomenon. Introjection refers to the opposite whereby a person internalises and reproduces an external object, behaviour or fantasy as that of their own (Perron 2005a, 1334–1336).
2 The idea of a masculinist and separatist lifestyle is of course not new. It has been discussed in relation to masculinity in film as a fantasy of narcissistic self-sufficiency by Steve Neale (1983). Neale argues that the male spectator engages in contradictory viewing and identification practices like assuming the active gaze of the male hero while also feeling inadequate and vulnerable himself. Such anxieties are defended against by mainstream Hollywood cinema in showing phallic weapons or fight scenes between men for example (see also Yates 2007). In the context of MGTOW, the men defend against feelings of lack and vulnerability by similarly assuming a fantasy of male self-sufficiency.
3 I am conscious of the fact that such a dialectic could (and has been) also explained through a Lacanian prism. For Lacan, sexuality itself functions as a kind of negative ontology, as Alenka Zupančič has shown (2017). She demonstrates through her famous 'coffee without cream – coffee without milk' joke (2017, 47–48) that 'without' something, or the lack of something, actually means 'with the lack of something' (ibid, 48). A total lack or entire absence is thus impossible for Lacanians. For MGTOWs and incels, *being without* women, rather than being truly alone, is thus a marker of the dialectics of desire and fantasy. In its negativity, both are able to hold on to the 'with-without' of woman.
4 Young-Bruehl develops Freud's basic three character types. In his characterology of the libidinal types (Freud 1932), Freud had argued that there are three main character types subjects can be grouped under: erotic, narcissistic and compulsive. Those depend on the level of investment of the libido within them. Young-Bruehl moves away from a pure focus on libido and develops a psychosocial conceptualisation of character types which take account of subjective and social dimensions.
5 Hysteria is a key and contested idea in the history of psychoanalysis. The early work of Freud and Breuer famously identified hysteria as a female condition. This led to justified criticism and debate within and beyond psychoanalysis. Feminists from the 1960s onwards critiqued Freud's sexism and problematic understandings of female sexuality (see Chapter 1). There is thus a sexual politics to the very concept of 'hysteria' and it is something that is socio-historically constructed (Veith 1965; Gilman et al. 1993). Juliet Mitchell has pointed out that male hysteria has historically been repressed in psychoanalysis. Over the past 50 years, hysteria has also steadily declined as a clinical diagnosis, but Mitchell makes the case for it to be taken seriously as a clinical condition. To her, eating disorders, borderline or multiple personality conditions can all be subsumed under hysteria. She particularly relates hysteria to conflicted sibling relationships (Mitchell 2000). For both Mitchell and Young-Bruehl, hysteria has sexual roots. It combines intense sexuality with a fear of destruction for the subject. This background to the term and how it is used by Young-Bruehl is important to keep in mind.

Chapter 6

The manifestos of mass shooters and the absent father

As noted in previous chapters, the manosphere has been associated with mass shootings and violence. Recent shootings by men have in particular been linked to a hatred of women in popular and scholarly discourses. For example, authors for the news websites *Vox* and *Daily Beast* as well as the newspaper *The New York Times* write:

> Rarely has the connection between sexual anxiety and right-wing nationalism been made quite so clear. Indeed, Breivik's hatred of women rivals his hatred of Islam, and is intimately linked to it. Some reports have suggested that during his rampage on Utoya, he targeted the most beautiful girl first. This was about sex even more than religion. (Goldberg 2017, online)

> Then in 2014, a self-identified incel went on a killing spree in Isla Vista, California.... The attacks were a turning point for the incel community. The killer's posts on PUAHate, a popular online forum among incels frustrated that pickup artist techniques weren't working for them, rendered the term 'incel' toxic.... But Rodger more than redefined the term 'incel': He helped reshape the ideas that the community would come to stand for, pushing its angriest and most nihilistic impulses to the fore. (Beauchamp 2019, online)

> [In 2018] Alek Minassian drove a truck into a crowd of pedestrians in downtown Toronto. Mr. Minassian, just before carrying out his attack, wrote a post on Facebook in which he proclaimed the arrival of an 'incel rebellion.'... This was an Islamic State-inspired attack minus the Islamic State ideology. (Cottee 2018, online)

In this chapter, I analyse the manifestos of two recent mass shooters:[1] Anders Behring Breivik and Elliot Rodger. Breivik detonated a bomb in Oslo and killed 69 young people on the nearby island Utøya in 2011. Elliot Rodger, who killed 6 and injured 14 UC Santa Barbara students in 2014, has

DOI: 10.4324/9781003031581-6

been recurrently referred to in the incel community. He is regarded as a hero by some incels and there are many memes about him (Witt 2020). Both manifestos are available online following a Google search. I do not intend to provide a platform for the hatred and mad ideas that are expressed within the manifestos, but to analyse them as a further step of the excessive escalations that we find on the internet and on social media today.[2] For some men, it is only a small step from being an incel to becoming a mass shooter. The Dayton mass shooter in the United States in August 2019 also reportedly had mentioned incels on his social media accounts. One of his victims included his transgender sibling who referred to himself as a male. The anti-Semitic shooter in Halle (Germany) in 2019 also referred to himself as an incel (Ware 2020).

Drawing on the work of the psychoanalyst Ruth Stein on Islamist terrorists (2010), I relate the mass shootings to the role of the (absent) father. Ever since Freud's *Totem and Taboo* [1912–1913] (1960), the famous tale of the origin of civilisation and ethics (the primordial father who is killed by his sons), the role of the father has received attention in psychoanalytic theory. Notable psychoanalysts besides Freud have paid attention to the father such as Lacan, Kohut, Bollas, Benjamin, Stein and many others (see Jones 2008 for an overview).

While the mother plays an equally, perhaps even more important role than the father for the men whom I discuss in this book (as the allegedly phallic mother who has castrated the sons in the first place), I wish to focus on the father. The role of the father is particularly crucial when thinking about the mass shooters like Breivik and Rodger. The father is equally important when considering masculinity and ideas of what it means to be a man today. It is the father who embodies and lives masculinity for the son.

Jessica Benjamin (1988), who I return to in the concluding chapter of this book, notes that it is through the relationality between father and son that separation and gender identification can occur. There is a special relationship between father and son which allows for recognition and (unconscious erotic) identification. In other words, the father serves as the boy's ideal. This process enables the boy to acquire a sense of self, a masculine identity and see himself as a desiring subject and a subject to be desired. For the manosphere, the father is the quintessential role model and implicitly expected to pass on a strong masculinity to the son; to hand down testosterone so that the boy can become an alpha male. If that process of male inheritance fails, as incels often lament, and the father was a 'betabux' as they call it (a beta male) for example, the rage against the father is immanent (see previous chapter). Incels in particular, as shown in Chapter 4, are obsessed with genetics and how their parents have apparently passed on undesirable body types and traits. As I discuss in this chapter, for the two mass shooters it is particularly the absent father who is significant.[3]

The real and fantasmatic role of the father

'On the cultural level', Stein writes, 'the father has been conceived as a lawgiver..., as well as a liberator and facilitator of desire and ambition' (Stein 2010, 75). In psychoanalytic terms, it is the father who acts as the third, and breaks the dyadic mother-infant relationship, and (together with the mother) enables an entry into the outer world, reality and language, as many thinkers have argued. The father (like the mother) in this context is always real *and* imagined; an internal object which is grounded in real and fantasmatic experiences. Stein notes that in psychoanalysis, the father has been regarded as 'a powerful, idolized, impervious entity who promises protection and metes out punishment' (ibid, 77). This is the archaic father who is nonetheless of an eerily presence in individual's psyches and in cultural discourses across the world today which embrace authoritarian and fascist ideas. Seen in this vein, the father of fantasy is indeed god-like; an omnipotent, phallic figure who is outside the law, in fact makes the law for others. Such a figure is of essential importance for understanding religious terrorism and, I might add, the symbolic (and at times real) terrorism as it occurs in the manosphere today.[4] The fantasy of the strong father is so prominent for some today, because of underlying crises in the social realm (see Chapters 2 and 4). Socio-economic crises have led to the unconscious desire for security, protection and punishment of the Other.

For Stein, Islamist terrorists seek to communicate something through their acts. Like the male mass shooters I discuss in this chapter, they wish to perform (in the sense of the word) an act of metaphysics: 'to give ultimate meaning to time and history through ever-escalating acts of violence which culminate in a final battle between good and evil' (ibid, 20).

For Stein, a key process in seeing God as a loved father is initiated by a sense of self-hatred being transformed into a love for God. She notes that Mohammed Atta, one of the 9/11 terrorists, had an 'overbearing, self-confident' (ibid, 26) father. Atta himself was extremely shy with women and everything connected to sexuality was 'felt by him to be defiled and therefore untouchable' (ibid). Atta's actions and mindset were partly motivated by a hatred of women. He was very close to his mother, and his father felt that Atta was soft as a result (ibid, 38). Atta came to despise women and everything soft and feminine. It needed to be killed. Islamist terrorism, as has been noted in the media, is in that sense not dissimilar from Breivik's worldview. Breivik too had retreated from sexuality and hated women and everything sexual. Simon Cottee argues that what incels and Jihadists have in common is sex and shame. He writes of Alek Minassian in the *New York Times*, who referred to incels online and killed others with his truck in 2018:

> The sense of shame from not being able to perform a culturally approved sex role may be a key to understanding his murderous rage.

It may also be another thread connecting him to other violent actors whose ideology is different from his own, yet whose actions are similar. It is not difficult to spot parallels with the world of jihadism, where women and sex are similarly fixated on to an extraordinary degree.... Like incels, jihadists similarly crave sex, but the circumstances surrounding its consummation are closely regulated by their religious norms, which prohibit sex outside of marriage and same-sex couplings. (Cottee 2018, online)

Ruth Stein would probably agree with such a statement. While I cannot comment on Islamist terrorists' relationship to sex, it is the relationship to the god-like father figure which is more significant in my opinion. The men who become Islamist terrorists and who are often suicide bombers form around a male bond. They are threatened by strong, modern women and empowered sexuality. God as a father

is imagined to be waiting there [in heaven] to redeem his sons' troubled souls and sweep away the doubts of their former selves. It seems as if the primitive father of Freud's primal horde has been resuscitated, or, better is still alive, and has come to embrace his sons – provided they unite against 'woman,' that is against the feminine principle of pleasure and softness (found both in Islamic women and in Western society), which is seen as feminized. (Stein 2010, 27)

This is a love for the father that presents itself in total submission, in all or nothing. The terrorists gain their strength from identifying with their father (God). They become his instrument and are at the same time killed by him. They regressively return to him and ask him to kill parts of their selves. They give up their own judgement and instead subscribe to the father who knows what is true and just. This 'ecstasy of self-obliteration' is seen as an act of love by the men. 'Not only did they "not kill their father"; they spared themselves the awareness of having committed a crime against the other humans and themselves. They "let the Father" kill them' (ibid, 41). I return to the role of the father for the two mass shooters in the course of this chapter.

There have been several publications from clinicians who have (psycho) analysed Breivik (see Tietze 2014 for a discussion) and Rodger (Langman 2014; Vito, Admire & Hughes 2018) and I discuss some of them in this chapter. In keeping to the objectives of this book, I pay particular attention to how women and the relationship between men and women are discussed in the manifestos. Breivik's manifesto in particular is first and foremost full of racist claims about multiculturalism and the alleged islamisation of Western cultures, something I do not discuss in great detail because it goes beyond the scope of this book. What unites both Rodger and Breivik is their hatred of the modern woman and of (leftwing) feminism in particular. Some commentators have specifically argued that Breivik's manifesto is primarily anti-feminist and against women, and only secondarily racist (Jones 2011; Goldberg 2017). Breivik used racism and specifically an anti-Islam stance to mask his misogyny and hatred of women, possibly so that he would appear more 'manly' in the eyes of fellow racists and white supremacists by discussing questions of immigration, national identity, 'cultural Marxism' and secondarily the alleged 'feminisation' of men and Western nations by feminists. Rodger was primarily misogynistic but also displayed some racist ideas in his manifesto.

As literature on school shootings has pointed out, mass shooters, who are almost exclusively male, harbour violent and misogynistic fantasies. Such fantasies lead to and influence the violent acts of killing that those men commit (Myketiak 2016; Murray 2017a, 2017b; Wilson 2017; Vito, Admire & Hughes 2018). The recent shootings of the past few years are significant in the way the shooters have made use of social media and the internet in broadcasting and communicating their actions and manifestos. I discuss two manifestos in this chapter.

Anders Behring Breivik

Anders Breivik's manifesto *2083: A European Declaration of Independence* (2011) is 1,515 pages in length. 'The title he gave that document, 2083, is a reference to the 1683 Battle of Vienna, in which the forces of European Christendom defeated the Ottoman Empire' (Richards 2014, 43). He believes that by 2083 Islam in Europe will be defeated a second time. Breivik's writing is full of racism and Islamophobia. He sees himself at the forefront of a 'Western European resistance' (Breivik 2011, 12). Europe and its cultural identity is threatened and will fall within '2 to 7 decades' (ibid) as a result of multiculturalism and immigration. Similarly to other fascist or racist ideologies, Breivik begins by introducing 'political correctness' as a form of left-wing indoctrination that has resulted in a suppression of reality. Those and many other passages were copied and pasted from other sources by Breivik (Richards 2014, 45). Like other racists, Breivik evokes a mythic past where everything was orderly where societies were safer, men behaved like gentlemen and there was no divorce. For him, as for Jordan Peterson and others, 'political correctness' is equated with 'cultural Marxism' which was allegedly advanced by the Frankfurt School and others (see Chapter 3). 'Political correctness' allegedly dominates schools, universities, the media and every other sphere of society. He goes on to criticise feminist, psychoanalyst and Marxist thinkers. From the outset, Breivik is anti-feminist and devotes a section to a 'discussion' (it is not a discussion in any nuanced sense) of his particular idea of radical feminism. Radical feminism is, according to him, responsible for media representations of superior women and inferior men, women are being supported in schools, at university, in the workplace, while men are being left behind. 1968 and the sexual revolution is also yet again isolated as a powerful signifier that brought about the evils of the contemporary world.

> Today, the feminisation of European culture, moving rapidly since the 1960s continues to intensify. Indeed, the present-day radical feminist assault through support for mass Muslim immigration has a political parallel to the their anti-colonial efforts. This current assault is in part a continuation of a century-old effort to destroy traditional European structures, the very foundation of European culture. (Breivik 2011, 36)

Breivik frequently mentions *Sex and the City* and other cultural texts as they have allegedly contributed to the feminisation of society, according to him. Man has to bow to the agenda of radical feminists who want to emasculate him. For him, there is an intellectual 'warfare against the European male' so that he is no longer able 'to defend traditional beliefs and values' (ibid, 36).

Breivik's mental state has been debated amongst clinicians. The psychiatric report that was compiled during his trial did not stipulate that he was psychotic while he was assessed. Some clinicians have argued that he is psychotic, others have disagreed (see Tietze 2014 for a discussion). A first psychiatric review concluded that he had paranoid schizophrenia, while a second diagnosed dissocial personality disorder.

Barry Richards (2014) argues that Breivik's worldview is not only characterised by a hatred of Islam, but by two crucial other aspects: a fragile masculinity and a sense of grandiosity. Richards argues that for Breivik, 'there is a deeper set of motives at work: a desire to counter a sense of humiliation and express rage. Through his violent acts, he tried to restore both his culture, as he saw it, and his manhood' (Richards 2014, 43). Richards describes the manifesto as full of delusions. Breivik claims to have re-established the Knights Templar military order so as to save Europe from Muslims, for example. The document is characterised by a 'cold omnipotence' (ibid, 43) with which he details how a violent uprising should commence. However, Richards argues that a deeper, underlying fear is key to understanding Breivik's motives and actions: a fragile masculinity. Islam is evoked as a mask to hide such fears. 'What terrifies him is the prospect of his brittle, besieged masculinity being engulfed in a society where sexuality and gender no longer take clear and predictable forms' (ibid, 45). Flooded by the forces of social change and by 'cultural Marxism', he fears that 'the distinction between masculinity and femininity will disappear' (ibid, 37). Like the Freikorps soldiers, Breivik feels a threat of disintegration, of his ego dissolving because of an apparently powerful Other. Richards argues that the target of the social democratic youth camp on Utøya can be understood in this way. Breivik saw sexually free youth whom he needed to kill in order to stop such ideology from being reproduced.

Siri Erika Gullestad (2017) has argued that inner (unconscious) motivations led Breivik to his actions. The discursive and ideological mobilisation of Islam or 'cultural Marxism' only serve to displace inner fantasies and experiences. They are projected out there, where already a war is going on, according to Breivik.

His own experiences with women, perhaps an (unconscious) aversion to or fear of them because he was rejected or experienced hurt, are projected outwards and turned into a general issue. The 'feminization of society', as he called it, has resulted in a weakened society that is unable to defend itself from external threats. His own family and friends had brought shame on him, as he writes. He claims that his members of his family (his half-sister and mother) engaged in sexual behaviour that he found unbearable (for instance having many different sexual partners during one's live). His family had in that sense shamed him by succumbing to the hedonistic, 'cultural Marxist' ideas that he is against. A very personal element of hurt informs his warped ideology.

Breivik, having already had a porous and boundaryless ego because of his (proto-incestuous) relationship with his mother (see below), was further threatened because of the empowered, modern woman who was represented by his half-sister and mother. It directly threatened his body, as Theweleit notes (Theweleit 2015, 107). In response to that, Breivik trained and toned his body, he constructed a body armour through building up muscle. Many sections in his manifesto are about advice to other 'warriors' on how they should use steroids, dieting, etc. to acquire the body that is needed for warfare.

Breivik writes about his idea of masculinity: 'Being male means having to prove something, to achieve something, in a greater way than it does for women' (ibid, 356). It goes on and on. 'I will postulate that being male first of all is some kind of nervous energy, something you need to prove' (ibid, 359). He eventually 'proved' what he could do by committing acts of terrorism. He had finally become a male in his eyes – 'the restless sex' (ibid, 359).

One should get an idea of Breivik's ideology and I do not wish to analyse his ideas further. His explicit anti-feminism and crude gender politics are very similar to those of the YouTubers and Reddit users I have discussed so far in this book. As with Theweleit, who argued that the soldier males were defending against psychosis through their fantasies and actions (see Chapter 1), Richards argues that Breivik seems psychotic, but is overall capable of (somewhat) coherent lines of arguments. Breivik provides an intellectual discussion of various themes which are highly rational in their irrationality, meticulously structured and apparently logically argued. He is a monster, who nonetheless has a sense of humour and dry irony.

Like incels (see Chapter 4) and the Distributist YouTuber (see Chapter 3) and other commentators, Breivik uses the language of biology and evolutionary psychology to discuss what he sees as the 'erotic capital' of women. 'Females have a significantly higher proportion of erotic capital than males due to biological differences (men have significantly more prevalent sexual urges than females and are thus easily manipulated)' (ibid, 1179). The same pseudo-scientific discourse is mobilised here (see Chapter 3). Like many white cis men, he feels that his masculinity has been threatened and destabilised by women. The erotic, seductive woman, who controls and seduces the man, is a frightening scenario for him, as it was for the Freikorps soldiers. Barry Richards provides a convincing summary of Breivik's defensive masculinity when he argues:

> Behind Breivik's contempt for Islam is an unconscious fantasy of masculinity under threat. Like all unconscious fantasies, this internal fear may bear little correspondence to any external reality, past or present. But it explains his abhorrence of contemporary sexual freedoms, with their threat, as he saw it, to the sovereignty of the patriarchal male, and his unmanageable hatred of the liberal state that he believes promotes these freedoms. To defend against his inner sense of weakness and vulnerability, he developed an extremely grandiose and omnipotent state of mind, complete with medals and world-historic missions. Breivik combines a catastrophically fearful, humiliated masculine self with a capacity for unchecked grandiosity and omnipotence. (Richards 2014, 47–48)

In his manifesto, Breivik created an image of himself as a potent, phallic warrior, belonging to an organisation that does not exist in reality. He interviewed himself in the manifesto. 'The way in which he carried out his crime, and the way his thoughts contextualised it, resembles role-playing, rather than political terrorism' (Knausgård 2015, online), the writer Karl Ove Knausgård has written. Breivik wanted to make himself seen, to represent himself to the world – like so many mass shooters – so that he would finally be seen as a real man. Only then could he be sure of his existence and that he would not disintegrate. He grew up with a mother who had been abused as a child. She was unable to fully relate to others, 'and her narcissistic traits were reflected in her son' (ibid). Breivik's parents had gotten divorced when he was 18 months.

> After the divorce, [the young boy] Anders slept in his mother's bed at night. His mother had made some half-hearted efforts to break this habit, but the unclear boundaries between mother and son remained. According to the police interrogations, Breivik – 'for a joke' – gave his

mother a vibrator when her relationship with a boyfriend ended in 2004, a fact that, indeed, cries out for an explanation. (Gullestad 2017, 209)

A few months before he carried out the terrorist acts, Breivik visited his stepmother and told her that he would soon make his father proud by doing something. Yet, Knausgård is adamant that 'Breivik's childhood explains nothing, his character explains nothing, his political ideas explain nothing' (ibid). He was an ordinary man until he became a mass murderer. Gullestad (2017) details Breivik's upbringing and youth. He never fully fit in at school and was isolated. 'It seems warranted to speculate that, on an unconscious level, the mother might have been experienced as symbiotically engulfing – a powerful figure endangering the core of his masculine identity' (ibid, 210). He had also lost his father. The inner chaos that resulted from the unclear boundaries between him and his mother needed to be protected against by creating a fantasy world. 'The heroic fantasy of being Justiciary Knight Andrew Berwick [a name Breivik adopted] also may serve to deny the feminine, weak (gay?) side of him' (ibid, 211).

Knausgård (2015) argues that it was the fact that Breivik was unseen, that he was hidden and hid himself from others – women in particular, I would add – that contributed to him becoming a killer. 'Breivik remained unseen, and it destroyed him. He then looked down, and he hid his gaze and his face, thereby destroying the other inside him'. Five years before 22 July, Breivik isolated himself and began creating a world of his own, which would ultimately be expressed in the manifesto. Like incels (and to a lesser degree MGTOW), it was this self-inflicted isolation that proved so fatal. A self-isolation in which he could create a fantasy world which would give rise to a new male, a new ego, a soldier. Gullestad argues that Breivik seems to have identified with an imagined almighty paternal authority, expressed in his pretending to be a policeman during the massacre' (ibid, 212). Breivik had finally placed himself above the law. Both acts of creating a fictional organisation and of being disguised as a policeman (the latter primarily so that he could kill as many individuals as possible) seem to suggest that he needed to designate himself as an X (as Young-Bruehl discusses about obsessional characters), he needed to belong to a wider collective: the Knights Templar and the police.

In 2015 Klaus Theweleit published *The Laughter of the Perpetrators: Breivik et. al.* (which has not been translated into English). In the book, he analyses killings and massacres by men and places particular attention on the laughter and enjoyment they got out of their actions. Theweleit similarly argues that Breivik framed himself in his manifesto not as an individual but as a 'member' (Theweleit 2015, 23, my translation) of an organisation. Breivik, suffering from the sense of grandiosity as he did, was further convinced that his actions were for the greater good of Europe, that he was redeeming Europe as a whole. Like the Freikorps soldiers, Theweleit notes that Breivik (and other men like him, this includes the kind of men I discuss in this book) need the totality, they need to create collectivity and collective rules in order to be fully born. Breivik's manifesto and his actions, the incels and MGTOWs online interactions, the YouTube videos by the alt-right, etc. seek to create respective, often specific, world orders. Such forms of collectivity are needed so that the men can achieve a sense of 'bodily equilibrium' or balance (ibid, 27), Theweleit argues. The others (and the Other) needs to be brought to a similar state, need to conform to the world order, so that it can be guaranteed and upheld. As a last resort this includes the annihilation of the Other, if they cannot be converted or forced. If the Stacy cannot be forced by law to be with an incel (which many incels dream up when their inceldom has been established), she needs to vanish, as those men think. Such processes are bodily processes but they transcend the individual body. Thus, a homeostasis must be established and even if only symbolically on the internet. This means that through writing about such themes, men can receive a momentary affective equilibrium, or relief. However, this is only temporary as they also depend on and desire other women, as I have also argued in the previous chapters.

Breivik acted in cold blood and with utmost sadism. Gullestad argued that killing for Breivik was sadistic. Like the Freikorps soldiers, he experienced it as a combination of aggression and lust. She writes that Breivik wanted to be seen in such a way, as a male soldier. But those of us who believe in peace and equality rightly refuse to do so. 'What the world notices, confronted with his ill deeds, is not what he wants us to see. What we see is unfathomable evil' (Gullestad 2017, 215). While Breivik's ideology can be seen as being conformist to that of the manosphere, he did not specifically refer to idioms or ideas from online communities within it. The next section of this chapter analyses Elliot Rodger's manifesto, who referred to himself as an incel, and who is frequently mentioned by incels in some of their posts.

Elliot Rodger

Elliot Rodger was 22 yeas old when he committed a mass shooting in Isla Vista, Santa Barbara (USA). He, as well as other mass shooters, is often mentioned by incels in their posts. Rodger also wrote a manifesto. He is of essential significance to the incel community and to understanding why some incels have taken the turn they did. Rodger was active on various online fora. For example, he frequented the forum PUAHate.com which served as a community to criticise the ideology of Pick up Artists. He used the term 'incel' many times online, as documented by the Southern Poverty Law Center. 'One day incels will realize their true strength and numbers, and will overthrow this oppressive feminist system' (2014, online), he wrote for example. For many incels, whether they really mean it or not, Rodger is one of them. Some write that they regard him as a martyr or hero who has put into action what others only ever write about online. He was a nobody who lived an unfulfilled and unseen existence which he defended against with a manic sense of superiority and grandiosity (as Breivik did). Like Breivik, Rodger left a presence on social media and uploaded YouTube videos for example. His manifesto was emailed by him to members of his family, friends and his therapist.

The school shooting expert and counselling psychologist Peter Langman has described Rodger as having 'psychotic' and 'psychopathic' traits. 'Elliot Rodger was neither floridly psychotic nor flagrantly psychopathic. He exhibited, however, both psychotic and psychopathic features' (Langman 2014, 2). Langman's analysis is based on Rodger's manifesto and needs, in my view, be read with some caution, because he did not assess him in person, as he killed himself during the shooting. I do not mean to say that I am disputing any of Langman's claims, I do not have the clinical expertise to do so. Yet, it remains difficult to assess someone's mental state from their writing alone.

Langman argues that Rodger had schizotypal personality disorder.[5] Rodger repeatedly describes his shyness, social anxiety and becoming self-conscious in front of others. He was extremely inhibited and unable to speak in front of others in class for example. Langman summarises his detailed analysis of Rodger:

> Elliot Rodger was a complicated person. He had traits of both psychotic and psychopathic shooters. He was masochistic and an injustice collector. He both envied and resented his peers, alternately feeling inferior and superior to them. He had a damaged sense of masculinity due to his short stature, physical weakness, lack of athletic abilities, and failure with women. He struggled with being biracial. He was also enraged at the thought that his siblings surpassed him. All these issues drove him to violence. (Langman 2014, 7)

Additionally, Langman argues (2014) that Rodger (beyond the two basic diagnoses of psychopathy and psychosis) was masochistic and an 'injustice collector' (who kept track of and wrote about all the apparent injustices from others he had to endure).

In my analysis of some parts of Rodger's 141-page-long manifesto, I pay particular attention to fantasies of women that he writes about. His manifesto is a kind of biography in which he discusses his upbringing.

A fundamental sense of (sexual) entitlement was at the heart of Rodger and it is also reflected in the incel community and other parts of the manosphere. He repeatedly refered to himself as a god in the manifesto, as '[m]agnificent, glorious, supreme, eminent… Divine!' (Rodger 2014, 135), or 'superior' (ibid, 1, 89, 90, 99, 102, 111, 132, 135). In reality, he was unnoticed, invisible and nonexistent to those who he desired the most and wanted to be with: girls and women.

Rodger was of mixed ethnic background, his father was white British and his mother was Chinese-Malaysian, who had moved to Britain when she was young. He was born in London and the family later moved to the United States. His father's family was allegedly 'prestigious' (ibid, 1). He structured his manifesto according to age periods and the period from 0 to 5 was 'happiness and bliss' (ibid, 2). Such words lay bare the sense of idealism and constructed nostalgia that he mobilised in order to later contrast it with his apparent cruel and miserable teenage life. His style of writing conveys a sense of grandiosity, vividness and plasticity. He wanted the reader to believe a particular narrative that he created. It begins with supposed bliss. His writing is soapy, mannered, kitschy and restrained.

Rodger's manifesto is not a manifesto, compared to Breivik's. It is not so much about justifying, or explaining his motives but rather a litany of a failed existence, as far as he was concerned. He hardly alluded to politics or other social factors. He painted a picture of his early life as one that destined him to achieve greatness, to be great, to be entitled. He created images of an idealised childhood in order to be able to dramatically contrast them with the 'darker' later chapters of his life. It is significant that he produced a written manifesto, by putting things into writing, he could further cement his fantasy world, literally write it into existence and so that others could see and witness it. After his seventh birthday, his parents divorced and, according to Rodger, this was life-changing for him:

> Because of my father's acquisition of a new girlfriend, my little mind got the impression that my father was a man that women found attractive, as he was able to find a new girlfriend in such a short period of time from divorcing my mother. I subconsciously held him in higher regard because of this. It is very interesting how this phenomenon works… that males who can easily find female mates garner more respect from their fellow men, even children. (Rodger 2014, 11)

While he wrote of his 'subconscious' here and that he valued his father's 'acquisition' (a term used deliberately by him to dehumanise women) of a new partner, the reality seemed a different one. One can interpret the above as expressing a hatred of his father, who had betrayed the family.

He was not one of the 'cool kids' at school; this, according to him, further decreased his self-esteem. Writing about the next ten years from the age of ten onwards, he noted: 'The pleasures of sex and love will be denied to me. Other boys will experience it, but not me. Instead, I will only experience misery, rejection, loneliness, and pain' (ibid, 21). He was of the opinion that 'sex should be outlawed' (ibid). 'It is the only way to make the world a fair and just place. If I can't have it, I will destroy it' (ibid). His feelings of inferiority were countered with feelings of superiority. He thought that he 'must be destined to change the world, to shape it into an image that suits me!' (ibid).

Rodger's manifesto is full of fantasies that he would eventually achieve the life he desired by becoming rich. Like many incels, he believed that wealth, wearing expensive clothes and driving luxury cars would automatically enable him to get a girlfriend. He moved to Isla Vista (close to Santa Barbara) to attend college. As he moved there, he presented a typical incel narrative:

> The more I explored my college town of Isla Vista, the more ridiculousness I witnessed. All of the hot, beautiful girls walked around with obnoxious, tough jock-type men who partied all the time and acted crazy. They should be going for intelligent gentlemen such as myself. Women are sexually attracted to the wrong type of man. This is a major flaw in the very foundation of humanity. It is completely and utterly wrong, in every sense of the word. As these truths fully dawned on me, I became deeply disturbed by them. Deeply disturbed, offended, and traumatized. (Rodger 2014, 84)

Once again, we see how self-pity and victimhood are mobilised by a man (just like incels and other men do) to justify his own apathy and toxicity. It is others who fail to see him, who have all the fun and pleasure while simultaneously denying it from Rodger. The kind of masculinity that he portrayed in his manifesto is one of defensive vulnerability and a kind of emotional self-reflexivity. While he showed forms of psychosis, he expressed his own shortcomings as being caused by others. It was other people who allegedly traumatised him. Rodger used the same kind of self-victimisation discourse that I have discussed in relation to other men in this book so far. His own inhibitions could not be seen as his own by him, but other people were made responsible for them. Something which had no basis in reality. At the same time, he was disinhibited and constructed destructive fantasies in which he had agency.

Fantasies of fascism

Rodger developed violent fantasies of killing females who had allegedly chosen to ignore him, and killing males who had taken females away from him. He concluded that he would never have a girlfriend and that there was no point to his life. He presented himself as being controlled by urges and hormones. He regularly masturbated and fantasised about beautiful girls while 'the entire town of Isla Vista erupted in raucous debauchery' (ibid, 110) around him. Like the soldier males Theweleit writes of, Rodger was controlled by an affective fragility that ate away at his ego boundaries and sense of self. It was marked by envy.

Even in his 20s, he presented himself as an immature, infantile boy who was controlled by his drives and beset by feelings of grandiosity and inferiority. His writing style, while elaborate and articulate, is at the same time childish, whiny and immature. Like other man of the manosphere, he presented a child-like sense of entitlement. It is only by having a gun that he felt like a soldier. All of this is coupled with misogyny and a completely distorted view on women. Incels have adopted the very same worldview as Rodger and it is debatable if such a shift in the community towards more aggression and destructiveness followed Rodger's actions or if they had such views all along. According to incels and him, women should not get to choose who they have sex with; instead men should make such choices because they are rational.

> In an ideal world, sexuality would not exist. It must be outlawed. In a world without sex, humanity will be pure and civilized. Men will grow up healthily, without having to worry about such a barbaric act. All men will grow up fair and equal, because no man will be able to experience the pleasures of sex while others are denied it. The human race will evolve to an entirely new level of civilization, completely devoid of all the impurity and degeneracy that exists today. (Rodger 2014, 136)

Rodger imagined an authoritarian, fascist-like society where women are 'quarantine[d]' in 'concentration camps' (ibid, 136). One cannot escape the phallic fantasy that is at the root of this imagery and his life in general. If only he would have had the phallus, everything would have been different. While Rodger displayed some racist tendencies (against people of colour for example) in his manifesto, it was not clear if he actively sympathised with fascism for example. The police report mentions some of the terms he searched for online (Brown 2015, 40–41). They included:

- Did Adolf Hitler have a girlfriend
- Adolf Hitler's childhood
- I've never had a female friend
- Adolf Hitler narcicist [sic]
- Adolf Hitler and the law of attraction
- If Hitler was born today
- If you were Adolf Hitler

From the above terms and how Rodger envisioned a fascist-like society in his manifesto, one could suggest that he wanted to become like Hitler, a powerful dictator who could create his own world. The fact that fascism was at least partially drawn on and identified with by Rodger (as the last few pages of the manifesto and some of the search results detailed in the police report suggest) is significant because it shows the same links between fascism and contemporary male ideologies online that I have discussed in previous chapters.

From redistribution to retribution: the absent father

A continued theme of the two manifestos by Breivik and Rodger – and of many of the narratives by the men I have written about in previous chapters, is that of a gendered *redistribution* of sex and power. Male phallic fragility is countered with demands for a redistribution of sexual power and prowess to men, specifically those men who have allegedly been denied it. Both Breivik and Rodger were alienated, lonely men who had retreated into a fantasy world and were heavy gamers. Breivik, unlike Rodger, did not mention any biographical rejections or hurt he experienced by women, but it might be that he consciously chose to exclude such narratives from his manifesto because they would make him appear weak and not like the alpha male he thought of himself as. The masculine identities of both are experienced as being threatened by women by them. As a result, and because of their grandiose sense of entitlement, they – along with incels and other groups – demand a redistribution of sex (and to a lesser degree men's rights). They have been denied sexual contact and relationships and, to them, it is a human right to have sex with all the hot girls they see on their screens and in the real world.

Breivik actively turned against such forms of demands, by retreating into a kind of voluntary celibacy, but his hatred of women may be symptomatic of his desire for a heterosexual relationship. He discusses a different kind of redistribution in his manifesto as he fantasises about the goods and assets of 'traitors' being redistributed once the 'new cultural conservative regime' (Breivik 2011, 1121) is in place. Rodger's idea of redistribution is, on the other hand, taken up by many incels as they dream of their inceldom (see Chapter 4). As we know, such forms of redistribution have not happened. There is no inceldom, and Europe is thankfully still as diverse and multicultural as it was in 2011 when Breivik sought to change history.

As I have outlined in the previous chapter, many men of today have complicated relationships with their parents. They complain that their desired potency was not handed down to them by their parents, and specifically by their *fathers*. Breivik had lost contact to his father and his relationship with his mother's new partner was also difficult (Berardi 2015, 60). In his 'interview' with himself in the manifesto, he writes that after making contact with his father, the latter was 'not mentally prepared for a reunion' (Breivik 2011, 1387). Elliot Rodger discussed his father many times in his writing as he detailed his family life. There are a few times when he actively criticised him instead of women:

> For those months, my father was dead to me. My mother was all I had left in this bleak world. (Rodger 2014, 67)

> My father effectively abandoned me at one of my most crucial points in my life. Though in fact, he was never really present in my life to

abandon me in the first place. When I think about it, he was always absent from my life. When my whole world took a downward spiral into darkness after I hit puberty, he never made any effort to save me. He just didn't care. (Rodger 2014, 73)

Fathers seem of essential significance for the two shooters discussed in this chapter and for many incel or MGTOW men in particular. Rodger hated his father for finding a new partner quickly after getting divorced. His father is the attractive male, in his eyes. There is thus scope for envy. The father also did not fulfil his fatherly role and Rodger felt abandoned by him. Whether this really was the case, is of course open to questioning. Rodger, as noted, was extremely inhibited and he presumably expected his father, who was (apparently) a successful producer, to hand down his healthy disinhibition to him so that he would become outgoing and confident.

As cultural legend dictates, it is the *father* that in a rite of passage shows the son what it means to be a man and how to become one (Benjamin 1988). Such a redistribution of phallic manhood has failed for some men today. (Does it ever really exist for anyone? Is it not just a fantasy?). The men of the manosphere blame women more than their fathers for it, because their fathers have already been 'betas' or turned into betas by women (or if their fathers were 'alphas', it is genetics that have affected the sons' looks).[6]

Redistribution of fatherly power to the son has failed. The signifier with its supposedly magically endowed qualities has been castrated so that it becomes re~~dis~~tribution. Retribution, or revenge, is a term used by Rodger (he named the day he commited the killings 'the Day of Retribution') and also by many incels (see Chapter 4). Breivik's whole manifesto is a kind of rationalisation of the violent retribution he carried out and advocated.

In his book, *Heroes,* on recent male killers (such as Breivik), Berardi evokes the role of the father in 1968. 1968 was a revolt against the symbolic and real father:

> What is the primary meaning of '68? After two world wars, after Hiroshima and Nagasaki, in 1968, young people, students, workers, intellectuals and women asserted, among other things, that humans must emancipate from mental slavery, and that mental slavery is essentially based on subordination to the Father. The authority of the father was viewed not only as the key tool of patriarchal oppression, but also of colonial violence and of capitalist exploitation. Seen through the prism of 1968, refusing and defusing the authority of the father, the transmission of its oppressive law and the obedience to its traditions was the first step in a social and sexual liberation from slavery. In the following two decades, society attempted and often succeeded in creating fraternal links of solidarity and freeing itself from patriarchal subjection. (Berardi 2015, 59)

One could say that following that emancipatory moment, there was a backlash, where a longing for a strong father returned. Too much alleged disinhibition of 1968 led to a desire for inhibition and authority (see Chapter 2). Today, at a time when some men feel anxious and castrated by a loss of the old entitlements and unable to manage the different representation by women and the feminine other, the return of the stong containing father is for some (such as those discussed in this chapter) desired more than ever.

In her study of religious terrorism Ruth Stein isolates the figure of the archaic father as highly significant when trying to understand the terrorist's mind. For Stein, the terrorist submits in total love to god as the father who awaits him in paradise or heaven. It is he who knows who is worthy under his eyes and who is not. Those who are not, the 'non-believers' for example, are seen as animals. For the terrorists, killing is seen as noble and good (Stein 2010, 33). This is exactly how Breivik saw his acts, as needed, as necessary in order to save Europe. Rodger did not proclaim such motives but he too, and incels with him, regarded women as animal-like, as inhuman that deserved to die. Stein writes that terrorism 'aims at fighting the very stance that opposes, or even tries to comprehend' (ibid, 37). This is certainly the case with the kind of manifestos I have discussed. They create a worldview that is placed under a giant glass cover, suctioned tight. *Impossible to penetrate but all too visible.* The same mechanisms are at place in incel or MGTOW fora where the other (a well-meaning woman, an understanding man, someone else offering advice or critique) is instantly banned after being abused. Terrorism 'attempts to terrorize thought itself' (ibid, 37).

The regression towards and desire of a strong father is somewhat similar (with different aims and outcomes) for fundamentalist terrorists and the kind of men I discuss in this book. Stein describes the father of Mohammed Atta (one of the 9/11 terrorists) as 'overbearing'; a man who regarded Atta as soft because he was extremely close to his mother. Breivik's father was absent, because of the parents' divorce and he had a difficult relationship with the mother's new partner. Rodger's parents divorced and he felt abandoned by his father, who was 'dead' to him. Their acts represent, at least in part, a longing for a strong father. A father who is introjected and idealised by them. A father who makes the law for everyone under him and whose only pleasure is fulfilled by his desire, which is absolute. This is the kind of *imago* father that incels and other men dream of today. A god-like father. The men both demand him and rage against him because they have not had such a father who could pass on his magic omnipotence to them. A father of limitless pleasure, charisma, wealth and attraction. A father who should likewise reign over all women and lead them to all men.

Real fathers are absent as *imagos*, or have otherwise failed. 'One time my mom told my dad to give me "the talk" about sex and buy me some condoms. He didn't do anything because he knew there was no chance I would sleep with anyone', one incel user writes (Reddit 2018k, online). 'How come ur dad reproduced and made an incel', a different thread states. A user replies: 'My dad is a 5'5 manlet [short man] bastard that didn't do shit except give me his manlet genes', a second writes 'chad-lite. My sister is a Stacy-lite and my brother is also chad-lite. And then there's me', someone adds. '6'1 robust classically handsome chad. Yale engineering degree and Harvard mba. Started and owned a software company. Now a real estate developer. He mogs [dominates] my entire life. Married a hapa [a person of mixed ethnic background] with soft features and male incel traits. I came out as a genetic recombination', another user replies (Reddit 2018l, online).

The acts of revenge and retribution are thus not only acts of terrorism against women, they are also aimed at the men's fathers. The real father is killed (at least in an unconscious fantasy) and a new, phallic father is envisioned and desired. For Breivik and Rodger, who see themselves as becoming alpha males in the act of killing, the father is unconsciously sought in order to be reunited with once more. Like the terrorists Stein writes about, the male shooters want to merge with a god-like father who will finally see them and recognise them as they kill others. It is the unconscious, identificatory love for an idealised father (who they did not have in real life) that in part drove them to their actions. Such actions are symptoms of a longing for a fatherly approval and recognition; something those men either did not experience or they felt they did not experience enough. Ruth Stein writes about the Islamist terrorist that he 'wants (unconsciously) *to change the father from persecutor into an idealized love object*, to reverse the rage and discontent (and the pain and suffering) into glory and narcissistic enhancement' (100, italics in original). I would argue that a similar dynamic is in place here.

A terrorist like Breivik wanted to change his father. He visited his stepmother a few months before he carried out the terrorist acts and told her that he would soon make his father proud by doing something (Gullestad 2017). Unlike the terrorists Stein writes about, the men discussed in this book not only want to be recognised by the father in the act of killing, they also want to *kill* the father as the ultimate proof of their strength and phallic omnipotence. Only by killing the father in an act of revenge, who has finally recognised them, can they surpass him. This is not the same as the killing of the primordial father that Freud postulated which ultimately brought about a shared sense of community and ethics.

For Breivik, incels and other men, the (unconscious) wish to kill the father is both an act of love and revenge. It figures as the ultimate test of courage at which end the son has fully individuated himself (Benjamin 1988). According to this fantasy, the mass shooter has both been seen as phallic by the father and can then feel recognised and empowered, because the father has been destroyed. He has become the father. In fact, he has become a god. Both Breivik and Rodger and many other male killers who commit mass shootings play god. Through their psychotic sense of grandiosity, they have given themselves a god-like status of deciding over life and death. It is the role of the phallic father who knows best and knows what is morally necessary. Breivik in particular produced endless 'arguments' both in court and in his manifesto, why it was necessary, indeed inevitable, to commit the actions that he committed. Those men find the ultimate power and valuation as an alpha male in the, in our eyes, impossible act: to kill another human being. Jessica Benjamin (1988) has argued that the father-son struggle is a struggle of two subjects who both wish to be absolute. The 'son is constantly taking the father inside himself, trying to become him' (Benjamin 1988, 220). It lays the foundation of patterns of domination, which the men of the manosphere reproduce in relation to women. It makes it impossible for those men to recognise someone outside of themselves. In such a relationship, 'the opposition between self and other can only reverse – one is always up and the other down' (ibid). The consequences of this are not only that the father becomes a fantasmatic object, but also the mother, as Benjamin writes. As she argues, both are reduced to objects that should be dominated; a dynamic that affects the whole lives of those men.

I would like to add that the father is not so much a leader, or *Führer*-figure. The narratives discussed in this book do not express such a sentiment. Incels in particular have created a culture for themselves (they did not necessarily grow up in one) that bears some resemblance to conservative Islam as Stein discusses it. These are cultures where the son is taught to be 'dismissive, even contemptuous, towards his mother, sister, and wife' (Stein 2010, 84): 'Deprived of identification with his mother as well, the son's shameful parts are projected onto others who are now treated with contempt, even violence' (ibid). The son's quest for his father's approval continues in different forms which are at the same time 'suffused with shame and self-loathing' (ibid). Unlike radical Islamists, the (mostly) white men discussed in this book do not submit to God, but it is the desire for an idealised father and the rage against a real (or perhaps differently fantasmatically constructed) father that works as an *affective force* that powers their bodies. It leaves them at the edge of disintegration. I argue that such desires remain largely unconscious, because we can see no, or very little, articulation of a leader-figure who could be seen as a father. Incels, MGTOW and other communities are leaderless. They do not idealise Trump or other leaders either. The desire to be shown the ropes and be raised by a phallic father is thus not displaced or projected onto someone else except an imagined father.

Conclusion

This chapter discussed two manifestos by misogynistic terrorists. Both men were, in their own ways, fascists who envisioned fascist, totalitarian societies in which women would be controlled and dominated by men. Breivik's and Rodger's mad ideas and their horrific actions are continuations of what many 'keyboard warriors' discuss online today. All such actions, whether they are symbolic-digital or real, are acts of *terrorism*. Terrorism, as Ruth Stein puts it, that terrorises thought itself and creates an impenetrable and yet visible and (to some) highly alluring worldview and fantasy structure. I have argued in the previous chapters that such a worldview is dependent on woman as an image and an idea that is at once destroyed and desired.

In this chapter, I have paid closer attention to the role of the father and how the striving for a particular fascist body and alpha masculinity is strongly connected to enacting revenge on the father for failing to provide such a body to his son. It is also connected to a perverse love of the father who should see and recognise his son in the moment that he is being surpassed and killed. Such an unconscious wish to kill and become the father is not connected to Oedipal elements, or to unconscious entanglements with the mother (although in Breivik's case such elements may have played a role given his well-documented dyadic and troubled relationship with his mother). Instead, it is pre-Oedipal and connected to regression towards an unborn state and the wish to be reborn as a strong man (see Chapter 1). Such a wish to be reborn may ultimately be connected to the main aspect of the actions of the male shooters: to kill women. To get revenge on women for allegedly not being able to become a new man, for not being able to be desired. In running amok, going on a rampage, those men must have been conscious of the fact that they could be killed. Rodger committed suicide. Only in dying, could he unconsciously hope to be reborn anew. In such acts, all boundaries are transcended, including the men's owns.

Some men have created their own fantasy worlds in which others (women) figure as symbolic and real targets for hatred and violence. Those men experience themselves and their boundaries as fragmented, shattered, threatened with disintegration, their psychic equilibrium in turmoil. They find refuge by calling themselves 'soldier', 'incel', 'MGTOW', 'Knights Templar', etc. They find refuge by forming male bonds around those signifiers, whether real or imagined. I have also argued that many of those communities are deeply infused with fascist and alt-right ideas, symbols, images and discourses. They are psychosocial symptoms of an era where authoritarian masculinity is widespread and where certain, obsessive men find themselves drawn to authoritarian ideas of racism, sexism and misogyny. As I have argued, such social aspects need to be understood on a bodily level too and those men are caught in a matrix of dis/inhibition that structures and also threatens their psychic homeostasis. Their bodies are in constant tension, bursting, exploding, restless. Such affective-bodily states are also situated, as I have noted so far in this book, in a wider visual culture of pornography, social media platforms like Instagram, hook-up apps like Tinder and an omnipresent sexuality. They are, particularly in the case of incels, related to mainstream pornography. Porn that misrepresents women as mindless, beautiful objects who only want to be fucked. MGTOWs and other men like Breivik respond to such an overload by trying to abandon women. Incels and men like Rodger respond to it by constructing and desiring a pornstar version of femininity.

Such forms of desire which are inherently structured by dis/inhibition could be responded to by a different form of self-disinhibition; by unloading the affectivity in a different way: through masturbation. Is shooting a displacement of ejaculation? The weapon as phallus. Rodger discussed masturbation in his manifesto. Masturbation is all that incels and MGTOWs have left. It fuels their fantasies. Can the demanded but unachievable enjoyment be sublimated and turned into a kind of *jouissance à un*? Probably not; for it is porn and masturbation that have, in part, helped shape the very (sexual) fantasies of many men today. Some men try to abandon pornography and masturbation and I discuss them in the next chapter. Their stories help us to further understand the technosexual male body as it is situated in a world of right-wing populism, the manosphere and ideological sexual neoliberalism.

Notes

1 The term 'mass shooter' refers to an individual who commits acts of gun violence in which multiple victims are involved (Myketiak 2016).
2 While both Breivik and Rodger do not belong to the manosphere as such, they are nonetheless often referred to by the different communities within the manosphere and in the case of Rodger in particular have had lasting influence on them. It is for that reason that they are included in this book.
3 Klaus Theweleit has also noted that fathers were mostly absent for the Freikorps men, perhaps they were not needed. For him, the Freikorps soldiers did not revolt against Oedipal fathers or sought to identify with them. They (unconsciously) wished to kill their parents in order to be reborn anew on the battlefield. Fathers are of little importance to them. In the context of his *Male Fantasies* books, the 'fatherless society' is relevant however. Some of the men of the Freikorps had lost their fathers in World War 1, while many others were World War 1 veterans (Bessel 1993; Donson 2010). Theweleit pays little attention to the role of the father as he focusses on the role women played in the soldiers' lives. The notion of the fatherless society extended beyond World War 2 in which many men lost their lives (Seegers 2015).
4 Jordan Peterson has of course been described as a father figure for some men of the manosphere (see Crociani-Windland & Yates 2020).
5 Schizotypal personality disorder (SPD) refers to a disorder which sees individuals unable to form relationships. They lack empathy and instead distrust others. Their behaviour is often eccentric and bizzare. They suffer from illusions, thought disorders and obsessive ruminations (Jakobsen et al. 2017).
6 We could also read the identification with (and revolt against) the father as a turning away from the mother, because it is the mother who those men would rage against. This argument would place the analysis in line with Oedipal conflicts and that the men turn towards the father as they have internalised the incest taboo.

Their hatred of women would thus be a hatred of their mothers. However, I specifically do not situate the men in Oedipal dynamics (see Chapter 1 and the Conclusion for an extended discussion on this). They turn against *both* parents and *specifically* against the father not because of Oedipal dynamics but because of an identification with the phallus and a struggle with masculinity. I follow Benjamin's (1988) critique of the Oedipus complex in that it pits women and men against each other via sexual difference (see my Chapter 1 and Conclusion). Benjamin's emphasis on the conflictual father-son relationship as a blueprint for domination is particularly useful for my analysis, as I have shown in this chapter.

Chapter 7

NoFap: masturbation, porn and phallic fragility

The previous chapter leaves us with an impasse. What is left to analyse after having written about some of the worst conceivable acts of killing women and men? Ending the last chapter by writing about masturbation led me to NoFap. The topic of masturbation and porn has acquired pressing currency in today's authoritarian capitalism and rise of the alt-right online. Some men on the alt-right specifically link masturbation to homosexuality and have argued that if men masturbate, they are gay. This chapter discusses data from the NoFap community and its official forum on NoFap.com. NoFap (which began on Reddit) is an online community for men and women who want to stop consuming pornography. Many of its thousands of registered users proclaim that they have a pornography and masturbation addiction. NoFap advocates to abstain from masturbation and porn for as long as users can so that they may eventually overcome their addiction. Users exchange tips and strategies on how to overcome their addictions. NoFap is perhaps the most progressive community of all examined in this book, because it presents far more nuanced and less openly (self-)destructive narratives than the others. There are also often diverse opinions within one thread and in general users actually discuss with each other. Threads can often be many pages long. It is debatable if one could count NoFap as part of the manosphere. It is overall not racist or anti-Semitic, but nonetheless often highly misogynist and toxic.

There have been major debates within feminist scholarship as well as other fields and paradigms on pornography and whether it is harmful to individuals or not (see Shrage 2005; Long 2012; Smith & Attwood 2014 for overviews). This chapter does not engage with such works in detail, because I am not interested in taking a particular position for or against pornography. While I do not want to question the NoFap men's pathological consumption of pornography and that it could lead them to some form of addiction, pornography can also lead to education and transformation of one's sexual identity (Albury 2014), something the men outrightly reject.

It also needs to be stressed that mainstream pornography is often violent, sexist, misogynist, racist, ableist and particularly abusive towards women

(McKee 2005; Fritz & Paul 2017; Shor & Seida 2019). It has been debated whether this results in consumers acting violent (Donnerstein 1984; Boyle 2005; DeKeseredy 2015), becoming addicted (de Alarcón et al. 2019), undergoing changes in their brains (Kühn & Gallinat 2014), or not (Voros 2009). I am neither in a position to argue for or against the use of pornography in relation to its addictive or brain-altering qualities. Writing in 2019, Rubén de Alarcón et al. conclude in their overview of research on porn addiction that 'despite all efforts, we are still unable to profile when engaging in this behavior becomes pathological' (de Alarcón et al. 2019, 1). In that sense, the question as to whether porn addiction actually exists is still debated by academic professionals (Voros 2009; Klein 2016).

While pornography research constitutes a niche within academia, the field of porn studies has emerged in the last 30 years (Williams 1989, 2004). Pornography, its representation (Attwood 2002; Schauer 2005; Boyle 2010; Paasonen 2011; Longstaff 2019), reception (Attwood 2005; McKee 2018; Attwood, Smith & Barker 2019), and wider cultural diffusion (Attwood 2017) have been researched by a growing number of academics through different approaches. Recent work has analysed the representations of masculinity within heterosexual (Hirdman 2007; Garlick 2010) and gay pornography (Burke 2016; Mercer 2017; Florêncio 2020; Rehberg 2019). Work has also focussed on how male porn users construct a sense of community on the internet (Lindgren 2010; Taylor & Jackson 2018). Some scholarship has drawn on psychoanalysis (Cowie 1992; Marks 1996; Butler 2004; Longstaff 2019; Varghese 2019, ed.). What matters for this chapter is that many men, and to a lesser extent women, *speak of themselves* as having a pathological, unhealthy addiction to porn. They want to end the addiction through the NoFap programme and by ending masturbation and porn consumption. Their narratives show that their fantasies have been heavily shaped by the porn industry (see Chapter 2) and, as many write, as a result their sex lives suffer or they find themselves unable to get aroused with a real partner.

There has been little substantial research on NoFap. The only two critical, qualitative studies to date are by Kris Taylor and Sue Jackson as well as by Marlene Hartmann (Taylor & Jackson 2018; Hartmann 2020) in which the authors use discourse analysis to examine how masculinity is constructed on NoFap (see also Taylor & Gavey 2019 for a related study that did not focus on NoFap). Taylor and Jackson (2018) argue that the NoFap users 'reject pornography to reconcile pornography use with particular expectations of normative masculinity' (ibid, 621). There is a 'struggle in defining masculinity' (ibid, 632) across NoFap and how it relates to ideas around hegemonic masculinity. This struggle articulates itself in emphasising the need for 'real' sexual relationships (as opposed to masturbation or watching virtual porn) as well as discussing the need to become more masculine, which means to embrace an alpha male type masculinity. This specifically includes heterosexuality which is equated with domination and innate, biological sexual difference (see also Hartmann 2020). Such findings very much resonate with the arguments I present in this chapter.

I contribute to such analyses by making the argument that masculinity is discussed as something that is specifically *threatened* by homoerotic feelings and extreme forms of porn and how this relates to the (fear of the) unconscious. This results in defence mechanisms, similarly as I discussed in previous chapters, whereby the men defend against their addictions through deploying a pseudo-scientific discourse. This presents them as victims of neuro-biological processes that render them helpless addicts. This is in line with my earlier discussions of the status of self-victimisation in this book. This status of the victim extends to discussions of particular forms of porn: gay porn, 'cuckold' porn and so-called 'sissy hypno' porn. I relate such narratives to Elizabeth Cowie's discussion of fantasy (Cowie 1997) as something that can shift within the cinematic viewing experience and afterwards. Cowie also argues that viewers can occupy multiple positions within the same viewing process and I connect this to how the NoFappers discuss their changing registers of dis/identification with male and female bodies and particular types of pornography.

At the same time, the narratives also reveal the creation of fantasies of symbolic power and agency in which women and feminism are being made to be responsible for the creation of sissy hypno porn in particular – a claim that is unsubstantiated. In this chapter, then, I focus on three particular themes that were present in the data: how pornography and desire in general are discussed by the men; their fears of becoming gay as a result of their consumption of hetero and gay pornography; and their discussion of the 'sissy hypno' and 'cuckold' porn genres. As with the previous chapters, a psychoanalytic perspective on the data shows the contradictory and complex fantasies that those men embody and circulate. NoFappers also discuss distinctly changing fantasies, as I show. I also continue to relate the data to the concept of dis/inhibition.

Following a brief discussion of the cultural history of masturbation and how it is discussed in psychoanalysis, this chapter examines material from NoFap.com.

The historical evils of masturbation

In *The Currency of Desire: Libidinal Economy, Psychoanalysis and Sexual Revolution*, David Bennett (2016) discusses the relationship between the (libidinal) economy and sexuality. He shows how sex itself was (and is) often (linguistically) equated with money where sexual organs are historically referred to as 'treasure' or 'bank', sexual intercourse as 'business' for example. In the 18th century, the physician Samuel-Auguste Tissot published *L'Onanisme*, a tract of sexuality and medicine. For Tissot, as Bennett points out, semen, and genital fluid, was a currency that needed to be retained. Specifically onanism was impoverishing and weakening the male body. It was 'as scandalous to spill one's sperm as it is to throw money out of the window' (Tissot 2015, 57, cited in Bennett 2016, 16). Physician's like Tissot saw semen as valuable, like money, that needed to be spend carefully and withheld from 'circulation' in the 'market'. In Freudian terms, sexuality, and in particular male ejaculation, was seen by many professionals and social commentators as an affective force that seeks affective discharge which should be contained within the body or abstained from. Libido was seen by sexologists as something that needed to be spent in moderation in order to conserve the body's energy. To an extent, Freud would draw on such early conceptualisations in his own theory of libido and the affective economy of the body, as Bennett notes. The psyche itself was a system of energy based on the retention and discharge of affect (Johanssen 2019). Bennett points out that, for Freud, libido functions almost like money as a general equivalent and medium of universal exchange. Libidinal energy can be spent, displaced or sublimated onto a variety of things or processes that are not directly related to sexuality.

The economy of sex and masturbation is thus an economy of caution and saving. The antithesis of masturbation was productive labour and often prescribed as a 'cure' for the 'disease'. Masturbation was a flight into fantasy, an escape from reality, which for many in the 17th and 18th centuries was seen as dangerous and fatal (see also Foucault 1978, 2003). Needless to say, such crusades were incorrect and ultimately futile, as time would tell. However, anti-masturbation discourse of a similar nature has made a comeback in some circles in a different fashion. It is no coincidence that NoFap, and other anti-porn communities, have emerged in the last few years. NoFap was founded in 2011 and there are, as I go on to show, some common denominators with the alt-right's misogyny and racism, the manosphere and other ideas that I have discussed so far in this book. NoFap itself is also regularly discussed by incels and MGTOWs. Before discussing NoFap data, I present some theoretical considerations in the next section.

Psychoanalysis, desire, masturbation and pornography

It was Freud, who was one of the first to discuss infantile sexuality without claiming it was inherently dangerous or damaging. In the *Three Essays on the Theory of Sexuality* (Freud 1981b), Freud specifically considered masturbation as an infantile sexual activity. For him, it represented the 'executive agency' of infantile sexuality (ibid, 189). Its erotogenic zone is the genital region and as the child develops sexually the other erotogenic regions lose their significance (see also Freud 1981d). Initially, autoeroticism (which is different from masturbation proper) is not object-dependent. Satisfaction may be obtained without the recourse to an object (for example the genitals).

Freud argued that the first form of autoeroticism is the sucking of the breast (Freud 1981b). The object is split and the autoerotic-sexual instinct is detached from non-sexual functions (which represent nourishment). The breast becomes the object of desire, because it 'comes to be desired in its absence' (Cowie 1992, 135). As the infant frees itself from dependence on the first object (the breast) and sees 'itself as an "object" for its own satisfaction' (Perron 2005b, 141), autoeroticism is no longer about pure drive satisfaction but about a merger of drive and object whereby the ego is cathected as an object in and for itself. 'This unifying movement then acts on another person during the initial "object choices" that will govern all later sexual life' (ibid). Laplanche and Pontalis note that 'auto-erotism is not the attribute of a specific instinctual activity (oral, anal, etc.), but is rather to be found in each such activity, both as an early phase and, in later development, as the component factor of *organ-pleasure*' (Laplanche & Pontalis 1973, 47, italics in original).

For Freud, infantile masturbation was also linked to the instinct for mastery (of sexuality). 'A certain amount of touching is indispensable (at all events among human beings) before the normal sexual aim can be attained' (Freud 1981d, 156). He also linked the instinct for mastery to *scopophilia*, the pleasure in looking and being looked at. This has been picked up by psychoanalytic film theorists such as Laura Mulvey who has linked *scopophilia* to filmic representation and how the male gaze is depicted on screen and how cinema was traditionally for the male gaze itself i.e. primarily a male audience (Mulvey 1975). I return to this discussion later in the chapter through the work of the psychoanalytic film theorist Elizabeth Cowie.

Coupled with excessive pornography consumption, masturbation can be thought of as an attempt by the subject to assume a phallic and sexual potency. Some argue that while masturbation may appear to be self-soothing and function as a means to discharge affects, it may also act as an aggressive-narcissistic attempt to seize back control of the self and to turn passivity into activity (Dodes 1990).

Another aspect about masturbation, and this is seldom if ever made in the literature or by Freud himself, is its possible link to affect. Freud's early 'discharge model' of affects (Johanssen 2019) practically lends itself to see masturbation as a pleasurable form of affective discharge which culminates in orgasm(s). Wilhelm Reich (1997) picked up on the role of masturbation and the orgasm for the subject. Writing about the Austrian Friedrichshof Commune and its leader Otto Muehl, Bennett notes:

> For Muehl, as for Reich, orgasm was the spending of an energy that could otherwise be hoarded or trapped in the body as a defence, forming an 'armour' that protected the subject against powerful emotions but blocked the natural, pleasurable impulse to discharge rather than save libido: a legacy of the patriarchal nuclear family and its taboos, such

character-armour was the foundation of the fascist state. (Bennett 2016, 213)

I would not be able to provide a better summary of Reich's (and by extension Theweleit's) ideas. For Reich in particular, orgasming (and masturbating) was a form of radical sexual politics (see Chapter 1). Reich's view of the orgasm relates to the wider themes of this book and the construction of a body armour as a defence mechanism, as I have discussed in the previous chapters. The men of NoFap are no different in this respect and regard abstinence from masturbation and pornography as an effective way to construct a body armour. In their cases this body armour is used to defend against non-heterosexual desire and the unconscious.

Pornography and masturbation (as I have shown via Freud) are not necessarily bad for the subject in itself. As the psychoanalyst Giorgio Tricarico (2018) writes:

> When porn is evoking such pristine joy, masturbation too may be experienced as a healthy, energising relationship with one's own body, a way to care for oneself, and not as a sad, solitary surrogate for sexual intercourse, a sort of tranquilliser for anxiety or depression, a compulsive necessity, and so on. The joyful sensation may persist alongside masturbation, in the form of a more confident feeling of being grounded, more attractive, and living in a world full of possibilities. (Tricarico 2018, 39)

Porn starts to become unhealthy if it is consumed excessively or used as a substitute object in order to mask a conflict, or mental health issue.

Given that fantasy is of central importance to both psychoanalysis and pornography, the subject has been of interest to psychoanalytic thinkers (see Introduction). In her classic work, Elizabeth Cowie (1992) argues that pornography is so alluring to the viewer, because the *desire to desire* draws the viewer in. Sexuality 'for psychoanalysis is not the upsurging of an instinct, a programmed response, but arises in the emergence of fantasy. As a result sexuality is characterised as a desire for pleasure, rather than simply the satisfaction of biological sex' (Cowie 1992, 136). Fantasy in that sense is what drives or perpetuates desire. Fantasy functions as a scene of and for desire. Both fantasy and desire can be closely connected to *scopophilia* and this has resulted in numerous feminist film and media scholars arguing how desire is constructed in film as a form of identification through the gaze for example (Mulvey 1975; Neale 1983; Doane 1987; Cowie 1997 and many others).

It is the wish to be aroused, and the wish to fantasise a scenario of sexual activity which pornography serves, so that the climax is a kind of interruption, though one which also maintains the system. The pleasure of sexual fantasy and pornography is desired for itself and not as a simple means to physical sexual gratification. (Cowie 1992, 136)

For psychoanalysis, then, the consumption of pornography is never only a matter of a means-end process, or of mere sexual gratification. Pornography facilitates the *desire to desire* (see Doane 1987). This has also been developed by Deleuze and Guattari when they argue that the desire to desire is desire in its originary, productive sense. When we speak of 'incest desire', 'patriarchal desire' or 'sexual desire', desire is already socially coded and has been repressed in its productive form (Deleuze & Guattari 1983a, 1983b). I think both Freudian/Lacanian and Deluzian-Guattarian accounts can exist in harmony here. Rather than the originary unconscious and with it desire being completely repressed, I would argue that it continues to exist even if desire is displaced onto particular myths or categories in psychoanalytic theory. I discuss fantasy and desire here in more detail because they are central concepts that I take up in this chapter in relation to sexuality and pornography. For Deleuze and Guattari, the Freudian unconscious is too orderly and representational, because Freud mobilised representational artefacts (myths, stories, etc.) to interpret the unconscious thereby prohibiting the radical potential of it both in practical and conceptual terms. This is useful to keep in mind when thinking about desire, which I predominantly use in the Freudian-Lacanian sense (see Introduction).

Psychoanalysis has also discussed addiction and specifically porn addiction (Savelle-Rocklin & Akhtar 2019). Addiction, and porn addiction, can be theorised and discussed from a variety of aspects: porn consumption as a way to avoid or manage intimacy, insecure attachment, avoidance, narcissism, disturbed object relations, repetition compulsion, a sense of mastery over the self, fantasies etc. are key here. Addiction may serve as a form of temporary relief from anxiety, depression, loneliness, or conflicts. It may provide a quick rush of pleasure and escapism. This chapter does not aim to contribute to such scholarship or to specifically theorise addiction, I therefore limit my discussion of it at this point. In the next section, I introduce NoFap and discuss some exemplary narratives of porn addiction by users.

NoFap: the promise of the phallus

The NoFap community is, in contrast to the incel and MGTOW communities, really more of a *community*, because detailed exchange of opinions and experiences takes place in the fora of NoFap.com. NoFap was founded in 2011 by the web developer Alexander Rhodes. Rhodes initially created the NoFap subreddit on Reddit and set up a dedicated website later on. What is remarkable about the official NoFap website is its entrepreneurial feel and corporate design. NoFap has an official logo which screams phallic power at the viewer: a red rocket that is being launched upwards. 'Get a new grip on life' the slogan underneath reads.

NoFap is also a copyrighted term and the website has its own shop that sells merchandise such as t-shirts. There is also an 'emergency' button that users can click. It opens up a page showing the following links which upon clicking randomly open motivating YouTube videos, memes, aphorisms or Reddit posts.

The forum and its sub-fora are the main part of the site. Many users have statistics in their signatures of how many days they have managed without porn or masturbation. Many advocate abstaining from masturbation and pornography entirely. The following user post is a good summary of NoFap:

> Masturbating still drains a vast amount of your energy and gives you nothing in return. Although it might relieve some pain and provides you some pleasure, it's still not worth it. Not to mention that it might get you back to watching porn, so you have to entirely eradicate it from your life. Just consider it a challenge that shows how strong you are. If you can't overcome this addiction, I doubt that you'll be able to overcome other obstacles in your life. (NoFap 2017a, online)

What is striking about many of the posts in the community is the orthodoxy with which the users advocate abstaining from masturbation altogether. The narratives are very similar to the ones Bennett (2016) discusses that conceive of the human body as an economic machine which needs to be kept in balance and needs to use its resources wisely, both in energetic and monetary terms. It is without question that if it becomes pathological and a form of repetition compulsion (to unconsciously work through particular conflicts), masturbation is unhealthy for the subject. If it takes centre stage and, coupled with porn consumption, it may make the subject less focused and energetic. I do not want to dispute such aspects when we think of masturbation and pornography as pathological and all-consuming. What seems noteworthy at least is the implicit *economism* with which the bad habits are discussed by the users. Apart from mental health issues, they cause procrastination, unproductivity and a draining of energy. NoFappers present themselves as *homo economicus* subjects who reproduce a phallic, neoliberal discourse of productivity and self-discipline. This is not meant as a critique, but it shows how they have internalised neoliberal values of self-reliance, willpower and a kind of pragmatic modification of the self (Walkerdine 2020). Such a discourse is similar to that of incels who draw on neoliberalism (see Chapter 4). However, while incels reject or have lost confidence in neoliberalism, NoFappers see neoliberal ideology as something to aspire to.

The NoFap forum is structured according to different thematic sub-fora: a forum on the lived experiences of those with porn addiction, a forum on 'rebooting' (i.e. recovering from porn addiction), a forum on 'success stories' and others. NoFap functions essentially as a self-help community which displays classic characteristics of pragmatic self-help philosophies: a focus on the problem and how to find the best solutions as a way forward (Johanssen 2012, 2013, 2017). Threads often reference mental health issues or other difficulties and users express that they used porn as a coping mechanism for example. The overall atmosphere and tone of the NoFap fora is supportive and positive. Users compete with each other who can have the longest 'streak', as they put it, without 'fapping' (masturbating). One user writes that he will 'prepare a new schedule from tomorrow onwards, so i can start being productive'. On Day 27: 'No PMO has helped me channel my energy elsewhere and concentrate on real life problems' (NoFap 2019a, online).

Many users discuss their problems in a pseudo-scientific, biologistic and highly rationalistic way (see also Hartmann 2020). Like the rest of the manosphere, they often refer to evolutionary psychology, and scientific papers to back up their claims (see my discussion of this in Chapter 3). Their porn addiction is presented as a stimulus-response dynamic that needs to be broken, so that they no longer associate porn with masturbation or sex. Many also link porn addiction to physical substance addiction, for example.

What is striking about many of the narratives is the instrumentality and cold rationality with which the users write about themselves. They only need to follow a few simple steps and all will be fine. NoFap replicates classic neoliberal self-help strategies that suggest to individuals that all they have to do is follow a few steps and their behaviour will be altered (Johanssen 2012). There is no space for the unconscious and that the porn consumption in itself may very well be a symptom of something else (relationship problems, or mental health issues for example).

While nuanced accounts are also very much present in the community, the overall atmosphere and tone of the discussions is one of manic, army-like discipline that often only knows schematic 'either – or' viewpoints. Overcoming the addiction is frequently called a 'battle', the NoFappers refer to themselves as 'soldiers', or 'brothers' who are 'fighting'. Not watching porn and masturbating is named 'surviving'.

The other man: fears of becoming gay

In their discourse analysis of NoFap data, Taylor and Jackson argue that 'it is noteworthy that there appears to be an unspoken agreement about the type of pornography users are abstaining from. That is to say that genres, gender representations, and sex acts often remain nebulous and ill-defined' (Taylor & Jackson 2018, 625). However, as I show in the following sections, NoFap users do discuss very specific porn genres and often specifically detail a journey through different genres over time (Hartmann 2020). Many discuss their consumption of heterosexual porn and also gay porn. Similar to many Christian fundamentalists (Dodson 2015) and some on the alt-right, one user writes that masturbation is equivalent to being gay and for that reason needs to be abstained from (NoFap 2019b). The user writes that 'sex fantasizing needs to go completely. Your mind needs to understand that sexual arousal is related to actual opportunities of having sex, not imaginary ones' (NoFap 2019b, online). Fantasy is completely deactivated and rendered impotent by the user. Isn't pleasure rather about *both* masturbation and other forms of sexual activity? On the surface, it appears that such sentences against masturbation and homosexuality are about embodying a particular masculinity. It is apparently *manly* not to masturbate, because one gets enough sex with a female partner. There is no need for autoeroticism. Being gay is also distinctly unmanly, the men claim. Such narratives can be seen as attempts to assume heterosexual masculinity (Taylor & Jackson 2018; Hartmann 2020).

However, underneath the surface are two dynamics at play, I argue: the (unconscious) fear of becoming or already being gay, because the NoFappers have already lost so much agency, porn could now turn them into anything. Secondly, a defence against the soft, homoerotic and female elements within those men. Those elements need to be expelled; they need to be labelled 'gay' or as pathetic, masturbatory. The only real enjoyment and arousal is through sex with a woman.

The use of the term 'addiction' is also relevant in this context. It adds to defensive discourses in which the men render themselves victims of something that is framed in a biological and scientific way (addiction). Similar to the other defensive strategies that I have discussed in this book (by incels for instance), the men present themselves as victims of something that has acquired a power over them. This could be pornography, women, feminism. A hegemonic sense of masculinity is threatened by the addiction. This also relates to masturbation specifically which is discussed as unmanly and not 'real' (see also Taylor & Jackson 2018). So-called 'real', 'hard' men don't need to masturbate. In fact, if they do and cannot overcome it, they will fail at everything else in life, as one user writes. The use of addiction as a particular scientific discourse is also significant because it relates to the use of science and evolutionary psychology, which I have discussed in Chapter 3, that seeks to cement ideologies of gender and sexual difference which seek to justify male dominance and, ultimately, patriarchy. Addiction, then, becomes a particular signifier which is used to both rationalise and defend against the excessive pornography consumption as something external, biological, feminine that those men are faced with. It turns them into victims of a flood of stimuli that they cannot control. This is similar to Theweleit's discussion of the feminine 'flood' that the male soldiers faced and sought to annihilate. Women were perceived as wild streams and floods which the male sought to banish from his life. At the same time, the soldiers were driven in their hunger for the red flood which they could destroy and neutralise (Theweleit 1989). According to the NoFap men, addiction is something that has come unto them; they cannot help it because their brains are hardwired to respond to sexual stimuli. At the same time, they want to move beyond their addiction because it has turned them into feminised, weak, gay men. They have failed as 'real' men (Bratich & Banet-Weiser 2019). The NoFap community promises a return to phallic power and 'real' masculinity for those men. We can see how defence mechanisms are mobilised in this community.

We could argue that such discourses are examples of retroactively repressing the originary unconscious as Deleuze and Guattari (1983a, 1983b) conceptualise it. The men use particular signifiers ('gay', 'extreme', 'addiction') in order to limit the productivity of their desire in its polymorphous-perverse form by self-diagnosing fears of becoming gay. Rather than seeing their responses to particular porn as being affective expressions of the unconscious, they try to understand and name them, because of the pathological nature of their porn consumption. This takes place because it is still taboo for those men to confess that they are attracted to porn (even though they have masturbated to it) as part of a complex and varied sexuality that may include homosexuality. However, there is more to this defence mechanism and I unpack it further below.

One can additionally argue that the fear of becoming gay becomes a rationalisation for the turning away from heterosexual porn, because it is another man who has sex with the woman. It is not the male porn viewer. While some may identify with the male porn actor and see themselves in his place, many other men seek to defend against this fact by mobilising fears of becoming gay. I do not dispute that such fears of a contagion, of becoming attracted to men are absent. They exist alongside a negation of the passivity of the porn consumer. He is watching someone else with the phallus. The fact that he is masturbating to another man having sex with a woman is unbearable. He should be in his place. As a result, the other man has to disappear. Of course, the question is whether such fantasies of heterosexual intercourse as the norm existed before the porn addiction or if they were amplified by it. Like incels, MGTOWs and other men today, some men cannot adapt to changing cultural norms when it comes to sexuality. Such changing cultural norms include the increasing visibility of queer and non-hetero sexuality in recent decades in popular culture (and porn) and the increase in declared LGBTQI+ orientations among Western populations (Bulman 2019). They also include trans and queer issues being discussed in the media, as well as a larger number of young people wishing to undergo gender reassignment surgery (Fielding & Bass 2018). All of those changing cultural norms have made sexual orientation more fluid and dynamic compared to previous decades (Hines 2018). Those developments feel threatening to the men; they threaten their fragmented egos.

Whether porn consumption has amplified (or animated, for a better term) the males' sexual fantasies to include homoerotic feelings and a less rigid sexual identity, or whether such feelings were always latent and had been *unearthed* by porn is a 'chicken or egg' question that is impossible to answer. For Freud, heterosexuality was a myth and depending on the other person, he argued that everyone was bisexual (Freud 1981b; Lemma & Lynch 2015). Bringing in psychoanalytic film theory at this point can help to further analyse such narratives.

Averting the other's gaze

The relationship to gay sexuality and seeing other men on screen can be further discussed via Elizabeth Cowie's *Fantasia* text (Cowie 1997). Drawing on Freud, Lacan, as well as Laplanche and Pontalis, Cowie argues that fantasy takes manifold and complex manifestations, one of which can include defences that are located within a particular fantasy. In our case this could mean that the act and fantasy of being aroused by men (who are either shown in heterosexual or gay porn) results in 'the most primitive defensive processes, such as turning round upon the subject's own self, reversal into its opposite, projection and negation' (Cowie 1997, 135). While it is beyond speculative to argue if the men of NoFap developed homoerotic fantasies and explored them through porn before or after having started to consume porn, they consciously articulate the need to repress such desires and fantasies by abstaining from porn/masturbation. The discussion of their fantasies and desires online and in particular their discussion of needing to end them can thus be seen as defences against such fantasies and practices.

Such fantasies are also often discussed in relation to thoughts on male, heterosexual porn actors:

> The thing is nobody talks about perspective, but the perspective you have when watching porn/erotica is deeply, deeply disturbing - you are actually inside the room next to other people fucking. Most porn movies show close-ups of actual intercourse and it's definitely not POV [point of view of the man] because of the angle. That means you're literally 2 or less feet away from a guy's junk and penetration itself. Sometimes the woman stares into the camera (at you), while she's being fu%ked by another guy. The act is extremely emasculating, even if you don't realize it. It's actually the woman you're sexually interested in and the woman you're attracted to getting owned by another male. Evolutionarily that means you failed and he won. He gets to reproduce and you didn't. He got her, you didn't. (NoFap 2019c, online)

Note how the post refers to evolutionary psychology and narratives of conditioning and evolution. The triangular, or triadic, perspective that is opened up through the post above is worthy of further analysis.

Cowie argues that fantasy and its filmic representation invites multiple forms of identification rather than just one where, for example, the male viewer only identifies with the male protagonist/gaze (Mulvey 1975). For Cowie, the gaze is mobile and fluid (see also Neale 1983). It has become perhaps even more mobile, fluid and fleeting in our current age where users are confronted with thousands of clips to choose from. Such a fluidity of the gaze also implies a fluidity of gender and sexuality (Minsky 1996; Maguire 2015). For Cowie, the viewer moves between different subject positions and this allows them to occupy both female and male, but also object and subject, active and passive positions. Cowie argues, drawing on Laplanche and Pontalis (1968) in particular, that cinema bears some relationship to primal fantasies (fantasies of seduction; the origin of sexuality and sexual difference; fantasies of castration).[1] 'Cowie's concept of fantasy enables the spectator to view a film as a staging and working through of these fantasies of the origins of subjectivity and sexual difference' (Yates 2007, 53), as Yates has argued in her analysis of cinematic representations of masculine jealousy. We could read the above posts which discuss the triadic relationship of the heterosexual (screen) couple and the viewer as fantasies of the primal scene (where the child finds their parents having sexual intercourse), but I think such an analysis goes a step too far and would make interpretations about those men that I could not make. I also would not argue that such porn scenes are used by the male viewers to conduct any substantial form of working through.

However, Cowie's emphasis on the shifting modes of fantasy and identification by viewers is helpful. While she uses it to theorise the viewing process itself, I would also point to the shifting aspects of fantasy before, during and after the viewing process. We can see how fantasies and acts of identification are multimodal and change over time. First, those men wrote that they were initially aroused by seeing *both* female and male bodies (heterosexual porn), as well as only male bodies (gay porn). As they realised their addiction, they sought to *disidentify* from such forms of identification.

Second, their fantasy changes towards one in which they take up the position of the passive voyeur who can only watch the couple in the room but cannot participate. This shows a desire to depart from such a fantasy in which the male porn consumer has become weak and is forced to watch the object of his desire (the woman) with another man. A more fluid form of sexuality and fantasy is thus policed and brought back into stringent heterosexual norms which result in a defence against homosexuality, and against the consumption of any heterosexual porn. This is coupled with (pseudo-scientific) narratives of weakness, having 'lost' to the alpha male porn actor, and being emasculated as a result.

Such posts are also implicitly coupled with envy of the other man in the videos, because he is able to have 'real' sex with the woman and the NoFapper is not. While fantasy is the '*mise-en-scene* of desire' (Cowie 1997, 143), we can see through the posts discussed in this section how it is dynamic, in flux and subject to a kind of deferred changing of meaning – the latter of which is done in the service of defending against the productivity of desire and the unconscious. Fantasy is thus shifting and subject to changes (we could say different forms of cathexis), over time. Many NoFappers feel not only ashamed because of their porn addiction, they feel emasculated because of it. They are weakened in their male identity, because they watch other people having sex. They feel deprived of their heterosexual masculinity because of porn. The first step in any addiction is to acknowledge it. NoFap is an important platform in this case and enables those men to come clean without being judged. They are understood and supported by other men.

However, the notion of identification, which seems such a powerful vehicle to enable porn consumption in the first place, is subsequently categorically denied in those narratives. In Lacanian terms, one can say that it is the Other's gaze that those men fear. It is not only that they defend against all those aspects that I have outlined (becoming gay, soft elements within them, watching porn), they also defend against the possibility that they are seen by the Other as masturbating to porn. Rather than identifying with the male porn actor and perhaps gaining a momentary sense of affective discharge and pleasure from it by *imagining* that it is them who are giving that female pornstar such apparently breath-taking orgasms or at least what it would be like to do so, they fear being caught in the act of looking at porn. It seems, Laura Mulvey's (1975) essay on the male gaze that structured cinematic representation and (unconscious) identification and audience spectatorship no longer applies to those men. They *disidentify*. They cannot bear to see the other man with the phallus and that they do not have it. They have come to realise that watching porn is pathetic and a flight from reality, as they see it. The phallus then becomes something that is desired (also in a homoerotic way, which is in itself defended against) and envied by those men, because they feel that they lack it. I have made similar arguments about the implicit appeal of fascism as a male homoerotic bond in Chapter 5. This desire of and defence against the Other's phallus is further negotiated by the men through the cuckold porn genre, which I discuss later in this chapter.

Additionally, the post quoted earlier (see page 177) is also significant because it exemplifies wider psychodynamics of the manosphere whereby the users perform a kind of super-ego function both for themselves and all the other users. They remind everyone that such forms of porn consumption are wrong, emasculating, and abnormal. The other users are directly addressed as 'you' by the men. In writing about their changing fantasies and presenting them essentially as defence mechanisms against the productivity of desire and the unconscious, as I have argued, the men move *beyond* defensive narratives and assume power and symbolic agency. Again, we see a pattern repeating itself which I discussed in Chapter 2, Chapter 3 on YouTubers, Chapter 4 on incels, Chapter 5 on MGTOW and incels and in Chapter 6 on the mass shooters: initial defence mechanisms and passivity are turned around into (fantasies of) symbolic power and agency. Such fantasies construct the body armour of those men. Of course this does not mean that such fantasies are left behind; the defence mechanisms remain and the body armour is always porous. While those men imply and play with their status of alleged victimhood, they all try to move beyond it in different ways. In the two posts quoted earlier, the men tell the others ('you') what is normal, what 'you' do and what constitutes the identity of a NoFap user. The same mechanisms are in place in the incel and MGTOW communities. Particular identities are constructed, circulated, policed and affirmed by everyone. Immanent to such identities is the creation of a specific version of reality (via fantasy) that is particularly based on excluding, hating and abusing women. This becomes fully evident when discussing another set of narratives. Narratives which are about particular extreme and fetish porn.

The sissy hypno conspiracy to weaken all men: the thing and the user unconscious

One niche genre is picked up again and again by many NoFappers: so-called 'sissy hypno' porn. It is a porn genre where images/sequences of women are periodically interrupted by images of naked males, penises and male ejaculation. It allegedly hypnotises men and turns them into females. Men discuss their consumption of such material as follows:

> Sissy Hypno is what brought me here and although I was only into it for a short time it seriously messed up my head. I was even questioning my gender and started acting all girly and giggly for a while. It is very evil stuff in my opinion. The stuff I was watching (although made by an amateur) was highly professional in terms of presentation, used upbeat music and the image overlays were targeted to exact the greatest amount of fear and novelty which resulted in massive spikes of dopamine which got me hooked very quickly. Please DO NOT view it because it will warp your mind massively. (NoFap 2017c, online)

NoFappers not only feel that certain porn genres are extreme, immoral and abnormal (something I would not necessarily dispute), but there is something far bigger behind them. It is an alleged effort to weaken all men:

> For those who don't know, sissy hypnosis porn is a sub-genre that leverages and amplifies viewers' innate feelings of shame and inadequacy for the purpose of causing harm. They are explicitly designed to make the viewer question their sexuality and gender, break down their self-esteem, and pull them further into shame and addiction. While many are of low quality, some are clearly the work of individuals with training in sound engineering, hypnotherapy, or both. I expect that some are made by certified clinical hypnotherapists who are exercising their own fetishes.

NoFap and phallic fragility 181

> They use images with subliminal text, multiple voice tracks, binaural beats, and other techniques to create an extremely powerful, addictive, and destructive experience. These videos are dangerous. (NoFap 2018, online)

Before analysing the alleged conspiracy behind sissy hypno porn in more detail, I wish to think about the wider psycho-technological consequences of NoFap.

The endless search is a key symptom of porn consumption and many users write that they spend significant amounts of time browsing videos. One can never quite find what one is looking for. There is an unbridgeable gap between a desire for a particular sexual scenario and what is offered by porn. Fantasy and desire never only operate in the ideational (representational) realm, they have distinctly affective components that always escape re-presentation. Porn thus fundamentally operates with an ideological promise that it can never fulfil: you, the user, will be provided with the realisation of your most inner erotic fantasies. For Lacanians, this refers to the lack the subject occupies in the Symbolic Order and the relationship to the Imaginary. Porn endlessly perpetuates the desire to desire, because of never ending possibilities of arousal. One allegedly better than the other. The notion of searching is of course a general characteristic, we could say *symptom*, of our contemporary technoculture. Patricia Ticineto Clough has theorised this in *The User Unconscious* (2018a). She writes:

> The user unconscious, I therefore have suggested, is a matter of affect, in psychoanalytic terms, the force of seeking lost (infantile) objects, operating, however, in a networked environment of objects that along side those lost are those that are not lost but rather are lively and not containable brought by datafication out of reach of human consciousness and bodily-based perception, that is, an environment of the endless availability of the search that in itself supersedes finding an object. This endless searchability supported by datafication is another way of posing the liveliness of objects or their other-than-human liveliness that suggests an embodiment of the I and the unconscious that is human and other than human, yet to be fully engaged as a matter of subjectivity and sociality. (Clough 2018b, online)

We live in a technoculture that works hard to eradicate the need to search so that automated processes (e.g. algorithms, artificial intelligence, user data analytics) offer us suggestions and solutions *before* we can even enter a keyword. Porn is a key force in this. The platform *PornHub* for example harvests users' data in order to provide them with a sophisticated re-commender system of what kind of porn they would like to watch. Their porn consumption is fundamentally, but not exclusively, shaped by algorithms.[2] It is a *machine* that makes their desires. For Clough, this would be emblematic of what she calls the 'user unconscious'. An unconscious that goes beyond the unconscious of classic psychoanalytic theory. It is an unconscious that is comprised of human and non-human dimensions, given our fundamental merging with technology. Her conceptualisation has 'unsettled the notion of internal objects' (Clough 2020, 125) of traditional psychoanalysis. The user unconscious is not only about lost objects and the search for them, but it is also about the search for new objects, a search that is alluring, nudging and seductive; brought into existence by both technology and the human body. Digital technologies thus alter the unconscious itself and have themselves unconscious qualities. The subject is therefore relational through the use of technology. This is not necessarily something negative in itself, but it becomes problematic if attachments to digital technologies become pathological or damaging for individuals. Such attachments articulate themselves in specific ways for the men of NoFap.

NoFappers are examples of what Wilhelm Reich called the 'machine-men' of fascism (Reich 1997, xix). Masturbation itself becomes a technosexual act which for those men is only possible in and through porn. The consumption of and masturbation to sissy hypno porn is thus partly facilitated by a user unconscious which lured the men towards it. The id's qualities of seeking pleasure at all costs are evident here. In addition, the sissy hypno porn has taken up residence in the user unconscious itself and is allegedly shaping it directly from there. Men are hypnotised and unconsciously manipulated, as they write: 'Now add to that the subliminal and subconscious as well as the direct & blatant programming & hypnosis of these more "extreme" & "next level dopamine rush" videos -that use flash images and music and beats to put the brain into a direct or semi hypnotic state' (NoFap 2019d), as one user expresses. Such a persecutory fantasy and anxiety is a symptom of the user's anxieties of his unconscious itself. He has become addicted to porn and his affective experiences of watching porn and living with the addiction are in psychoanalytic terms experiences of bodily dispossession and loss of agency (Johanssen 2019). It is the unconscious itself that he fears because it harbours unknown and unpredictable forces. An unconscious that has been coupled with technology and is, in part, literally shaped and controlled by non-human elements (algorithms, big data analytics, porn videos).

This question of *not knowing* is a fundamental aspect of psychoanalysis. We cannot know everything about ourselves. This is unbearable to those men. They need to know. Someone must know! Why has this happened to them? Who knows? Someone must! 'I don't know what that would specifically be as I stated in another post ... something "spiritual" or psychological maybe or something else??', one user asks. The unconscious is a void, a non-place that is never fully knowable, let alone representable in an ideational form to human subjects. 'I don't know', writes the user and suspects 'something'. Something 'spiritual' or 'psychological' or 'something else'. It is noteworthy how that particular user attributes no human action behind that kind of porn, but spheres or forces. A *something*.

We can unpack this further with Freud's (Freud 1953) and Lacan's notion of *das Ding* (the Thing). Das Ding refers to the secret centre of desire. A core of desire which is inaccessible for the subject. By way of analogy, we could say that this secret centre is similar to the secret workings of a machine, where we cannot get access to the engine but this engine enables the machine to function. Like algorithms today which are fundamentally inaccessible for ordinary users. For Lacan, das Ding refers to an originary, libidinal base of the unconscious in its polymorphous perversity. Das Ding means something beyond signification and imagination. It is a lost object that the subject nonetheless searches for and tries to find again. It is close and yet distant. Das Ding sets desire in motion and, as Allison Horbury notes, Lacan developed this idea further with his notion of the *objet petit a*. The difference between both is, as he explains in his *Seminar on Anxiety* that the *objet a* 'embodies the dead end of desire's access to the Thing' (Lacan 2014, 271). A route that is necessarily blocked, because the Thing is inaccessible and this inaccessibility in a sense animates *objet a* or sets it in motion. In this case, the endless search for more porn in the hope of discovering *objet a* and, ultimately, the Thing.

For Horbury, porn functions along 'the polymorphous perversity of the partial drives – oral, anal, genital, invocatory, and especially scopic – and their search for substitutive pleasures in a medium or aesthetic modality that does not (necessarily) fill out these drives beforehand with ideals via elaborate plots or scenarios' (Horbury 2019, 91). While porn relates to part-objects (mouths, breasts, phalli, anuses) and the satisfaction of particular drives (oral, anal, genital, scopic) through a system of signification which operates through those two registers, there is always something emanating from and revolving around the Thing which remains beyond the ideational and representational (in Lacanian terms, the Real). As she argues:

> Insofar as the pornographic aesthetic intractably represents those Real part-objects, drives, and erotogenic orifices that metonymically 'stand in' for the Thing, their particular presence may be said to simultaneously 'encircle' a gap in the symbolic that nevertheless signifies a 'third meaning' for the viewer. (Horbury 2019, 94)

The very consumption of porn is thus inherently tied to the unconscious and to (unconsciously searching for) and finding 'porn one thought one was looking for, and what one finds erotic in it may not be obvious to another' (ibid, 94). For Horbury, who draws on Lacan, there is an ethics in pornography that can actually reveal the subject's desire to them:

> Where pornography's intractable aesthetic can be of ethical import is

> where it can teach the subject something about the truth of their desire and objet a beyond socio-symbolic values of 'good' representations, or politically 'bad' pornography.... What arises, then, is the question at the heart of a psychoanalytic ethics regarding the subject's relation to das Ding and their management of desire: is the subject's super-ego injunction on enjoyment stronger than their commitment to the truth of their desire?
>
> What defence might be mounted to manage the lack of distance in pornography's push towards the real polymorphous perversity of the drives? (Horbury 2019, 94–95)

While pornography, as I have argued, may shape a subject's desire, and not necessarily reveal it, it nonetheless has a strong relation to the Thing and the fundamental perverse core of the unconscious and the drives. In encountering such pornography, the NoFappers mount particular defences against their own consumption/addiction of it by questioning who is behind it, because they cannot comprehend or know their unconscious motives for watching it. They cannot comprehend their addictive, endless searches for porn. We can underline this further with Lacan's only other explicit discussion of the Thing (apart from *Seminar VII*) in *Seminar X* when he writes about anxiety: 'Not only is it [anxiety] not without object, but it very likely designates the most, as it were, profound object, the ultimate object, the Thing' (2014, 311). In that sense, there is a key relationship between anxiety and the Thing, which is expressed for the NoFappers in the way I have discussed above for example. Not having access to the Thing, or rather having access to the Thing which in itself remains inaccessible nonetheless, results in anxiety for them. They want to know the secret core of their desires and cannot. As a result, they resort to speculating who is behind the porn.

For the NoFap users, affective forces, the Thing, beyond human comprehension are behind the sissy hypno porn. Other users affirm such a view when they write:

> They know they are going to hell and they want other people to steer away from god's path. I don't know if you are agnostic or atheist but it is related to spirituality what these people are doing. If you go behind the scenes you will see that many of the times, these people are worshiping Satan. (NoFap 2019e, online)

> Call me crazy, but this proves that porn is inherently demonic. The reason why many men lose in the war against porn is that it attacks your soul as well as your mind and body. Demons are able to enter inside your body through obscene images (such as violence, sexual deviancy, the occult, ect.).... We are at war, brothers, so don't let your guard down! Not even for a second! (NoFap 2019f, online)

It is interesting that the devil is evoked here. Freud wrote of demonic forces that they are 'derivatives of instinctual impulses that have been repudiated and repressed' (Freud 1981f, 72). They are 'bad and reprehensible wishes' (ibid). While the particular porn videos the NoFappers write about may be very well described as 'demonic', are they perhaps referring to their own demons, unleashed by their unconscious here too? For Freud, the figure of the devil is a father figure (as is God). The father is the prototype for both God and the devil. For Freud and Lacan, the super-ego is also related to the father, as it is the father, who in the nuclear family, lays down the rules (this is of course no longer such an exclusive case today). It is thus a demonic father that articulates itself in the NoFapper's super-egos. A devil-like super-ego that knows how wrong it is to watch such porn and yet does nothing to stop the (equally demonic) id from pursuing it. It is the ego which finds a solution in this dynamic by calling out the demonic forces that are behind the videos rather than within the men themselves. The army of NoFap is 'at war', but are those men not at war with themselves?

The need to name *someone*

Rather than naming spherical, demonic, affective forces that relate to the Thing as being behind such content, many other men resort to naming individuals who have a sense of omnipotence and control over them. In reflecting on a loss of agency (as the men themselves allude to), they turn it into an effort of mind control and domination of men on the part of sissy porn producers. There must be an Other at work behind the scenes with far more darker motives. The men's own paranoia about their porn addiction – and their fears of their unconscious – is thus projected onto an Other. This is another defence mechanism that seeks to shift responsibility to someone else rather than to the men themselves. Someone else is rendered responsible and the men can thus remain free of self-blame or shame:

> *Who is behind sissy hypno stuff and what is their actual goal?*
> All together [sissy hypno porn content] looking like an organised propaganda wave rather than pathetic amateur attempts of some weird fetish small community. And inevitably the question arises: who's paying for this and Why? What are they trying to achieve with such a strange global online social experiment?
> On 1st, superficial glance, I speculated it must be some Western mogul supporting the radical left. One of those sponsoring LGTB agenda, deconstruction of gender roles and so on. But looking more closely, the content contradicts the left-wing narrative on many counts…. (NoFap 2019g, online)

Similar to blaming the Jews, women or others, fascistic tendencies are evident in the above post and the manosphere more widely (see previous chapters). There is a global world revolution, a global social experiment financed by a hidden power, a hidden agenda, the user writes. With Young-Bruehl (1996) we could read such narratives as displaying some obsessive qualities (see Chapter 5). An 'organised propaganda wave' is at work, as one user writes. The above user wonders if 'LGBT' groups or a Western mogul supporting the radical left are behind it, but he finds obvious contradictions in his own theory. Other users speculate that the agenda is purely money-driven, or just an angry person with a lot of time on their hands. Soon enough, other users affirm the original poster's question. One writes that 'there is an elite above the government that keep us a certain way to benefit them'. This elite allegedly control the media, the government and society in order to oppress the majority of people. 'I feel they don't change or encourage certain Porn, technology and social media as they know how the brain works and know how it affects us'. Sissy porn is part of their plan. 'Who is behind this? Yes you could simply say just follow the money.... But I would not be surprised if there was actually something more sinister behind it. But I dont really know. But it's a disturbing trend for sure in my opinion', a third person wonders.

Another user insists that 'someone must be sponsoring their works' because 1, 2 or even 10 people could not create the mass of content that exists out there 'even if they work day and night'. Sissy porn is described here as a flood, as streaming, bombarding the internet, male bodies and the NoFappers' unconscious – like Theweleit's soldier males perceived the red flood of women. The men are frightened by such force and threat to their egos. Rationalising and finding *someone* behind it may bring them some peace, as the below post exemplifies:

> It's mainly LGBTQ and fundamentally something that aims to disconnect sex from gender. If they push this stuff and make men into 'females' it means their ideology is correct and they won.... A man will never ever be a woman, nor will a woman be a man.... Sissy hipno ultimately aims to emasculate men and make women masculine. They want to make sex/gender a 'social construct' that is 'maliciously assigned at birth'. It's also pushed by 3rd wave feminism as 'woman empowerment'. (NoFap 2019h, online, emphases in original)

From the perspective of the above user, the weakening and emasculating effects of such videos are allegedly actively desired by women, feminists, LGBTQI+ people. Such narratives are examples of further active fantasies that the men employ whereby they render somebody else responsible for orchestrating a great conspiracy to weaken all men. None of this is true of course. While there are some users who disagree with such points in the above thread, many agree with them. 'It could be a feminist agenda to destroy men', one muses. 'So if we talk about who to blame, I think that lgbt activism, third wave feminism and gender theory are to blame', another adds. 'There's also definitely an attack on white men too, they're always the butt of jokes in movies and/or commercials etc. They even laugh at themselves now', one writes (NoFap 2019h).

Here, one can argue that such conspiracy theories are symptomatic of a persecutory super-ego that has 'outed' those men as 'sissies' or 'cucks' and punished them. They cannot fully accept that t*hey* themselves are behind their porn consumption. Rather than granting agency to their unconscious and its perverse drives, they grant it to other forces or groups that are allegedly out there to weaken and control men. In that sense, many NoFappers are identical to incels, MGTOWs and other men of the manosphere and the alt-right today. At some point, it is the Other who is to blame for it all. While such fantasies are defensive, they at the same time also create a new reality in which particular groups are behind this type of content. Such narratives are thus another example of how defence mechanisms and symbolic power are intertwined. The implicit fascist and racist dimensions of the above posts are further unpacked in the next section.

The cuck: a racist fantasy from porn to the manosphere

While no current data on the ethnicities of NoFap.com users exists, it seems that most are male, 'white, heterosexual..., living in the USA or western Europe' (Hartmann 2020, 2). In 2012, 72% of NoFap users who completed a survey on their socio-demographic background, referred to themselves as Caucasian (see https://nofap.com/about/community/). The background of the users is important to consider in so far as their narratives at times overlap with similar racist discussions that incels engage in when it comes to an understanding of their bodies and masculinity.

Sissy hypno porn is about degrading the viewer and another genre similarly plays with feelings of humiliation and shame: Cuckold porn depicts scenes where a white man (the 'cuck' or cuckold) is forced to watch a white woman, who is portrayed as his wife or girlfriend, have sex with another man (who is most often black). Such content also regularly features the 'husband' being degraded and verbally abused.

The theme of the cuckold genre, which is relatively niche but growing in mainstream porn (Lokke 2019) has racist and racialised connotations that are important to discuss. It gained in popularity following the election of Barack Obama as U.S. president in 2009 (Lokke 2019, 218) and thus suggests an un/conscious response to changing social life. It may articulate itself in relation to white supremacy and racist fantasies of white people that the white race would be in decline in the United States under an African-American president (see Chapter 2). Cuckold porn could be seen as an unconscious way of working through such anxieties which specifically extend to include racist fantasies of the white phallus being overtaken or replaced by the black phallus (Pegues 1998; Doane 1999; Crawford 2008; Stephens 2014).[3]

The cultural figure of the cuck can be regarded as a (sexual) failure of the white phallic man. Not only is his wife unfaithful, he is 'forced' to watch her having sex with another man. He is thus considered an overall failure and this impression is amplified by the other (male) who sees him in a passive position (Sinclair 1993). 'At its most basic, the cuckold is used to explore the anxieties of a wounded patriarchy, whose fears of sexual failure are made benign through mockery' (Lokke 2019, 213).

This form of mockery takes on a particular salience in our political moment of post-Trump politics which signified a forceful break with the Obama era. The term 'cuck' was particularly used during the online culture wars from 2015, for example in the form of racist memes by Trump supporters and the alt-right to refer to Liberal and Left men. It was also transformed into the term 'Cuckservative' to denote conservatives who failed to get behind Trump (Nagle 2017).

Since he came to power, Trump has not only rolled back achievements of the Obama administration (Marsden 2019) but the election of a misogynist and racist white male has led to a renewed sense of power for his (mostly) white supporters. In the wake of the U.S. Black Lives Matter protests in the summer and autumn of 2020, Trump's apathy and deliberate negation of police brutality have led to white armed racists taking to the streets, hoping to incite a civil war.

In Chapter 4, I argued that incels construct the white, fascist Chad as an ideal type which they ultimately desire. They also often refer to themselves as 'cucks' to describe their alleged weak and fragile egos. Other men of the manosphere, such as MGTOWs, also use the term to refer to weak men who have been allegedly 'cucked' by women into obedience. The term is used by NoFap users both metaphorically and literally: they refer to themselves as cucks metaphorically – weak men who lack a phallic masculinity because of their porn addiction – and literally when they write of their consumption of cuckold porn itself.

As with other men of the manosphere, the ideal form of masculinity the NoFap men aspire to is white and phallic. The cuck is used as a self-descriptor in a similar effort to name the type of masculinity the men feel they have. This act of naming, however, is underpinned by racism and situates the white body in relation to a fantasmatically constructed ultra-phallic male black body. This also needs to be seen in relation to the racist dynamics of interracial pornography which often replicate an oppressive master-slave relationship.[4] Yet, the fact that the active male in the cuckold videos is black, may provide 'some solace for the white male' (Lokke 2019, 216), as the viewer can occupy a fantasmatic position of weakened but nonetheless white masculinity. If the black male body is perceived in racist and stereotypical terms by viewers, and the NoFap men in particular, they can assume a position of some racist symbolic power in which they occupy the status of the white, if weakened, male. A white male who may be momentarily subordinated as the cuck, but who ultimately still belongs to a 'superior' race compared to non-white ethnicities, as the men think.

Given the ambivalent homoerotic fantasies which I have discussed earlier, NoFap men may also identify with and desire the exoticised black male in the videos. This may have attracted them to this genre, but they defend against such homoerotic feelings. While Lokke notes that the viewer could identify with any of the three of the performers in cuckold porn (see also Ward 2015), the men of NoFap ultimately seem to identify mostly with the cuck in an act of masochistic self-punishment. They can nonetheless maintain some remaining sense of agency because they consume porn which shows the white male being 'betrayed' by a black male. The blame is shifted to the woman and the black man in such fantasies. The husband's wife has cheated on him and he is a helpless onlooker. This marks a difference to the sissy hypno porn genre which, for the NoFappers, is entirely degrading and castrating.

The alt-right and the men of the manosphere more widely take the cuckold sex scene as an image representative of Western culture and masculinity as a whole. White men have been 'cucked' by feminist women, Left and Liberal governments, men who are not white, etc. The porn script of the cuckold scene is used as a defensive fantasy of traditional white masculinity and against anything that threatens it. The same transferring from porn to wider social life is also observable in the NoFap community when men move from discussing the literal cuck (themselves as porn consumers) to the metaphorical one:

> Most women won't admit it, but they want strong men in their lives. Men capable of solving problems, making decisions, and voicing their opinions, despite the fact it might upset someone. Feminism only really exists in places where the men are cucks. (NoFap 2019j, online)

> Considering we've been living in decades of peace in the western world, the men have all gotten soft. Then come the third world migrants who take advantage of European women because the European men are too cucked and obedient to their globalist overlords. (NoFap 2019k, online)

Anders Breivik made similar claims about the alleged decline of Western civilisation (see previous chapter). The modern white male has become a cuck and/or sissy, weakened by various Others. 'Millions of men are trained intro cuckoldry'. (NoFap 2019i, online) by consuming sissy hypno, cuckold or other kind of niche porn, writes one user. The use of the term 'cuck' by

NoFap users, incels, MGTOWs and other men of the manosphere is in that sense the same as other words they use to lament their inadequate masculinity: incel, beta male, etc. However, the usage of the word cuck comes with a particular racialised and racist fantasy which makes the overlap of the manosphere with racist and fascist online communities all the more apparent. The figure of the cuck is used to construct a racist fantasy in which white men have been weakened by a dominant union of feminist women, Jews, refugees, BIPOC individuals and people on the Left. This sense of weakness explicitly includes sexuality and a defence against changing times. As with sissy hypno porn, many NoFap users think that the cuckold porn genre itself is used in order to manipulate or brainwash men into becoming weak.

This fantasmatic shift from a masochistic ('I am the cuck, help me fight my addiction', as a user might say) to a sadistic fantasy ('I have been cucked by others') marks a change from inhibition to disinhibition whereby a sense of agency is reattained by those men and blame is shifted onto the Other.

A note on masochism

I argue that the intense speculations of who is behind the sissy porn conspiracy, which I discussed earlier, as well as discussions of men being 'cucked' by feminists and others are in fact expressions of the desires of those men on NoFap to know what (or who) is behind their consumption of such kinds of porn. This means that they seek to both know and to defend against their unconscious and the desires that may be stirred up by the knowledge of those users who are similarly drawn to the content of porn sites. Why were they attracted to this type of content in the first place, the men wonder? They frame it as a natural progression from 'vanilla' porn towards extreme porn, but this seems too superficial. Sissy porn is inherently sadistic, because it degrades the man in the harshest terms. Cuckold porn, while arguably less harsh, is also about degradation and humiliation. I do not want to dispute that such porn or sexual practices may be arousing for some men, women, nonbinary individuals or couples, what matters is that it is seen as so damaging to the NoFappers' mental health by themselves. Such sadism, is initially responded to by masochism. At the point of their consumption of such content, the men displayed highly masochistic tendencies. They masturbated to being humiliated and insulted, and found it pleasurable. This is similar to the cuckold porn videos I discussed a moment ago.

Sissy hypno videos are inherently perverse in the psychoanalytic sense of the term (Stein 2005). In *A Child is Being Beaten*, Freud discusses masturbation in connection with masochism. The masochist masturbator (a 'pervert', as Freud calls him) finds himself to be presented with 'unbearable intensity' (Freud 1981e, 197). In attempting intercourse with a woman, he finds himself to be impotent. He wants to become a woman.

We could postulate that such dynamics are also in place for the NoFappers. The fantasies are precisely enacted in the sissy hypno porn videos and the NoFap men respond to them by masturbating to them. Could this then be a case of the real sexual desire which the subject did not know of and which is revealed through porn, as Horbury writes? Rather than wanting to become a woman, it may be that it is the supposedly punishing and humiliating aspects of sissy and cuckold porn that those men were attracted to. It is as if they unconsciously *want* to be caught by someone (wife, girlfriend, mother, sister, friend) so that their consumption would finally be revealed and could end. This would be the ultimate disinhibition which, so it is hoped, would help with other inhibitions beyond the screen. The act of being caught is itself both arousing and anxiety-inducing for the men (Kahr 2008; Waldon 2011). It is only amplified through the consumption of cuckold porn in which the white male is allegedly humiliated by others. There may thus be fantasies of masochism and being dominated by women at the heart of such porn for viewers. However, the men have not been caught, or if they have, they have nonetheless joined NoFap to put an end to all of this themselves. At the same time, sissy and cuckold porn promise, like fascism, an end of responsibility as they represent a domination of the male viewer who is hypnotised, brainwashed, humiliated and rendered helpless. He can give up responsibility and power and submit to an other who tells him what to do. Nonetheless, the NoFappers wish to assume a sense of responsivity and relationality towards women again.

Conclusion: the perverse technoculture of phallic entitlement

This chapter focussed on the online community NoFap, a community that is on the fringes of the manosphere. Nonetheless, there are some similarities to other communities such as incels and MGTOW as I have shown. I discussed particular themes present in the data and focussed on the shifting and dynamic nature of fantasies (Cowie 1997) that those men detail in relation to their desires and consumption of pornography. As in the previous chapters, a similar psychodynamic pattern of dis/inhibition was also present in the NoFap data which illustrates the contradictory and shifting discourses that incorporate defence mechanisms, self-victimisation as well as the creation of a toxic reality which embraced particular forms of masculinity as well as toxic views of women and others.

NoFap is an inherently neoliberal product, similar to other self-help groups, in which users think of their bodies and themselves in economic terms. They place an emphasis on conscious manipulation of their bodies by seeking mutual support and sublimating their urges towards more productive avenues. Have those men really overcome their addictions? Have those, who have not relapsed, not supressed it rather than left it fully behind? The addiction as symptom has been consciously inhibited, but unless its underlying dimensions and causes are addressed, it will return. NoFappers continuously encourage each other and demand that their activities are sublimated into more productive activities, so that the energy can be retained. It seems that their porn consumption is excessive and damaging to them and they demonstrate more self-awareness and openness than many of the other men I have discussed in this book. In that sense, they are a positive, important community that potentially also enables working through for the men. We could also read their porn use of particular genres (gay porn, cuckold porn, sissy hypno porn) as a progressive act of *queering* their own sexualities (and affirming the polymorphous qualities of the unconscious), which they then defend against upon realising what they have done by actively wanting to turn away from it. However, I don't think such an argument would allow for enough complexity that is needed to think about this community. I do not want to condemn porn or porn consumption *per se*. We could also argue that in fact porn may have helped NoFappers to learn and come to terms with particular desires or fetishes. As Alison Horbury argues:

> pornography can afford a confrontation within those particular inhibitions that limit the realizing of libidinal enjoyment, but can also encourage us to brave our internal censorship in order to access the particularity of our desire. (Horbury 2019, 96–97)

However, as NoFappers themselves attest, their consumption has become too excessive and pathological and the steps they have taken to realise their libidinal enjoyment have led to problems and conflicts for them. Horbury's well-argued point may thus only apply to pornography that is consumed non-pathologically.

As I have argued, the speculations of who is behind the sissy porn conspiracy as well as their racist usage of the term 'cuck' reveal fears of their unconscious and its productive force. It is those speculations that are problematic, because they resort to fascist stylistic devices of isolating an Other who is pulling the strings in the background.

It is also discussions of feminism, women and masculinity that show NoFap's proximity to the other communities and men discussed in this book. There are many specifically anti-feminist posts that this chapter could not discuss. NoFappers express the same entitlement as all the other men of the manosphere.

A further psychoanalytic concept helps us to make sense of those men: perversion (Stein 2005; Kahr 2008; Waldon 2011). They implicitly (and at times explicitly) refer to their *own* perversions that they want to get rid of. They wish to repress their desires (whether they have been created by porn or not is irrelevant in that respect) so that they can focus their attention on something else. This is how perversion is linked to culture for Freud. Its energy is reconstituted as sublimation, as Stein (2005) notes. I have argued elsewhere (Johanssen 2019, Chapter 6) that we live in a perverse culture of big data analytics where social media companies de/humanise us by turning us into data, all under the guise of self-discovery, care and communication. In that context, I have also quoted Ruth Stein who wrote about perversion and representation:

> there are two basic ways to destroy or negate the human body in its undivided, whole aliveness: one is to represent/show it as cut into parts, flayed, excrementalized bloodied, reduced to senseless flesh; the other is to render it into a mechanized and digitalized entity, a robotized mechanism, occasionally multiplied into an anonymous crowd of uniform, faceless robots. (Stein 2005, 778)

Is not the same true for contemporary masculinities and gender relations? The NoFappers have manoeuvred themselves into perverse forms of relatedness (to online porn), which they want to escape from. They are likewise turned into an army of anonymous, masturbating porn consumers in front of their screens. All the same, while their data are being collected to fine-tune the algorithms of the porn streaming platforms. Yet, *they* also claim to live in a kind of perverse culture where they have been co-opted by feminism in a 'perverse pact' (Stein 2005, 787) of supporting equality and female empowerment while they are being exploited and oppressed by women in return. They have already become the sissys or cucks. They feel that they are dominated and oppressed by women. Such a sentiment is articulated time and time again in the manosphere, but is of course untrue. Similar sentiments are discussed by the YouTubers in relation to sexuality and specifically homosexuality (see Chapter 3). Incels and MGTOWs also articulate similar ideas about male oppression. The men of NoFap feel they are in a perverse relation where women have become men and men have become women. They claim that they have been hypnotised into becoming weak females or cucked into becoming weak men – while masturbating to such fantasies. They now want to escape both their dependence on the fantasy of the sissy hypno/cuckold porn video and the alleged 'reality' of having been made a sissy or cuck by women.

I would reject such 'arguments'. The men, and incels, MGTOWs and others, may feel that this is the case, but I argue that at the same time, it is *them* who wish to initiate a perverse pact with women. They want to have the phallic potency so that they can live out the 'normal' porn scenes and their (sanitised) heteronormative fantasies. Behind such dynamics are thus ultimately narcissistic fantasies of power for the men. Fantasies where the men are in charge and can get the women to do what they want. This resembles a master-slave relationship which is as abusive as the one-sided online posts in which women are only discussed but have no opportunity to answer back to.

However, the difference to incels, MGTOWs, Breivik, Rodger and many other men is that at least the NoFappers articulate their desire of women and loving relationships. NoFappers desire a dyad and wish to be with women. Nevertheless, they need to let go of their paranoid and toxic fantasies about women, LGBTQI+ individuals and 'beta' men. The men would need to enter into a dialogue and relationship with women so that both sides can understand that the other is not to blame for everything. They also need to let go of their fantasies of domination and embrace a masculine identity that is necessarily fragile and contradictory in itself and can be supported by other humans. Such a perspective provides us perhaps with a glimpse of hope. We can move beyond a violent binary where women are abused online and men assume a sense of illusionary agency through such acts. At the end of the day, all those men discussed in this book long for one thing: *recognition*. Such themes have been explored by the psychoanalyst Jessica Benjamin. I turn to her in the Conclusion chapter.

Notes

1 This term refers to fantasy formations that the young infant had 'inherited' in relation to scenes of castration, parental intercourse, and seduction (Laplanche & Pontalis 1973, 331–333).
2 The coupling of porn and big data has also led to an increase in more niche and extreme porn in recent years. For instance, 'incest porn' has been increasing in popularity, as an Esquire article in 2018 noted, but it seems that this was because a trend was spotted in the search terms and more advertisements were displayed which in turn led studios to produce more incest porn and users to watch it. A loop that no one can get out of (O'Neill 2018). The terms 'big data', 'data analytics' and 'algorithms' refer to automated processes whereby digital (user) data are analysed by social media and other online platforms (see Johanssen 2019: Chapter 6 for more discussion and definitions).
3 Such racist fantasies have of course a much longer history which goes back to the years of racial segregation in the United States in the late 19th century, a segregation which still persists in many areas such as schooling or residential housing today (Rothstein 2017).
4 It is beyond the scope of this chapter to go into further detail here (for critical discussions of racialised and interracial porn, see Capino 2006; Dines 2006; Williams 2009; Miller-Young 2010).

Conclusion: from dis/inhibition to recognition – a space for hope?

> And it is not only, or just, conflict the uninhibited have to bear; it is also the possibility of being suffused with feeling, or what Freud calls 'a continual flood of sexual fantasies'. This is an interesting phrase in that presumably a *continual* flood ceases, eventually, to be called a flood, and becomes, say, a lake, or a river. In other words, following the image, sexual fantasy would become in time no longer invasive or overwhelming; it would be just what we were, what was in our minds, or just what our minds were.... We would no longer feel flooded, we would be a flood. (Phillips 2013, 192, italics in original)

> What then are our men really repressing? How does their unconscious really function? What does it actually desire and what does its production really look like? (Theweleit 1987, 215)

Now that we have reached the final chapter, I wish to offer further reflections.

The world has changed significantly since the time I began work on this book in 2018. As I write this Conclusion in the autumn of 2020, the world has been dominated by the novel Coronavirus. Feelings of despair, alienation and anxiety have manifested themselves for many people. Significant economic crises have already or will hit many countries. COVID-19 and its responses by governments also seem to have divided people along those who believe science and those who do not believe the virus really exists.

Numerous countries have also recently seen Black Lives Matter protests against racist violence and oppression. In times like these, the internet and online cultures have only expanded their reach into the lives of many. Subjects have used social media and other platforms for organising, collaborating and other forms of solidarity. Many have felt connected through digital technology as they were forced to stay at home during lockdowns. Yet, the corner of the internet known as the manosphere continues to attract men who join different communities in order to discuss their hatred of (cis women. Some isolated and recently unemployed men, may have turned to the manosphere as they are stuck at home.

Writing this book has not been easy as I was confronted with deeply troubling and toxic narratives that formed the basis of my analyses. I was perhaps only able to write it because I embody a form of white masculine privilege which establishes a barrier or buffer between myself and those men I wrote about, something which is harder to do for those who are at the receiving end of abusive narratives. At the same time, I reproduce patriarchy at least to some degree simply by being a male who is living in neoliberal capitalism.

Reflecting on the different chapters, it is hard to see much hope, care or something positive emanating from them. It is a relatively easy task to critique those men, as I have done throughout, and to deconstruct their narratives. Some may argue that a book with such detailed analyses is not necessary because it reproduces the symbolic and real violence which is endemic to those communities. I would argue against such a position. We must confront the uncomfortable and offensive nature of certain online cultures and many online interactions more generally. I feel that we can only do so adequately by reproducing some of the narratives that those men create. I would argue that it is particularly a psychoanalytic perspective which allows for a detailed engagement and goes beneath the surface of those narratives to try and get an insight into those men's psyches. If we were to merely reject, negate or ignore the incel, MGTOW, NoFap and other communities within the manosphere, we would in a sense reproduce a similar binary and paranoid-schizoid worldview that they hold. The purpose of critique, as I see it, is to unmask their ideological and flawed worldview. To me, this form of critique also involves a detailed analytical engagement with actual data rather than only a theoretical analysis.

What is more challenging is to go beyond a critical or dismissive stance. If we only critique the manosphere we may risk reproducing the very core of their own ideology: that those men feel alienated, misunderstood or dismissed by the rest of society.

We must also ask ourselves what our own psychic investment in critiquing, attacking or dismissing the manosphere says about us. Psychoanalysis holds the view that there is never a pure subject without any inherent destructiveness or toxic fantasies. While there are of course vast differences between the manosphere and most other heterosexual men and women as well as LGBTQI+ individuals, psychoanalysis encourages us to go beyond a stance which would outcast or split those communities from the rest of the internet and society. A much more difficult task is to hold 'them' and 'us' together. This requires a new perspective, which I develop in this Conclusion by drawing on Jessica Benjamin. She writes:

> There is more implied in the ability to hold opposites than merely recognizing one's own capacity for destructiveness or wrong action.

There must also be an ability to tolerate the possible incursion of the badness that has been identified with the Other into the good that has been identified with the self: the so-called primitive or early feelings of discarding and projecting that which is abject, faecal, disgusting in the human body have to be countered by an acceptance of bodily or psychological weakness within self and other. Otherwise what dominates is the powerful impulse to project it outward into a vile and dangerous Other who must be kept out of the self and excluded from the group at all costs. (Benjamin 2018, 225)

Such an ability to tolerate the bad parts of the self and Other fundamentally applies to the manosphere but it also applies to everyone else. This is challenging. As I was thinking about a more relational, tolerating and even hopeful perspective on the men discussed in this book, I initially struggled to see it. I did not want to understand or empathise with those men. I thought this would open up a naïve, sanitised perspective of letting go of differences. A perspective that would argue that if we only could try and understand each other more, all toxicity and alienation would subside. Such a view contradicts the complex theory of the human subject that different psychoanalytic thinkers have developed. Aggression and toxic fantasies will always remain, but so will love, care and hope. Yet, I attempt to move towards a more relational and perhaps hopeful perspective. In this Conclusion, I summarise the key arguments of this book and then move on to a discussion of a different perspective: one of possible hope and mutual recognition.

Sexuality and its discontents

Sexuality is not a straightforward subject, encounter, or experience. No matter what different forms it may take. This book is about the psychoanalysis of particular men, with specific defense mechanisms and fantasies – and it seems they are many – and how they talk about, experience and constantly circle around sexuality. This book is also about how sexuality changed with the sexual revolution of the late 1960s, and throughout recent history up until the present day. For all of us, sexuality may remain one of the most puzzling and existential aspects of human life. Even if we live in the most sexually liberated of all times in the Western world, Wilhelm Reich proved to be wrong and our supposed liberation has not brought the envisioned social change or equal society.

Even in its accessible and digital-facilitated form today, sexuality is highly pleasurable and immensely difficult to navigate at the same time. This quantum of pleasure that was amplified but also problematically lived with in the original sexual revolution and somewhat continued, perhaps differently channelled, by our contemporary age, is desired by those who have not had it, or have not had enough of it, or have had it only with themselves or in the virtual realm: An army of machine-like, technosexual, algorithmic men. Those men articulate their particular embodiment using different platforms and collectives today, be it on YouTube, be it in the incel subreddits and fora, the MGTOW subreddit and forum, the many MRA subreddits and fora, the Red Pill or PUA communities, the alt-right and fascist circles, in the NoFap communities or wherever else we may find those men. Some have sworn never to be with or touch a woman again, some have sworn that women are the enemy, some have demanded that women change, some have wanted to turn back time to a different era, some have muttered their dreams of finally being with a woman, some have cried out at their hopeless inward directedness and addiction to porn. And, worst of all, some have killed others, often women, in states of cold rationality, psychosis and delusion.

This book began with a discussion of history. History not only in terms of the origins of the sexual revolution, but also in terms of the origins of German fascism. Klaus Theweleit's monumental *opus* served as a setting or scenery against which I developed the wider scenes and formations that this book has unfolded. Those men today and the males of 1920s and 1930s Germany were not the same – and yet, there are many similarities between them. Soldier-like masculinity and patriarchy have long roots. The manosphere today may be unique in its specific historical, social and, above all, technological contexts; but the affective character of its members is by and large somewhat similar as the soldier males analysed in Theweleit's two volumes. While most of the online men are not real solders or killers, they dream to be as strong and are haunted by the ghosts of such men who once lived or of those who are amongst them. While the German soldier males were asexual beings who detested everything sexual, the online men are sexually charged up and damned up to the point of bursting. At the same time, they too struggle with the sexual and sensual. They revolt against it and wish to annihilate everything that is seductive which they cannot control.

The push and pull of the unconscious

The men of the manosphere lack a full connection to their own bodies and are not in touch with what they feel and really are. Klaus Theweleit argued that the soldier males actively worked against pleasure and everything pleasurable. 'Attitudes of asceticism, renunciation, and self-control are effective defenses' (1989, 7); such attitudes are different for the various kinds of men discussed in this book. While they all abstain from pleasure to differing degrees, they simultaneously seek and demand pleasure, sexuality and enjoyment. While Theweleit's men sought to repress the desire to desire because they feared their unconscious, I claim that the situation is more complex for the men of the manosphere. They fear their unconscious and its unpredictable productivity. I think this has become particularly clear from my analysis of NoFap. They equally fear and desire women. At the same time, their bodies are powered by the desire to desire and by the perpetuation of the Thing. They seek pleasure in symbolically destroying and castrating the other, while seeking to repress their fears and anxieties of no longer existing. It is this movement of toing and froing, of pulling back and pushing in – of dis/inhibition – that both distances them from and brings them closer to their unconscious. The same occurs in the soldier male when he takes action.

> It is not specific contents that he represses; instead, he subjects the unconscious itself, the whole desiring production of the unconscious, to repression. Inside this man is a concentration camp, the concentration camp of his desires. (Theweleit 1989, 6)

The desire to desire also manifests itself in the need to express (in written form) what the men discussed in this book feel and think about women. Reality becomes reality (for them) through posting. A virtual reality that is so *disembodied* and hollow and at the same time so *full of bodies* in images, videos, texts. They must write about it, not only to establish collective bonds, but to remind themselves of what they should really focus on, of what matters. Their language is pure defense against the other – and this also means, to different degrees, defense against themselves. Such writings serve the purpose to strengthen their body armour and combat feelings of disintegration. *This is who I am, this is who I write myself to be.* It is an ego that is pre-formed, constitutive of various building blocks that I have outlined (YouTube influencers, porn, social media, conspiracy theories, the altright). It is given to the men and they assume its form, constantly reminding themselves what they are here for and what it means to be an incel, a MGTOW or a NoFapper.

Going online and interacting with others in the communities not only spreads the messages, it also serves as a reality check: *I still exist and my thoughts appear before me in written form.* It gives those men a sense of agency and feeling of collective tranquillity that they lack beyond the internet. Such language has, as Theweleit writes, the purpose to maintain the self and destroy the other. In that sense, we can confidently name the reality that such language creates as *fascist*. Reality that kills and deanimates everything that it sees as beyond itself. It kills life itself and creates new worldviews and fascist totalities. It constantly dreams up a future (inceldom, MGTOW without women, life without porn addiction) that may never arrive. Those men are thus in constant states of *becoming* in the Deleuzian sense. A becoming that needs to be fixed in discourse so that it can be upheld and worked towards (whether in reality or fantasy). They feel that they *deserve* something, but that something is lacking. Just like the men who would become soldiers and killers in the Weimar Republic.

Many of the men discussed in this book reflect on their own upbringing, their parents, and so on. The NoFappers in particular are highly reflexive and self-critical. They are very able to make associative links between themselves and their parents, childhood memories, or conflicts in their youth. This book then has shown how the men I discussed are the product of defenses and fantasies which relate to socio-cultural issues. In paying attention to history, social change and specific data, we can see how the fantasies are both ahistorical-universal (as I showed through my theoretical framework of Theweleit, Reich and Young-Bruehl) as well as highly situated in contemporary developments. Such a perspective adds a level of complexity to existing research and shows what kind of men are behind the anonymous online posts. Their fantasies need to be seen in relation to changing neoliberalism and how it has become insecure and precarious for many following the 2008 financial crisis (see Chapter 4). Furthermore, their fantasies are particular responses to changing sexual culture, the online mass distribution of porn, and the dynamic role of women and feminism in society (see Chapters 2 and 7 in particular). Their fantasies are also fundamentally shaped by the alt-right and fascist ideology (see Chapters 3, 4 and 5 in particular). I also linked those discussions to early conflicts and the role of the parents in those men's lives (Chapters 5 and 6). The role of race is also crucial in the narratives of the manosphere and I analysed its racialized and racist fantasies (see Chapters 2, 4 and 7). Such fantasies have been amplified by the alt-right and the Trump administration which have enabled racist anxieties around a threat of traditional white masculinity to come to the surface and be expressed on the internet and beyond.

In addition, the ever-present dialogue of two inner, conflicting voices and affective states of dis/inhibition is attempted to be silenced by conscious written expression, but it is never fully silenced and the contradictions creep into the words and phrases and settle down in the discourses. All men are incapable of forming meaningful object relations. And all the while, the machine of desire runs on. The men become machines, partly brought into being by the user unconscious (Clough 2018a) and the technology of social media which they inhabit.

Many of today's men want to become men of steel; steel facilitated by algorithms and data centres that host the social media and forum platforms. Their machine-like egos are not least formed by the different communities themselves and the identities that are moulded within them. It is clear what it means to be incel, what it takes to be a real MGTOW, when one can call oneself a true follower of NoFap. Like binary code, the characteristics of those subcultures are set. All it needs is some users who can embody them.

Capitalism and the utopia of big data

Reflecting further on the wider arguments I made in this book, I could have expanded more on the broader connective tissue that not only holds the manosphere together but links it to contemporary techno-social dimensions more generally. There is a particular *libidinal* and technological logic inherent to the manosphere, social media and online culture, and wider contemporary politics (see Rambatan & Johanssen 2021 for further discussions of this). While the manosphere and other cis men I analysed in this book embody their own affective states that relate to specific socio-economic dimensions, there are also much broader developments which relate to the increasing dominance of surveillance and tech as part of authoritarian capitalism. A discussion of those developments is useful because it relates the particularities of the manosphere to broader social changes in relation to the role of technology in capitalism today.

At various times in this book (see Chapters 3 and 7, for example) I discussed the pseudo-scientific discourses of the manosphere. For example, how crude theories from evolutionary psychology are used to naturalise sexual difference and allegedly inherent female and masculine behaviour. Such pseudo-scientific discourses are deployed to lend authority to the wider claims the men make. Needless to say, the theories are fantasies. They serve as very potent fantasies nonetheless, which the men draw on to justify their ideologies.

Such fantasies also relate to wider (phallic) desires for a utopian form of politics and capitalism that are driven by science, big data, artificial intelligence and the logic of the computational (Golumbia 2009; Johanssen 2019: Chapter 6; Jutel 2019, 2020). The men of the manosphere may embody a particular user unconscious (Clough 2018a), but this user unconscious is more widely reflected in contemporary life. It is shaped by an ideology of techno-utopian liberalism that is present in the realm of politics. This point has been made most succinctly by the Lacanian theorist Olivier Jutel (2019, 2020).

Jutel argues that we are in the midst of a post-political moment in which real politics, that is normally characterised by contradiction, antagonism and specific actions, is replaced by a technoliberal culture in which complex data-driven processes have become the driving force of election campaigns and administrations. Politics makes use of sophisticated big data analytics procedures in order to automate governance itself. For Jutel, this was both exemplified in the data-driven Clinton campaign which placed an emphasis on rational politics and data analytics while avoiding real issues, as well as in the Cambridge Analytica scandals and debates on how the Trump election and the Brexit vote were allegedly facilitated by manipulation of voters on social media. We could also think of the British Prime Minister Boris Johnson's former chief adviser Dominic Cummings, who sought to modernise the civil service by wanting to bring in 'weirdos and misfits' who should be experts in data analytics and AI (Syal 2020).

Politics is shaped by a 'computational view of the social' (Jutel 2019, 179) and regarded as something that can be mastered via technology. It is distinctly influenced by the technocratic utopianism of Silicon Valley and the power of Google, Facebook, Amazon and other tech companies. Truth itself becomes data-driven and something that can best be achieved through data accumulation and surveillance. In the examples of the Trump campaign or Brexit and across politics, social media and technology are both seen as useful instruments for politicians and feared or exploited as tools for political manipulation. There is thus a contradiction at the heart of such a perverse fantasy which sees technology as both the clean solution and dirty threat to politics. For politicians, it is about assuming a position of power through technology. This fantasy of data-driven politics masks the antagonism at the heart of politics. Reality is not something that can be adequately modelled and simulated via digital means. Difference itself becomes sanitised (Rambatan & Johanssen 2021). At the heart of such a view is, similar to the manosphere, a phallic sense of mastery and dominance of the other and truth itself.

This form of data-driven politics also masks the inherently exploitative and violent goals of much data-driven technology today. As Jutel argues, social media and big data technology have immensely contributed to increased surveillance, discrimination and oppression of the last decade (see also Clough 2018a). A surveillance that is often directed against minorities, LGBTQI+s and women.

The logic of the data-driven post-political is mirrored across the communities of the manosphere, for example in the cold and calculative manuals of Pick Up Artists and Red Pillers, the crude pseudo-scientism of incels, MGTOW and NoFap, the distorted historical analyses of alt-right and reactionary YouTubers as well as in the manifesto by a mass shooter like Breivik. Such men all embody a sense of phallic technological mastery in so far as they have constructed fully functional and self-contained worlds which they inhabit. They are the masters in such fantasy worlds where they construct their own language and code words, laws and relations. This form of mastery is distinctly *technological* insofar as it articulates itself in the neat and aestheticized creation of fora, memes, clips and text-based narratives. It comes into being in the virtual realm.

This (desire for) mastery also shows itself in the endless desire of the manosphere to accumulate and share data – both in relation to pseudo-science that 'proves' the men's worldviews, and in relation to data about their 'enemies' (for example, newspaper articles that allegedly show how women or others have behaved in ways that prove the views of the manosphere). Such practices are data-driven whereby some kind of objective truth is allegedly produced by endlessly circulating articles, videos, memes, pictures and posts that cement the worldviews of the different manosphere communities.

This machinic core of those men's psyches and their communities thus relates to contemporary society on a wider level. It is not specifically unique to the manosphere or politics, but reveals itself as the underlying libidinal logic of social media which are based on excessive data accumulation and surveillance for profit maximisation (Fuchs 2014). It is the very ideology of commercial social media like Facebook or YouTube that the more users share about themselves, the more they will be rewarded with a sense of recognition (Balick 2014). While this can be seen as positive and enable users to feel connected and valued, the underlying motives of social media companies are about making money through advertising that feeds on user data. It is perhaps no coincidence that the term 'big data' sounds phallic in itself (Johanssen 2019: Chapter 6).

While the rise of social media platforms of the past 15–20 years has enabled users to create online identities and connect with each other, it has also established a particular sense of the online self which is often about portraying a perfect subject, for example on Instagram. The ability to portray oneself as desirable, well-connected, happy, fit, beautiful, etc. makes for a new kind of social capital that is reflected across and desired by subjects from all backgrounds and genders (Rambatan & Johanssen 2021). This includes a shiny and polished display of bodies – what incels call 'lookism'. Its flipside are communities of the manosphere that portray a grotesque version of the average social media user: dirty, disrespectful and ruthless. The men of the various spaces of the manosphere fail to see that the seemingly perfect acts of self-presentation of others are performative. They could also be seen as acts of communal displays of bodies in times of neoliberal precarity, as Jamie Hakim (2019) has argued for instance. There are of course also many practices of self-presentation on social media that foreground authenticity and the complexity of the self (Balick 2014).

While the manosphere may have successfully created particular virtual worlds, in most cases, the fantasy of mastery and data-driven truth does not translate into real life. Incels have not ascended to 'inceldom', NoFap users have not outlawed porn in society, MGTOWs will always be in contact with women in some way. The very formulation of such a techno-solutionist fantasy thus reaches its limits and can never be fully realised. This failure drives further hatred and abuse of women, minorities or others who threaten it. Perhaps paradoxically, this rupture of the fantasy can also present us with some hope.

Beyond doer and done to

Now that I have sufficiently analysed the different men and their states of dis/inhibition, it is time to think about possibilities of moving beyond the deadlock that they themselves have entered into. This Conclusion is also an opportunity to think about hope or if there are different conceptualisations of subjectivity that go beyond the analytical types that I have put forward in this book. I do so by drawing on the work of Jessica Benjamin (1988) and her conceptualisation of intersubjective recognition (see also Honneth 2012). Incidentally, together with Anson Rabinbach, Benjamin wrote the foreword to the English translation of *Male Fantasies 2*, the second volume of Theweleit's books (Theweleit 1989).

To paraphrase Adam Philips (who I quoted at the beginning of this Conclusion): How can those men turn from feeling flooded to becoming a flood, or a still lake? Is it possible? It is particularly apt to include a discussion of recognition and of Benjamin's work at this point.

A key dimension of us as, what we could call, ethical subjects is that 'we are able to recognize the other in ourselves' (Benjamin 1988, 169). Benjamin develops a theory of recognition by critically reworking the Oedipus complex and the role of the mother and father for the boy/girl as identificatory objects (see Chapters 1 and 6, where I discuss aspects of this). Benjamin places an emphasis on the pre-Oedipal rather than the Oedipal phase of the infant. Briefly put, she argues that the Oedipus complex results in a (conceptual) devaluation of the mother in psychoanalysis and an emphasis on the father, who is responsible for enabling the child to shift their desire towards him. As the phallus takes on such an important value within the theory of the Oedipus complex, it devalues female sexuality. 'Thus, masculinity is defined in opposition to women, and gender is organized as polarity with one side idealized, the other devalued' (ibid, 168). While I cannot reproduce the detail of Benjamin's commentary on and criticism of the Oedipus complex here, it seems as if the men discussed in this book have internalised exactly the same pattern which Benjamin critiques above. While she acknowledges the importance of the phallus (see my discussion in Chapter 1), she problematizes its status as an all-powerful symbol within psychoanalytic theory and society at large. The problem with the Oedipal mode, then, is its assertion of sexual *difference* or, as Benjamin calls it, 'polarity' (ibid, 169). Man and woman remain united in (conceptual) opposition rather than truly united in recognition. One could also interpret the manosphere men's relations with femininity as Oedipal relations which struggle and oscillate between separation and proximity to femininity – and ultimately the mother. The hatred and love of all females that those men express could be read as symptomatic of Oedipal conflicts, early fears of an engulfing, castrating mother, a hatred of the mother, or an envy of the womb and women's reproductive capacity. My emphasis on the role of the parents, and the father in particular, who those men wish to kill could equally be read as the manifestations of Oedipal conflicts, or the breaking up of the parental dyad so that those men can be with their mothers, or their wish to kill the father in order to individuate themselves from their parents.

However, those arguments reproduce the Oedipal model that Benjamin critiques and only further pit men and women against each other. Following such a logic as discussed above, one would argue that the men have not learned to desire in the 'correct' (i.e. heterosexual, respectful, reflexive) way and have not learned to aspire to notions of femininity and masculinity following the Oedipal stage. However, this leaves no space for a different perspective and also reproduces a heteronormative logic, which from Benjamin's perspective repudiates the qualities associated with the fantasy mother and what is culturally associated with femininity.

I have also extensively drawn on Theweleit's argument about the pre-Oedipal phase that the men he writes about are stuck in. Their egos are fragmented and they depend on other mechanisms to form an ego. Their egos are also held together by fascism. I have made a similar argument about the men of the manosphere. While I cannot definitively say if their egos are fragmented, I think it is clear from my analyses that they use the internet, their respective communities (incel, NoFap, MGTOW, etc.) as body armour which to a degree holds their egos together. Such construction of body armour is characterised by dis/inhibition and always remains porous. This porosity is a chance.

Emphasising the pre-Oedipal, then, as both Benjamin and Theweleit do, may open up a different perspective that goes beyond binaries. Benjamin argues that psychoanalysis and the Oedipus complex in particular 're-presents life chiefly as a process of bodies doing to or being done to by other bodies, and the phallus is the principal doer (or done to in the case of castration anxiety)' (ibid, 124). While I have used the phallus as an analytical category in this book, it is important to move beyond it now in order to think about an analytical perspective that can open up if not solutions but perhaps more hopeful viewpoints upon the themes that I have discussed. Letting go of the phallus also allows us to place an emphasis on feminine desire and agency.

Benjamin has continued to explore the theme of recognition in her books (Benjamin 1988, 1995, 1998, 2018). She has constructed an intersubjective and relational psychoanalysis which draws on a range of psychoanalytic thinkers and schools. She has particularly developed an emphasis on what she calls 'the Third' in her most recent work (Benjamin 2018). Her work has been very influential for the relational turn in psychoanalysis in the United States in particular (Beebe & Lachmann 2003) and for psychoanalytic theory in general. Benjamin's concept of the Third denotes a position where a subject recognises the other as a subject who is both same and different to themselves. It means that feelings and ideas can be shared between them (Benjamin 2018, 4).

This Conclusion, then, shows a shift in my perspective from a broadly Freudian-Lacanian prism to Benjamin's relational psychoanalytic angle which to some degree is positioned against Freud and Lacan. This shift in perspective introduces another dimension to the analyses which neither Freudian nor Lacanian accounts could provide.

Benjamin's concept of the Third was actually inspired by Lacan's use of the term (Lacan 1975) to describe a dimension beyond the dyad of two subjects (Benjamin 2018, 26). However, she critiques Lacan's emphasis on the father which suggests an equation of the Third with paternal authority and Oedipal dynamics. 'Thus, I contend that thirdness is not literally instituted by a father (or other) as the third person; it cannot originate in the Freudian [and Lacanian] oedipal relation in which the father appears as prohibitor and castrator' (Benjamin 2018, 27), Benjamin writes. This critique also marks a move away from the phallus as a central concept for Freud and Lacan in particular which may be useful to undertake in this Conclusion as well in order to open up a different perspective on the material I have examined in this book. Additionally, Freudian conceptualisations of the human subject do not fully take into account more relational perspectives of intersubjectivity (Johanssen 2019, 21) and post-Freudian thinkers, Lacan among them, have done much to address this. Benjamin's work is of particular value for this Conclusion because of the way she has reconceptualised early intersubjective (gender) relations, as I discuss in the coming sections. She goes beyond pre-Oedipal dynamics to develop a relational understanding of subjectivity and psychoanalysis (Benjamin 2018).

Due to limits of space, I cannot extend my discussion of this important intersubjective aspect of her work and encourage the reader to read Benjamin directly. Her work is particularly relevant for our current sociopolitical moment which is characterised by division, polarisation and destructiveness. This is amplified not only by the manosphere and alt-right politics, but by Trump himself who thrives on denial and social violations, and operates with a binary logic of doer-done to (Benjamin 2018, 6–7, 248).

While Benjamin has developed and advanced her intersubjective theory of psychoanalysis over many decades, I mainly focus on her *The Bonds of Love* book as it laid the foundations for her work and places a useful emphasis on questions of sexuality, masculinity and femininity (Benjamin 1988).

The pre-Oedipal model of recognition: in/dependence and discovery

Benjamin begins her book by arguing that we can already find recognition in the pre-Oedipal stage, the early stage of the infant's life. In placing an emphasis on pre-Oedipal development, an emphasis is also placed on the mother rather than the father of the Oedipal stage. For the newborn (and young) baby, recognition takes two forms: the mother recognises the baby as her own and the baby recognises the mother (and father and siblings) as their parents, at least the mother thinks (or projects) the baby's sounds, looks, movements, etc. as forms of recognition. From the moment the baby is born, they recognise their mother's voice which they remember from hearing in the womb. Needless to say, recognition is central to human experience and is perhaps the foundation of any ethics (Singh 2019). This does not mean that recognition is a kind of idealised state without conflict or contradiction. Benjamin stresses that there is no original 'pure culture of intersubjectivity' (ibid, 223) that is subsequently corrupted by conflict. Recognition implies both conflict and harmony, separation and unity. Applied to my analyses, it seems at first that it is precisely recognition that those men lack and also cannot give to the other. They lament being invisible, ignored, rejected, mistreated by women and respond by misrecognising them in turn. As I show in my subsequent discussion, we can nonetheless see signs of recognition and specifically a *desire* for it within those men. In our present age of data-driven communication, recognition has acquired an increasing importance in relation to ethics and how subjects present themselves and communicate with each other using digital technologies (Balick 2014; Singh 2019; Crociani-Windland & Yates 2020).

Benjamin rejects a psychoanalytic understanding of more commonly held ideas of initial wholeness of mother and infant (as exemplified for example by thinkers like Anzieu 1989 or Mahler 1979) towards separation and individuation. She reformulates recognition not as freedom from the other but as being in a relationship with the other that allows for mutual recognition and independence. A key exception to other schools within psychoanalysis here is D. W. Winnicott and his notion of the transitional space which is essentially a space in which the infant is both recognised and allowed to be independent by the mother. It is also a space for the infant to feel recognised and experience recognition via the transitional object they play with, either with or without the mother being present (Winnicott 2002). Recognition is a reflexive mode which includes a response from the other towards us and also 'how we find ourselves in that response' (ibid, 21). Recognition is thus essential for psychic functioning and health. Object-relations psychoanalysis and intersubjective approaches allow for a conceptualisation of recognition that is particularly useful for this book. At first, the discourses that I have presented may seem antithetical to recognition or any kind of relationality. They are destructive, toxic and hateful. They specifically close down any recognition while often simultaneously demanding it (as incels do for instance). This seems to leave us with an impossible situation without recognition, not least because actual women are mostly excluded from the spaces I have written about.

However, I think if we open up the analytical perspective to recognition we may find traces or hints of it within the data I analysed. One question to begin with is: Does the naming of the other already imply recognition, or a desire for recognition? Does the discussion of women (even if they are insulted, given particular names like 'femoids', etc.) warrant a first act of (desire for) recognition, or perhaps *misrecognition* of the other? Such questions are important because they enable us to move beyond perspectives of negation or annihilation of women which I have discussed in this book.

While real women are absent from the discourses I have analysed, they are all the more present as fantasies within them. Women are constantly named, evoked, desired, (ab)used and played with in those male fantasies. Women are omnipresent while being attempted to be rejected or excluded from the men's lives. At the same time, they are intensely desired. More discussion of Benjamin is needed here before applying her insights to the manosphere.

'At the moment of realising our own independence, we are dependent upon another to recognise it' (ibid, 33), writes Benjamin about the infant. She draws on D. W. Winnicott, who stresses that the infant becomes independent in the transitional space and learns to be alone in the presence of another (real or material) object (Winnicott 2002). Benjamin has subsequently developed her theory of intersubjective recognition further with her concept of *the Third*, which she defines similarly to Winnicott's transitional space (Benjamin 2018). The men of the manosphere, as I have argued, cannot leave women behind. They are dependent on them as fantasies which they need to constantly discuss online. This also enables a sense of recognition, or the desire for recognition, to emerge. The men are dependent on the fantasy of woman, because it is the woman who may (eventually) recognise them and validate their existence. The problem is that this is something they cannot bring themselves to acknowledge. It possibly remains unconscious to them. Instead, they produce discourses and fantasies that are all about the impossibility to acknowledge the other as a subject in their own right. They cannot acknowledge the other as existing independently and not as an other that exists for them. All of the different communities and men instead construct an other that is there to serve them; as an obedient femininity that should prop up the men's fragmented egos. While they may desire nothing more than recognition, they resort to destruction of the other. Such acts seem to close down any possibility for recognition, mutual understanding, or dialogue. It would seem that if the men desire recognition it is a particular form of recognition: submission. The men, fuelled by their fascist body fantasies, dream up scenarios in which they are the dominant men who are admired and cared for by submissive women. This form of recognition is sado-masochistic and fascist where women are constructed as *having* to desire their own submission. However, such fantasies of recognition are defensive and close down any opportunity for real recognition or mutual respect and an unbiased discovery of the other. A real woman is absent and replaced with a fantasy that allows for the control of woman.

One could argue that those men are stuck in (or regress to) an early phase of development where the infant thinks of themselves as omnipotent and misrecognises themselves. This has been conceptualised in different ways by Kohut, Klein, Lacan, Winnicott and others. Such a phase is overcome as the infant interacts more with those around her and develops. All men discussed in this book thus embody a distinctly immature subjectivity that is about (a desire for) omnipotence and dominance over women. One could perhaps also make the argument that the communities I analysed constitute toxic transitional spaces in which men can feel supported by each other and perform/play with particular identities. There is a kind of inward recognition whereby the men only recognise each other and validate each other as a means of survival.

As I have stressed throughout this book, the men's fantasies are inherently contradictory and porous in themselves. They do not fully allow for the complete control or domination of women, because they are marked by dis/inhibition as well as desire and something that somewhat comes close to love. As the fantasies I have examined are so contradictory, they may present an opportunity to break the endless 'vicious circle' (Benjamin 1988, 220) of domination. The fantasies in themselves allow for glimpses of recognition to emerge from them.

While such fantasies do not negate women, they need to be seen in relation to my discussion of fascism and obsessive characters (Chapters 4 and 5). They also need to be seen in relation to a heavily policed form of heteronormativity, which I particularly discussed in Chapter 7, that essentially argues that heterosexuality *itself* is about male dominance and female submission – in the bedroom and beyond. Such a perspective has been amplified by socio-economic conditions of changing neoliberalism (see Chapter 4) and by the rise of Trump, general online misogyny and the alt-right. The misogynist men fail to see that our world has, at least to some degree, moved beyond such archaic times and gender relations. This form of sado-masochistic, heteronormative recognition thus functions to defend against a kind of queer sexuality (Chapters 3 and 7) and the productive force of the unconscious. Yet, there is more to such fantasies.

Destruction as recognition?

At the same time, such acts and fantasies of destruction that I have described in this book can also be seen as expressions of a desire for genuine recognition. Benjamin notes (via Winnicott) that the infant learns to meaningfully relate to an object by first destroying it (see also Honneth 2012 who draws on Winnicott in his theory of recognition). The young infant gradually learns that objects (for example the mother) exist externally and not just in her mind. They exist in their own right. For Winnicott, this transition involves fantasies of destroying the object. This means that the other has to be destroyed in fantasy, inside, in order to be recognised outside. We can think of omnipotent fantasies of destruction that test if the other survives them. If they do, they really exist outside of the infant's fantasy world. This means that the other has 'survived' destructive fantasies and recognises the infant. If the infant had been able to completely negate the other, they would not be there to recognise them. In that sense, fantasmatic destruction is the foundation of any intersubjective recognition. It 'is a movement into intersubjective space, the bursting of the illusion of omnipotence with limits of the world, and the difference of others' (Balick 2014, 109).

Can we not draw an analogy here to the fantasies of the manosphere? Are the men not constructing particular fantasies of destruction of women, *because* they desire recognition? Most of them, apart form the mass shooters, do not completely negate the female other. They destroy her in fantasy but also desire her both in fantasy and as a real subject. If they would completely negate the other, the other would not be there to recognise, see and desire those men. 'In adulthood, destruction includes the intention to discover if the other will survive' (1988, 38), Benjamin writes. In this perspective, destruction and the violation of the other can include attacking 'the other's separate reality in order to finally discover it' (ibid, 68). The men of the manosphere play a kind of virtual peekaboo – or *fort-da* – of negation and affirmation. It marks the beginning of a desire for recognition and discovery – and perhaps of some form of hope.

I appreciate that such arguments may be hard to accept for some and that readers may respond that I am reading too much into the data I have presented. The arguments may seem contradictory at first. It may be argued that I have attempted to 'humanise' those men or that I have defused their toxic narratives. However, I argue that such a perspective, as I have developed it in this chapter so far, opens up an angle to think about the desire for recognition that those men have. They fail to achieve real recognition, because they do not (wish to) discover a shared reality with the outside object (ibid, 88). The tragedy is that the object (women) only exists in the fantasies of those men. Women are absent from their communities and it seems that many also have no meaningful contact with women beyond the internet. Nonetheless, the men wish to achieve recognition and relationality and this presents us with some hope.

The fact that those fantasies are voiced and circulated online is also significant. While misogyny of course takes place beyond the internet, social media and online fora enable forms of recognition, as Aaron Balick (2014) has argued. It is through acts of self-representation and communication on the internet that subjects express a desire for recognition and can, *eo ipso*, be recognised by others. Balick argues that the playful creation of identities on social media for example is so attractive for users, because others can respond through comments, likes, shares, etc. and thereby express appreciation of such identities. This is the case for progressive spaces online when it comes to LGBTQI+ communities for instance, but it is also the case for the manosphere where men create particular destructive identities which are recognised by other men. The fact that others are excluded from such male communities is an act of aggression, but it also needs to be seen as inherent vulnerability those men have. They exclude others because they feel misrecognised or fear that others won't recognise them and challenge their identities if they were to enter the manosphere. Such psychodynamics perhaps help us to understand the immense psychic energy and time that those men invest in their respective communities. They spend a lot of time producing toxic narratives, as I have shown, but they also spend considerable time discussing and reinforcing what it precisely means to be an incel, a MGTOW or a NoFap user. This need for continuous reaffirmation also points to the porousness and fragility of those identities. The attempts at continuously fixing their fragmented identities erect an unclimbable wall between them and those outside of the manosphere. Yet, the attempts show all the more how much they desire recognition and a sense of wholeness. It needs to be stressed that the very creation of their toxic identities undermines recognition by the other. However, this does not mean that they would not deeply desire a sense of recognition which goes beyond the immediate one of their male communities.

With Benjamin, we can particularly read the desire for sex that incels and NoFappers endlessly discuss as a desire for recognition. In erotic union, the self and other can feel intertwined, merged and whole. The ultimate point of sexual intercourse, it is often alleged, is to experience a kind of transcendent wholeness and for the self and other to become one. Such a desire for sex, Benjamin argues, 'is really a form of the desire for recognition' (ibid, 128). This also implies a reconfiguration of desire, not as something that is forever pushing and pulling *ad inifinitum* in the Lacanian sense, but as desire for erotic union. Achieving mutual pleasure with and in the other is a form of mutual recognition. It is a form of recognition that does not privilege the phallus, or masculinity or femininity. This, for Benjamin, opens up a new perspective for female desire in particular, because it is not rooted in the phallus, or in submission to the man. This means that men themselves need to let go of the phallus and embrace a different, perhaps more feminine version of subjectivity and in particular sexuality. In short, they need to accept the power of their unconscious and should not defend against non-heteronormative sexualities for example as the NoFap men still do. In Chapter 2, I discussed Jamie Hakim's recent work on the portrayal of male bodies via digital media (Hakim 2019). Hakim analyses the celebrity male nude leak via social media platforms, the rise in (homo)eroticised imagery on platforms such as Instagram by hetero and gay young men, and the 'chemsex' practices of gay men. Such kinds of masculinities are inherently more vulnerable, contradictory and communal than the type of masculinity that I have analysed in this book, because Hakim reads them as responses to post-2008 neoliberal precarity. They show perhaps that a different kind of masculinity which is about embodiment, desire, as well as a display of vulnerability is possible. A masculinity that is more communal and reflexive than the manosphere. Certain kinds of geek masculinity also fall in such a category. In her recent critical discussion of *Male Fantasies*, Laura U. Marks reaches a similar conclusion. She argues that Theweleit's books did not open up space for a different kind of masculinity which could counter that of the Freikorps.

> There are lots of cultures and subcultures of men who don't cultivate or reject the armoured ideal [of the Freikorps soldiers, or alpha masculinity]. In North American societies, there are slackers, dropouts, 'sensitive men' (sometimes). Bears and puppies who push back against the gay hard body-cult. Born males who reject the gender and try out a third path. 'Lesbian boys'. Stylish men. Men who grow old gracefully. Men at ease with their sexuality. Gentle fathers. Gamers who manage to balance the imaginary body adventuring in virtual space and the soft, flabby, physical body at the console. There are so many kinds of lovely men. (Marks 2020, 117)

If only the men of the manosphere could see those kinds of men as role models.

The curiosity that those men of the manosphere hold and the fundamental wish to discover women provides us perhaps with some hope. The men would need to arrive at a nuanced understanding of reality that grants others independence as well as dependence. They would need to become more open minded in order to truly discover women and a reality that is different to their own. They need to reach a position of the Third and this fundamentally requires *surrender* (Benjamin 2018). Surrendering to the other means 'freedom from any intent to control or coerce' (Benjamin 2004, 7) while accepting, caringly affirming I would add, the difference of the other. Likewise, women would need to enter into a dialogue with those men with a similar kind of open mindedness, something that may be difficult to ask for, but recognition requires two subjects.

As I argued, we could read the manosphere's fantasies as attempts to see if the women would survive them. For the most part, women have survived them, not least because they are absent from those online communities. At the same time, sexism and misogyny is now commonplace in many spaces on the internet and beyond where women and men interact. No one can expect or demand that women should engage with those kinds of men, unless they changed their tone, style and abusive language and behaviour. Women have responded to the kind of misogyny and sexism that I have discussed in this book with anger, rage, despair, apathy and also humour. I have no definitive answer to the many problems this book has explored.

'I know that the armoured, disembodied hateful subjectivity Theweleit analysed thrives on and cannot be theorized away. But I must believe that it is an artefact of history' (Marks 2020, 118), Laura U. Marks writes in her discussion of Theweleit and the current threat of fascism in many parts of the world. One day, the manosphere is also going to be history.

***

Another woman should have the last word. One possible answer how to respond to the men is: love. I close with Alexandria Ocasio-Cortez and parts of a speech she gave following the El Paso shooting in the United States in August 2019:

What I have to say to the young men and increasingly some of the young women in this country that are falling into the grips of white supremacy that find themselves getting radicalized in a funnel of vitriol towards Latinos, towards immigrants, towards African Americans, towards all people, Black, towards all people, Jewish, towards all people of different faiths, what I have to say to you is come back! Because there is a mother waiting for you, I know it. I know there's a teacher waiting for you saying what happened to my kid? What happened to my friend? And we will always be here and hold space for you to come back. We will love you back. You are not too far gone, and I know that this society is isolating, I know that this society creates depression, I know that the lack of opportunity here, from Brownsville to El Paso.... This is not just about assault weapons, this is about gun violence in all of our communities. So whether it's from misogyny or whether it's from racism, you're not more of a man with a gun. You're not more of a man if you are capable of violence. You are not stronger if you tear another life down.... We're gonna have to go deep, we need to go deep.... We need to learn to love bigger to bring them back. (Anwar 2019, online)

I end this book with the reproduction of a famous meme which can also be found in the manosphere:

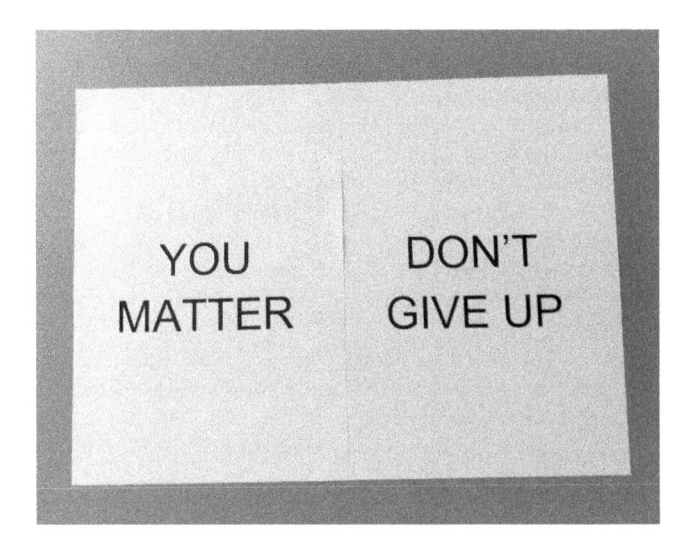

Figure 1 Sometimes it is just a question of perspective.

Bibliography

Abel, E., Christian, B. and Moglen,H. (1997, Eds.). *Female Subjects in Black and White: Race, Psychoanalysis, Feminism*. Berkeley: University of California Press.
Adorno, T. W. (1970). Freudian Theory and the Pattern of Fascist Propaganda. *Psyche: Zeitschrift für Psychoanalyse und ihre Anwendungen*, 24(7), 486–509.
Adorno, T. W., Frenkel-Brunswik, E., Levinson, D. J. and Sanford, R. N. (1950). *The Authoritarian Personality*. New York: Harper & Brothers.
Adorno, T. W. and Horkheimer, M. (1947). *Dialectic of Enlightenment: Philosophical Fragments*. Amsterdam: Querido.
Adorno, T. W. and Horkheimer, M. (1989). *Dialectic of Enlightenment*. London: Verso.
Albury, K. (2014). Porn and Sex Education, Porn as Sex Education. *Porn Studies*, 1(1-2), 172–181.
Allan, J. A. (2016). Phallic Affect, or Why Men's Rights Activists Have Feelings. *Men and Masculinities*, 19(1), 22–41.
Allyn, D. (2001). *Make Love, Not War: The Sexual Revolution: An Unfettered History*. London: Routledge.
Almog, R. and Kaplan, D. (2017). The Nerd and His Discontent: The Seduction Community and the Logic of the Game as a Geeky Solution to the Challenges of Young Masculinity. *Men and Masculinities*, 20(1), 27–48.
Anderson, B. (1991). *Imagined Communities: Reflections on the Origin and Spread of Nationalism*. London: Verso.
Anwar, M. (2019). AOC's Speech To White Supremacists Is So Passionate & Inspiring. *Elite Daily*. https://www.elitedaily.com/p/aocs-speech-to-white-supremacists-is-so--passionate-inspiring-18567176.
Anzieu, D. (1989). *The Skin Ego*. New Haven, CT: Yale University Press.
Aron, L. and Starr, K. (2013). *A Psychotherapy for the People: Toward a Progressive Psychoanalysis*. London: Routledge.
Attwood, F. (2002). Reading Porn: The Paradigm Shift in Pornography Research. *Sexualities*, 5(1), 91–105.
Attwood, F. (2005). What Do People Do with Porn? Qualitative Research into the Consumption, Use, and Experience of Pornography and Other Sexually Explicit Media. *Sexuality and Culture*, 9(2), 65–86.
Attwood, F. (2009). *Mainstreaming Sex: The Sexualization of Western Culture*. London: IB Tauris.

Attwood, F. (2011). The Paradigm Shift: Pornography Research, Sexualization and Extreme Images. *Sociology Compass*, 5(1), 13–22.
Attwood, F. (2017). *Sex Media*. Cambridge: Polity.
Attwood, F., Smith, C. and Barker, M. (2019). Engaging with Pornography: An Examination of Women Aged 18–26 as Porn Consumers, *Feminist Media Studies*, 21(2), 173–188.
Auestad, L. (2012, Ed.). *Psychoanalysis and Politics: Exclusion and the Politics of Representation*. London: Karnac Books.
Auestad, L. (2014, Ed.). *Nationalism and the Body Politic*. London: Karnac Books.
Auestad, L. (2017). Speech, Repetition, Renewal. In: Auestad, L. and Kabesh, A. T. (Eds.). *Traces of Violence and Freedom of Thought*. Basingstoke: Palgrave Macmillan, pp. 17–34.
Aust, S. (2008). *Baader-Meinhof: The Inside Story of the RAF*. Oxford: Oxford University Press.
Baader, M. S., Jansen, C., König, J. and Sager, C. (2017, Eds.). *Tabubruch und Entgrenzung. Kindheit und Sexualität nach 1968*. Cologne: Böhlau Verlag.
Bainbridge, C. (2008). *A Feminine Cinematics: Luce Irigaray, Women and Film*. Basingstoke: Palgrave Macmillan.
Bainbridge, C. (2012). Psychotherapy on the Couch: Exploring the Fantasies of *In Treatment*. *Psychoanalysis, Culture and Society*, 17(2), 153–168.
Bainbridge, C. (2013). The Spectacle of Envy and Femininity in the Press: A Psycho-Cultural Approach. In: Martin-Albo, Á. M.-A. and Gregorio-Godeo, E. (Eds.). *Culture and Power: Identity and Identification*. Newcastle: Cambridge Scholars Publishing, pp. 217–232.
Bainbridge, C. (2019). Box-Set Mind-Set: Psycho-Cultural Approaches to Binge Watching, Gender, and Digital Experience. *Free Associations: Psychoanalysis and Culture, Media, Groups, Politics*, 75, http://freeassociations.org.uk/FA_New/OJS/index.php/fa/article/view/253.
Bainbridge, C. (2020). Who Will Fix It for Us? Toxic Celebrity and the Therapeutic Dynamics of Media Culture. *Celebrity Studies*, 11(1), 75–88.
Bainbridge, C. and Yates, C. (2005). Cinematic Symptoms of Masculinity in Transition: Memory, History and Mythology in Contemporary Film. *Psychoanalysis, Culture, & Society*, 10(3), 299–318.
Bainbridge, C. and Yates, C. (2011, Eds.). Therapy Culture/Culture as Therapy. Special Edition. *Free Associations: Psychoanalysis and Culture, Media, Groups, Politics*, 62, http://freeassociations.org.uk/FA_New/OJS/index.php/fa/issue/view/5.
Bainbridge, C. and Yates, C. (2012, Eds.). Media and the Inner World: New Perspectives on Psychoanalysis and Popular Culture. Special Issue. *Psychoanalysis, Culture & Society*, 17(2). 113–119.
Bainbridge, C. and Yates, C. (2014, Eds.). *Media and the Inner World: Psycho-cultural Approaches to Emotion, Media and Popular Culture*. Basingstoke: Palgrave Macmillan.
Balaji, M. (2009). Owning Black Masculinity: The Intersection of Cultural Commodification and Self-Construction in Rap Music Videos. *Communication, Culture & Critique*, 2(1), 21–38.
Balick, A. (2014). *The Psychodynamics of Social Networking: Connected-Up Instantaneous Culture and the Self*. London: Karnac Books.

Bandinelli, C. and Bandinelli, A. (2021). Love me, Tinder: Enjoying Dating Apps in Neoliberal Societies. *Psychoanalysis, Culture & Society*, 26(2).

Banet-Weiser, S. (2018). *Empowered: Popular Feminism and Popular Misogyny*. Durham: Duke University Press.

Banet-Weiser, S. and Miltner, K. M. (2016). #MasculinitySoFragile: Culture, Structure, and Networked Misogyny. *Feminist Media Studies*, 16(1), 171–174.

Beauchamp, Z. (2019). Our Incel Problem. *Vox*. https://www.vox.com/the-highlight/2019/4/16/18287446/incel-definition-reddit.

Beebe, B. and Lachmann, F. (2003). The Relational Turn in Psychoanalysis: A Dyadic Systems View from Infant Research. *Contemporary Psychoanalysis*, 39(3), 379–409.

Belle, C. (2014). From Jay-Z to Dead Prez: Examining Representations of Black Masculinity in Mainstream Versus Underground Hip-hop Music. *Journal of Black Studies*, 45(4), 287–300.

Benjamin, J. (1988). *The Bonds of Love: Psychoanalysis. Feminism, and the Problem of Domination*. New York: Pantheon Books.

Benjamin, J. (1995). *Like Subjects, Love Objects: Essays on Recognition and Sexual Difference*. New Haven, CT: Yale University Press.

Benjamin, J. (1998). *Shadow of the Other: Intersubjectivity and Gender in Psychoanalysis*. London: Routledge.

Benjamin, J. (2004). Beyond Doer and Done to: An Intersubjective View of Thirdness. *The Psychoanalytic Quarterly*, 73(1), 5–46.

Benjamin, J. (2018). *Beyond Doer and Done To. Recognition Theory, Intersubjectivity and the Third*. London: Routledge.

Bennett, D. (2016). *Currency of Desire: Libidinal Economy, Psychoanalysis and Sexual Revolution*. London: Lawrence & Wishart.

Berardi, F. B. (2015). *Heroes: Mass Murder and Suicide*. London: Verso.

Berbrier, M. (2000). The Victim Ideology of White Supremacists and White Separatists in the United States. *Sociological Focus*, 33(2), 175–191.

Bergner, G. (2005). *Taboo Subjects: Race, Sex and Psychoanalysis*. Minneapolis: University of Minnesota Press.

Berns, N. S. (2017). *Framing the Victim: Domestic Violence, Media, and Social Problems*. London: Routledge.

Besana, T., Katsiaficas, D. and Loyd, A. B. (2019). Asian American Media Representation: A Film Analysis and Implications for Identity Development. *Research in Human Development*, 16(3-4), 201–225.

Bessel, R. (1993). *Germany after the First World War*. Oxford: Oxford University Press.

Bhabha, H. K. (1994). *The Location of Culture*. London: Routledge.

Bhattacharyya, G. (2015). *Crisis, Austerity, and Everyday Life: Living in a Time of Diminishing Expectations*. Basingstoke: Palgrave Macmillan.

Bhavnani, K. K. (2001, Ed.). *Feminism and "Race"*. Oxford: Oxford University Press.

Billig, M. (1995). *Banal Nationalism*. London: Sage.

Bion, W. (1963). *Elements of Psycho-Analysis*. London: Heinemann.

Blevins, K. (2018). Bell hooks and Consciousness-Raising: Argument for a Fourth

Wave of Feminism. In: Ryan Vickery, J. and Everbach, T. (Eds.). *Mediating Misogyny. Gender, Technology, and Harassment*. Basingstoke: Palgrave Macmillan, pp. 91–108.

Blodgett, B. and Salter, A. (2018). Ghostbusters Is for Boys: Understanding Geek Masculinity's Role in the Alt-Right. *Communication, Culture & Critique*, 11(1), 133–146.

Boag, S. (2012). *Freudian Repression, the Unconscious and the Dynamics of Inhibition*. London: Karnac.

Boehme, H. M. and Isom Scott, D. A. (2020). Alt-White? A Gendered Look at "Victim" Ideology and the Alt-Right. *Victims & Offenders: An International Journal of Evidence-based Research, Policy, and Practice*, 15(2), 174–196.

Boyle, K. (2005). *Media and Violence: Gendering the Debates*. London: Sage.

Boyle, K. (2014). Feminism and Pornography. In: Evans, M., Hemmings, C., Henry, M., Johnstone, H., Madhok, S., Plomien, A. and Wearing, S. (Eds.). *The Sage Handbook of Feminist Theory*. London: Sage, pp. 215–231.

Boyle, K. (2010). Porn Consumers' Public Faces: Mainstream Media, Address and Representation. In: Boyle, K. (Ed.). *Everyday Pornography*. London: Routledge, pp. 146–158.

Bratich, Z. and Banet-Weiser, S. (2019). From Pick-up Artists to Incels: Con(fidence) Games, Networked Misogyny, and the Failure of Neoliberalism. *International Journal of Communication*, 13, 5003–5027.

Brickman, C. (2003). *Aboriginal Populations in the Mind: Race and Primitivity in Psychoanalysis*. New York: Columbia University Press.

Bridges, T. and Pascoe, C. J. (2014). Hybrid Masculinities: New Directions in the Sociology of Men and Masculinities. *Sociology Compass*, 8(3), 246–258.

Brigley Thompson, Z. (2020). The (Alt) Right to Rape: Violated white Masculinities in the Alt-Right, and the Film Nocturnal Animals. *Feminist Media Studies*, 20(1), 104–118.

Brown, B. (2015). *Isla Vista Mass Murder. May 23, 2014. Investigative Summary*. Police Report. https://web.archive.org/web/20150220034256/http://www.sbsheriff.us/documents/ISLAVISTAINVESTIGATIVESUMMARY.pdf.

Bulman, M. (2019). Number of People Identifying as Lesbian, Gay or Bisexual Hits Record High, Figures Show. *The Independent*. https://www.independent.co.uk/news/uk/home-news/lgbt-lesbian-gay-bisexual-uk-sexuality-office-national-statistics-ons-a8738356.html.

Burke, N. B. (2016). Straight-acting: Gay Pornography, Heterosexuality, and Hegemonic Masculinity. *Porn Studies*, 3(3), 238–254.

Butler, J. (1990). *Gender Trouble and the Subversion of Identity*. London: Routledge.

Butler, J. (1993). *Bodies that Matter: On the Discursive Limits of "Sex"*. London: Routledge.

Butler, J. (2004). The Force of Fantasy: Mapplethorpe, Feminism, and Discursive Excess. In: Butler, J. and Salih, S. (Eds.). *The Judith Butler Reader*. Oxford: Blackwell Publishing, pp. 183–203.

Cameron, D. (2015). Evolution, Language and the Battle of the Sexes: A Feminist Linguist Encounters Evolutionary Psychology. *Australian Feminist Studies*, 30(86), 351–358.

Campbell, J. (2000). *Arguing with the Phallus—Feminist, Queer and Postcolonial Theory: A Psychoanalytic Contribution.* New York: St Martin's Press.
Capino, J. B. (2006). Asian College Girls and Oriental Men with Bamboo Poles: Reading Asian Pornography. In: Lehman, P. (Ed.). *Pornography: Film and Culture.* New Brunswick, NJ: Rutgers University Press, pp. 206–219.
Chamberlain, P. (2017). *The Feminist Fourth Wave: Affective Temporality.* Basingstoke: Palgrave Macmillan.
Chang, W. Y. and Glynos, J. (2011). Ideology and Politics in the Popular Press: The Case of the 2009 UK MPs' Expenses Scandal. In Dahlberg, L. and Phelan, S. (Eds.). *Discourse Theory and Critical Media Politics.* Basingstoke, London: Palgrave Macmillan, pp. 106–127.
Chasseguet-Smirgel, J. (1986). *Sexuality and Mind.* New York: New York University Press.
Cheng, A. A. (2001). *The Melancholy of Race: Psychoanalysis, Assimilation and Hidden Grief.* Oxford: Oxford University Press.
Ciclitira, K. (2004). Pornography, Women and Feminism: Between Pleasure and Politics. *Sexualities*, 7(3), 281–301.
Clarke, S. (2003). *Social Theory, Psychoanalysis and Racism.* Basingstoke: Palgrave Macmillan.
Clarkson, J. (2005). Contesting Masculinity's Makeover: Queer Eye, Consumer Masculinity, and "Straight-Acting" Gays. *Journal of Communication Inquiry*, 29(3), 235–255.
Clough, T. P. (2018a). *The User Unconscious: On Affect, Media, and Measure.* Minneapolis: University of Minnesota Press.
Clough, T. P. (2018b). From the Cyborg Manifesto to the User Unconscious. A Commentary by Patricia Ticineto Clough. *Public Seminar.* http://www.publicseminar.org/2018/08/from-the-cyborg-manifesto-to-the-user-unconscious/.
Clough, T. P. (2020). By the Skin of Our Machines: Psychoanalysis Beyond the Human, A Dialogue Between Patricia Clough and Jacob Johanssen. *Capacious: Journal For Emerging Affect Inquiry*, 2(1-2), http://capaciousjournal.com/article/by-the-skin-of-our-machines/.
Cohen, P. (2002). Psychoanalysis and Racism: Reading the Other Scene. In: Goldberg, D. T. and Solomos, J. (Eds.). *A Companion to Racial and Ethnic Studies.* Malden: Blackwell. 170–201.
Coleman, G. (2014). *Hacker, Hoaxer, Whistleblower, Spy: The Many Faces of Anonymous.* London: Verso.
Collins, P. H. (2004). *Black Sexual politics: African Americans, Gender, and the New Racism.* London: Routledge.
Connell, R. W. (1987). *Gender and Power. Society, the Person and Sexual Politics.* Cambridge: Polity.
Connell, R. W. (1995). *Masculinities.* Cambridge: Polity.
Connell, R. W. and Messerschmidt, J. W. (2005). Hegemonic Masculinity: Rethinking the Concept. *Gender & Society*, 19(6), 829–859.
Copjec, J. (1994). *Read My Desire: Lacan Against the Historicists.* Cambridge, MA: MIT Press.

Copjec, J. (2002). *Imagine There's No Woman. Ethics and Sublimation.* Cambridge, MA: MIT Press.
Cottee, S. (2018). Sex and Shame: What Incels and Jihadists Have in Common. *New York Times.* https://www.nytimes.com/2018/04/30/opinion/sex-shame-incels-jihadists-minassian.html.
Cowie, E. (1992). Pornography and Fantasy. In: Segal, L. and McIntosh, M. (Eds.). *Sex Exposed: Sexuality and the Pornography Debate.* London: Virago, pp. 132–152.
Cowie, E. (1997). *Representing the Woman. Cinema and Psychoanalysis.* Basingstoke: Macmillan Press.
Cox, M. (2017). The Rise of Populism and the Crisis of Globalisation: Brexit, Trump and Beyond. *Irish Studies in International Affairs,* 28, 9–17.
Crawford, M. N. (2008). *Dilution Anxiety and the Black Phallus.* Columbus, OH: The Ohio State University Press.
Crenshaw, K. (1989). Demarginalizing the Intersection of Race and Sex: A Black Feminist Critique of Antidiscrimination Doctrine, Feminist Theory and Antiracist Politics. *University of Chicago Legal Forum,* 8(1), 139–167.
Crenshaw, K. (1992). Race, Gender, and Sexual Harassment. *Southern California Law Review,* 65(3), 1467–1476.
Crenshaw, K. (1993). Beyond Racism and Misogyny: Black Feminism and 2 Live Crew. In: Matsuda, M., Lawrence, C. R., Delgado, R., Williams Crenshaw, K. (Eds.). *Words That Wound. Critical Race Theory, Assaultive Speech, and the First Amendment.* Boulder, CO: Westview Press, pp. 111–132.
Crociani-Windland, L. and Yates, C. (2020). Masculinity, Affect and the Search for Certainty in an Age of Precarity. *Free Associations: Psychoanalysis and Culture, Media, Groups, Politics,* 78, 105–127.
Dalal, F. (2001). Insides and Outsides: A Review of Psychoanalytic Renderings of Difference, Racism and Prejudice, *Psychoanalytic Studies,* 3, 43–66.
Dalal, F. (2013). *Race, Colour and the Processes of Racialization: New Perspectives from Group Analysis, Psychoanalysis and Sociology.* London: Routledge.
Daniels, J. (2009). *Cyber Racism. White Supremacy Online and the New Attack on Civil Rights.* London: Rowman & Littlefield International.
Daub, A. (2018). The Return of the Face. *Longreads.* https://longreads.com/2018/10/03/the-return-of-the-face/.
Dean, J. (2009). *Democracy and Other Neoliberal Fantasies.* Durham: Duke University Press.
Dean, J. (2010). *Blog Theory: Feedback and Capture in the Circuits of Drive.* Cambridge: Polity.
Dean, T. (2000). *Beyond Sexuality.* Chicago: The University of Chicago Press.
de Alarcón, R., de la Iglesia, J. I., Casado, N. M. and Montejo, A. L. (2019). Online Porn Addiction: What We Know and What We Don't—A Systematic Review. *Journal of Clinical Medicine,* 8(1), 1–20.
deCook, J. R. (2018). Memes and Symbolic Violence: #proudboys and the Use of Memes for Propaganda and the Construction of Collective Identity. *Learning, Media and Technology,* 43(4), 485–504.
deCook, J. R. (2021). Black Pill Epistemology, Castration, and the Archive in the Incel Wiki. *Psychoanalysis, Culture & Society,* 26(2).

DeKeseredy, W. S. (2015). Critical Criminological Understandings of Adult Pornography and Woman Abuse: New Progressive Directions in Research and Theory. *International Journal for Crime, Justice and Social Democracy*, 4(4), 4–21.

de Lauretis, T. (1994). *The Practice of Love: Lesbian Sexuality and Perverse Desire*. Bloomington: Indiana University Press.

Deleuze, G. and Guattari, F. (1983a). *Anti-Oedipus. Capitalism and Schizophrenia*. Minneapolis: University of Minnesota Press.

Deleuze, G. and Guattari, F. (1983b). *A Thousand Plateaus. Capitalism and Schizophrenia*. Minneapolis: University of Minnesota Press.

Denisova, A. (2019). *Internet Memes and Society: Social, Cultural, and Political Contexts*. London: Routledge.

De Visser, R. O. (2017). "I'm Not a Very Manly Man" Qualitative Insights into Young Men's Masculine Subjectivity. *Men and Masculinities*, 11(3), 367–371.

De Wiele, C. E. and Campbell, F. (2019). From Swiping to Ghosting: Conceptualising Rejection in Mobile Dating. In: Hetsroni, A. and Tuncez, M. (Eds.). *It Happened on Tinder: Reflections and Studies on Internet Infused Dating*. Amsterdam: Institute of Network Cultures, 158–175.

Dines, G. (2006). The White Man's Burden: Gonzo Pornography and the Construction of Black Masculinity. *Yale JL & Feminism*, 18, 283.

Doane, M. A. (1987). *The Desire to Desire. The Woman's Film of the 1940s*. Bloomington, IN: Indiana University Press.

Doane, M. A. (1999). Dark Continents: Epistemologies of Racial and Sexual Difference in Psychoanalysis and the Cinema. In: Evans, J. and Hall, S. (Eds.). *Visual Culture. The Reader*. London: Sage, pp. 448–456.

Dodes, L. M. (1990). Addiction, Helplessness, and Narcissistic Rage. *The Psychoanalytic Quarterly*, 59(3), 398–419.

Dodson, B. (2015). Masturbation. In: Bolin, A. and Whelehan, P. (Eds.). *The International Encyclopedia of Human Sexuality*. 10.1002/9781118896877.wbiehs288.

Donnerstein, E. (1984). Pornography: Its Effect on Violence against Women. In: Malmuth, N. M. and Donnerstein, E. (Eds.). *Pornography and Sexual Aggression*. Cambridge, MA: Academic Press, pp. 53–81.

Donson, A. (2010). *Youth in the Fatherless Land: War Pedagogy, Nationalism, and Authority in Germany. 1914-1918*. Cambridge, MA: Harvard University Press.

Dunham, L. and Aptow, J. (2012-2017). *Girls*. TV Series.

Eichhorn, K. (2019). *The End of Forgetting. Growing Up with Social Media*. Cambridge, MA: Harvard University Press.

Engel, J. (2006). *The Epidemic: A Global History of AIDS*. New York: Harper Collins.

Elliot, P. (2014). Psychoanalysis. *TSQ: Transgender Studies Quarterly*, 1(1–2), 165–168.

Evans, D. (2006). *An Introductory Dictionary of Lacanian Psychoanalysis*. London: Routledge.

Evans, E. (2016). What Makes a (Third) Wave? How and Why the Third-Wave Narrative Works for Contemporary Feminists. *International Feminist Journal of Politics*, 18(3), 409–428.

Fakhry Davids, M. (2011). *Internal Racism: A Psychoanalytic Approach to Race and Difference*. London: Red Globe Press.

Faludi. S. (1999). *Stiffed: The Betrayal of the Modern Man*, London: Chatto & Windus.
Fang, N. (2020). Feeling/being 'Out of Place': Psychic Defence Against the Hostile Environment. *Journal of Psychosocial Studies*, *13*(2), 151–164.
Fanon, F. (1967). *Black Skin, White Masks*. London: Pluto.
Farrell, T., Fernandez, M., Novotny, J. and Alani, H. (2019). Exploring Misogyny across the Manosphere in Reddit. Proceedings of the 10th ACM Conference on Web Science. 10.1145/3292522.3326045.
ffytche, M. and Pick, D. (2016, Eds.). *Psychoanalysis in the Age of Totalitarianism*. London: Routledge.
Fielding, J. and Bass, C. (2018). Individuals Seeking Gender Reassignment: Marked Increase in Demand for Services. *BJPsych Bulletin*, *42*(5), 206–210.
Fielitz, M. and Thurston, N. (2019, Eds.). *Post-Digital Cultures of the Far Right: Online Actions and Offline Consequences in Europe and the US*. Bielefeld: Transcript Verlag.
Filipovic, J. (2007). Blogging While Female: How Internet Misogyny Parallels Real-World Harassment. *Yale Journal of Law & Feminism*, 19, 295–304.
Fincher, D. (1999). *Fight Club*. Film.
Florêncio, J. (2020). *Bareback Porn, Porous Masculinities, Queer Futures. The Ethics of Becoming-Pig*. London: Routledge.
Forscher, P. S. and Kteily, N. S. (2020). A Psychological Profile of the Alt-right. *Perspectives on Psychological Science*, 15(1), 90–116.
Foucault, M. (1978). *The History of Sexuality. Volume 1: An Introduction*. New York: Pantheon Books.
Foucault, M. (1980). Body/Power. In: Gordon, C. (Ed.). *Power/Knowledge. Selected Interviews and Other Writings. 1972-1977*. New York: Pantheon Books, pp. 55–62.
Foucault, M. (2003). *Abnormal: Lectures at the Collége de France, 1974–1975*. London: Verso.
Fountain, A. (2019). Men of Color Are Creating Their Own Manospheres, & Their Misogynistic Violence Is Going Ignored. https://racebaitr.com/2019/06/18/men-of-color-are-creating-their-own-manospheres-their-misogynistic-violence-is-going-ignored/.
Fraser, N. (2017). The End of Progressive Neoliberalism. *Dissent*. https://www.dissentmagazine.org/online_articles/progressive-neoliberalism-reactionary-populism-nancy-fraser.
Freud, S. (1915). The Unconscious. *The Standard Edition of the Complete Psychological Works of Sigmund Freud. Volume XIV. On the History of the Psycho-Analytic Movement, Papers on Metapsychology and Other Works*. London: The Hogarth Press and the Institute of Psycho-Analysis, pp. 159–215.
Freud, S. (1932). Libidinal Types. *The Psychoanalytic Quarterly*, 1(1), 3–6.
Freud, S. (1949). *Inhibitions, Symptoms and Anxiety*. London: The Hogarth Press and the Institute of Psycho-Analysis.
Freud, S. (1953). On Aphasia. *A Critical Study*. New York: International Universities Press.
Freud, S. (1960). *Totem and Taboo*. Empire Books. London: Penguin Books.
Freud, S. (1981a). Project for a Scientific Psychology. *The Standard Edition of the Complete Psychological Works of Sigmund Freud. Volume I. Pre-Psycho Analytic*

Publications and Unpublished Drafts. London: The Hogarth Press and the Institute of Psycho-Analysis, pp. 283–346.

Freud, S. (1981b). Three Essays on the Theory of Sexuality. *The Standard Edition of the Complete Psychological Works of Sigmund Freud. Volume VIII. A Case of Hysteria. Three Essays on Sexuality and Other Works*. London: The Hogarth Press and the Institute of Psycho-Analysis, pp. 130–231.

Freud, S. (1981c). Some Character-Types Met with in Psycho-Analytic Work. *The Standard Edition of the Complete Psychological Works of Sigmund Freud. Volume XIV. On the History of the Psycho-Analytic Movement, Papers on Metapsychology and Other Works*. London: The Hogarth Press and the Institute of Psycho-Analysis, pp. 309–333.

Freud, S. (1981d). From the History of an Infantile Neurosis. *The Standard Edition of the Complete Psychological Works of Sigmund Freud. Volume XVII. An Infantile Neurosis and Other Works*. London: The Hogarth Press and the Institute of Psycho-Analysis, pp. 7–104.

Freud, S. (1981e). 'A Child is Being Beaten': A Contribution to the Study of the Origin of Sexual Perversion. *The Standard Edition of the Complete Psychological Works of Sigmund Freud. Volume XVII. An Infantile Neurosis and Other Works*. London: The Hogarth Press and the Institute of Psycho-Analysis, pp. 175–176.

Freud, S. (1981f). A Seventeenth-Century Demonological Neurosis. *The Standard Edition of the Complete Psychological Works of Sigmund Freud. Volume XIX. The Ego and the Id and Other Works*. London: The Hogarth Press and the Institute of Psycho-Analysis, pp. 67–106.

Freud, S. (1981g). A Note Upon the 'Mystic Writing Pad'. *The Standard Edition of the Complete Psychological Works of Sigmund Freud. Volume XIX. The Ego and the Id and Other Works*. London: The Hogarth Press and the Institute of Psycho-Analysis, pp. 225–232.

Fritz, N. and Paul, B. (2017). From Orgasms to Spanking: A Content Analysis of the Agentic and Objectifying Sexual Scripts in Feminist, for Women, and Mainstream Pornography. *Sex Roles*, 77(9-10), 639–652.

Fromm, E. (1941). *Man for Himself: An Inquiry into the Psychology of Ethics*. New York: Holt, Rinehard, and Winston.

Frosh, S. (1994). *Sexual Difference: Masculinity and Psychoanalysis*. London: Routledge.

Frosh, S. (1995). Masculine Mastery and Fantasy, or the Meaning of the Phallus. In: Elliott, A. and Frosh, S. (Eds.). *Psychoanalysis in Contexts: Paths Between Theory and Modern Culture*. London: Routledge, pp. 89–105.

Frosh, S. (2005). *Hate and the 'Jewish Science'. Anti-Semitism, Nazism and Psychoanalysis*. Basingstoke: Palgrave Macmillan.

Frosh, S. (2006). *For and Against Psychoanalysis*. Second Edition. London: Routledge.

Frosh, S. (2011). Psychoanalysis, Anti-Semitism and the Miser. *New Formations*, 72, 94–106.

Frosh, S. (2016). Studies in Prejudice: Theorizing anti-Semitism in the Wake of the Nazi Holocaust. In: Ffytche, Matt (Ed.). *Psychoanalysis in the Age of Totalitarianism*. London: Routledge, pp. 28–41.

Frosh, S., Phoenix, A. and Pattman, R. (2001). *Young Masculinities: Understanding Boys in contemporary Society*. Basingstoke: Palgrave Macmillan.
Frost, L. (2001). *Sex Drives: Fantasies of Fascism in Literary Modernism*. Ithaca: Cornell University Press.
Fuchs, C. (2014). *Digital Labour and Karl Marx*. London: Routledge.
Fuchs, C. (2018). *Digital Demagogue: Authoritarian Capitalism in the Age of Trump and Twitter*. London: Pluto Press.
Garlick, S. (2010). Taking Control of Sex? Hegemonic Masculinity, Technology, and Internet Pornography. *Men and Masculinities*, 12(5), 597–614.
George, S. (2014). From Alienation to Cynicism: Race and the Lacanian Unconscious. *Psychoanalysis, Culture & Society*, 19(4), 360–378.
George, S. (2016). *Trauma and Race: A Lacanian Study of African American Racial Identity*. Waco, TX: Baylor University Press.
Gerhard, J. (2001). *Desiring Revolution: Second-Wave Feminism and the Rewriting of Twentieth-Century American Sexual Thought*. New York: Columbia University Press.
Gherovici, P. (2017). *Transgender Psychoanalysis: A Lacanian Perspective on Sexual Difference*. London: Routledge.
Giddens, A. (2009). *Sociology*. Sixth Edition. Cambridge: Polity Press.
Giffney, N. and Watson, E. (2017, Eds.). *Clinical Encounters in Sexuality. Psychoanalytic Practice & Queer Theory*. Goleta, CA: Punctum Books.
Gilbert, J. (2013). What Kind of Thing Is 'Neoliberalism'? *New Formations*, 80 / 81, 7–22.
Gill, R. (2007). Postfeminist Media Culture: Elements of a Sensibility. *European Journal of Cultural Studies*, 10(2), 147–166.
Gill, R. (2013). Postfeminist Sexual Culture. In: Steiner L., McLaughlin L. and Carter C. (Eds.). *The Routledge Companion to Media and Gender*. London: Routledge, pp. 607–617.
Gill, R. (2016). Post-Postfeminism? New Feminist Visibilities in Postfeminist Times. *Feminist Media Studies*, 16(4), 610–630.
Gill, R. (2017). The Affective, Cultural and Psychic Life of Postfeminism: A Postfeminist Sensibility 10 Years on. *European Journal of Cultural Studies*, 20(6), 606–626.
Gilman, S. L., King, H., Porter, R., Rousseau, G. S. and Showalter, E. (1993). *Hysteria Beyond Freud*. Berkeley: University of California Press.
Gilmore, D. D. (1990). *Manhood in the Making: Cultural Concepts of Masculinity*. New Haven: Yale University Press.
Ging, D. (2017). Alphas, Betas, and Incels: Theorizing the Masculinities of the Manosphere. *Men and Masculinities*, 22(4), 1–20.
Ging, D. and Siapera, E. (2019, Eds.). Gender Hate Online. Understanding the new Anti-Feminism. Basingstoke: Palgrave Macmillan.
Glynos, J. and Mondon, A. (2016). The Political Logic of Populist Hype: The Case of Right-Wing Populism's 'Meteoric Rise' and its Relation to the Status Quo'. *POPULISMUS Working Paper Series*.
Goldberg, M. (2017). Norway Massacre: Anders Breivik's Deadly Attack Fueled by Hatred of Women. *The Daily Beast*. https://www.thedailybeast.com/norway-massacre-anders-breiviks-deadly-attack-fueled-by-hatred-of-women.

Golumbia, D. (2009). *The Cultural Logic of Computation*. Cambridge, MA: Harvard University Press.
Gotell, L. and Dutton, E. (2016). Sexual Violence in the "Manosphere": Antifeminist Men's Rights Discourses on Rape. *International Journal for Crime, Justice and Social Democracy*, 5(2), 65–80.
Gottzén, L., Mellström, U. and Shefer, T. (2019, Eds.). *The Routledge International Handbook of Masculinity Studies*. London: Routledge.
Grant, L. (1993). *Sexing the Millennium: A Political History of the Sexual Revolution*. Glasgow: Harper Collins.
Gray, P. W. (2018). 'The Fire Rises': Identity, the Alt-Right and Intersectionality. *Journal of Political Ideologies*, 23(2), 141–156.
Gray, R. T. (2004). *About Face: German Physiognomic Thought from Lavater to Auschwitz*. Detroit, MI: Wayne State University Press.
Greedharry, M. (2008). *Postcolonial Theory and Psychoanalysis: From Uneasy Engagements to Effective Critique*. Basingstoke: Palgrave Macmillan.
Greene, V. (2019). All They Need Is Lulz: Racist Trolls, Unlaughter, and Leslie Jones. In: Webber, J. A. (Ed.). *The Joke is on Us. Political Comedy in (Late) Neoliberal Times*. London: Lexington Books, pp. 37–64.
Grigg, R., Hecq, D. and Smith, C. (2015, Eds.). *Female Sexuality. The Early Psychoanalytic Controversies*. London: Karnac Books.
Grosz, E. A. (1994). *Volatile Bodies: Toward a Corporeal Feminism*. Indiana University Press.
Grosz, E. A. (1995). *Space, Time and Perversion: Essays on the Politics of Bodies*. London: Routledge.
Guillaumin, C. (2002). *Racism, Sexism, Power and Ideology*. London: Routledge.
Gullestad, S. E. (2017). Anders Behring Breivik, Master of Life and Death: Psychodynamics and Political Ideology in an Act of Terrorism. *International Forum of Psychoanalysis*, 26(4), 207–216.
Günther, H. F. K. (1933). *Kleine Rassenkunde des Deutschen Volkes*. https://www.velesova-sloboda.info/archiv/pdf/guenther-kleine-rassenkunde-des-deutschen-volkes.pdf.
Hakim, C. (2010). Erotic Capital. *European Sociological Review*, 26(5), 499–518.
Hakim, J. (2019). *Work that Body. Male Bodies in Digital Culture*. London: Rowman & Littlefield International.
Hanna, B. (2018). Challenge Mode: Overcoming Sexism in the Games Industry. *Screen Education*, (89), 44–49.
Hartmann, M. (2020). The Totalizing Meritocracy of Heterosex: Subjectivity in NoFap. *Sexualities*, 24(3), 409–430.
Hartzell, S. L. (2018). Alt-White: Conceptualizing the "Alt-Right" as a Rhetorical Bridge Between White Nationalism and Mainstream Public Discourse. *Journal of Contemporary Rhetoric*, 8(1/2), 6–25.
Haider, S. (2016). The Shooting in Orlando, Terrorism or Toxic Masculinity (or Both?). *Men and Masculinities*, 19(5), 555–565.
Hall, S. (1993): Cultural Identity and Diaspora. In: Rutherford, J. (Ed.). *Identity, Community, Culture, Difference*. London: Lawrence and Wishart, pp. 222–237.
Hawley, G. (2017). *Making Sense of the Alt-Right*. New York: Columbia University Press.

Heidenry, J. (1997). *What Wild Ecstasy: The Rise and Fall of the Sexual Revolution*. New York: Simon & Schuster.
Heino R., Ellison, N. and Gibbs, J. (2010) Relationshopping: Investigating the Market Metaphor in Online Dating. *Journal of Social and Personal Relationships*, 27(4), 427–447.
Hellinger, D. C. (2019). *Conspiracies and Conspiracy Theories in the Age of Trump*. Basingstoke: Palgrave Macmillan.
Hermansson, P., Lawrence, D., Mulhall, J. and Murdoch, S. (2020). *The International Alt-Right: Fascism for the 21st Century?* London: Routledge.
Herzog, D. (2005). *Sex after Fascism, Memory and Morality in Twentieth-Century Germany*. Princeton, NJ: Princeton University Press.
Hills, M. (2002). *Fan Cultures*. London: Routledge.
Hines, A. (2019). How Many Bones Would You Break to Get Laid? "Incels" Are Going Under the Knife to Reshape Their Faces, and Their Dating Prospects. *The Cut*. https://www.thecut.com/2019/05/incel-plastic-surgery.html.
Hines, S. (2018). *Is Gender Fluid? A Primer for the 21st Century*. London: Thames & Hudson.
Hirdman, A. (2007). (In) Visibility and the Display of Gendered Desire: Masculinity in Mainstream Soft-and Hardcore Pornography. *NORA—Nordic Journal of Women's Studies*, 15(2-3), 158–171.
Hodapp, C. (2017). *Men's Rights, Gender, and Social Media*. London: Rowman & Littlefield International.
Honneth, A. (2012). *The I in We. Studies in the Theory of Recognition*. Cambridge: Polity.
Hook, D. (2004). Racism as Abjection: A Psychoanalytic Conceptualisation for a Post-Apartheid South Africa. *South African Journal of Psychology*, 34(4), 672–703.
Hook, D. (2006). 'Pre-discursive' Racism. *Journal of Community & Applied Social Psychology*, 16(3), 207–232.
Hook, D. (2008). Postcolonial Psychoanalysis. *Theory & Psychology*, 18(2), 269–283.
Hook, D. (2018). Racism and Jouissance: Evaluating the "Racism as (the Theft of) Enjoyment" Hypothesis. *Psychoanalysis, Culture & Society*, 23(3), 244–266.
Hook, D. (2020). White Anxiety in (Post) Apartheid South Africa. *Psychoanalysis, Culture & Society*, 25, 612–631.
Horbury, A. (2015). *Post-Feminist Impasses in Popular Heroine Television: The Persephone Complex*. Basingstoke: Palgrave Macmillan.
Horbury, A. (2019). A Psychoanalytic Ethics of the Pornographic Aesthetic. *Porn Studies*, 6(1), 87–99.
Horney, K. (2015). The Dread of Woman: Observations on a Specific Difference in the Dread Felt by Men and Women Respectively for the Opposite Sex. In: Grigg, R., Hecq, D. and Smith, C. (Eds.). *Female Sexuality: The Early Psychoanalytic Controversies*. London: Karnac Books, pp. 241–252.
Horrocks, R. (1994). *Masculinities in Crisis: Myths, Fantasies, and Realities*. Basingstoke: Palgrave Macmillan.
Huffer, L. (2013). *Are the Lips a Grave? A Queer Feminist on the Ethics of Sex*. Columbia University Press.
Hunte, Z. (2019). 'Female Nature, Cucks, and Simps': Understanding Men Going Their Own Way as Part of the Manosphere. http://www.diva-portal.org/smash/record.jsf?pid=diva2%3A1331052&dswid=6085.

Humphries, D. (2009, Ed.). *Women, Violence, and the Media: Readings in Feminist Criminology*. Lebanon, NH: Northeastern University Press.

Hsieh, L. (2012). A Queer Sex, or, Can Feminism and Psychoanalysis Have Sex without the Phallus. *Feminist Review*, 102(1), 97–115.

Incels.co. (2018). Who Is the Enemy to You? https://incels.co/threads/poll-who-is-the-enemy-to-you.49499/.

IncelWiki. (2020). Chad. https://incels.wiki/w/Chad.

Irigaray, L. (1985). *The Sex Which Is Not One*. Ithaca, NY: Cornell University Press.

Irigaray, L. (1993). *An Ethics of Sexual Difference*. Ithaca, NY: Cornell University Press.

Jakobsen, K. D., Skyum, E., Hashemi, N., Schjerning, O., Fink-Jensen, A., & Nielsen, J. (2017). Antipsychotic Treatment of Schizotypy and Schizotypal Personality Disorder: A Systematic Review. *Journal of Psychopharmacology*, 31(4), 397–405.

Jane, E. (2014). 'Back to the Kitchen, Cunt': Speaking the Unspeakable about Online Misogyny. *Continuum*, 28(4), 558–570.

Jane, E. (2016). *Misogyny Online: A Short (and Brutish) History*. London: Sage.

Jane, E. (2018). Systemic Misogyny Exposed: Translating Rapeglish from the Manosphere with a Random Rape Threat Generator. *International Journal of Cultural Studies*, 21(6), 661–680.

Jardina, A. (2019). *White Identity Politics*. Cambridge University Press.

Jeffreys, S. (1990). *Anticlimax: A Feminist Perspective on the Sexual Revolution*. New York: The Women's Press and New York University Press.

Jenson, J. and De Castell, S. (2013). Tipping Points: Marginality, Misogyny and Videogames. *Journal of Curriculum Theorizing*, 29(2), 72–85.

Johanssen, J. (2012). Subjects in Labour. A New Self in 'My Strange Addiction'. In: Henderson, D. (Ed.). *Psychoanalysis, Culture and Society*. Newcastle: Cambridge Scholars Publishing, pp. 144–162.

Johanssen, J. (2013). We Shall Overcome. The Posthuman Discourse as a Symptom of Today's Negation of the Unconscious. In: Rambatan. B. and Johanssen, J. (Eds.). *Cyborg Subjects: Discourses On Digital Culture*. Seattle, WA: Createspace Publishing, pp. 42–52.

Johanssen, J. (2016). Not Belonging to One's Self: Affect on Facebook's Site Governance Page. *International Journal of Cultural Studies*, 21(2), 207–222.

Johanssen, J. (2017). Immaterial Labour and Reality TV: The Affective Surplus of Excess. In: Briziarelli, M. and Armano, E. (Eds.). *The Spectacle of 'Free' Labor: Reading Debord in the Context of Digital Capitalism*. London: University of Westminster Press, pp. 197–208.

Johanssen, J. (2019). *Psychoanalysis and Digital Culture: Audiences, Social Media, and Big Data*. London: Routledge.

Johanssen, J. and Krüger, S. (2016). Digital Media, Psychoanalysis and the Subject. Special Issue. *CM: Communication and Media*, 38(11). http://aseestant.ceon.rs/index.php/comman/issue/view/467/showToc.

Jones, M. (2017). Expressive Surfaces: The Case of the Designer Vagina. *Theory, Culture & Society*, 34(7–8), 29–50.

Jones, S. (2016). "Extreme" Porn? The Implications of a Label. *Porn Studies*, 3(3), 295–307.

Jones, C., Trott, V. and Wright, S. (2019). Sluts and Soyboys: MGTOW and the Production of Misogynistic Online Harassment. *New Media & Society*, Online First. 10.1177/1461444819887141.

Jones, J. C. (2011). Anders Breivik's Chilling Anti-feminism.' *The Guardian*. https://www.theguardian.com/commentisfree/2011/jul/27/breivik-anti-feminism.

Jones, K. (2008). The Role of Father in Psychoanalytic Theory: Historical and Contemporary Trends. *Smith College Studies in Social Work*, 75(1), 7–28.

Jutel, O. (2019). Civility, Subversion and Technocratic Class Consciousness: Reconstituting Truth in the Journalistic Field. In: R. Overell and Nicholls, B. (Eds.). *Post-Truth and the Mediation of Reality. New Conjunctures*. Basingstoke: Palgrave Macmillan, pp. 177–202.

Jutel, O. (2020). Blockchain, Affect and Digital Teleologies. In: Boler, M. and Davis, E. (Eds.). (2020). *Affective Politics of Digital Media: Propaganda by Other Means*. Routledge, pp. 101–115.

Kahr, B. (2008). *Sex and the Psyche: The Truth About Our Most Secret Fantasies*. London: Penguin Books.

Kanwal, G. and Akhtar, S. (2018). *Intimacy: Clinical, Cultural, Digital and Developmental Perspectives*. London: Routledge.

Keller, J., Mendes, K. and Ringrose, J. (2016). Speaking Unspeakable Things. Documenting Digital Feminist Responses to Rape Culture. *Journal of Gender Studies*, 27(1), 22–36.

Keller, J. and Ryan, M. (2014). Call for Papers: Problematizing Postfeminism. http://arcyp.ca/archives/4244.

Kelly, A. (2017). The Alt-Right: Reactionary Rehabilitation for White Masculinity. *Soundings* 66, 68–78.

Keskinen, S. (2013). Antifeminism and White Identity Politics: Political Antagonisms in Radical Right-Wing Populist and Anti-Immigration Rhetoric in Finland. *Nordic Journal of Migration Research*, 3(4), 225–232.

Kershaw, I. (1998). *Hitler. 1889-1936: Hubris*. London: Penguin Books.

Khanna, R. (2003). *Dark Continents: Psychoanalysis and Colonialism*. Durham: Duke University Press.

Kimmel, M. (2008). *Guyland: The Perilous World Where Boys Become Men*. New York: Harper.

Kimmel, M. (2013). *Angry White Men: American Masculinity at the End of an Era*. New York: Nation Books.

Klein, M. (1988a). *Love, Guilt and Reparation and Other Works. 1921–1945*. London: Virago.

Klein, M. (1988b). *Envy and Gratitude and Other Works. 1946–1963*. London: Virago.

Klein, Ma. (2016). *His Porn, Her Pain: Confronting America's Pornpanic with Honest Talk about Sex*. Santa Barbara, CA: Praeger.

Knafo, D. and Lo Bosco, R. (2017). *The Age of Perversion: Desire and Technology in Psychoanalysis and Culture*. London: Routledge.

Knausgård, K. O. (2015). Inside the Warped Mind of Anders Breivik. *The Telegraph*. https://www.telegraph.co.uk/news/2016/07/22/anders-breivik-inside-the-warped-mind-of-a-mass-killer/.

KnowYourMeme.com. (2018). Virgin vs. Chad Meme. https://knowyourmeme.com/photos/1265119-virgin-vs-chad.
Koulouris, T. (2018). Online Misogyny and the Alternative Right: Debating the Undebatable. *Feminist Media Studies*, 18(4), 750–761.
Kovel, J. (1984). *White Racism: A Psychohistory*. Columbia University Press.
Kray, T. R. (2018). By Means of Seduction: Pickup-Artists and the Cultural History of Erotic Persuasion. *NORMA*, *13*(1), 41–58.
Kristeva, J. (1982). *Powers of Horror: An Essay on Abjection*. New York: Columbia University Press.
Kristeva, J. (1998). Experiencing the Phallus as Extraneous, or Women's Twofold Oedipus Complex. *Parallax*, *4*(3), 29–43.
Krüger, S. (2017). Unable to Mourn Again? Media(ted) Reactions to German Neo-Nazi Terrorism. In: Auestad, L. (Ed.). *Shared Traumas, Silent Loss, Public and Private Mourning*. London: Karnac Books, pp. 59–76.
Krüger, S. (2018). Violence and the Virtual. Right-wing, Anti-asylum Facebook Pages and the Fomenting of Political Violence. In: Krüger, S., Figlio, K. and Richards, B. (Ed.). *Fomenting Political Violence - Fantasy, Language, Media, Action*. Basingstoke: Palgrave Macmillan, pp. 75- 102.
Krüger, S. (2021). Anal Sexuality and Male Subcultures Online. *Psychoanalysis, Culture & Society*, 26(2).
Krüger, S. and Johanssen, J. (2014). Alienation and Digital Labour—A Depth Hermeneutic Inquiry into Online Commodification and the Unconscious. *Triple C: Communication, Capitalism & Critique. Open Access Journal for a Global Sustainable Information Society*, 12(2), 632–647.
Krüger, S., Figlio, K. and Richards, B. (2018, Eds.). *Fomenting Political Violence*. Basingstoke: Palgrave Macmillan.
Kühn, S. and Gallinat, J. (2014). Brain Structure and Functional Connectivity Associated with Pornography Consumption: The Brain on Porn. *JAMA Psychiatry*, 71(7), 827–834.
Kupers, T. A. (2005). Toxic Masculinity as a Barrier to Mental Health Treatment in Prison. *Journal of Clinical Psychology*, 61, 713–724.
Lacan, J. (1972–1973). *The Seminar. Book XX. Encore. The Limits of Love and Knowledge*. New York, NY: Norton.
Lacan, J. (1974–1975). *RSI*. Unpublished Seminar.
Lacan, J. (1975). *The Seminar of Jacques Lacan, Book I: Freud's Papers on Technique, 1953–54*. New York: Norton.
Lacan, J. (1977). *The Four Fundamental Concepts of Psychoanalysis*. London: Karnac Books.
Lacan, J. (2014). *Anxiety. The Seminars of Jacques Lacan. Book X*. Cambridge: Polity.
Lacan, J. (2020). *Écrits*. London: Routledge.
Lamerichs, N., Nguyen, D., Melguizo, M. C. P., Radojevic, R., Business, C. and Lange-Böhmer, A. (2018). Elite Male Bodies: The Circulation of Alt-Right Memes and the Framing of Politicians on Social Media. *Participations*, *15*(1), 180–206.
Lane, C. (1998, Ed.). *The Psychoanalysis of Race*. New York: Columbia University Press.

Langman, P. (2014). Elliot Rodger: An Analysis. *The Journal of Campus Behavioral Intervention*, 2, 5–19. https://www.rescarchgate.net/profile/Peter_Langman/publication/294090690_Elliot_Rodger_An_Analysis/links/56be443f08ae2f498ef62a5e.pdf.

Laplanche, J. and Pontalis, J.-B. (1968). Fantasy and the Origins of Sexuality. *The International Journal of Psycho-Analysis*, 9, 1–18.

Laplanche, J. and Pontalis, J.-B. (1973). *The Language of Psycho-Analysis*. New York: Norton.

Lawrence, E. and Ringrose, J. (2018). @NoToFeminism, #FeministsAreUgly, and Misandry Memes: How Social Media Feminist Humor is Calling Out Antifeminism. In: Keller, J. and Ryan, M. E. (Eds.). *Emergent Feminisms: Complicating a Postfeminist Media Culture*. London: Routledge, pp. 211–232.

LeGates, M. (2001). *In Their Time: A History of Feminism in Western Society*. London: Routledge.

Lehmann, Z. (2015-2018). *Casual*. TV Series.

Lemma, A. (2017). *The Digital Age on the Couch. Psychoanalytic Practice and New Media*. London: Routledge.

Lemma, A. and Lynch, P. E. (2015, Eds.). *Sexualities: Contemporary Psychoanalytic Perspectives*. London: Routledge.

Lewis, R. (2018). *Alternative Influence. Broadcasting the Reactionary Right on YouTube*. Report. https://datasociety.net/output/alternative-influence/.

Liff, S. and Wajcman, J. (1996). 'Sameness' and 'Difference' Revisited: Which Way Forward for Equal Opportunity Initiatives? *Journal of Management Studies*, 33(1), 79–94.

Lin, J. L. (2017). Antifeminism Online. MGTOW (Men Going Their Own Way). In: Frömming, U. U., Köhn, S., Fox, S., and Terry, M. (Eds.). *Digital Environments: Ethnographic Perspectives Across Global Online and Offline Spaces*. Bielefeld: Transcript Verlag, pp. 77–96.

Lindgren, S. (2010). Widening the Glory Hole: The Discourse of Online Porn Fandom. In: Attwood, F. (Ed.). *Porn.com: Making Sense of Online Pornography*. New York: Peter Lang, pp. 171–185.

Long, J. (2012). *Anti-Porn: The Resurgence of Anti-Pornography Feminism*. London: Zed Books.

Longstaff, G. (2019). Bodies that Splutter–Theorizing Jouissance in Bareback and Chemsex Porn. *Porn Studies*, 6(1), 74–86.

Lokke, G. (2019). Cuckolds, Cucks, and Their Transgressions. *Porn Studies*, 6(2), 212–227.

Lumsden, K. and Harmer, E. (2019, Eds.). *Online Othering: Exploring Digital Violence and Discrimination on the Web*. Basingstoke: Palgrave Macmillan.

Luepnitz, D. (2003). Beyond the Phallus: Lacan and Feminism. In: Rambaté, J.-M. (Ed.). *The Cambridge Companion to Lacan*. Cambridge: Cambridge University Press, pp. 221–237.

Lyons, M. N. (2017). *Ctrl-Alt-Delete: The Origins and Ideology of the Alternative Right*. Somerville, MA: Political Research Associates. https://www.politicalresearch.org/2017/01/20/ctrl-alt-delete-report-on-the-alternative-right.

MacInnes, J. (1998). *The End of Masculinity: The Confusion of Sexual Genesis and Sexual Difference in Modern Society*. Philadelphia: Open University Press.

Maguire, M. (2004). *Men, Women, Passion and Power*. Revised Edition. London: Routledge.
Maguire, M. (2015). *Men, Women, Passion and Power: Gender Issues in Psychotherapy*. London: Routledge.
Maguire, S. (2001). *Bridget Jones Diary*. Film.
Mahler, M. (1979). Autism and Symbiosis: Two Extreme Disturbances of Identity. *Infantile Psychosis and Early Contributions: The Selected Papers of Margaret S. Mahler. Volume 1*. London: Jason Aronson.
Main, T. J. (2018). *The Rise of the Alt-Right*. Washington: Brookings Institution Press.
Manne, K. (2018). *Down Girl. The Logic of Misogyny*. Oxford: Oxford University Press.
Mantilla, K. (2013). Gendertrolling: Misogyny Adapts to New Media. *Feminist Studies*, 39(2), 563–570.
Mantilla, K. (2015). *Gendertrolling. How Misogyny Went Viral*. Santa Barbara, CA: Praeger.
Marcuse, H. (1955). *Eros and Civilization*. Boston, MA: Beacon Press.
Marcuse, H. (1964). *One-Dimensional Man: Studies in the Ideology of Advanced Industrial Society*. Boston: Beacon.
Marks, L. U. (1996). Straight Women, Gay Porn, and the Scene of Erotic Looking. *Jump Cut*, 127–136.
Marks, L. U. (2020). Which Came First, Fascism or Misogyny? Reading Klaus Theweleit's Male Fantasies? In: Gandesha, S. (Ed.). *Spectres of Fascism: Historical, Theoretical and International Perspectives*. London: Pluto Press, pp. 109–119.
Marsden, L. (2019). Pushing Back the Obama Legacy: Trump's First Year and the Alt-Right-Evangelical-Catholic Coalition. In: Olivia, M. and Shanahan, M. (Eds.). *The Trump Presidency. From Campaign Trail to World Stage*. Basingstoke: Palgrave Macmillan, pp. 85–109.
Marwick, A. E. and Caplan, R. (2018). Drinking Male Tears: Language, the Manosphere, and Networked Harassment. *Feminist Media Studies*, 18(4), 543–559.
May, R. and Feldman, M. (2019). Understanding the Alt-Right: Ideologues, 'Lulz' and Hiding in Plain Sight. In: Fielitz, M. and Thurston, N. (Eds.). *Post-Digital Cultures of the Far Right: Online Actions and Offline Consequences in Europe and the US*. Bielefeld: Transcript, pp. 25–36.
Massanari, A. (2017). #Gamergate and The Fappening: How Reddit's Algorithm, Governance, and Culture Support Toxic Technocultures. *New Media & Society*, 19(3), 329–346.
Mayer, V. (2013). The Feminization of US Media Work. In: Steiner L., McLaughlin L. and Carter C. (Eds.). *The Routledge Companion to Media and Gender*. London: Routledge, pp. 51–60.
McGowan, T. (2004). *The End of Dissatisfaction. Jacques Lacan and the Emerging Society of Enjoyment*. New York: State University of New York Press.
McKee, A. (2005). The Objectification of Women in Mainstream Pornographic Videos in Australia. *Journal of Sex Research*, 42(4), 277–290.
McKee, A. (2018). Porn Consumers as Fans. In: Booth, P. (Ed.). *A Companion to Media Fandom and Fan Studies*. London: John Wiley & Sons, pp. 509–520.

McKey Carusi, R. (2020). *Lacan and Critical Feminism. Subjectivity, Sexuation, and Discourse.* London: Routledge.

McQuarrie, M. (2016). Trump and the Revolt of the Rust Belt. USAPP–American Politics and Policy Blog. https://blogs.lse.ac.uk/usappblog/2016/11/11/23174/.

McRobbie, A. (2004). Post-Feminism and Popular Culture. *Feminist Media Studies*, 4(3), 255–264.

McRobbie, A. (2007). Postfeminism and Popular Culture: *Bridget Jones* and the new Gender Regime. In: Tasker, Y. and Negra, D. (Eds.). *Interrogating Postfeminism. Gender and the Politics of Popular Culture.* Durham: Duke University Press, pp. 27–39.

McRobbie, A. (2008). Young Women and Consumer Culture: An Intervention. *Cultural Studies*, 22(5), 531–550.

McRobbie, A. (2009). *The Aftermath of Feminism: Gender, Culture and Social Change.* London: Sage.

Mercer, J. (2017). *Gay Pornography: Representations of Sexuality and Masculinity.* London: IB Tauris.

Messerschmidt, J. W. (2018). *Hegemonic Masculinity: Formulation, Reformulation, and Amplification.* London: Rowman & Littlefield International.

Messner, M. A. (1998). The Limits of "The Male Sex Role" An Analysis of the Men's Liberation and Men's Rights Movements' Discourse. *Gender & Society*, 12(3), 255–276.

Messner, M. A. (2016). Forks in the Road of Men's Gender Politics: Men's Rights vs Feminist Allies. *International Journal for Crime, Justice and Social Democracy*, 5, 6–20.

Miller, J.-A. (1994). Extimité. In: Bracher, M., Alcorn, M. W., Cortell, R. J. Massardier-Kenney, F. (Eds.). *Lacanian Theory of Discourse: Subject, Structure and Society.* New York: New York University Press, pp. 74–87.

Miller-Young, M. (2010). Putting Hypersexuality to Work: Black Women and Illicit Eroticism in Pornography. *Sexualities*, 13(2), 219–235.

Minsky, R. (1996). *Psychoanalysis and Gender.* London: Routledge.

Mirrlees, T. (2018). The Alt-Right's Discourse on "Cultural Marxism": A Political Instrument of Intersectional Hate. *Atlantis: Critical Studies in Gender, Culture & Social Justice*, 39(1), 49–69.

Mitchell, J. (1974). *Psychoanalysis and Feminism: A Radical Reassessment of Freudian Psychoanalysis.* London: Allen Lane.

Mitchell, J. (2000). *Mad Men and Medusas. Reclaiming Hysteria.* New York: Basic Books.

Morgan, A. (2019). The Real Problem with Toxic Masculinity Is That It Assumes There Is Only One Way of Being a Man. *The Conversation.* https://theconversation.com/the-real-problem-with-toxic-masculinity-is-that-it-assumes-there-is-only-one-way-of-being-a-man-110305.

Morgan, S. L. (2018). Status Threat, Material Interests, and the 2016 Presidential Vote. *Socius*, 4, 1–17.

Moss, Donald (2003, Ed.). *Hating in the First Person Plural: Psychoanalytic Essays on Racism, Homophobia, Misogyny, and Terror.* New York: Other Press.

Mountford, J. B. (2018). Topic Modeling the Red Pill. *Social Sciences*, 7(3), 1–16.

Mulloy, D. J. (2020). *Enemies of the State: The Radical Right in America from FDR to Trump*. London: Rowman & Littlefield International.

Mulvey, L. (1975). Visual Pleasure and Narrative Cinema. *Screen*, 16(3), 6–18.

Murray, J. L. (2017a). The Role of Sexual, Sadistic, and Misogynistic Fantasy in Mass and Serial Killing. *Deviant Behavior*, 38(7), 735–743.

Murray, J. L. (2017b). The Transcendent Fantasy in Mass Killers. *Deviant Behavior*, 38(10), 1172–1185.

Mutz, D. C. (2018). Status Threat, Not Economic Hardship, Explains the 2016 Presidential Vote. *Proceedings of the National Academy of Sciences*, 115(19), 4330–4339.

Myketiak, C. (2016). Fragile Masculinity: Social Inequalities in the Narrative Frame and Discursive Construction of a Mass Shooter's Autobiography/Manifesto. *Contemporary Social Science*, 11(4), 289–303.

Nagle, A. (2017). *Kill all Normies. Online Culture Wars from 4chan and Tumblr to Trump and the Alt-Right*. Winchester: Zero Books.

Nakamura, L. (2015). The Unwanted Labour of Social Media: Women of Colour Call Out Culture as Venture Community Management. *New Formations*, 86, 106–112.

Neale, S. (1983). Masculinity as Spectacle. *Screen*, 24(6), 2–17.

Neill, C. (2019). Masculinity in Crisis: Myth, Fantasy and the Promise of the Raw. *Psychoanalysis, Culture & Society*, 25(1), 4–17.

Neumark Hermann, S. (2019). *The Discursive Style and Reactionary Politics of the Manosphere*. Doctoral dissertation. https://summit.sfu.ca/item/19345.

Nicholas, L. and Agius, C. (2018). #Notallmen, #Menenism, Manospheres and Unsafe Spaces: Overt and Subtle Masculinism in Anti-"PC" Discourse. In Nicholas, L. and Agius, C. (Eds.). *The Persistence of Global Masculinism: Discourse, Gender and Neo-Colonial Re-Articulations of Violence*. Basingstoke: Palgrave Macmillan, pp. 31–59.

Niethammer, L. (1979). Male Fantasies: An Argument for and with an Important New Study in History and Psychoanalysis. *History Workshop*, 7, 176–186.

No author (2013). Disinhibition. In: VandenBos, G. R. (Ed.). *APA Dictionary of Clinical Psychology*. Washington, DC: American Psychological Association, p. 177.

NoFap. (2017a). Alternatives to Porn When Masturbating. https://www.nofap.com/forum/index.php?threads/alternatives-to-porn-when-masturbating.115405/.

NoFap. (2017b). Alternatives to Porn When Masturbating. https://www.nofap.com/forum/index.php?threads/alternatives-to-porn-when-masturbating.

NoFap, (2017c). What Is Sissy Hypno Porn. https://www.nofap.com/forum/index.php?threads/what-is-sissy-hypnosis-porn.115145/.

NoFap. (2018). Sissy Hypno Horror Avoid. One Doctors Struggle. https://forum.nofap.com/index.php?threads/sissy-hypno-horror-avoid-one-doctors-struggle.196675/.

NoFap. (2019a). Starter Guide on Being a Real Man. Just My Opinion. https://nofap.com/forum/index.php?threads/starter-guide-on-being-a-real-man-just-my-opinion.210441/#post-1846025.

NoFap. (2019b). Shemale Gay Porn Is the Natural Progression from Straight Porn. https://www.nofap.com/forum/index.php?threads/shemale-gay-porn-is-the-natural-progression-from-straight-porn.235514/.

NoFap. (2019c). Watching Others F-uk While Masturbating Is Actually a Very Disturbing. https://nofap.com/forum/index.php?threads/watching-others-fu-k-while-masturbating-is-actually-a-very-disturbing-act-possibly-triggering.226323/#post-2 005691.
NoFap. (2019d). Who Is Behind Sissy Hypno Stuff and What Is Their Actual Goal. Page 2. (https://www.nofap.com/forum/index.php?threads/who-is-behind-sissy-hypno-stuff-and-what-is-their-actual-goal.220974/page-2.
NoFap. (2019e). Who Is Behind Sissy Hypno Stuff and What Is Their Actual Goal. Page 2. https://www.nofap.com/forum/index.php?threads/who-is-behind-sissy-hypno-stuff-and-what-is-their-actual-goal.220974/page-2.
NoFap. (2019f). Who Is Behind Sissy Hypno Stuff and What Is Their Actual Goal. Page 3. https://www.nofap.com/forum/index.php?threads/who-is-behind-sissy-hypno-stuff-and-what-is-their-actual-goal.220974/page-3.
NoFap. (2019g). Who Is Behind Sissy Hypno Stuff and What Is Their Actual Goal. https://nofap.com/forum/index.php?threads/who-is-behind-sissy-hypno-stuff-and-what-is-their-actual-goal.
NoFap. (2019h). Who Is Behind Sissy Hypno Stuff and What Is Their Actual Goal. https://www.nofap.com/forum/index.php?threads/who-is-behind-sissy-hypno-stuff-and-what-is-their-actual-goal.220974/.
NoFap (2019i). Shemale/Gay Porn Is the "Natural" Progression from "Straight Porn". https://www.nofap.com/forum/index.php?threads/shemale-gay-porn-is-the-natural-progression-from-straight-porn.235514/.
NoFap (2019j). Starter Guide on Being a Real Man (Just my Opinion). https://nofap.com/forum/index.php?threads/starter-guide-on-being-a-real-man-just-my-opinion.210441/.
NoFap (2019k). Fall of Modern Men. https://nofap.com/forum/index.php?threads/fall-of-modern-men.240413/.
Nunn, L. (2019). *Sex Education*. TV Series.
Ogden, T. (2004). On Holding and Containing, Being and Dreaming. *International Journal of Psychoanalysis*, 85(6), 1349–1364.
Olito, F. (2019). How the Divorce Rate Has Changed Over the Last 150 Years. Insider. https://www.insider.com/divorce-rate-changes-over-time-2019-1.
O'Neill, L. (2018). Incest Is the Fastest Growing Trend in Porn. Wait, What?. *Esquire*. https://www.esquire.com/lifestyle/sex/a18194469/incest-porn-trend/.
O'Neill, R. (2015). Feminist Encounters with Evolutionary Psychology: Introduction. *Australian Feminist Studies*, 30(86), 345–350.
O'Neill, R. (2018). *Seduction: Men, Masculinity and Mediated Intimacy*. London: John Wiley & Sons.
Ostow, M. (1996). *Myth and Madness: The Psychodynamics of Antisemitism*. New Brunswick, NJ: Transaction Publishers.
Ott, B. L. (2017). The Age of Twitter: Donald J. Trump and the Politics of Debasement. *Critical Studies in Media Communication*, 34(1), 59–68.
Ouellette, L. and Banet-Weiser, S. (2018). Media and the Extreme Right: Editors' Introduction. *Communication, Culture & Critique*, 11(1), 1–6.
O'Keefe, T. (2016). Making Feminist Sense of No-Platforming. *Feminist Review*, 113(1), 85–92.

Overall, C. (1992). What's Wrong with Prostitution? Evaluating Sex Work. *Signs: Journal of Women in Culture and Society*, 17(4), 705–724.

Paasonen, S. (2011). *Carnal Resonance: Affect and Online Pornography*. Cambridge, MA: MIT Press.

Pearson, E. (2019). Extremism and Toxic Masculinity: The Man Question re-posed. *International Affairs*, 95(6), 1251–1270.

Pegues, C. (1998). Piece of Man: Redefining the Myths around the Black Male Phallus. In: Atkins, D. (Ed.). *Looking Queer: Body Image and Identity in Lesbian, Bisexual, Gay, and Transgender Communities*. New York: Harrington Park Press, pp. 259–275.

Perron, R. (2005a). Projection. In: de Mijolla, A. (Ed.). *International Dictionary of Psychoanalysis*. Detroit, MI: Thomson Gale, pp. 1334–1336

Perron, R. (2005b). 'Autoeroticism'. In: de Mijolla, A. (Ed.). *International Dictionary of Psychoanalysis*. Detroit, MI: Thomson Gale, p. 141.

Petro, P. (1988). Review of Male Fantasies. Volume I: Women, Floods, Bodies, History by Klaus Theweleit. *SubStance*, 17(3), 77–78.

Phillips, A. (2013). Against Inhibition. In: *One Way or Another*. London: Penguin, pp. 177–202.

Phillips, W. (2015). *This is Why We Can't Have Nice Things: Mapping the Relationship between Online Trolling and Mainstream Culture*. Cambridge, MA: MIT Press.

Pinchevski, A. (2019). *Transferred Wounds: Media and the Mediation of Trauma*. Oxford: Oxford University Press.

Pollock, G. (1988). *Vision and Difference: Femininity, Feminism and the Histories of Art*. London: Routledge.

Preciado, P. B. (2018). *Countersexual Manifesto*. Columbia University Press.

Proctor, W. and Kies, B. (2018). On Toxic Fan Practices and the New Culture Wars. *Participations*, 15 (1), 127–142.

Quindeau, I. (2018). Masculinity Concepts in Psychoanalysis. *Internationales Archiv für Sozialgeschichte der deutschen Literatur*, 43(2), 377–386.

Rambatan, B. and Johanssen, J. (2021). *Event Horizon. Sexuality, Politics, Online Culture, and the Limits of Capitalism*. Winchester: Zero Books.

Rasmussen, B. and Salhani, D. (2010). A Contemporary Kleinian Contribution to Understanding Racism. *Social Service Review*, 84(3), 491–513.

Ravetto, K. (2001). *The Unmaking of Fascist Aesthetics*. Minneapolis: University of Minnesota Press.

Reddit. (2018a). Sometimes I Fantasize. https://www.reddit.com/r/Braincels/comments/98s1ti/sometimes_i_fantasize_about_having_dbz_or_bleach/.

Reddit. (2018b). Foid Whore Revenge Feels So Good. https://www.reddit.com/r/Braincels/comments/bs7wfy/foid_whore_revenge_feels_so_good/.

Reddit. (2018c). Sweet Fucking Revenge from an Ascendedcel. https://www.reddit.com/r/Braincels/comments/c19tga/sweet_fucking_revenge_from_an_ascendedcel/.

Reddit. (2018d). Don't Think a Lot of You Guys Understand The. https://www.reddit.com/r/Braincels/comments/9awobp/i_dont_think_a_lot_of_you_guys_understand_the/.

Reddit. (2018e). When You Post About Being Shocked. https://www.reddit.com/r/BlackPilledNormies/comments/9k395o/when_you_post_about_being_shocked_by_the_absolute/.
Reddit. (2018f). My Chad Brothers. https://www.reddit.com/r/Braincels/comments/98hz2h/my_chad_brothers/.
Reddit. (2018g). Daydreaming About the Life I Would Have Wanted. https://www.reddit.com/r/Braincels/comments/c6ffwa/daydreaming_about_the_life_i_would_have_wanted/.
Reddit. (2018h). What's Your Background. https://www.reddit.com/r/Braincels/comments/99pxh4/whats_your_background/.
Reddit. (2019a). Chadlite Jawline. https://www.reddit.com/r/Incelselfies/comments/9ffz6j/chadlite_jawlinenormie_jawline_or_a_fucking/.
Reddit. (2019b). What They're Actually Like. https://www.reddit.com/r/MGTOW/comments/cc17gc/what_theyre_actually_like/.
Reddit. (2019c). You Can Do It Too. https://www.reddit.com/r/MGTOW/comments/cbxkxl/you_can_do_it_too/.
Reddit. (2019d). I Am Honestly Three Times More Happier Since I Follow MGTOW. https://www.reddit.com/r/MGTOW/comments/cbqpd6/i_am_honestly_three_times_more_happier_since_i/.
Rehberg, P. (2019). More than Vanilla Sex: Reading Gay Post-Pornography with Affect Theory and Psychoanalysis. *Porn Studies*, 6(1), 114–128.
Reich, W. (1933). *Massenpsychologie und Faschismus. Zur Sexualökonomie der politischen Reaktion und zur proletarischen Sexualpolitik.* Kopenhagen: Verlag für Sexualpolitik.
Reich, W. (1997). *The Mass Psychology of Fascism.* London: Souvenir Press.
Reichardt, S. (2007). Klaus Theweleits "Männerphantasien": ein Erfolgsbuch der 1970er-Jahre. *Zeithistorische Forschungen/Studies in Contemporary History*, 3(3), 401–421.
Reid, R. C., Carpenter, B. N. and Fong, T. W. (2011). Neuroscience Research Fails to Support Claims that Excessive Pornography Consumption Causes Brain Damage. *Surgical Neurology International*, 2. https://www.ncbi.nlm.nih.gov/pmc/articles/PMC3115160/.
Renold, E. and Ringrose, J. (2012). Phallic Girls? Girls' Negotiation of Phallogocentric Power. In: Landreau, J. C. and Rodriguez, N. M. (Eds.). *Queer Masculinities.* Berlin: Springer, pp. 47–67.
Renold, E. and Ringrose, J. (2017). Pin-Balling and Boners: The Posthuman Phallus and Intra-Activist Sexuality Assemblages in Secondary School. In: Allen, L. and Rasmussen, M. L. (Eds.). *The Palgrave Handbook of Sexuality Education.* Basingstoke: Palgrave Macmillan, pp. 631–653.
Rentschler, C. A. (2014). Rape Culture and the Feminist Politics of Social Media. *Girlhood Studies*, 7(1), 65–82.
Reny, T. T., Collingwood, L. and Valenzuela, A. A. (2019). Vote Switching in the 2016 Election: How Racial and Immigration Attitudes, Not Economics, Explain Shifts in White Voting. *Public Opinion Quarterly*, 83(1), 91–113.
Richards, B. (2014). What Drove Anders Breivik?. *Contexts*, 13(4), 42–47.

Riggs, D.W. (2005). Psychoanalysis as a 'Postcolonising' Reading Practice. In: Riggs, D. W. (Ed.). *Taking up the Challenge: Critical Race and Whiteness Studies in a Post-Colonising Nation.* Adelaide: Crawford House, pp. 33–59.

Ringrose, J. and Lawrence, E. (2018). Remixing Misandry, Manspreading, and Dick Pics: Networked Feminist Humour on Tumblr. *Feminist Media Studies*, 18(4), 686–704.

Ringrose, J. and Renold, E. (2012). Slut-Shaming, Girl Power and 'Sexualisation': Thinking Through the Politics of the International SlutWalks with Teen Girls. *Gender and Education*, 24(3), 333–343.

Rivers, N. (2017). *Postfeminism(s) and the Arrival of the Fourth Wave: Turning Tides.* Basingstoke: Palgrave Macmillan.

Roberts, S. (2014, Ed.). *Debating Modern Masculinities: Change, Continuity, Crisis?* Basingstoke: Palgrave Macmillan.

Robinson, S. (2000). *Marked Men: White Masculinity in Crisis.* New York: Columbia University Press.

Rose, J. (1986). *Sexuality in the Field of Vision.* London: Verso.

Ross, K. (2011, Ed.). *The Handbook of Gender, Sex, and Media.* London: John Wiley & Sons.

Rothstein, R. (2017). *The Color of Law: A Forgotten History of How Our Government Segregated America.* New York: Liveright.

Rustin, M. (1991). *The Good Society and the Inner World.* London: Verso.

Ruti, M. (2018). *Penis Envy and Other Bad Feelings: The Emotional Costs of Everyday Life.* New York: Columbia University Press.

Said, E. (1978). *Orientalism.* New York: Pantheon.

Saitō, T. (2011). *Beautiful Fighting Girl.* Minneapolis: University of Minnesota Press.

Salazar, P. J. (2018). The Alt-Right as a Community of Discourse. *Javnost-The Public*, 25(1-2), 135–143.

Salter, M. (2018). From Geek Masculinity to Gamergate: The Technological Rationality of Online Abuse. *Crime, Media, Culture*, 14(2), 247–264.

Salter, A. and Blodgett, B. (2017). *Toxic Geek Masculinity in Media: Sexism, Trolling, and Identity Policing.* Basingstoke: Palgrave Macmillan.

Samuels, A. (2018). Masculinity, Psychoanalysis and Politics. In: Petersen, H. (Ed.). *Love and Law in Europe.* London: Routledge, pp. 127–146.

Sanday, P. R. (1992). *Fraternity Gang Rape: Sex, Brotherhood, and Privilege on Campus.* New York: New York University Press.

Sanday, P. R. (2007). *Fraternity Gang Rape: Sex, Brotherhood, and Privilege on Campus.* Second Edition. New York: New York University Press.

Sandman. (2016). Rejecting Her – MGTOW. YouTube Video. https://www.youtube.com/watch?time_continue=32&v=dIbj1uUQ6Ys.

Savelle-Rocklin, N. and Akhtar, S. (2019, Eds.). *Beyond the Primal Addiction: Food, Sex, Gambling, Internet, Shopping, and Work.* London: Routledge.

Schaefer, E. (2014, Ed.). *Sex Scene: Media and the Sexual Revolution.* Durham: Duke University Press.

Schauer, T. (2005). Women's Porno: The Heterosexual Female Gaze in Porn Sites "for Women". *Sexuality and Culture*, 9(2), 42–64.

Schmitt, M. (2018). From Privilege to Precarity (and Back): Whiteness, Racism and the New Right. *Coils of the Serpent: Journal for the Study of Contemporary Power*, 2, 48–64.
Schneider, P. (1974). Die Sache mit der "Männlichkeit". Gibt es eine Emanzipation der Männer? *Kursbuch*, 35, 103–132.
Schrupp, A. (2017). *A Brief History of Feminism*. Cambridge, MA MIT Press.
Scott, J. W. (1988). Deconstructing Equality-versus-Difference: Or, the Uses of Poststructuralist Theory for Feminism. *Feminist Studies*, 14(1), 33–50.
Scoular, J. (2004). The 'Subject' of Prostitution: Interpreting the Discursive, Symbolic and Material Position of Sex/Work in Feminist Theory. *Feminist Theory*, 5(3), 343–355.
Sedgwick, E. K. (1993). *Tendencies*. Durham: Duke University Press.
Seegers, L. (2015). 'Dead Dads': Memory Narratives of War-related Fatherlessness in Germany. *European Review of History: Revue Européenne D'histoire*, 22(2), 259–276.
Segal, L. (1990). *Slow Motion: Changing Masculinities, Changing Men*. London: Virago Press.
Segal, L. (1999). *Why Feminism? Gender, Psychology, Politics*. New York: Columbia University Press.
Semerene, D. (2016). The Female Target: Digitality, Psychoanalysis and the Gangbang. *CM: Communication and Media Journal*, 38(11), 217–242.
Semerene, D. (2021). Creampied to Death. Ejaculative Kinship in the Age of Normative Data Flows. *Psychoanalysis, Culture & Society*, 26(2).
Seshadri-Crooks, K. (2000). *Desiring Whiteness: A Lacanian Analysis of Race*. London: Routledge.
Sheehi, L. (2020). The Reality Principle: Fanonian Undoing, Unlearning, and Decentering: A Discussion of Fanon's vision of Embodied Racism for Psychoanalytic Theory and Practice. *Psychoanalytic Dialogues*, 30(3), 325–330.
Shor, E. and Seida, K. (2019). "Harder and Harder"? Is Mainstream Pornography Becoming Increasingly Violent and Do Viewers Prefer Violent Content? *The Journal of Sex Research*, 56(1), 16–28.
Shrage, L. (2005). Exposing the Fallacies of Anti-Porn Feminism. *Feminist Theory*, 6(1), 45–65.
Sigusch, V. (1998). The Neosexual Revolution. *Archives of Sexual Behavior*, 27(4), 331–359.
Sinclair, A. (1993). *The Deceived Husband: A Kleinian Approach to the Literature of Infidelity*. New York: Oxford University Press.
Sinclair, S. and Steinkoler, M. (2019). *On Psychoanalysis and Violence. Contemporary Lacanian Perspectives*. London: Routledge.
Singh, G. (2019). *The Death of Web 2.0: Ethics, Connectivity and Recognition in the Twenty-First Century*. Routledge.
Smith, C. and Attwood, F. (2014). Anti/Pro/Critical Porn Studies. *Porn Studies*, 1 (1-2), 7–23.
Snider, N. (2020). Anti-Racism in Our Institutes: Opportunities and Challenges. *Contemporary Psychoanalysis*, 56(2), 418–437.
Snyder-Hall, R. C. (2010). Third-Wave Feminism and the Defense of "Choice". *Perspectives on Politics*, 8(1), 255–261.

Sontag, S. (1981). Fascinating Fascism. In: *Under the Sign of Saturn*. New York: Vintage Books, pp. 73–108.

Southern Poverty Law Center. (2014). Shooting Suspect Elliot Rodger's Misogynistic Posts Point to Motive. https://www.splcenter.org/hatewatch/2014/05/23/shooting-suspect-elliot-rodgers-misogynistic-posts-point-motive.

Southern Poverty Law Center. (No Year). Male Supremacy. https://www.splcenter.org/fighting-hate/extremist-files/ideology/male-supremacy.

Squirrel, T. (2018). A Definitive Guide to Incels Part Two: The A-Z Incel Dictionary. https://medium.com/@timsquirrell/dictionary-of-hate-the-a-z-of-incels-23cb431f0788.

Stamps, D. L. (2020). B(l)ack By Popular Demand: An Analysis of Positive Black Male Characters in Television and Audiences' Community Cultural Wealth. *Journal of Communication Inquiry*. 10.1177/0196859920924388.

Stanley, L. (2014). 'We're Reaping What We Sowed': Everyday Crisis Narratives and Acquiescence to the Age of Austerity. *New Political Economy*, 19(6), 895–917.

Stanley, J. (2018). *How Fascism Works. The Politics of Us vs. Them*. New York: Random House.

Star, D. (1998-2004). *Sex and the City*. TV Series.

Starck, K. and Luyt, R. (2019). Political Masculinities, Crisis Tendencies, and Social Transition: Toward an Understanding of Change. *Men and Masculinities*, 22(3), 431–443.

Stein, R. (2005). Why Perversion? "False Love" and the Perverse Pact. *The International Journal of Psychoanalysis*, 86(3), 775–799.

Stein, R. (2010). *For Love of the Father: A Psychoanalytic Study of Religious Terrorism*. Stanford, CA: Stanford University Press.

Stephens, M. A. (2014). *Skin Acts: Race, Psychoanalysis, and the Black Male Performer*. Durham, NC: Duke University Press.

Suler, J. (2004). The Online Disinhibition Effect. *Cyberpsychology & Behavior*, 7(3), 321–326.

Sundén, J. and Paasonen, S. (2020). *Who's Laughing Now? Feminist Tactics in Social Media*. Cambridge, MA: MIT Press.

Syal, R. (2020). Dominic Cummings Calls for 'weirdos and misfits' for No 10 jobs. The Guardian. https://www.theguardian.com/politics/2020/jan/02/dominic-cummings-calls-for-weirdos-and-misfits-for-no-10-jobs.

Tate, C. (1996). Freud and His "negro": Psychoanalysis as Ally and Enemy of African Americans. *Journal for the Psychoanalysis of Culture & Society*, 1(1), 53–62.

Tate, C. (1998). *Psychoanalysis and Black Novels: Desire and the Protocols of Race*. New York: Oxford University Press.

Taylor, K. and Jackson, S. (2018). 'I Want that Power Back': Discourses of Masculinity within an Online Pornography Abstinence Forum. *Sexualities*, 21(4), 621–639.

Taylor, K. and Gavey, N. (2019). Pornography Addiction and the Perimeters of Acceptable Pornography Viewing. *Sexualities*, 10.1177/1363460719861826

The Daily Wire. (2018). *The Sexual Revolution Ruined Everything It Touched*. https://www.youtube.com/watch?v=pYmDAac0CiI.

The Distributist. (2016). *The Lies of the Sexual Revolution (parts 1-4)*. https://www.youtube.com/watch?v=5wuBQa86nj0.

Theweleit, K. (1977). *Männerphantasien 1. Fluten, Körper, Geschichte*. Frankfurt am Main: Verlag Roter Stern.
Theweleit, K. (1978). *Männerphantasien 2. Männerkörper – Zur Psychoanalyse des Weißen Terrors*. Frankfurt am Main: Verlag Roter Stern.
Theweleit, K. (1987). *Male Fantasies. Volume 1. Women, Floods, Bodies, History*. Minneapolis: University of Minnesota Press.
Theweleit, K. (1989). *Male Fantasies. Volume 2. Male Bodies: Psychoanalyzing the White Terror*. Minneapolis: University of Minnesota Press.
Theweleit, K. (1990). *...ein Aspirin von der Grösse der Sonne*. Freiburg: Jos Fritz Verlag.
Theweleit, K. (2015). *Das Lachen der Täter: Breivik ua: Psychogramm der Tötungslust*. Salzburg: Residenz Verlag.
Thomadaki, T. (2019). Getting Naked with Gok Wan: A Psychoanalytic Reading of How To Look Good Naked's Transformational Narratives. *Clothing Cultures*, 6(1), 115–134.
Tietze, T. (2014). The Breivik Controversy: Politics, Terrorism and Psychiatry. *Australasian Psychiatry*, 22(4), 383–385.
Tissot, S. (2015). *Diseases Caused by Masturbation*. New York: Gottfried and Fritz.
Tricarico, G. (2018). *Lost Goddesses: A Kaleidoscope on Porn*. London: Karnac.
Tuhkanen, M. (2010). *The American Optic: Psychoanalysis, Critical Race Theory, and Richard Wright*. New York: SUNY Press.
Turkle, S. (2011). *Alone Together: Why We Expect More from Technology and Less from Each Other*. New York: Basic Books.
Tuters, M., Jokubauskaitė, E. and Bach, D. (2018). Post-truth Protest: How 4chan Cooked Up the Pizzagate Bullshit. *M/C Journal*, 21(3). https://doi.org/10.5204/mcj.1422.
Udupa, S. (2019). Nationalism in the Digital Age: Fun as a Metapractice of Extreme Speech. *International Journal of Communication*, 13, 3143–3163.
Vacker, B. (2019). The 20th Anniversary of Fight Club and The Matrix: Two Futures All Around Us in 2019. *Medium*. https://medium.com/@barryvacker/the-20th-anniversary-of-fight-club-and-the-matrix-two-futures-all-around-us-in-2019-511fad554864.
Vadolas, A. (2009). *Perversions of Fascism*. London: Karnac.
Van Valkenburgh, S. P. (2018). Digesting the Red Pill: Masculinity and Neoliberalism in the Manosphere. *Men and Masculinities*, 24(1), 84–103.
Varghese, R. (2019, Ed.). Porn on the Couch: Sex, Psychoanalysis, and Screen Cultures/Memories. *Porn Studies* Special Issue. https://www.tandfonline.com/toc/rprn20/6/1.
Veissière, S. P. L. (2018). "Toxic Masculinity" in the Age of #MeToo: Ritual, Morality and Gender Archetypes across Cultures. *Society and Business Review*, 13(3), 274–286.
Veith, I. (1965). *Hysteria. The History of a Disease*, Chicago: University of ChicagoPress.
Vemuri, A. (2018). "Calling Out" Campus Sexual Violence: Student Activist Labors of Confrontation and Care. *Communication Culture & Critique*, 11(3), 498–502.
Vendée Radio. (2018). *The New Left, 1968 and the Sexual Revolution*. https://www.youtube.com/watch?v=oeB7qTn9Sik.

Vito, C., Admire, A. and Hughes, E. (2018). Masculinity, Aggrieved Entitlement, and Violence: Considering the Isla Vista Mass Shooting. *NORMA*, 13(2), 86–102.
Voros, F. (2009). The Invention of Addiction to Pornography. *Sexologies*, 18(4), 243–246.
Wachowski, A. and Wachowski, L. (1999). *The Matrix*. Film.
Waldon, E. (2011). *Playing with Dynamite. A Personal Approach to the Psychoanalytic Understanding of Perversions, Violence, and Criminality*. London: Karnac Books.
Walkerdine, V. (2020). Neoliberalism. In: Stavrakakis, Y. (Ed.). *Routledge Handbook of Psychoanalytic Political Theory*. London: Routledge, pp. 380–391.
Walton, J. (2001). *Fair Sex, Savage Dreams: Race, Psychoanalysis, Sexual Difference*. Durham: Duke University Press.
Walton, S. J. (2012). Anti-Feminism and Misogyny in Breivik's "Manifesto". *NORA-Nordic Journal of Feminist and Gender Research*, 20(1), 4–11.
Ward, J. (2015). *Not Gay: Sex Between Straight White Men*. New York: New York University Press.
Ware, J. (2020). *Testament to Murder: The Violent Far-Right's Increasing Use of Terrorist Manifestos*. International Center for Counter-Terrorism. https://www.jstor.org/stable/pdf/resrep23577.pdf.
Warzel, N. (2019). How an Online Mob Created a Playbook for a Culture War. *The New York Times*. https://www.nytimes.com/interactive/2019/08/15/opinion/what-is-gamergate.html.
Weder, C. (2016). *Intime Beziehungen. Ästhetik und Theorien der Sexualität um 1968*. Göttingen: Wallstein Verlag.
Weiss, S. F. (1990). The Race Hygiene Movement in Germany. 1904-1945. In: Adams, R. T. (Ed.). *The Wellborn Science. Eugenics in Germany, France, Brazil, and Russia*. Oxford: Oxford University Press, pp. 8–50.
Wendling, M. (2018). *Alt-Right: From 4chan to the White House*. London: Pluto Press.
Wetzel, D. (2020). The Rise of the Catholic Alt-Right. *Journal of Labor and Society*, 23(1), 31–55.
White, M. (2019). *Producing Masculinity: The Internet, Gender, and Sexuality*. London: Routledge.
Williams, L. (1989). *Hard Core: Power, Pleasure and the "Frenzy of the Visible"*. Berkeley, CA: University of California Press.
Williams, L. (2004, Ed.). *Porn Studies*. Durham: Duke University Press.
Williams, L. (2009). Skin Flicks on the Racial Border: Pornography, Exploitation, and Interracial Lust. In: Thornham, S., Bassett, C. and Marris, P. (Eds.). *Media Studies: A Reader*. Third Edition. New York: New York University Press, pp. 71–105.
Wilson, L. C. (2017, Ed.). *The Wiley Handbook of the Psychology of Mass Shootings*. London: John Wiley & Sons.
Winnicott, D. W. (2002). *Playing and Reality*. London: Routledge.
Wilz, K. (2016). Bernie Bros and Woman Cards: Rhetorics of Sexism, Misogyny, and Constructed Masculinity in the 2016 Election. *Women's Studies in Communication*, 39(4), 357–360.
Witt, T. (2020). 'If i cannot have it, i will do everything i can to destroy it.' The Canonization of Elliot Rodger: 'Incel' Masculinities, Secular Sainthood, and Justifications of Ideological Violence. *Social Identities*, 26(5), 675–689.

Wodak, R. (2015). *The Politics of Fear: What Right-Wing Populist Discourses Mean.* London: Sage.
Yates, C. (2007). *Masculine Jealousy and Contemporary Cinema.* Basingstoke: Palgrave Macmillan.
Yates, C. (2015). *The Play of Political Culture, Emotion and Identity.* Basingstoke: Palgrave Macmillan.
Yates, C. (2019). The Psychodynamics of Casino Culture and Politics. *Journal of Psychosocial Studies,* 12(3), 217–230.
Yates, C., Richards, B. and Sergeant, A. (2020, eds.). Psychosocial Reflections on Fifty Years of a Cultural and Political Revolution. *Free Associations: Psychoanalysis and Culture, Media, Groups, Politics,* 78, http://freeassociations.org.uk/FA_New/OJS/index.php/fa/issue/view/28/.
Young-Bruehl, E. (1996). *The Anatomy of Prejudice.* Cambridge, MA: Harvard University Press.
Žižek 1993 Žižek, S. (1993). *Tarrying with the Negative.* Durham: Duke University Press.
Žižek 1994 Žižek, S. (1994). *The Metastases of Enjoyment.* London: Verso.
Žižek 1997 Žižek, S. (1997). *The Plague of Fantasies.* London: Verso.
Zuckerberg, D. (2018). *Not All Dead White Men. Classics and Misogyny in the Digital Age.* Cambridge, MA: Harvard University Press.
Zupančič, A. (2017). *What is Sex?* Cambridge, MA: The MIT Press.

Index

A
absent father 144–45, 47, 158–59
absent presence 16, 29, 41, 140
addiction 20, 56, 58, 74, 83–4, 166–68, 172–76, 179, 181–82, 184–85, 188, 190, 192, 198–99
Adorno, Theodor W. 36–7, 82, 87–8
affect: affective discharge 46, 93, 109, 169–70, 179; affective equilibrium 153; affective tension 33, 58, 109, 132; and Freud 12, 15–6, 46
affirmation 45, 49, 98, 108, 126–27, 210
agency 16, 28, 41, 50, 55, 69, 73–4, 89, 102, 106–08, 113, 120, 135, 142, 156, 168–69, 175, 180, 185, 187, 189–90, 194, 199, 205
algorithm 12, 7, 20, 77, 181–83, 193–94, 200
alpha (male) 71, 90, 96, 110, 112, 114, 145, 158–59, 161–63, 167, 178, 212
alt-right 4, 6–11, 16, 18, 20, 22, 36, 41, 50, 60–7, 70–1, 73–84, 88, 90, 94–5, 97–8, 100, 103, 106–08, 112–16, 118, 123, 125, 129–30, 133, 136–37, 142, 153, 163, 166, 169, 187–89, 198–200, 202, 206, 209
anal 131–32, 170, 183
The Anatomy of Prejudices 19, 38, 126, 130
Anders Breivik 4, 19, 20, 41, 62, 74, 94, 144–54, 158–62, 164, 190, 194, 202
annihilation 127, 153, 208
anti-feminist 658, 61, 94–5, 124, 148, 192
anti-masturbation 20, 168–9
anti-Semitic 6, 23, 35, 41, 61, 64, 86–8, 98, 100, 108, 112–14, 120, 145, 166
anxiety 5, 36, 44, 85, 120, 133, 140–42, 144, 154, 171–72, 182–84, 191, 195, 205

archaic father 146, 160
ascending 112
authoritarian 5, 16, 28–9, 36–8, 40, 49, 57, 61, 70, 87, 93, 106–07, 136, 138, 146, 157, 163, 166, 201

B
BDSM 124, 137–38
Benjamin, Jessica 21, 31–32, 73, 145, 162, 194, 196–97, 204–12
beta (male) 25, 59–60, 90, 109–10, 123
Big data 20–1, 182, 193–94, 201–03
biology 6, 97, 151
BIPOC 11, 36, 74, 190
black 20, 22–3, 35, 64, 80, 110–11, 120–21, 187–89, 195, 213
black pill 8, 10, 71, 103, 105, 117, 124
ody armour 16–7, 29, 42–3, 47–8, 103, 107, 118–19, 137, 150, 171, 180, 199, 205
boundaries 43–4, 69, 127, 141, 151–52, 156, 163
boy 15, 31, 118, 132, 145, 151, 156, 204

C
capitalism 5, 9, 38–9, 49, 53, 70, 82, 90–1, 93, 95, 104, 106, 116, 136, 142, 166, 196, 201
castration 12, 14–5, 23, 31, 42, 46, 69, 117, 127, 133, 178, 194, 205
chad 44, 64, 71, 97, 102, 106, 109–14, 117, 121, 135, 139–40, 161, 188
character 19, 37–40, 94, 131, 133, 135–36, 140–41, 152, 198
character type 16, 19, 28–9, 37–40, 122, 130, 134
child 32, 40, 57, 151, 157, 169, 178, 204
cis 17, 19, 24, 27, 33, 36, 38, 61, 63, 70, 77, 85, 94, 112, 125, 151, 195, 201

class 21, 33, 40, 57, 59, 61–62, 82, 96, 105, 122, 154
cleaning 43, 131
computational 21, 201–02
confidence 19, 66, 69, 92, 101, 105, 116–117, 173
conspiracy theories 11, 78, 95, 187, 199
contagion 4, 35, 85–6, 110, 176
Cowie, Elizabeth 167–68, 170–72, 177–79, 191
crisis (of masculinity) 18, 59, 61–3, 69, 108, 142
cuck 9, 59, 63, 97, 111, 168, 187–90, 192, 193
cuckold porn 20, 168, 179, 187–93
cultural Marxism 11, 76, 81–82, 148–50

D
defensive 18, 33, 41–2, 44, 74, 77, 80, 97, 105–06, 114, 116, 128, 151, 156, 175, 177, 180, 187, 189, 208
defense mechanisms 14, 16, 18, 28, 38, 42, 83, 87, 197
denial 126–27, 206
Deleuze, Gilles 14–5, 27,38, 172, 176
desire to desire 15, 171–72, 181, 198–99
destroy 9, 41–42, 65, 81, 87, 99, 102, 107, 113, 116–17, 128, 135, 140, 149, 152, 155, 161,163, 176, 187, 193, 199, 209–10
destructive 18, 26, 29, 33–5, 41, 60, 90–1, 102, 113, 134, 139–41, 156, 181, 207, 209–10
devil 82, 185
dirty 17, 86, 132–35, 202–03
dis/inhibition 3–4, 15–7, 29–30, 37, 43–44, 46–8, 56, 72, 74, 76, 98, 106, 109, 120, 122, 127, 135, 142, 163–64, 168, 191, 195, 199–200, 203, 205, 209
disidentification 178–179
disintegration 3, 17, 44, 46, 48, 69, 119, 149, 162
doer–done to 73, 203–06
dominance 31–32, 41, 55, 60, 77, 79, 81, 100, 127, 137, 175, 201–02, 209
double-bind 135
drive 14, 100, 170

E
ego 16–7, 28–9, 42–5, 47, 51, 118–20, 141, 149–50, 152, 156
enjoyment 35–6, 50–1, 67, 86, 92, 112, 126, 152, 164, 175, 184, 192, 198

entitlement 3, 12, 64, 74, 77, 90, 104–05, 118, 154, 157–58, 191–92
envy 15, 51, 156, 159, 179, 204
erotic capital 92, 151
erotics 122, 136
eugenics 114–15
Europe 2, 17, 51–2, 63, 87, 114, 136, 148–49, 152, 158, 160, 187, 189
evolutionary psychology 18, 90–1, 151, 174–75, 178, 201

F
family 8, 16, 37, 40, 49, 93, 114, 139–40, 150, 154–55, 158, 170, 185
fantasies of transformation 18, 103, 109–114, 117, 166
fantasmatic 17, 35–7, 68, 72, 74, 108, 113, 126–27, 146, 162, 189, 190, 209
fantasy world 110, 130, 152, 155, 158, 163, 202, 209
fascism: and Fascist 1–2, 4–5, 7–10, 16, 18–19, 22–5, 28–53, 60, 62–3, 66, 72, 74–5, 80–3, 85–8, 93–4, 97–8, 101, 103, 106–07, 112, 114–20, 122, 130, 136–41, 146, 148, 157, 162–63, 171, 186–88, 190, 192, 198–99, 200, 208; and Hitler 1, 5, 28, 34, 36–8, 115, 157; and images 8, 18, 22, 63, 107, 114, 133; and National Socialism 36, 137; and Nazi Germany 28, 36–37, 39, 53, 86, 112–13, 126; and Nazism 5, 17, 37, 138; and vocabulary / language 23, 61, 86, 97–8, 100, 199
father 15–6, 19–20, 23, 31–2, 40–1, 44, 50, 53, 59–60, 84, 100, 122, 139–40, 144–48, 152, 155, 157–65, 185, 204, 206, 212
feminism 2, 4, 6, 8, 11, 14, 18–19, 26, 36, 39, 50, 52, 56–61, 64, 66, 68–9, 71, 73, 75–77, 79–80, 83, 88–91, 104, 123–24, 139, 142, 148, 168, 175, 186–87, 192–93, 200
feminization 59, 150
Fight Club 8–10
financial crisis 18, 70, 101, 105, 107, 116, 200
flood 46, 133, 175–76, 186, 195, 204
Foucault, Michel 37, 49, 53, 82–83, 138, 169
4Chan 1, 7, 10, 95, 97, 102, 106, 112, 118
fragile 4, 9, 20, 47, 149, 188, 194
fragmented ego 16, 29, 42–4, 48, 51, 119, 134, 137, 176, 208

Frankfurt school 23, 33, 36–7, 82, 148
Freikorps 17, 37–8, 40–2, 46, 50–1, 113, 117–18, 133–36, 138, 141, 149, 151–53, 164, 211
Freud, Sigmund 3, 13–6, 19, 24, 30–4, 38, 43–8, 50, 57, 122, 130–31, 143, 145, 147, 161, 169–72, 173, 177, 183, 185, 191, 193, 205–06

G

Gamergate 10–1, 65, 99–100, 102
gay 69–70, 77, 82–8, 138, 152, 166, 168, 174–77, 179, 211
gay porn 20, 167–68, 175, 177–78, 192
Geek masculinity 52, 59, 65–6, 70, 211
gender: feminine 13, 41, 43, 50, 52, 59, 70, 134–35, 139, 146–47, 152, 160, 175, 205, 211; femininity 1, 13, 18, 20, 30, 32, 58, 65–6, 70, 88, 96–7, 103–04, 149, 164, 204–05, 208, 211; masculine 13–4, 21, 36, 52, 59–60, 66, 69, 100, 105–06, 110–12, 117, 131, 134, 138, 145, 151–52, 158, 167, 178, 186, 194, 196, 201; masculinity 1–2, 7–10, 12–3, 18, 20, 22, 28, 30, 32–3, 37, 41, 47, 49, 52–3, 56, 58–66, 69–75, 77, 79, 81, 88, 90, 96, 98, 103–04, 106, 107–08, 111–13, 122, 138, 142–43, 145, 149–51, 154, 156, 163, 165, 167–68, 175–76, 179, 187–92, 198, 200, 204–05, 206, 211
Germany 5, 17, 21–3, 28–9, 34, 36–9, 49–52
girl 15, 31, 45, 66, 108, 144, 204
grandiosity 107, 149, 151–52, 154–56
Guattari, Felix 14–5, 27, 37–8, 172, 176

H

hegemonic masculinity 18, 20, 53, 58, 60, 65–6, 70, 75, 98, 104, 106, 167
heterosexuality 12–3, 30,79, 94, 103, 168, 177, 209
history of feminism 57–60, 76
history of the sexual revolution 51–57
homosexuality 30, 37, 55, 76, 80, 82, 84–5, 87, 93–4, 100, 111, 138, 166, 175–76, 178, 193
hook-up apps 3, 142, 163
humour 67, 97, 101–03, 106, 112, 116, 150, 212
hypergamy 91, 124
hypergamous 90–1, 93
hysteria 143

hysterical 1, 19, 38, 122, 130, 133–35, 140

I

id 44, 47, 185
ideal type 136, 188
identification 14, 20, 36, 40, 43, 71, 102, 141, 143, 145, 162, 164–65, 168, 171, 178–79
identity 3, 7, 13–4, 21, 35–6, 39, 41, 60–3, 65, 78, 81, 94, 97, 100, 105, 116, 127, 133, 136, 141, 145, 148, 152, 156, 177, 179–80, 194
ideology 3, 5, 12, 19, 25, 39, 49, 62–3, 68, 73, 82–3, 89, 92–3, 95, 101, 104–07, 110, 115, 142, 147, 150, 153, 173, 186, 196, 200–01, 203
imago 19, 40, 122, 135, 140, 160
immature 109, 124, 156–57
irony 66–7, 97, 102–03, 106, 116, 150
Islamist 19, 145–47, 161

J

Jew 4, 17, 41, 45, 64, 81–2, 87, 110, 112–13, 115, 126, 133, 137, 186, 190

K

Killing 17, 20, 42, 44, 47, 85, 137–38, 140, 144, 148, 152–53, 156, 159–61, 166

L

Lacan, Jacques 14–5, 21, 27, 31, 34–5, 50, 145, 177, 183–85, 205–06
lack (Lacan) 15, 32, 34, 50, 143, 179, 181, 188
law 5, 45, 55, 57, 97, 123, 146, 152–53, 157, 160
leader 5–6, 20, 37, 57, 118, 141, 162, 170
LGBTQI+ 2, 11, 74, 81, 176, 187, 194, 196, 202, 210
libido 43, 143, 169–70
love 40, 56, 83, 102, 122, 125, 131–32, 135, 137, 142, 146–47, 155, 160–61, 163, 197, 204, 209, 212

M

Mahler, Margaret 38, 42, 51, 207
Male Fantasies 3, 17, 28, 36–44, 49, 53, 94, 164, 204, 211
male gaze 31, 67–8, 170, 179
male sexual privilege 79
manifesto 2, 19, 96, 144–59

masculine strength 51, 106, 110–14, 117, 138
masochism 137, 190–91
The Mass Psychology of Fascism 28, 37–8
mass shooter 41, 44, 47, 62, 64, 71, 74, 76, 94, 106, 142, 144–65
mastery 21, 24, 110, 170, 172, 202–03
masturbation 9, 20, 47, 123, 164, 166–94
masturbation and psychoanalysis 169–72
The Matrix 8–9, 71, 81
memes 7, 9, 63, 97, 100–02, 113, 144, 173, 188, 202
Men's Rights Movement 6–7, 18, 26, 39, 52, 57–9, 72, 76, 100, 129
mental health 69, 97, 101, 104–05, 116, 171, 173–74, 190
metrosexual 59
misrecognition 207
mother 21, 31–2, 40–1, 51, 59, 121, 139–40, 145–46, 150–52, 155, 158, 160–65, 191, 204–7, 209, 213

N
Nazi 22, 28, 36–9, 53, 86–7, 110, 112–15, 126, 137–38
negation 132, 176–77, 188, 208, 210
neoliberalism 18–9, 39, 51, 58–9, 62, 71, 76–7, 88, 91–4, 101, 105–07, 116–18, 120, 142, 164, 173, 200, 209
1968 18, 23, 29, 37, 49, 50, 52–8, 72, 77–8, 81, 83, 133, 149, 159–60
Normie 7, 25, 97, 102

O
obsessional 19, 38, 122, 130–36, 140–41, 152
Oedipal 32–3, 40, 51, 163–65, 204–06
omnipotence 74, 98, 113, 149, 160, 161, 185, 209–10
orgasm 55, 170–71

P
parental 19, 33, 40, 49, 53, 122, 140, 194, 204
parents 23, 40–1, 55, 122, 139–40, 145, 151, 155, 158, 160, 164–65, 178, 200, 204, 206
pathological 131, 166–67, 173, 176, 182, 192
penis 15, 31

perversion 193–94
phallic 12, 15, 17, 20–1, 24, 31–2, 50, 66, 77, 79, 92–3, 103, 105, 111, 128, 133, 138, 141, 143, 145–46, 151, 157–59, 161–62, 170, 173, 176, 188, 191, 194, 201–03
phallus 14–15, 19, 23–4, 31–2, 42, 50, 63, 66, 92, 105, 140, 157, 164–5, 172, 176, 179, 188, 204–06, 211
physiognomy 114–15
Pick Up Artists 8, 11, 101
Pizzagate 78–9, 95
political correctness 11, 63, 100, 148
politics 2, 6–7, 16, 20–1, 25, 41, 52–4, 57, 62–3, 76, 81, 143, 150, 155, 171, 188, 201–03, 206
polymorphous perversity 94, 183–84
populism 2, 4–6, 13–14, 22, 36, 49, 61, 113, 164
populist 4, 14, 30, 36, 47, 136
porn 3–4, 7, 18, 20, 47, 50, 56–7, 66–9, 71, 73–4, 76, 78, 80, 83–4, 97, 99, 114, 135, 137, 163–64, 166–94, 198–200, 203
porn addiction 56, 83–4, 167, 172–74, 176, 179, 185, 188, 199
porn culture 18, 50, 66–70
postfeminism 18, 31, 50, 66–70, 88, 92, 142
potency 12, 77, 90, 158, 170, 194
powerlessness 62, 98, 107, 135
prejudice 3, 13, 19, 28, 35, 37–8, 51, 64, 122, 125–27, 130–31, 134
pre-Oedipal 21, 43, 163, 204–06
pseudo-science 35, 114
psychosis 43, 46, 113, 150, 154, 156, 198
psychosocial 2–3, 12, 17, 33–4, 39–40, 48, 50, 73, 99, 101, 107, 130, 143, 163

Q
QAnon 78–9, 95
queer 20, 30–1, 54, 68–70, 77, 80, 86, 94, 99–100, 176, 192, 209
queer theory 31, 54, 69

R
race 18, 22–3, 33–7, 50, 57, 61–2, 64, 97, 111, 114–15, 120, 188–9, 200
race and psychoanalysis 33–7
racism 6, 10, 13, 19, 22–5, 30, 33–8, 50, 53, 60–4, 72, 80, 103, 111, 120, 127–28, 130, 148, 163, 169, 188

246 Index

racist 6–7, 20, 23, 34–6, 41, 51, 61–4, 66, 82–3, 86, 98, 101–02, 107, 110–11, 118, 140, 147, 148, 157, 166, 187–90, 192, 194–95, 200
reborn 41, 44, 140, 163–64
recognition 21, 30, 32, 50, 145, 161, 194, 197, 203–12
red pill 8, 10, 12, 101, 103, 109, 123, 198
Reddit 1–2, 7–8, 10–11, 18, 19, 26, 81, 85, 96–7, 99–100, 102, 106, 109, 116–20, 129, 150, 166, 172–73
redistribution 158–62
Reich, Wilhelm 3, 16, 28–9, 37–8, 47, 53–5, 82, 137, 142, 170, 182, 197
rejection 98, 101, 106, 109, 116, 123, 127, 155
relief 43, 47–8, 109, 153, 172
repression 16, 37, 40, 45, 49, 137, 199
retribution 158–62
revenge 18, 47, 97, 99, 107–08, 110, 118, 159, 161, 163
right-wing 2–6, 13–4, 22, 30, 36, 45, 63, 70, 81, 97, 103, 112–13, 136, 144, 164
right-wing extremism 3, 5, 7, 24
Rodger, Elliot 4, 19–20, 41, 47, 62, 74, 94, 96, 144–45, 147–48, 153–161, 163–64, 194

S

sadism 137, 153, 190
sadomasochistic 45, 132
scopophilia 170–71
self-hatred 64, 106, 120, 146
self-help 8, 20, 174, 192
self-image 119
self-pity 24, 44, 97–8, 102–03, 108, 116, 156
self-victimisation 14, 24, 36, 44, 74, 97, 102–03, 106, 108, 114, 135, 156, 168
separatism 123
Sex and the City 66, 84, 149
sexual difference 31–2, 127–28, 165, 168, 175, 178, 201, 204
sexual revolution 2, 4, 17–8, 23, 28–9, 37, 50, 52–60, 69, 71, 73–4
sexism; theories of sexism: 126–129; sameness sexism 128; difference sexism 128
siblings 54, 206
sissy hypno porn 20, 168, 180–87
snowflake 8, 10
social capital 203

soldier 5, 17, 37–44, 46–8, 50, 53, 85, 97, 113, 117–18, 130–7, 139–41, 149–53, 156–57, 163–64, 174–75, 186, 198–200, 212
solitude 19, 123, 125–26, 129–30
split 40–2, 46, 51, 58, 130, 170, 196
Stacy 47, 64, 97, 102–03, 107, 110–16, 134–35, 153, 161
strength 3, 19, 38, 59–60, 63, 74, 106–07, 110–12, 117, 124, 134–35, 138, 147, 153, 161
subject positions 106, 120, 178
submission 31–2, 55, 124, 137, 147, 208–09, 211
super-ego 19, 45, 47, 133, 179, 184–85
supremacy 5, 18, 50, 52, 62, 81, 107, 188, 213
surveillance 21, 201–03
symptom 3, 45, 174, 181–82, 192

T

terrorist 9, 11, 19–20, 63, 78, 145–47, 152, 160–62
theft of enjoyment 36, 50, 86
Theweleit, Klaus 3, 15–7, 22–3, 28–30, 36–44, 46–51, 53–54, 64, 72, 85–7, 94, 97, 110, 113, 117–19, 130–34, 136–40, 150, 152–53, 156, 164, 171, 175–76, 186, 195, 198–200, 204–05, 211–12
The thing 180–87
The third 32, 146, 205–06, 208, 212
toxic masculinity 7, 60, 73, 75
transgender 30, 69, 145
triadic 178
Trump, Donald 2, 6, 11, 22, 61–2, 70, 78–9, 95, 115, 125, 162, 188, 200–02, 206, 209

U

upbringing 16, 29, 40–4, 53, 72, 139–40, 152, 154, 200
user unconscious 20, 180–82, 200–01

W

war 11, 39–40, 43, 49, 51, 60, 79, 113, 150, 164, 185, 188
weak 9, 63, 79, 98, 100, 107, 112, 128, 150, 152, 158, 169, 176, 178–80, 187–90, 193
Weimar Republic 17, 41, 53, 87, 200
white 2, 4, 6, 10, 13, 18, 21–3, 25–6, 33–6, 41, 45, 50, 52, 57, 59, 61–4, 66,

68, 71, 73–5, 77–82, 85, 93, 96, 98–101, 107–08, 111, 114–15, 120, 141, 148, 151, 155, 162, 187–90, 196, 200
working through 22, 49, 178, 188, 192, 204

Y
Young-Bruehl, Elisabeth 3, 13, 19, 22, 24, 28–30, 34, 37–8, 47–8, 99, 122, 126–28, 130–32, 134–37, 140–41, 143, 152, 186, 200
YouTube 2, 7–8, 69, 76–84, 85–9, 94–5, 97, 100, 123, 129, 140, 142, 153–54, 173, 198–9, 203

Z
Žižek, Slavoj 34, 36, 86, 92, 126–27